Malaysia's
VISION
2020

Malaysia's
VISION
Understanding
the Concept,
Implications and
Challenges
2020

Edited and Introduction by
Ahmad Sarji Abdul Hamid,
Chief Secretary
to the Government of
Malaysia

Pelanduk
Publications

Published by
Pelanduk Publications (M) Sdn Bhd
24 Jalan 20/16A, 46300 Petaling Jaya
Selangor Darul Ehsan
Malaysia.

Perpustakaan Negara Malaysia
Cataloguing-in-Publication Data
National Seminar on "Towards a Developed and
Industrialized Society: Understanding the Concept,
Implications and Challenges of Vision 2020" [1991:
Genting Highlands, Pahang]
Malaysia's vision 2020: understanding the concept,
implications and challenges / introduction by
Ahmad Sarji Abdul Hamid.
Includes bibliographical references.
ISBN 967 978 471 1
1. Wawasan 2020—Congresses. 2. Economic forecasting
—Malaysia—Congresses. 3. Malaysia—Economic policy
—Congresses. 4. Malaysia—Forecasting—Congresses.
I. Malaysia. Unit Penyelidikan Sosio Ekonomi.
II. Title.
338.95950112

Printed by
Eagle Trading Sdn Bhd
81 Jalan SS25/32, 47301 Petaling Jaya
Selangor Darul Ehsan
Malaysia.

Contents

Introduction

Understanding the Concept, Implications and Challenges of Malaysia's Vision 2020

Ahmad Sarji Abdul Hamid

Malaysia has come a long way since its first five-year socio-economic plan which sets the direction and pace for national development. Guided by its success in implementing the subsequent five-year plans as well as the New Economic Policy which spanned a twenty-year period since 1970, Malaysia has now moved on to a new and more challenging phase in nation-building. Today, Malaysia is guided by Vision 2020. Vision 2020 envisions Malaysia as a fully developed nation by the year 2020, developed not only economically but also politically, socially and spiritually.

A shared vision is indeed a critical prerequisite for successful nation-building. A vision is a mental image of a future state of being which can be clearly perceived to be better or more attractive than the present state. It acts as a desirable goal or ideal, seen as worthwhile to work towards. It gives an insight into the direction which a nation needs to move, just as an identified destination gives direction to a journey. A well-defined vision gives focus and direction to the formulation of current programmes and in turn links current actions to the achievement of future goals. A shared vision acts as a magnet by pulling together the diverse forces of a nation towards a common pole. It should therefore be inspirational and help to establish a common national aspiration. Nations whose people are not bound together or led by a common vision have been known to flounder like rudderless ships at sea. In the process of building a nation, therefore, a key task of the leadership is to establish a common or shared vision.

Malaysia has been fortunate in this respect. It has leadership with the foresight and courage to set a long-term vision which acts as the rallying point for the nation as a whole. Vision 2020 can be said to have captured the imagination of the Malaysian people as a desirable goal to work towards. At the same time, it is not just a grandiose dream. It is a realistic programme which draws on past achievements and known potentials of the nation and provides the right impetus for national development in the current, turbulent era.

However, the process of translating the Vision into reality needs to be addressed effectively. This process must allow for discussion and exchange of views and opinions on the various aspects involved. This is essential to ensure that the concept of the Vision, the benefits to be accrued from the achievement of the goals therein and the means of achieving these goals are well understood by all. At the same time, discussion ensures that a variety of perspectives, experiences and expert opinions revolving around the matter are gathered and taken into consideration to fine-tune the concept and the means to achieve the desired goals. Consultation and discussion are also invaluable for gathering widespread consensus and support for the common mission through the participation and active involvement of various interest groups whose support is crucial to the successful implementation of the strategies and programmes involved. The process of garnering support and commitment to the Vision works on the realm of the mind and the imagination, where inspiration and persuasion become the key to overcoming mental barriers rather than coercion. In Malaysia, such a process of consultation and discussion has gathered momentum.

Much of the discussion generated revolves around the need to effectively address the nine major challenges which need to be met on the journey towards achieving Vision 2020. These challenges range from the need to establish an economy that is competitive, dynamic, robust and resilient to the evolution of a united Malaysian society that is democratic, just, moral, liberal, peaceful and progressive. These challenges pertain to several major fronts as well as new frontiers covering the political, economic and social realms. This presents a multifaceted and demanding agenda for change and action, one which certainly cannot be addressed effectively by any individual group. A well co-ordinated and orchestrated plan of action is *sine qua non*.

Malaysia's Vision 2020: Understanding the Concept, Implications and Challenges is one such effort where the process of consultation has been initiated and where various key issues involved in the move towards Vision 2020 have been identified for discussion. It contains valuable insights into the nature of the concept of Vision 2020 as seen by the architect of the Vision himself, namely, Dr Mahathir Mohamad, the Prime Minister of Malaysia. Chapter 1 encapsulates the views and comments of the Prime Minister on the Vision, which is further revealed and explained through his answers to the questions posed to him by various prominent personalities from the public and private sectors. Through these, readers will be able to get a more in-depth understanding of what Vision 2020 stands for and the plethora of issues to be addressed by the nation in striving towards this Vision.

These issues have also been posed to prominent members of the public sector, the private sector, the academia and other interest groups to ensure that they are perceived and evaluated from different points of view. This book contains the views, opinions and recommendations of a variety of high-level representatives of the public sector, the private sector as well as the academia on issues such as the achievement of the desired economic growth, the enhancement of science and technology and human resource development.

One critical factor for success in making Malaysia a fully developed nation by the year 2020 will be the achievement of a high level of economic growth. The targets for economic growth which will act as forerunner and set the overall pace are embodied within the Second Outline Perspective Plan, 1991-2000 and the Sixth Malaysia Plan, 1991-1995. The Second Outline Perspective Plan and the Sixth Malaysia Plan are important blueprints for translating the broad and general policies of Vision 2020 and the National Development Policy into tangible programmes and achievements within the coming years. In Chapter 2, Encik Abdul Ghafar Baba, the Deputy Prime Minister, addresses the various policies and programmes which need to be implemented to ensure the achievement of the given goals. Mohd Sheriff Mohd Kassim, the Secretary-General of the Ministry of Finance, explains the linkages among the Second Outline Perspective Plan, the National Development Policy and the Sixth Malaysia Plan and how these in turn fall into place in the move towards the goals of Vision 2020. Mohd Sheriff provides data on the major macro as well as sectoral development targets established under these plans in Chapter 3. He also highlights the strategies and programmes which will be implemented to ensure the necessary structural transformation and growth of the economy while at the same time meeting the distribution and equity objectives and aspirations of the nation. Growth with equitable distribution of economic opportunities and wealth remain the key objectives of development policy in Malaysia.

Both the Second Outline Perspective Plan and Sixth Malaysia Plan established a high-growth target. To put Malaysia on the right track to achieve the goal of a developed nation, the country's economy will need to grow at an average rate of 7.0 per cent per annum in real terms over the Second Outline Perspective Plan period. Growth will be achieved mainly through accelerated industrial development and an export-based manufacturing sector. Implicitly, the private sector continues to be the engine of growth in the economy. The high-growth strategy is projected against a scenario of high rates of domestic savings, private investment and rapid growth of exports. Constant monitoring of the situation, both domestic and external, and quick responses through appropriate measures such as trade, tariff and fiscal policies will need to be undertaken to ensure the achievements of the planned targets in these areas. At the same time, the high-growth strategy will need to be tempered with appropriate counter strategies to combat inflationary pressures and prevent overheating of the economy due to strong aggregate demand. Associated problems such as the tightening of the labour market and rising wages will also need to be addressed.

The export-led growth of the economy and Malaysia's intent to enter global markets will face increasing pressures from the overall tendency towards regionalism and protectionism as evidenced by developments in North America and Europe. Although protectionist pressures have led to new initiatives in multilateral trade negotiations within the General Agreement on Tariffs and Trade's Uruguay Round, continuous initiatives in this area are called for. At the same time, in the light of the sluggish growth of the North American and European economies, Malaysia will need to explore new avenues of trade. Malaysia's success in making significant inroads into the high-potential markets of Eastern Europe, China and other non-traditional markets will depend greatly on the aggressive initiatives of the private sector. On the whole, the private sector will need to be efficient and willing to take bigger risks and new approaches to revitalize corporate performance. It would need to match the competitive advantages of its global rivals, rationalize product lines to capture global economies of scale, improve the quality of products and accelerate research and development to produce new product lines.

These and other major economic issues are covered in Chapter 8 by Ali Abul Hassan Sulaiman, the Director-General of the Economic Planning Unit of the Prime Minister' Department. Dr Lin See-Yan, the Deputy Governor of Bank Negara Malaysia, the central bank of Malaysia, discusses the Malaysian government's role in mobilizing and channelling funds towards the productive sectors of the economy to stimulate and sustain growth in Chapter 9. He also examines such issues as managing the savings and investment gap and other related issues. Malek Merican, a prominent business personality, discusses various issues involved

in Malaysia's entry into global trade in Chapter 7. He discusses
what he feels are various viewpoints and approaches to the challenge of establishing a prosperous society with an economy that
is fully competitive, dynamic, robust and resilient. He highlights
the need for well-developed securities and capital markets as well
as the need for improved regulatory authorities which can improve the functioning of an open market economy.

The critical efforts on the part of the private sector to put
Malaysia into the world market would need to be fully supported
and facilitated by the public sector under the umbrella of the
Malaysia Incorporated Policy. The Malaysia Incorporated Policy
will continue to be emphasized as a major vehicle for public sector-private sector collaboration and co-operation in furthering the
cause of national development. Constant consultation, joint
projects and the development of close rapport between the two
sectors will continue to be key factors for economic success.
Ernest Zulliger, a prominent business personality and formerly
the President of the Malaysian International Chamber of Commerce and Industry, emphasizes the importance of the Malaysia
Incorporated Policy as a key forum for joint discussion and action
between the public and private sectors.

On its part, the public sector would need to undergo major
structural and attitudinal transformation to effectively play its assigned roles as pacesetter and facilitator to the private sector. Its
major efforts would need to be in the area of creating a conducive
environment for the growth of private enterprise and
entrepreneurship. In this context, the streamlining or abolition of
rules, regulations and procedures which are found to hinder the
efficiency and growth of the private sector will need to be an on-
going exercise. Efforts at improving the quality and productivity
of agencies involved directly in facilitating the private sector will
need to be continued. Computerization and automation will need
to be accelerated to enhance productivity in public sector agencies. Training programmes will need to be expanded and intensified to upgrade staff productivity. These efforts are expected to
contribute significantly to improvement in the delivery of services
to the private sector. In Chapter 15, Dr Abdullah Abdul Rahman,

the Director-General of the Malaysian Administrative Modernization and Management Planning Unit of the Prime Minister's
Department, describes the role to be played by the public sector
in facilitating the private sector as well as the expectations of the
nation in evolving a more competitive private sector. He also emphasizes the need for further collaboration between the public
and private sectors, especially in the development of small- and
medium-sized industries as a new frontier in Malaysia Incorporated.

A major area of focus during the coming years will be the accelerated development of science and technology. Emphasis
should be given to the role of science and technology in research
and development, especially where it pertains to the development of the agriculture and industrial sectors. The more effective
utilization of current technology and the absorption of new technology will need to be intensified to assist the industrialization
process and in enhancing the international competitiveness of
the nation. In this context, policies to provide a more conducive
environment for innovation and the application of technology
will need to be implemented. Public sector-private sector collaboration in the area of research and development will also need
to be encouraged. At the same time, current efforts at enhancing
science and technology education in schools should be continued
and improved. Emphasis should be placed on the study of mathematics and science at an early stage of education which is known
to have a strong impact on the students' aptitude for an interest in
engineering and technology-related subjects later. Continued emphasis should simultaneously be given to vocational training,
especially in terms of ensuring a better match between the skills
produced by the vocational schools and the skills required by industry. Electronics should be given more emphasis in view of the
very wide application in industry. Polytechnics and universities
should expand and intensify programmes in the field of
electronics.

Another area for emphasis is computer education and technology. Computer literacy programmes should be expanded and
intensified at all levels of education to ensure a sufficient supply of

manpower in this area, especially in view of the forecast of increased demand and shortage in this area. With the emphasis on computerization by the Malaysian government and private sector agencies, efforts should also be channelled to the development of the local software industry to meet rising demand in this area and to reduce the heavy dependence on software technology from abroad.

A more comprehensive and effective human resource development programme needs to be emphasized. Such a programme should be closely guided not only by the manpower needs of the nation but also by the kind of society envisaged in Vision 2020. Thus, initiatives in the area of human resource development would not only need to focus on the development of a workforce with a broad skill base to meet the demands of the new and varied industries emerging in Malaysia, but should also focus on the inculcation of positive work ethics and a good culture. This includes such aspects as the development of a people which is caring, united, confident, liberal and tolerant. The key role of science and technology development is dealt with by Dr Omar Abdul Rahman, Science Adviser to the Malaysian government and Yokio Shohtoku of the private sector, while issues on human resource development is discussed by prominent educationists Dr Othman Yeop Abdullah and Professor Ungku Abdul Aziz as well as by business leader C.D. Roxburgh.

The importance of moral and ethical values in the government as well as in business has been discussed extensively by Dr Noordin Sopiee, Dr R. Thillainathan and Professor Dr Syed Othman Al-Habshi while the need for discipline is the crux of Robert Kuok's discussion.

Having enunciated and propagated the Vision, it is also important to establish the process and infrastructure to support the achievement of the set goals. Appropriate plans, programmes and strategies have to be formulated to guide the movement in the desired direction. The implementation of these has to be supported by the necessary rules, regulations and procedures which will ensure adherence to the set process and minimize derailment along the way. These programmes, strategies and regulations would need to be monitored and evaluated from time to time to take into consideration changes in the light of new circumstances.

The formulation of strategic plans and programmes to successfully overcome the challenges and obstacles in these areas requires in-depth thinking, planning and strategizing. Solo efforts would not be able to meet the demands of this immense task. Inputs from many sources are required. At the same time, the plans and actions implemented in each of these areas need to be linked and orchestrated such that each does not go off on a tangent. We need to know the overall scheme as well as how each component fits into the other to make a cohesive and coherent whole. There must be complete understanding, consensus and co-operation between the various players based on a sense of give-and-take in the realization of higher national goals. All these can only be achieved if there is continuous and frank communication and exchange of views, ideas and information between the key thinkers, planners and players. This book is therefore an effort to bring together the thoughts, ideas, views and aspirations of several prominent members of the public and private sectors and the academia regarding the attainment of the goals of Vision 2020. As such, it will make a very significant and valuable contribution to the growing body of literature which deals with the concept of Vision 2020 and the many facets involved in translating this Vision into reality.

This book is valuable insofar as it represents the cumulative expertise and experience of prominent and successful personalities who have been actively involved in the development of both the public as well as the private sectors in Malaysia. Such expertise and experience have been applied to strategize the modus operandi towards the achievement of Vision 2020. It is timely in assisting the process of moving towards the desired goals.

1

Views and Thoughts of Dr Mahathir Mohamad, the Prime Minister of Malaysia

Dr Mahathir Mohamad: Firstly, I would like to thank you for organizing this seminar and for inviting me to close it. It is obvious that there is a great deal of interest in this seminar and in Vision 2020.

The Vision was conceived with an open mind and without any fanaticism or religious inspiration whatsoever. It is merely a means of determining a target that was announced early this year.

When this Vision was first made known, there was some uncertainty whether the people in this country would accept it. It is obvious now that Vision 2020 has become the focus of attention

---

*   This is an edited version of the dialogue between Dr Mahathir Mohamad, the Prime Minister of Malaysia, and participants at the seminar on "Towards a Developed and Industrialized Society: Understanding the Concept, Implications and Challenges of Vision 2020", where he enriched the seminar with his knowledge, wisdom and views by responding to issues, questions and doubts raised. He cleared many doubts and, in doing so, laid to rest many apprehensions expressed.

of the whole country, including academicians, administrators, politicians and even people in the villages now talk about Vision 2020. Whether all of us understand it is another matter, though. The fact is that we now have the targets of Vision 2020 to look forward to, and to focus our attention towards the achievement of the target. The question that must be asked is whether this is an achievable target.

Of course, there will be much scepticism as to whether Malaysia can become a developed country in thirty years' time and the other question that ought to be asked is, "What is a developed country?" Do we say that if our per capita income reaches beyond US$10,000 then we become developed? What if the US dollar is devalued against the Malaysian Ringgit, in which case we can be developed in maybe five years? In fact, the US dollar has been valued upwards and as a result, of course, our growth has become stunted in terms of US dollars. In terms of Malaysian Ringgit, we have been growing, but in terms of US dollars, which is the measurement used throughout the world, we have decelerated somewhat, and if the US dollar continues to be revalued upwards, our progress would be further slowed down. Therefore, this unit of measurement is not really a perfect unit of measurement.

What we need to look at is at our own achievements, whether we have a better quality of life, whether we have achieved higher standards in terms of education and in terms of well-being. I think that is important. But in order to quantify it, we have said that we would like to double our per capita income, or our GNP [Gross National Product] every ten years and it has been calculated that if we achieve an average growth of 7 per cent per year then we will be able to achieve an 800 per cent growth over a period of thirty years and this would mean that we have achieved the status of a developed country. That is only a measurement, but if we stick too rigidly to this measurement, we may feel disappointed at the end of that period, although I doubt whether I will be around to feel disappointed then. But the important thing is that everybody is now interested. We have created a great deal of interest in this objective of becoming a developed nation in thirty years. This great interest in itself is an achievement and will contribute towards the achievement of the target. If there has been no interest, if after announcing Vision 2020, and that was the end of it, nobody talked about it, nobody discussed it, people forgot about it, obviously we are not going to achieve anything. But we must be grateful that there is this great interest. Sometimes, the interest is a little too great in the figure 2020. For example, some people talk of having a 2020 walkathon, whatever that might mean. Maybe somebody will produce a 2020 toothpaste, but such things will happen and we should not be unduly bothered about it and I do hope that this will not be too much of a distraction for us.

However, this hall where we are today is called the 2020 Hall, and I think there is some reason for this. For one thing, of course, it is dedicated to the year 2020 when we hope to become a developed country. Secondly, it is also the place where this first seminar on 2020 is held and therefore they have a right to use the figure 2020. Additionally, I would like to point out that I was here just before I left for Venezuela almost two weeks ago and they were busy working on this hall and this hall was designed, planned and built in two and a half months. That is an achievement. If we can achieve that kind of growth, that kind of ability to construct a hall of this kind in two and a half months, then we can construct this country at the same rate.

You may have heard of the five-star hotel we built in Langkawi in four months and I do not mean the construction in four months. I meant the total planning, designing, engineering, ordering of all the equipment, etc. were all done in four months and in that four months, but for the rain, it would have been ready with three hundred rooms, but as it is, only 170 rooms were ready and I think that deserves a place in the *Guinness Book of World Records*. But another hotel, a three-star hotel, which we decided to build half way through the building of the five-star hotel, because suddenly we realized that there were not enough rooms in Langkawi, the hotel was built in 53 days and it has three hundred rooms. I think that is a record also and should go into the *Guinness Book of World Records*.

By the way, the Proton car has also achieved the status of being quoted in the *Guinness Book of World Records*, not as a Proton car, of course. It happens to be the car that was used by GEC of England to travel to twelve EC [European Community] countries in the shortest possible time, knocking eleven hours off the last record. The car was not mentioned but the picture was there and the picture was of a Proton car. Thus, although it was the travel time that was listed as a record in the *Guinness Book of World Records*, still we should remember that the Proton car was the one that was used. So we are capable of achieving this kind of dramatic results and because of that I think it is quite possible for us to achieve developed country status by the year 2020, provided of course, we all dedicate ourselves to this.

Now, apart from our interest and dedication and our obvious capacity to do things and do things well and quickly, the reason why we think we should target for a developed country status in the year 2020 is because the basic infrastructure is there, it is in place. We have a good administrative machinery, maybe not the best in the world but then I don't know which country has the best administrative system in the world. But we do have a good administrative machinery in place. It is experienced, well-organized and open-minded. It is able to accept new ideas, in fact, even to change completely its attitude and be willing to work with the private sector in the spirit of Malaysia Incorporated. Of course, as you suggested there should be improvements in this area. They should work more closely and I think the administrators are open to suggestions, and they are, I am quite sure, willing to make the necessary adjustments. So in terms of administration we have the basic infrastructure.

Politically, I think again we may not have the perfect system but at least we have a system that has been able to provide stability and directions for this country. Everybody has to acknowledge that Malaysia is politically stable. It may not have the perfect system, the perfect democracy, as defined by some people. There are certain practices which are condemned by others. But the main thing is that Malaysia is stable and it is stable in a very unstable environment. If you look around the world, there are not many countries with a multiracial population which are stable. If you look at Northern Ireland, Lebanon or India or Sri Lanka and a few other countries which are not so often mentioned, you will find that if there is a mixed population, then there is a tendency towards instability. Sometimes, of course, this will result in prolonged civil wars, and in all kinds of activities which tend to destabilize the situation and create an atmosphere that is not conducive to economic growth. But in Malaysia since Independence, apart from 1969, we have been very stable and this stability can contribute greatly towards the achievement of a developed country status by the year 2020.

We have a very tolerant society. Although we say that the Chinese, the Malays and the Indians have different cultures, different religions, I think, by and large, these communities are tolerant. They put up with a lot of things which such communities do not put up with in other countries. Although Malaysia is described as a Muslim country and officially it is declared to be, and Islam is said to be the official religion of the country, yet what other people fail to mention is that the constitution clearly states that other religions may be practised in peace and as a result Kuala Lumpur has more churches and temples of all kinds than one would see in other countries where Islam is not the religion. Despite the fact that there are many Muslims, mosques are very difficult to put up and every time they want to put up a mosque there is a protest, although the Muslim population may be big.

In Malaysia, despite the fact that Islam is the official religion and the majority of the people are Muslims, people of other religions practise their religion without hindrance. They are able to put up their churches and their temples, sometimes in places they should not put up their temples, including of course, government quarters. Sometimes these temples are put up, quite illegally. It is very difficult to remove them. You have to compensate them after they have done something that is wrong. Otherwise you cannot move them. But the government does not send in earthmovers to remove them because they have done something illegal. Rather, we negotiate with them and try to give them a place elsewhere. That is the measure of the tolerance of the government as well as the people of various religions of this country. This is related to the stability of our society. It is true that we work together and then go home to our homes which are different from the rest. In other countries too, they work together and they go home to their own homes. You cannot go home to somebody else's home. Thus, the political, economic, social and administrative infrastructures are in place.

In addition to that, the physical infrastructure is also in place. We have built roads, railways, ports, airports, water supply and electricity. There is a possibility that they are inadequate, but it is possible for us to upgrade all these infrastructural facilities. And therefore when we talk about a growth of 7 per cent, it is not something that is sheer imagination. These infrastructural facilities are in place and will enable us to grow.

Additionally, of course, we have gas. Gas pipelines have already been put in place and we have our own supply of petroleum. A very essential part of growth of the economy is fuel and we have our fuel. For a long time I think, until the year 2020, we should have our own petroleum. Of course, if you ask Petronas they will tell you we have only twenty years supply, but they said that in the year 1970, so by now we should have nothing. But they keep on saying twenty years all the time. So I should hope by the year 2020 we should still have enough petroleum for our own use. So you can see, all the basic infrastructures are in place to enable us to progress towards a developed country status by the year 2020.

What is important now is whether the people are ready to make use of this infrastructure and to adapt to the rapidly growing economy. If we are willing, if we have the necessary value system, of which there has been some discussion, about ethics, etc., if the value system is correct, I am quite sure we can achieve the target we have set for ourselves. Now, the value system is extremely important, at least to my mind. If you read history, you will find various people achieve greatness over a period of time and then disappear from our history books.

There was a time when the Persians were great, achieved greatness, built a great empire and then for some reason or other they disappeared. The Greeks did the same. So did the Romans, the Arabs, the Chinese and the Europeans, of course. The British, for example, built an empire on which the sun never sets. So people can achieve greatness and if we look for the reasons for their achievement, we will see that during the period they grew rapidly and achieved greatness, they had certain set of values which contributed towards that achievement. They were brave, willing to take risks, had good ethics, were disciplined and had other attributes which enabled them to move forward and achieve greatness.

Look again at the Japanese and Germans who lost the war. Japan was totally destroyed. Bombs were dropped on Hiroshima and Nagasaki. The Japanese have apologized for attacking Pearl Harbour. But of course no apologies are needed from dropping atomic bombs on Hiroshima and Nagasaki because that is natural. But the fact is that despite the total destruction of their country Japan and Germany are today the world's most powerful economies. Those who won the war are not as great as those who lost the war. So again this is proof that present weakness does not mean weakness forever. Provided we are willing to work hard and possess good ethical values, we can also achieve the kind of targets we have set for ourselves.

In conclusion, before you ask me questions, I would like to say that the target is achievable, provided of course all of us are willing to work towards the target. The infrastructure is in place. All that needs to be done is to apply ourselves to this task.

I am glad that not only Malaysians are interested in the targets of Vision 2020 but those who have business interests in Malaysia are also equally keen. They have voiced their support and have contributed towards building up Malaysia and we would like to thank them because we know that we cannot achieve the target we have set for ourselves alone.

It is quite all right to accept foreign technology. Although, of course, some people say foreigners are not willing to transfer technology to us. Before we get angry with them, let us ask ourselves whether we are willing to transfer our technology 100 per cent to others. For example, would we like to give all the best clones for rubber or palm oil to some countries in Latin America which are in the same latitude? I don't think we will give the best. I know we will always select between the ones we do not want and the ones we want. We are never going to give others the best so don't be surprised if others don't give us their latest technology. They are not willing to give. This is the way things are.

We have to accept half the technology and build on it and perhaps in time we will be ahead of them, as the Japanese are now in many areas ahead of the people who supplied them the original technology. So I would like to thank non-Malaysians for their support and their interest and together, Malaysians and non-Malaysians, we can work towards achieving the targets we have set for ourselves by the year 2020.

So I would like to thank you very much for giving me this opportunity to give my views and I will be happy to answer any questions that you may have.

Muhammad Ghazali Shafie: I was an ex-Chairman of one of the sessions and I must say that sitting here, these last two days, we have read all the papers, and we have heard the presentation of the papers. To me all the papers had a fairly high standard of preparation. The papers were all well designed, but more than that, I found that they were written very sincerely, as the Japanese would say "from the heart" or *kokorokara*. Perhaps you will see that the heart is the one that matters, not the brain. Of course, others will disagree with that. We had a big debate on the heart and the brain, but the Japanese used *kokorokara* very sincerely and in good faith. In our discussion, sometimes we went into the realm of philosophy and metaphysics. Nonetheless we sometimes also meandered. We talked of Hindu temples, of Chinese education and waterfalls. But then, when we measured all these against the background of the *Rukunegara* [the rules or principles that serve as a guide to good citizenship], we found that they were all genuine and all pass the test. As one of the Chairmen, I feel extremely grateful to the paper presenters. I think the papers should be kept as records.

We did get involved, Sir, I want to report to you, in the problems of semantics. Yesterday, for instance, someone used the word "sharing". Somebody reacted very quickly. Sharing what? Wealth? We have talked about this for last twenty years. I think it is a problem of semantics. If the world "sharing" comes about from the report of the NECC [National Economic Consultative Council], the Malay word for "sharing" will be *berkongsi untung nasib*, not *berkongsi duit atau kekayaan*, that is, the sharing of fate and destiny and this leads to the point which you made that we should have a *Bangsa Malaysia* [Malaysian Society].

Unless we are prepared to share our fate and destiny it will not be possible to talk about our *bangsa*. We already have *warga* or citizenship but that is a legal document. We can make it through a legal process for a person to be a citizen. But to be a *bangsa* there must be a motive. It must come from inside. I think we should talk a little bit more on this because this has become a rather sensitive issue. I have experienced in 1945, 1946 and 1947. Many Malays have asked who wants to share the *warga* with the non-Malays? Now they are saying, who wants to share the *bangsa* with the non-Malays. So we need to discuss a little more to see what is the difference and how we arrive at this. It is good to remind ourselves that even Hang Tuah did not say *Bangsa Melayu*. What he said was *"Melayu tidak akan hilang di dunia."* To my mind, we do not have a *bangsa*. We have a *rumpun*. Certainly we got involved in the problems of semantics, because we talked a little about *bangsa*.

I think we should really have a thorough discussion on the subject of National Unity because, this in fact, Sir, is the number one challenge in Vision 2020. National unity is not confined only to people. It also refers to the relationship between state and the federal, and amongst states.

You have touched on the question of ethics and morals. I certainly have a little bit more. We had very good papers on the subject of morals and ethics and I must say I am very impressed, as there are many things I did not know before. For instance, I learned how Hindu temples have been built and which god to invite. Twenty years ago, this would have been a very sensitive issue. We are able to talk about this now, and this goes to show the maturity of the nation after twenty years of NEP [New Economic Policy]. But we still need to talk and to give a deeper meaning to all these points on ethics and morals. As you rightly said, the glories of all the previous people were because they had very clear and strong ethics and morals, and I have pointed this out in one of my interventions. So, ethics and morals are really not intended for the workplace only.

We always say that we must copy Japanese ethics. We are talking about ethics and morals for the whole country, the whole nation and for everybody at all levels. Therefore we arrive at another conclusion. That when we talk of leadership by example, we mean leadership by good example. But one thing I did discover is that, we did not discuss in great detail that the road to Vision 2020 is bristled with the very thorny elements that might conduce towards non-unity or disunity. We have to look and examine this, whether we can maintain the kind of unity that we have achieved so far. We should really go beyond into greater depths in understanding national unity.

That is why we have recommended, as Yang Berbahagia Tan Sri Dato' Seri Ahmad Sarji Abdul Hamid said, that the Ministry of Education is to play even a greater role in inculcating ethics and morals. Now we have different schools and we confuse the kids. We must have a common one and the education system should be prepared to take care of these things. When it comes to moral class, we ask the Muslims to go to one side and non-Muslims the other. Surely, there are universal standards that can be evolved from all these value systems to make it into a truly Malaysian value system. I think we should give a little more work to the Ministry of Education to see to this.

In discussing globalization and open market, we all agreed that there must be globalization. We all agreed that there must be an open market. There should not be any protectionism. In fact, we are talking of lifting our own protectionism. But there is one thing I want to report to you, and not all of these things are that easy. We may find that the open market system has indeed been constricted especially when trade and aid have got to go through some conditionalities. Aid and trade are the things that would conduce development. We may not need so much of aid, but certainly we need a lot of trade and if the doors are closed to us then that might constrict or rather inhibit the growth towards 2020.

We did elude to the point where we had a great deal of hope on institutions like GATT [General Agreement on Tariffs and Trade] and Uruguay Rounds. I did not have the occasion, however, to remind our colleagues in this conference that Uruguay Rounds came in 1974. It came in 1974 because in 1973 there was an oil crisis. There was a jacking up of prices by the oil producing countries. In order to placate that and to borrow time, and also in order to subvert the oil prices, the bigger developing countries agreed to Uruguay Rounds. But please look into the records. They agreed to hundreds of resolutions but not one of them was implemented. And when the oil producing countries and oil prices were thoroughly subverted they refused to talk anymore of Uruguay Rounds.

Now they are coming back to Uruguay Rounds. You know why, because we have begun to talk about EAEC [East Asia Economic Caucus] with China and Japan, that is, something that is frightening the Western and industrial world. They may be able to bully the Japanese. Nobody asked the Japanese to apologize but they go on apologizing. You know the British occupied this country. We never asked them to apologize. Neither the Philippines asked the Americans to apologize, but the Japanese want to apologize. The point is, they can bully the Japanese but they cannot bully the Chinese and the Chinese are coming to play a bigger role and if they don't get into EAEC, the scheme of things that Malaysia is proposing, they may get into a more difficult place, like the non-aligned conference, if it is turned into a movement of the South.

Look at the veto power the movement of the South will have in the United Nations. These are the things that is worrying them and you can be sure that whatever we do, even towards Vision 2020, you will still find resistance, constrictions and also subversion. You see today we worked and discussed as if the market is going to be the same all the way through. It is not going to be the same.

We do need to think, Sir, of a review, as Tan Sri Ahmad Sarji Abdul Hamid said, of our Industrial Master Plan. As mentioned by Mr Prime Minister, we should be thinking of not only how to improve ourselves in terms of modern industry, but we should also think of alternative markets and the industries that fit into the markets, while we go into the high-tech industries. We also talked about Malaysia Incorporated. Now we have our own apprehensions about this. For one thing we thought the word "incorporated" which was used by other people, applied to the Japanese economy. The Americans started coining them. So they found that we in the government and the private sector are riding on each other's back. This I find is difficult to understand. You can't ride on one's back. They want to divorce the idea of free trade with government intervention. More than that, if the Incorporated concept is going to work it has got to work for the whole nation.

You also find that because of our constitution, the state governments are sovereign. I have noticed that many state governments send all sorts of missions abroad. So the point is that, not only they are sovereign, we also get governments that are opposed to the centre. We know now that there are two governments that are opposed to the centre. What happens if they don't comply with the idea of sharing fate and destiny. They may think that they have their own fate and destiny. And likewise, Sir, we also mentioned about the local authorities and the way they implement their laws. It is correct, that they have their laws to implement, but do they take into account Vision 2020 and the achievement of the NEP, for example, the raising of rates as we mentioned yesterday. How does this have an impact on Vision 2020 and what has been achieved in terms of national unity through NEP during the last twenty years.

So what we need, Sir, and I must suggest this to Tan Sri Ahmad Sarji Abdul Hamid, that we should organize more of this kind of meetings, perhaps confine the subjects to a little less than what we have been doing during these last three days. Have it regularly, for no other reason except that we need to continuously keep our Vision in constant check because things can get outmoded very quickly. That is number one. Number two, we need to monitor what everybody is doing, what the government is doing and what the private sector is doing. By sitting together, our experience for the last few days has shown that we have tremendous maturity. We were able to discuss even sensitive subjects. So I would suggest, Sir, we do this monitoring more regularly through meetings like this, and I will recommend at least once a year.

Dr Mahathir Mohamad: Thank you very much. I was trying my best to find out what the question is. So if I answer the wrong thing you must excuse me for I do not really know what the question is.

But firstly on the question of *Bangsa Malaysia*. If Malaysia is a great nation, then people will want to identify themselves as Malaysians. As a matter of fact I have noticed a change. I have non-Malay civil servants coming up to me, saying that they are very proud to be Malaysians. Now, wherever we go we are recognized, we are respected, and because of that they will tell people, I am a Malaysian. But if Malaysia is a country that is a gross failure, unstable, poor and with poorly educated people, no one wants to be identified as Malaysians. Therefore, it is important that we build this country and achieve the status of a developed country.

I don't mind saying this but the fact is that when the British were here a lot of people wanted to be identified with the British. Some of them even developed a very artificial Oxford accent and they used to hold their pipes the way the British held their pipes. Why? The reason is very simple. In those days, the British were regarded as successful people. No one wants to be identified with failures. In fact, those people who imitated the British liked to be called Englishmen, if possible.

The same applies to this country. If this country achieves its target of becoming a developed nation by the year 2020, then people will say they are Malaysians. There is no need to append the word *bangsa* or race, just Malaysians. To me, I think that is good enough.

Then the question of national unity that will also come about without having to force. I notice that more non-Malay girls are wearing *baju kurung* and Malay *kebaya* now, not because someone asked them to and I think we shouldn't ask them to, but they are wearing them because there is a sense of identity with this country, not with the Malays, at least with this country. That is why to me it is far more important to focus on the development of this country rather than to be sidetracked with controversial issues.

Perhaps it is good if we can have just one school using just one language, but it is a sensitive matter. If we get ourselves distracted by this issue about what language and what schools, etc., in the end we will not be able to focus on development, and of course we will not be able to achieve the status we are aiming for. If we don't achieve, then the idea of unity would become even less attractive.

No one wants to be identified with failure. So let us not be distracted. Let us focus on developing this country. God willing we will achieve unity in the end. On the other hand, if we try to force unity, it will not just come about. You cannot just drag people together and say, "now unite". It just does not happen. You know if they do not fall in love with each other, it is very difficult for us to tell them, "now you are in love with each other and you have to be by order of the government". It does not work that way.

The other thing is that we are not perfect. That is something that we must accept. We are God's creatures and we are not perfect. Whether we are animals or humans, we are not perfect. And so our plans, our designs, our targets, are also not perfect, and our progress towards our target will also not be perfect. We will be making mistakes all the way. But we will have to make corrections. The important thing is to have a target, so that at least we can go in that direction. If we have no target at all, we may be going in an opposite direction and that will be disastrous for us. So now that we have found a target, we will have to take steps in that direction, sometimes we take smaller steps, sometimes we may have to sidestep and sometimes even, we may have to go backwards one pace, in order to go forward two paces, but we will progress if we really apply our minds and our energy towards achieving these targets.

Of course the methods we use may not be correct all the time. For example, we talk about Malaysia Incorporated, it may well be that government officers will become corrupted by the private sector, once they get too close. We have got to watch them very carefully, because there may be a danger in this concept of Malaysia Incorporated, working together between government and the private sector.

government officers tend to keep away from the private sector because they fear being accused of corruption and of favouring. But then once you know people, if you happen to agree with a proposal, because it is a good proposal, it does not prevent one from saying that you are favouring someone. This is bound to happen. But then the other way is also equally bad too, that is, to keep the private sector from the public sector and to keep them as far apart as possible in order that no one will be corrupted or even appear to be corrupted. That too is bad because it will stifle growth. It will not achieve the kind of growth that we are aiming for.

So since both are imperfect, let us choose the imperfect one that leads to something better than the other imperfect alternative. So if we accept the imperfections of all our moves, I think we will not be too far wrong and too far off target. The reason why the government has changed the idea on the separation between the public and the private sector is because, between the two, the government feels that it is better if the government works together with the private sector, than if the government is forever supervising the private sector from a distance and always disagreeing.

There is always this feeling that if I put my signature to that document, he is going to become a millionaire, I am going to get my *gaji* [salary], the same amount and it is not going to improve. Now we have told the government officers that if you help the private sector to make more money, we are going to tax the private sector, so that we pay you better. Not as much as you would get if you get it directly of course, but this is much safer, safer than if you play around and get directly for yourself. It is better this way. Please make sure that the private sector succeeds and makes as much money as possible, because we always say that we have a 35 per cent share in all private enterprise, in terms of the tax they have to pay. If you lose that's your business. If you make money that's our money. So why shouldn't we help you. That kind of approach is not perfect either. So if we accept that most approaches are imperfect, then we will try as much as possible to be perfect. What we achieve will be fairly considerable and in that way, we can move on towards our target.

There will be international problems, GATT Rounds, etc., etc., but the thing is how do we deal with them? How do we prepare ourselves to deal with them? Assuming that the American market is closed to us completely, say, 100 per cent closed to us, we will lose 18 per cent of our total trade. That would be disastrous, but if we know how to adjust ourselves, it won't be a disaster for long. This is the reason why we are cultivating other markets.

I did not go to Latin America just to have a holiday. I met a lot of useful people. But we have been looking around, and it is surprising that there is so much business to be done. The problem is to persuade Malaysians to do business with those people. We are too comfortable. Why bother about selling abroad, when we can build two condominiums and make millions of dollars. Let us stay at home. Because we feel very comfortable at home, we do not want to venture abroad, but if we don't venture abroad, then our capacity to grow, our capacity to overcome decisions made by others, decisions beyond our influence will be very limited. So we should think of the GATT Rounds as going to fail. What do we do about it? Even if it succeeds, how do we take advantage of it. In other words, we must be able to deal with problems as they come. In fact, we should prepare ourselves for the worst scenario. If this is going to happen what do we do, or should we do things earlier so that when it does happen, we will be quite prepared for it. You become proactive, and by being proactive, I think we would lessen the impact of decisions made by others which are not within our control.

So I feel that it is better to look at ourselves rather than to look at others. Of course there would be a lot of criticism that we do all the wrong things. If you read some of the reports on Malaysia, you will find that we have done nothing right, but those who criticize us and say we have done nothing right are not doing any better either. In fact, they are doing worse than us. So I am not going to be worked up by them if we want to achieve our target. I think we can do it.

Of course you can hold seminars, but not too many, otherwise, we'll be talking all the time, and not doing anything. Once a year is okay but not too many seminars, because we must give a chance for all our decisions to be attended to and worked at before we begin to say that it is not going to work. If we see some of the projects that we have, if we are to succumb to their criticisms against our projects, I think we will never be anywhere. When we decided to go into heavy industries, people said it was crazy; Malaysia is a developing country, how can we go into heavy industries? Well I can assure you that the heavy industries we have started are getting heavier and heavier, and one day we are going to have heavy industries worthy of being named heavy industries. But as Confucius says when he is not so confused, a journey of a thousand miles begins with one step, so we have made not just one step, I think we have made many steps.

Ahmad Sarji Abdul Hamid: Ghazali Shafie also asked how we manage the two state governments and the local authorities under them.

Dr Mahathir Mohamad: Well, we are a democracy and these things happen. They want to do something, we want to do something. There are bound to be conflicts, but of course we will find a way around. I do not say that we have a definite, immediate solution but people will soon come around to thinking that all these things are not worthwhile. The kinds of government that we have had, where there is the same party at both the state and the federal level, is better than the kind of confrontational governments between the state and the federal level. Even a federal government that is very democratic but yet very weak is not going to help us either. If we have a country which is ruled by a minority government, it is still a government, but then it will not be stable.

Many people criticize us for being undemocratic. For example, I think it was stated in the *New Straits Times* this morning that we like to be like the Japanese, where the LDP [Liberal Democratic Party] had been in power since the end of the war. Apparently the suggestion is that because the LDP has been in power and is voted by the majority of the Japanese, it is not quite democratic. Somehow or other, the idea is that democracy must involve changes in government, whether people like it or not. If people don't like changes then they are not democratic. But as far as we are concerned, so long as people want this government, we will continue.

But if they prefer another government, they are welcome to it. They prefer another government in one state and they have made their choice, but then do not complain after that. You have to sleep in the bed that you have made. Don't say why is it that you do not get as much help from the federal government. When you voted, you were quite aware that if you don't work with the federal government than you stand to lose a few things. We will see how long it is going to last. We also don't know whether we will continue to be in power at the federal level. Maybe the Barisan National would lose. Maybe this country would be ruled by PAS [Parti Islam Se-Malaysia], PBS [Parti Bersatu Sabah] or even DAP [Democratic Action Party]. Who knows, they might become popular. But it if the people want it, then it is up to them. That is democracy.

Mohd Ramli Kushairi: Over the last two days as Tan Sri Dato' Seri Ahmad Sarji Abdul Hamid has said the participants have discussed extensively the nine challenges contained in Vision 2020, and I must say as a participant, the wide range of eminent participants coming from the government, private sector, the banking industries and from the universities, showed how serious and how interested they are in pursuing and exploring the goals of Vision 2020 and they have proposed some ideas how these goals can be attained.

I meant to ask four questions, but you have ably answered two of those, leaving me with only two. Firstly, has the country and society reached that level of maturity to openly and constructively discuss Vision 2020? Secondly, political stability is so important for economic progress and underpinning that stability is security, a credible defence and a good law and order situation. Would you then consider security as the tenth challenge? Thank you, Mr Prime Minister. May I, before I conclude, pay tribute to the organizers for having offered us excellent facilities for this seminar and I think we have achieved a lot during these two days.

Dr Mahathir Mohamad: Firstly, the question of whether society has reached that stage of maturity to appreciate what they have to do in order to achieve the target we have set for ourselves. I think they have. I have been to many countries in the world. I have talked to people and I do not see anything about the Malaysian society which shows that they are not ready for the kind of tasks that they have ahead of them. In fact, the level of achievement that we have attained at present signifies a sophisticated society, a society that understands how it works and how it should work in order to achieve certain objectives.

Malaysia is at this stage today not by accident; it is by design. Right from the beginning, right from the start of Independence, we set out to correct certain imbalances, to attend to certain needs and to plan for the development of this country. Many countries have plans, but you will find not many of them implement these plans or achieve the targets that they have planned for.

Socialism became very popular after the War and in all socialist states, the five-year plan is mandatory. But as you know a lot of socialist and communist states, where central planning is a *sine qua non* of their ideology, have not achieved anything. In fact, socialism and communism are all wrong, and it has not got them anywhere, despite their planning. That is because they thought that mere planning will achieve things. Planning alone will not achieve things. The people must be sophisticated enough to understand what the plan entails and what they have to do to achieve the targets that are planned for. Therefore, in Malaysia, people plan and implement plans. We have reached a certain stage today where no one can say that Malaysia has not achieved a considerable degree of development.

When we became independent, the per capita income at that time was US$300. Now the per capita income is US$2,000 to US$2,300, or thereabouts. It has increased many times, more than what we expect to achieve in the next thirty years. In the 35 years of independence, we have in fact grown much faster than what we are planning for in the next thirty years. What we are saying is that in the next thirty years our per capita income should increase to RM26,000. But the per capita income between the time we gained independence to the present time has increased from US$300 to US$2,500. That is a considerable increase. I think if we can achieve that we can also achieve our targets. The people are aware of this. They have been able to successfully implement this both at the government and private levels.

At one stage, growth was almost entirely due to government expansionary budgeting. But now, I remember about ten years ago, we decided that it should be the private sector which should contribute to growth and now it is happening. Growth today is due to private sector expansion, not the government sector. In fact, the government is trying to reduce its own contribution towards growth, because we do not want to borrow too much money in order to keep expanding the economy. So the private sector as well as the government sector is very much aware of what they are doing. So the level of sophistication is there. The ability to plan and to implement is there. So I would say that the country and the society has reached that kind of maturity and sophistication which makes formulating a target for the next thirty years something achievable.

On the question of security, law and order, I think in this country we are very concerned about security, law and order. We do not allow things to get out of hand before we step in and stop the slide towards disorderly behaviour. Of course we still have the ISA [Internal Security Act] and we have been criticized for it by everyone. But we have a choice. We can do without the ISA and have a disorderly society which will stifle growth, or we can have the ISA and have an orderly society without denying democratic rights too much. It must be remembered that this government has gone to numerous elections where the ISA was an issue and the people voted for this government with a big majority which means that the people as a whole approve of the ISA. Now if democracy means majority opinion, then the majority supports ISA, simply because the majority wants a stable and orderly society. So even if people say we are not democratic, I am quite prepared to argue against them because it is the people's choice. The majority of the people want security, law and order and if they have to have a law like the ISA then they will have it, and they will support the government that believes in having a law that will enable the slide towards disorderliness and breakdown in law and order to be arrested early.

In 1987, there was a lot of tension in Kuala Lumpur. We forget things very easily. In 1987, people were not sending their children to school. People were stocking food because they thought that riots were going to come about. People planned to leave the country on a certain day because they thought on that day there will be riots in Kuala Lumpur and May 1969 may be repeated. When one mad soldier shot two people, everybody shut their shops because they were frightened. But the government stepped in and arrested a lot of people, a hundred people, including some members of the government, and everything became normal again. The people realized that the government is willing to use the law to prevent any disorderliness or any breakdown of law and order in this country. Therefore people feel secure.

Now, security in terms of foreign invasion, I don't think there is much of a possibility at this point in time. We have sufficient arms to defend ourselves, but we can never have sufficient arms to really prevent a country like China from invading and conquering this country. However, they must also know that is a shortlived kind of operation as Iraq found out. You invade another country you are doing something that the rest of the world does not approve and the rest of the world gang up against you and I don't think China wants to do that. Our attitude towards China is said to be the same. But I feel that China now has learnt its lessons. The present leaders of China are not so dogmatic, not so ideological. They are quite prepared to live with capitalism. In fact, the areas that they have declared as special areas are growing faster than Malaysia.

China now is interested in providing a good life for the Chinese. I don't think they are interested in conquest anymore. Conquering is out of date now. So, I don't think there are any threats. That is why I am not too worried that the Americans are getting out of the Clarke Air Base and the Subic Naval Base in the Philippines. They are not coming to Malaysia, of course, but if they want to repair their ships here, why not, and we can make a little bit of money from them. That is not political. It is pure economics. So I don't think much about security threats from outside. There will be some people who want to propagate some ideology or some kind of religious interpretation, but I am quite sure we can deal with those problems. So I am not worried about security. We are quite prepared to deal with most possibilities. So the situation is, to my mind at least and to the government, quite stable and we expect this situation to continue into the future.

Ramon Navaratnam: Sir, I would agree with Tan Sri Ghazali Shafie and Dato' Ramli Kushairi that we have had an exceedingly stimulating seminar and still come out with cool heads and I think as I learned from Islamic values "a kind heart". Tan Sri Dato' Seri Ahmad Sarji Abdul Hamid has taken some of the wind from my sail, with the points he introduced earlier this morning, but let me, Sir, with your permission, raise some issues so as to draw on your wisdom and your visionary views. What I believe comes out clearly from this seminar is that your nine strategic challenges to achieve Vision 2020 can be overcome, mainly by adopting a more open and aggressive human resource development policy. As you have just said, Sir, we are blessed with all the prerequisites, but it will depend on whether the Malaysian people will rise to the occasion and to the challenges. This, I believe, Sir, would entail further improvements to the education system. I would therefore ask, Sir, whether you consider it appropriate to accept *inter alia* the following ideas which were expressed at the seminar.

Firstly, to review our education curriculum in conjunction with the private sector, to make it even more relevant to the manpower needs and the value system that we need to promote even more strongly a united Malaysian nation and a scientific and progressive society.

Secondly, Sir, to rapidly increase our skilled manpower resources through the introduction of distance education or open university scheme, although, I concede this may impinge on the issue of balance, at least in the short term.

Thirdly, to give the private sector a bigger role to play in setting up more universities and polytechnics within the framework of the National Education Policy.

And fourthly, Sir, to provide more university places to hundreds of our best and brightest students whom we lose to Singapore every year.

Finally, Sir, as you are well aware, there is a great deal of analytical and technical homework to be done to achieve the Vision 2020 objectives. As an ex-civil servant, Sir, I say with pride that the EPU [Economic Planning Unit] and the Treasury have done impressive socio-economic projections up to the year 2020 as they have indicated to us during the seminar. Perhaps, Sir, if I may suggest, they could carry out further analysis to breakdown the 2020 targets into five-year and preferably annual targets which the EPU and the Treasury could closely monitor under your guidance to ensure success in achieving Vision 2020.

Dr Mahathir Mohamad: Whenever we try to do something, we have to take all factors into consideration. As I said just now, you cannot achieve economic growth in an unstable society. Therefore, although when we talk about 2020 we seem to focus on the economic aspect of that target, we also have to consider the political aspect. It is no good becoming developed only to have everything torn to pieces because of differences between the people in the country. Therefore, when we consider the question of education, for example, although logically we should have just one language and one school, the fact remains that this is a sensitive issue and we should not try to abolish some schools just because we want to have one school system.

We have to be very careful about that because if we don't, then the country becomes unstable and when the country becomes unstable, despite our skills, we are not going to succeed in developing the country. This is the first thing that we have to remember. The fact remains that, this country's people are Malays, Chinese and Indians and there are differences economically among them, apart from cultural differences. If they are able to develop together at the same pace there should be no problem. The fact remains that people are different. Culturally, they are different.

The Chinese have a culture that is conducive towards economic success. This is not a culture that is unique to the Chinese. The Malays can also acquire that culture but it takes time. I think to a certain degree the Malays in this country, the Ibans, the Kadazans and others too, have begun to absorb some of the Chinese culture with regard to doing business. But it is a process that takes time, and we cannot force the pace. We can help it along the way, but we cannot force it by taking legislative action, for example. We have to live with these differences.

There is a feeling among the Bumiputeras that they are as yet incapable of competing with the non-Bumiputeras. This is a fact of life. We know that people are different. Supposing we take the Penans and put them among the Germans, give them the same education, give them everything in equal doses that you give to the Germans, do you really think that the Penans will be able to achieve what the Germans have achieved? I don't think so. Despite the fact that they are together, people and races, take many years to develop. Some develop faster than others, and this is a fact that we have to live with and we have to make allowance for. That is why in this country we must always be conscious of the need to balance things.

We would like to give opportunities to everyone irrespective of race. But if by so doing, we create too much of an imbalance, we are going to have a lot of resentment, and then resentment can explode into racial strife, antagonism, instability, and this will definitely hamper the progress towards economic growth. So we are not going to achieve despite the fact that we seem to be working towards achievement; we will not achieve the targets we have set for ourselves simply because we are looking purely at the economic angle and not the political angle, not sensitive to the sensitivities of the communities. In Malaysia, this has to be attended to all the time.

We have been very careful in this country, not to favour any group too much. We often say in Malaysia that when everybody is unhappy then we are doing the right thing. It is funny to say but if we find suddenly that all the Chinese are happy, we can be sure that the Malays are unhappy and they are going to do certain things which will disturb the stability and the peace of this country. Similarly, if we favour the Malays to the point where they are very, very happy, the Chinese are not going to be happy, the Indians are not going to be happy, and that again will lead to instability. We cannot make all of them happy because all of them want everything for themselves without regard for the others. So obviously it is not possible for us to have a totally happy society in this country.

So the best we can achieve is a partially unhappy society. Everybody is against the government, the Chinese say the government is favouring the Malays, the Malays say, see the government is giving all the contracts to the Chinese and the Indians say we remain as rubber-tappers forever and ever. Of course it is not true because a lot of the doctors in the hospitals are Indians and there are more Indian lawyers in this country, whether for better or for worse, than we have Chinese or Malay lawyers. So, there are people who will be complaining all the time and I think that is a good situation. If that is the situation, then we can progress, but any attempt made to focus entirely on economic progress without due regard to racial sensitivities may in fact obstruct that economic progress.

The government has and can easily accept the idea that we should review the school curriculum. In fact, we are doing that right now. We have asked the Ministry of Education to concentrate on manual and living skills rather than on learning too much about history and arts and all that because we are going to have an industrialized society. Fine, if you can have people who can write good novels and all that. We need a few of them but not too many. But mainly we need people who are skilful in the use of their hands, who can look at the computer and not feel frightened by it; they know what it is, they know how it works, that is why we are introducing computer science. We are making people more familiar with machines, engines and electronic parts. That is part of the revision that has already been carried out. But of course we welcome any new ideas that can improve the process of preparing the future generation for the kind of industrialized society that we are going to have. So I would welcome private sector participation in the formulation of new curriculum for our schools and even the universities.

We can have distance learning, that is not a problem, but distance learning is only suitable for the kind of theoretical learning that is mainly focused on the arts. To learn mechanical things from a distance is a little bit difficult. Although with the aid of computers it is now much easier, but, we have already decided that we should institute distance learning. And this is a great way to not only prepare people who have less opportunity but those who have missed their opportunity can relearn and readjust to a society that stresses on mechanical and electronic skills rather than on reading, writing and appreciation of the arts.

We have also decided that the private sector can actually set up universities. We said that the government is not in the position to provide the universities that the country needs. It is not so easy to set up a private university. The problem always is getting the teaching staff. We can put up the buildings, but teaching staff is another thing. In fact, Genting Highlands is planning to put up a college which can provide the kind of higher education that is of the same status as a university.

We have, for example, allowed Tunku Abdul Rahman College to have twinning arrangements with foreign universities. We in fact encourage the setting up of schools and tertiary institutions in this country by the private sector. The government, as you know, wants to withdraw from being too involved in this kind of thing. The more the private sector is involved in education the better for us. We don't have to spend so much money. And I think it would be better because the private sector would know what kind of education it would like the people to have because it wants them to serve them.

In the past we set up universities in order to provide the recruits for the government to become administrators. That is why the government was keen. By the way, there are others who also went to the university and who do not work for the government. Before, if you were sent to a university, it meant that you would be employed by the government. You come out of the university and you wait to be called up. In fact, if you're not called up to work for the government in less than one month you would say, look how inefficient the government is, until of course you become a part of the government, then you are a part of that inefficiency.

But we welcome private sector initiatives on providing university education. But it must of course conform with our education policy. We cannot have a university here which is totally Russian. We must pay attention to *Bahasa* and other things and the curriculum must be something that is acceptable to this country. If you're going to teach communist ideology, for example, I am sorry to say, we cannot allow, but if you want to do comparative politics and study both communism and capitalism and find out which one is better and it's already been proven that communism is not the better one, it's okay.

As far as upgrading every year the work on achieving Vision 2020, well I think this is something that we can all do. You can have your seminar here and the government is prepared to listen.

This government listens to people. We do not get here without listening to the people. We don't have very original ideas. Most of our ideas in government are obtained from the private sector. That is why we talk about Malaysia Incorporated and all that. It's all somebody else's ideas. As Tan Sri Ghazali said, it was applied to Japan. Well, it may be regarded as a bad thing as far as the United States' view of Japan is, but as far as we are concerned it is a good thing. If the Japanese government can work with the private sector and develop Japan, why can't we do the same. Nobody is stopping America from doing the same. America Incorporated, it will be a great thing. It might even be able to challenge Japan.

Ernest Zulliger: Mr Prime Minister, you have recently been travelling quite a bit all over the world and you are certainly aware of what is going on in the continents and in regard to a country's opening a legislation and opening their frontiers for foreign investments. In certain quarters, it is said that the need for investments far exceeds the funds which are actually available to cope with all these new investments required not only in Russia, Eastern Europe, Middle East, South America, Africa, but also everywhere. Well, you also are fully aware of the various trade blocs and other alliances which are being formed. My question is, do you think that this evolution might have an impact in the future years on firstly, investments from abroad into Malaysia and secondly, whether certain export markets which have been relatively easily accessible to Malaysia, might not be that easily accessible anymore because these trade blocs might have certain requirements for national content, and this might make things very much more difficult. So from there, it would appear that being a small nation with a small population and domestic market, there is an urgent need to expand and enlarge our domestic and our regional markets and of course also all over the world.

Now we have been reading that the Asean [Association of Southeast Asian Nations] economic ministers had proposed a free-trade zone which within fifteen years should bring custom duties down to zero. I have expressed during this seminar that in my view this is far too long a period, particularly when we see how fast things are moving in other countries. The question that arises is that, we know within Asean not every country has the same urgency and the same priority. Our country has eighteen million people and would this impediment not be overcome by Malaysia, for example, taking initiatives to form on its own certain bilateral or multilateral trade agreements, be it within the Asean or Asian region or with countries outside this continent.

Dr Mahathir Mohamad: I think there is this worry about the amount of funds available for investments when so many countries are now opening up their borders and inviting foreign participation in their economies. For example, the Latin American countries have now decided to allow foreign participation in their economy. And they have gone the whole way. They have allowed full foreign participation in their economies to the extent that they are quite willing to have their utilities run by foreign companies.

When we talk about privatization in Malaysia, we mean that we will sell a government facility to the local private sector. First we corporatize, then we sell off shares to the locals. Of course, some foreigners also come in but generally we are thinking in terms of locals taking over, but in Argentina, Chile, Brazil and Venezuela, when they say privatization it means selling their telephone companies to IT&T [International Telephone & Telegraph] or AT&T [American Telephone & Telegraph] and selling their airlines as just outright sales to foreign countries because they need the cash to pay off their debts. So in a way they are much more open than we are. And they should become very attractive. But people take time to accept that they have now accepted the system. They are not yet very comfortable with these countries.

So although some funds will flow towards these Latin American countries, there will be sufficient, I mean most people would be more keen to invest in a known country, a country like

Malaysia which is already known for its record of being friendly with foreign investors. Ever since Independence we have been friendly with foreign investors, so they feel much more comfortable here than they would feel in Latin America. So, we feel that we still have a good chance to attract foreign capital.

The same can be said about Eastern Europe. Not many people are going to Eastern Europe simply because they are not very certain about the ideology, the understanding of the free market system and the capacity of the government which is taking over from the previous communist government. They are not very certain about that. And the infrastructure is not yet in place. So while they may shunt some money for aid, I don't think they are going to invest such a great deal of money in these countries.

Nevertheless, whatever little that they put in will be a minus for us. But the Japanese are not yet attracted towards these countries and our investments are largely from Japan, Taiwan and now Korea and European investments in Malaysia as well as American investments which are not yet that big. Not as big as it used to be, it's getting less and less by comparison to Taiwan, Japan and Korea. Therefore, we can expect investment money to flow into Malaysia. It may be less but we ourselves cannot deal with such big investments, for example, in 1990 they say that total investment proposals amounted to 40 billion dollars. Of course, those are proposals, but for every dollar that is invested in this country, the government has to spend at least 10 cents by way of infrastructure. And if 40 billion dollars come in, we have to spend 4 billion dollars and we don't have that kind of money. So I think for the moment I am not worried about the amount of money flowing into this country but in time it is going to be reduced. But by that time we hope that domestic investments will be able to generate sufficient funds and domestic investors will be able to have sufficient funds to invest in new industries. However, I am not an expert in this area but this is my view after having travelled to Latin America, the Caribbean and some countries in Europe. I think we still have several years left before we are deprived of investment funds which can contribute towards our growth.

Now with regard to trade blocs, this is a worrisome thing. Trade blocs are definitely being formed. There is no good denying that there are trade blocs. The European Community is a trade bloc, so is Nafta [North American Free Trade Area]. What we need to do is of course to find loopholes and to find some leaks, some breaks in the wall that they have built up and we can to a certain extent still maintain our exports to these countries. But in the mean time it is necessary for us to find new markets and encourage our people to seriously look into these markets.

Many are doing business with the countries of the North so if they are doing business with the countries of the North, they must have a market. We should go in and try to compete with the countries of the North. I think we have the capacity if we really try. Many of them are very keen in trading with Malaysia. There is a lot of goodwill there and we should exploit that goodwill. But it will not happen if our people are not willing to take risks. Some people say that if there is no risk, there will be no gain but some of our people are so used to having no risk at all in Malaysia, and they are not going to go abroad. Here, there is always the government which can be asked to give certain policies which will facilitate business. When we go abroad we cannot ask those governments to do things which will make it profitable for you but I think if others can do business with these countries we can do business with them also. So we must actively shift our markets now so that when eventually certain markets become closed, as I think they will, we will have other markets open to us.

We should of course expand our domestic market. One of the things we have decided was to have a population of seventy million. Seventy million is not bad if the seventy million work and produce things. But seventy million people sleeping and doing nothing is not going to be good for the country. We expect people to work hard and be productive. So seventy million is a population that Malaysia can well afford considering its size. It has to be remembered that when the government said seventy million it is not now. We said that we should achieve seventy million people who have the money to spend. Then, of course, the domestic market will contribute to growth. Even now the domestic market is contributing more towards growth than before.

Asiah Abu Samah: We have been mulling over Vision 2020 since February, Mr Prime Minister, and we in Education in particular, have been having very thought-provoking and discussions as late as a few days ago, and as early as almost immediately after your speech to the Malaysian Business Council.

There are a number of issues that worry us, Mr Prime Minister. There is one issue that is very much at the heart and core of education, that my colleagues and I are grappling with. Now, your very first statement of Vision, rather the backdrop to the nine *cabaran* or challenges, you talked of a strong united nation that is economically vibrant and competitive that contributes strongly towards the building of a science and technology culture, founded on the inculcation of deep ethical and moral values with a very strong caring strain in our society.

I gather what has been worrying us in Education as well as this seminar is that there will be sections of the population that will be able to and that will have these attributes you have so wisely envisioned. But there will also be sections of the population, to our mind, who will still be struggling to be there in the year 2020. We have talked of an open economy, and personally, I am still grappling with the concept.

But from what I understand, Mr Prime Minister, we have moved from certain precepts, certain principles or orientation even of policy from the New Economic Policy to the National Development Policy which goes more for openness, for excellence, for competitiveness and for quality. We who are in the planning group are very conscious, Mr Prime Minister. We are working very hard towards this. But the realities of the situation is that there are certain developments that will take some time and I know too well in education, it is like that. That urban schools will develop faster than rural schools.

We have had five Malaysia Plans, Mr Prime Minister. We have had all kinds of strategies and yet we are still getting a situation where rural schools, if I can be more frank, where *sekolah-sekolah kebangsaan* [national-type schools], for example, are lagging far behind some other schools.

Many of us are very sincere about the caring society, about the development of values, based on strong spiritual foundation, *pembangunan insan yang harmonis dan seimbang* [the development of a harmonious and balanced society] which is at the heart of the education philosophy, *Falsafah Pendidikan Negara* [National Education Philosophy]. But how far are all of us committed to this, Mr Prime Minister. There is a feeling that some of us will be pursuing this more strongly than others. Some of us will be going more for economic, scientific and technological development which I know you will say, Mr Prime Minister, that this will have to depend on the ethical and moral values but we have also seen such development taking place that are almost divorced of ethical and moral values, and yet we still consider them as development. This is a very basic issue to me that we are grappling with in the process of trying to arrive at that scenario that you have painted.

I think there have to be a great deal of discussions and commitments. There has to be a greater understanding of those who are in the slower strand of development by those who are in the faster lane. I am not saying that those in the faster lane should slow down, but they should probably help. By helping, I mean understanding the reality of the weaknesses and the problem that those in the slower lane are facing. I am saying this, Mr Prime Minister, because sometimes we feel that this understanding is somewhat wanting. I could be much more concrete than that, but I like to believe that I am being understood. For those who have been following yesterday's discussion I think this is much more deeply understood. I think this is very crucial to us in the world of education. There is no problem working with the private sector. We have been working already, Mr Prime Minister, in our curriculum planning. We have been involving so many parties from so many walks of life. There is no problem about that but it is the problem of implementation. It is the problem of commitment and understanding in terms of issues I am talking about.

Dr Mahathir Mohamad: Thank you very much for bringing up what is a very worrisome aspect of this target that we have set for ourselves. In fact, at the recent UMNO [United Malays National Organization] meeting, I mentioned this thing that it will not do to have a developed society in the year 2020, when the Bumiputeras will be left behind, very undeveloped. I don't think I have the answer but I feel the situation is not as bleak, as it was, when we started. In the days when we were extremely worried about whether the Malays and Bumiputeras can keep up with the pace of development in the early days, our conclusion was that they will not. But we have seen progress.

We have seen the Bumiputeras, the rural people, become exposed to new ways of doing things and being able to adjust to new things. I have noticed that they are as skilful as anybody. In terms of learning how to do work, they can learn it as fast and in certain instances they are faster than other people. But what I notice and what worries me is the attitudes towards work and the material aspects of life. Sometimes we see them running away from reality because they feel that they cannot cope and this is due to the value system. We are brought up with this value system which does not prepare us to face reality and we tend to retreat.

The value system of a community normally develops by itself. It is changing all the time. At some stage it will be good and other stages it will be bad. We see changing value systems all over the world. The people who have been very successful before have now acquired value systems which will negate their success. In fact, we see in the West, for example, a very radical change is taking place in the value system where there is apparently a loss of pride in their own abilities and in their own way of life.

You know, if you were to go to New York, you see a city that is decaying right in front of your eyes, and there is no effort made to stop the process of decay. We see a city that is unsafe. Nobody can walk around at night without being molested and if you are molested in the city, people will just look at you, and not come to your rescue. There is a loss of moral values. This is not the same society that built America before. The pioneering society, of course from the Red Indians point of view, was not very good but from the American viewpoint this was a great society. This was a society that built America, a society made up of immigrants who came and were willing to face all odds and build the nation but that has now changed.

We also see this change among other communities in other parts of the world. These are changes which take place unconsciously as a result of circumstances. We know, for example, the Arabs before they became Muslims were among the most quarrelsome people. They used to have feuds for ages until they have forgotten why they quarrelled with each other, but all they know is that when this *Kabilah* meet that *Kabilah* they must fight. Then they became Muslims and became united. They built the great Islamic empire and the process of change goes on and having built the empire, they deteriorated. They no longer hold the values of the religion they profess to believe in and now they are back to the same old thing. An Iraqi cannot see a Kuwaiti without wanting to murder him. Only the same *Kabilah* thing except on a grander scale. So, values change and as the values change, the people change and their achievements also change. The same people who lived in caves before can compete with the most civilized Romans.

So I think, if we appreciate the fact that values play a big role towards making a society achievement-oriented, then we cannot wait for the values to change by itself. They do change. The Malays and Bumiputeras of today are not the same as the Malays and Bumiputeras of yesterday. They have changed. Sometimes for the better and sometimes for the worse. As you can see the number of drug addicts among young Malay boys. They copy and if left to themselves they will copy some of the values that are not good for them. For example, the Americans feel guilty about the way they treat the Blacks, so in order to become more identified with the Blacks they have an Afro hairdo. That is their psychological problem. Why should we have an Afro hairdo? But you see our Malaysian boys too having Afro hairdo. Fashionable, but you don't know that this is a reflection of American guilt to overcome what they have done to the Blacks. So they say, "Black is beautiful and Afro is beautiful." They know it is ugly but they do it, and our people left to themselves will just copy without knowing the reason why. So we cannot afford to have the Bumiputeras absorb value systems on their own or change their value systems on their own.

We have to actively foster good value systems because I feel we can overcome some of their weaknesses. We can implant and develop good value systems among the Bumiputeras or the people in the rural areas. Since you are shy to mention Malays and Bumiputeras, I will mention it to you. I know what is on your mind. You say you know, I know, I will say I know. Actually this is what the government is doing.

We want to actively change their value system. We have devoted RM100 million for this process. We are setting up centres where we will take people and tell them why this value system is bad and why this is good and why you should practice this value system and not that. For example, we have taken workers to these centres and explained to them why they should not go on strike, because this is not going to contribute to their well-being at all. It will only make their leaders very happy. Because then they can collect more money and enjoy a better life but they themselves are going to contribute to their own downfall because once their own products are no longer competitively priced they cannot expand anymore and they will lose out in the end.

We have to explain this thing to them because we cannot expect them to reason these things out themselves. For example, the old concept of a trade union is that by having a trade union you can threaten your employer to give you better pay. If they don't then you go on strike and you assume that by going on strike you do damage to the employer but you also do damage to yourself. If you go on strike and get too big a pay and you produce things which are too costly, which are not competitive, in the end you are going to lose out and if a country is not competitive, not productive, then everybody will lose out and when everybody loses out, the workers lose out also. That kind of convoluted reasoning is not possible for the average worker. You have to tell him. So, what we try to do is to take groups of young people and tell them what is right and what is wrong and what is good and what is bad. It works sometimes. It does not always work. But we do see a change in them.

All the workers in Proton, three thousand of them have been inculcated with new values, work ethics and new ideas of how they can benefit from working. And they work very hard and even people who do not think we have done, we have produced our own car, think that the Proton is a good car. So it is a tribute to the changed attitude of the workers. You see them coming to the factory before time. You don't see them coming on time but before time, then they have a discussion, set their targets, say their prayers and then they start work. It is a new attitude towards work and the same thing can be applied towards learning.

If you orientate the child to the importance of learning, then he will be able to achieve success. But you cannot leave this to parents. Parents are uneducated, in terms of psychology. You can allow parents to inculcate values to a certain extent but left to themselves they really do not know. The average parent does not know what is good for his own child. He does not really teach the child to absorb good values. Sometimes parents are very careless. The average working-class parent just brings up his child any way he feels. He has no programme to put into the child a certain set of values which will ensure that the child will succeed.

I have always made this difference between the Chinese child and the Malay child. The Chinese child stands behind the counter and sells goods. The Malay child gets money from papa and mama and goes there, gives the money and gets the goods. That's his relation to money. Money is a convenience for getting something. Instead of having to carry a sack of rice he just carries money. Much more easy. Put them in the pocket and go and do something. What he is doing is to change something for something else. No profits and no losses are involved. But the Chinese child is taught from the beginning that you have to sell at a price. So the training from the very beginning is different. That is why now in the school we ask the school to teach children how to buy and sell. Get the Malay child behind the counter and not in front of the counter. You have two different communities not only divided because of ethnic origins but divided culturally and by training and if you want them to achieve, you have to give the same kind of training. Otherwise they cannot achieve.

I wrote a book called the *The Malay Dilemma* where I talked a lot about the hereditary factor and how Malays tend to marry within their own relatives. It does not happen anymore nowadays because they are all spread out. So, that hereditary factor is no longer there. But the exposure is not there. So I think that it may not resolve the whole problem but it can solve some of the problem. We must have a concerted effort to teach the young Bumiputeras what is good for them, how they can compete and why they should compete, this should not be left to the parents. But if we actively do this, I think we can solve some of the problems.

Now, I have told this story a thousand times to many people. When I was the Minister of Education, I thought that the people are most suited to change the character of the children will be the teachers. But there are thousands and thousands of teachers and I doubt whether they understand the need to inculcate good values. They know how to teach geography, history, maths and all that but good values is not part of the subject for teaching. So I thought that these teachers are sure to understand good values and teach the children good values so that they will become successful when they grow up. But you cannot talk to the teachers. So whom do you talk to. You talk to the people who teach the teachers. That is to say the lecturers in the colleges. Even then the numbers are very big. So I thought the best thing for me was to talk to the principal of the teacher training colleges. And I talked to them and explained to them the way I am explaining now about the need to inculcate new values so that they can do this and that. I am sorry to say that at the end of my one-hour lecture on why it is important to inculcate new values, one of the principals got up and said the problem is that the pay is not enough. Obviously the one-hour lecture was a waste of time. So I gave up.

That is why now we think in terms of actually training people to give talks to workers, students, teachers and the like. We are picking them out, we are going through this process now. I will be meeting a number of lecturers and I must say that we began with the ministers in the Cabinet. Of course we want the ministers also to have good values. I do not know whether you agree that they have good values. But we have the first batch that is made up of ministers of Cabinet, deputy ministers, Chief Secretary, Chief of Armed Forces, Chief of Police and all of them spent three days in Port Dickson during which we had talks and discussions on what constitutes good values and why we should propagate them. I do not know whether this has any effect or not, but I would like to think that it had some effect.

So while I cannot give an assurance that this will resolve the problems and therefore the fear that you have, I feel that one of the solutions at least is to actively propagate good values and expose them to the realities of life early among the Bumiputeras, whether they are from the rural or urban areas. This is the worry of all educationists in the Ministry. I understand that. I was the Minister of Education before and before I became a Minister I was one of those who was very concerned about this. But I am still concerned and I think we must make this attempt to change their attitude because people are the same. It is their values and culture rather than ethnicity which influence the success or otherwise of any community.

Geh Ik Cheong: May I join the others in first thanking and appreciating and in fact admiring what Tan Sri Dato' Seri Ahmad Sarji Abdul Hamid and Dr Mohd Yusof Ismail have done in organizing this seminar. Mr Prime Minister, because you have said that nothing is more important than the development of human resources, we have spent a lot of time and attention on this subject and it has been tied up with aspects of moral and ethical values.

I know that you are a great admirer of Japanese ethics and work ethics and what they have achieved in their country. I too share your admiration for the Japanese. Now I like to share with you one of my observations on what I think has made the Japanese education system so successful. In Japan, they provide 30 per cent tertiary education for their people. Amongst this 30 per cent tertiary education, there is a very large number of what they call Junior Universities which are principally directed to the female population. In their statistics, ever since 1978, the enrolment of women in tertiary education has overtaken the enrolment of men. Women now constitute 32 per cent of the eligible age and men, 27 per cent.

In these junior universities, the women are educated to be good mothers and in fact, in family responsibility, in the education of the child, the mother is almost wholly responsible, with the workaholic husband coming back after the child has gone to bed. Now we talked about moral and ethical requirements and not just the economic requirements of human resources. But they are all part of human resources and I think whatever we may sayboils down to education by educated parents.

The child always learns his first concepts of language and actions from the mother and in fact in the early pre-school days the child has mastered a speaking language, to be able to do all the things at home. It has in fact done most of the development it needs to do in coping with living in this world. Now of course education then takes over but during the years of education the child is still very strongly under the influence of the mother. In fact, until the child is married and even after marriage, it still depends on the mother. So, a well educated female population is a very important asset to the development of a country.

Now, the other aspect I would like to bring up is that we have made a lot of macroeconomic plans and we have made all sorts of master plans and industrialization and all that, but you have recognized and so has OPP2 [Second Outline Perspective Plan] and the Sixth Malaysia Plan that in fact human resource is the foundation for anything that a nation can do. There has been talk about a Royal Commission. I wonder whether that is necessary because I mean it is very time consuming and it brings up possibly not very relevant issues.

I have seen a very good paper by Dato' Dr Othman Yeop Abdullah where he set out some methodologies and a very scientific approach on how we can analyse our human resource requirements. In fact, if we want to approach Vision 2020 we have got to try to classify, quantify, analyse what human resource requirements and needs of Vision 2020 are. This is very difficult to do but as you say nothing is ever perfect.

In spite of its imperfections should we not consider the drawing up of a Human Resource Development master plan and keep on incorporating and reviewing this at each of our five-year plan periods. I am sure it will draw attention to a lot of our shortcomings. I mean it is true that in the past few days I have always been misunderstood that I am criticizing our educational achievements. Far from it, I am just appreciative how much more has to be done. Let us try to quantify, classify and analyse it and then knowing the needs of the country, assess what we can do to fulfill those needs. Because, if we don't get started we are not going to make much headway.

I think we have achieved a lot. We must have achieved a lot in education. Otherwise we would not be where we are today. But Dato' Dr Othman has said that locally we provide 7 per cent of the tertiary needs of the country, compared with the average of 30 per cent for those of NICs [Newly Industrialized Countries] and developed countries. Now I am saying let us realize what the needs are and analyse and try and put in figures what needs to be done in terms of Vision 2020.

Mr Prime Minister, you have mentioned the need for balance in this country. Even in a very homogeneous society like Japan, of course not everybody can be a scientist, a technologist, or a doctor, nor do we want in this country to say the Indians should be doctors and lawyers. We do not necessarily want that, but knowing the needs of the country, surely we can then see that a nation is a whole spectrum of activities. Some people are better in one type of activity, while some are better in another type of activity. This can be blended and we can strike the balance when we know what the needs are. Not everyone needs to be a doctor or a Prime Minister. You can be a number of things because the whole society needs a spectrum of skills and talents, and in fact some of these balances can be adjusted if you know your needs and what you can do towards fulfilling them.

I have had the honour of working with you in the development of PNB [Permodalan Nasional Berhad] and you know how rapidly Malays have been able to assimilate and understand values of savings, investments, dealing with the capital and financial market and computers. You have seen a whole spectrum of Malay ability developing there given the opportunity for education. This is the whole crux of it. We could do with more educational facilities. We can never have enough. Every time we talk about this we encounter the problem that there are not enough teachers. There are constraints.

But I think when we talk about Vision 2020 we are talking of the next generation. Let us make a start ensuring that we will have enough teachers, we will have enough educational facilities, so that different ethnic groups in the country don't feel deprived that they have to compete for scarce facilities. I know it is costly. But as you have said the private sector can play a part. You are very liberal about this now which I think is a watershed. The government has not been as liberal about private sector's participation in education as you are now. Maybe, we need to see to all these needs, how much can be fulfilled by the public sector. How much the private sector has to rise up so that they know the directions that they are going and the rules under which they can assist in the development of the educational facilities.

Dr Mahathir Mohamad: I agree with you that the most important thing is human resource development and here ethics play a big role. You mentioned about how the women in Japan are educated to be good mothers. When we say that we assume that the people who are going to teach the women of Japan understand what a good mother should do. In other words, we will have to have teachers who understand that. It is already a part of the Japanese culture to give that role to the mothers. It is no great problem for them to teach women how to be good mothers and how to inculcate good values in their children. They are not changing but are passing on a set of ethical values which they already have which needs perhaps to be re-emphasized. So the teachers just continue the process of educating the mothers as their duty to their children. Even if their fathers do not come back, it does not really matter because the mother is there to look after their children and to get them to study hard. In fact, Japanese mothers are known to drive their children to suicide by insisting that they must study hard, work hard and they must eventually end up in Tokyo University because that is the highest institution they have and some children cannot stand the pace, stand the pressure and they commit suicide. The numbers in Japan are said to be big. But that does not deter them from pushing their children to achieve success. So it is the ethics of an achievement-oriented society. That is already there and is passed on to the next generation.

Here what we want to do is to actually change the ethical values. We are saying that the mothers do not know what is good for their children and not only that, we are saying the people who are going to teach the mothers do not know. The teachers themselves do not know. Pardon me for saying so. Our teachers may be good in teaching mathematics, geography, or whatever, but are they qualified to teach good ethical values to our children. Is there a special course that is compulsory for every teacher to understand, what is good and what he or she must impart to the children? There is as far as I know no class devoted to this and if there is a class, the teachers must be specially prepared for this and if the teachers are to be prepared for this, then the lecturers in the teachers training colleges must know what they have to teach the teachers, who can then teach the mothers, if you like. This is not being done systematically.

That is why we try to do it through other means – non-conventional means, like taking them for five or six days or one week trying to inculcate new values, change their values and that is not easy. It is much more easy to emphasize existing values than to change values and to say what you are doing now is wrong and you must do this and not that. That is much more difficult. And the people who will pass on this set of values must be specially trained for that. If we can do that, than we can produced good human resources.

As you know, Japan is a resourceless nation and it has been inculcated in the minds of the children that their role is to bring in raw materials from abroad, process it, add value and export it in order to survive. This has been inculcated in the mind of every Japanese child but in Malaysia we do not have this problem. We are a resource-rich country. I mean it does not require much effort in order to be alive in this country. You can get fish from the rivers or the padi fields. There is always food around. Plenty of food. Nobody starves in Malaysia.

I remember in 1974 when I became Minister of Education there was this story about one child who died of starvation in Baling. I said this is not possible, not in Malaysia and sure enough it is not possible. It was a big fib told by these people who wanted to become heroes, including our present Minister of Finance.

Life being so easy it does not require that kind of resilience that is needed in the Japanese child. They would not be able to prosper if they don't have the willingness to work hard, to sacrifice for a good future and the Japanese have got this idea that the most disgraceful thing is to be ashamed. You know if you are ashamed of something you should actually commit *harakiri*. I am not suggesting we should do that but the Japanese still have this sense of shame. I mean there are still people who will throw themselves off the sixth floor if they have been accused of embezzling company funds. Of course, nowadays they come back. They don't do that anymore but the sense of shame is very deeply ingrained in the Japanese mind. So to fail is something that cannot be tolerated because if you fail you may have to commit *harakiri*. You may have to punish yourself. You may feel disgraced and all that kind of things.

Nowadays we have a society which is shameless. You know they go to jail, serve a sentence and they come out and they feel happy about it. They go around and behave as if nothing has happened. We have that kind of people around. I remember when I was a boy, to have a relative who has gone to jail is something so shameful. You want to be disassociated and do not want to mention his name. But nowadays they are invited to big functions and all that. They come and they are quite happy about it. It's nothing and there is no sense of shame. Not only the people concerned but the others also have no feeling of shame. But the Japanese have this strong sense of shame or *malu*, which makes them try to achieve, but we don't have that value and we do not implant that kind of value in the children. We can't expect the mothers to do that.

The Japanese force the children to achieve because if not the whole family is ashamed. Not only the child, the whole family and the child sometimes commits suicide simply because of that. He cannot do it. So he says life is not worth living. But we don't have that kind of society here. In Malaysia, if somebody fails you pat him on the back. "Never mind you will do something better next time." Next time he fails you pat his back again. He goes around having a nice time. He doesn't bother to study. We need to have a little bit of the sense of shame. This must be implanted and inculcated in the children. And I think that can best be done of course by trained teachers. I don't expect the mothers to be able to do that. Not at the moment because our society tolerates shame. I am not worried about that. Before you don't like to go and visit your relatives in jail. But now you openly go there and also demonstrate in front of the jail. You don't mind if people know that your relative is inside. It is not their fault that they are inside. It is the government's fault.

So this kind of thing, this kind of value system is very, very important if you are going to have the kind of human resources that we need. Whether he is a Malay, a Chinese or an Indian, if he has the correct value system I am quite sure he can achieve. A Malay child with a correct value system can achieve more than the Chinese child with the wrong value system. I am quite sure that is so. But the problem is a problem of numbers. There are a lot of Malays who have done well. Some have become bankers. Some have brokerage companies which have done very well. But there are a lot who have not done well.

The great fear among the Bumiputeras is that they will live in their own country where they have to serve others, where they will have to be cooks and drivers to others. This is their great fear. We have to assess the fear. We have to make sure that they are equally capable of achieving and this is not being helped by the Ali Baba methods where you go to a Malay and tell him, "I will give you the money, you go and sleep." Then of course he will become an idiot for the rest of his life because he has never been exposed to the problems of managing a company. He gets money and so why bother. Ask the government for another license, get more money and then sell the license. If you do this you are sabotaging the development of Bumiputeras. So please don't do that. If you want to take a Malay as your partner, then make him work. Make him feel the pain of it. Use his money. If he loses money, it will be his money. Don't tell him you don't have to do anything at all, like "You just go and get the license from the government and I will do everything." If you do that, you are going to sabotage our efforts. So these are factors which can contribute towards the development of the kind of character that we need in this country. We are worried still about this thing. That is why we still have to have some government control over education.

We will allow the private sector to participate in having educational facilities but we would like you to conform to the government's policy. People who are capable of getting good education should not be prevented from doing so because, as the Malays say, if "we try to grasp flour it is going to trickle between the fingers anyway" and that is precisely what is happening. But if all communities are conscious of their duties to the other communities and if they sincerely help, I think we will have lesser problems of disparities within our society. Until that time we have to continue to ensure that the identification of race with economic function will have to be eliminated consciously by the government and also by the private sector.

Dr Kamaruddin Hj Kachar: My question is on the maximum utilization of developed human resources. When we talk of human resources two aspects are taken into account. One is upgrading of personnel in the knowledge, skills and professionalism plus developing their positive attitudes. Secondly, is the utilization of trained personnel. The question is how could we ensure maximum utilization of trained personnel knowing that there is a brain drain to foreign countries. This obviously shows their lack of love and loyalty for their country. Furthermore, quite a number of trained personnel indulge in disciplines apart from the one which he or she was trained for, for example, one Ph.D. holder in Town Planning went around teaching and commercializing Islam.

Thirdly, Mr Prime Minister, is non-utilization of the expertise. For example, quite a number of our trained personnel have been influenced by some extreme groups of religious teaching. This is not the fault of the education system. I am glad that the Arqam group is banned but it is only after many years. This group, Mr Prime Minister, recruits their members mainly from the science and social science group.

Dr Mahathir Mohamad: Firstly, with regard to the brain drain. This happens everywhere. It does not only happen in Malaysia. Singapore which is supposed to be a haven for these people also loses a lot of people. There is no favouring the Malays in Singapore. In fact, Malays are not favoured at all. They are not allowed to join the airforce because they might learn how to fly an aircraft. They are not allowed to become officers but the brain drain is by the other citizens and they go off to Australia believing that life is better in Australia. They found that it is not so good now. Some of them want to come back but that is their choice. We have the English migrating to America and the Americans living in Paris.

I do not know whether they are less patriotic or not but everybody wants to find that something which he thinks good for himself. It is only later that he realizes that what appears to be good or what appears to be green is not so green after all. I am not worried about these people who want to migrate. They can migrate. But I feel quite sure if this country does well, these people will not want to go off so quickly and whether their not going off is good for us or not is another thing. I am not quite sure.

Now, the problem of our students being influenced by deviant teachings of Islam. This is really because we ourselves have not paid any attention to the teaching of religion. Some of us who are concerned about this are not knowledgeable about our own religion and because we are not knowledgeable we are not in the position to tell the teachers of Islam, the teachers of religion in the schools, what they should be teaching and because we don't oversee them then what they teach the children is either inadequate or wrong. And some of these students who go to the university are completely without a basic knowledge of Islam and because of that they are gullible. They accept somebody's definition of religion as the truth and they get easily influenced and they forget their obligations as required from a good Muslim and therefore they leave their studies or even if they are qualified they decide they are not going to be materialistic. They want to devote their life to religion. But of course they don't mind travelling in trains and aeroplanes which are built by materialistic people but we are not in a position to correct them because we ourselves have got a poor understanding of the religion.

We don't study religion enough in order to argue with them on a religious basis. You can't argue with them and say, "Look, you must be prosperous, you musn't be wearing this *Jubba* [robe] and this green turban." Why can't they? What's wrong with that? If they want to wear a green turban because they think it is part of the religion. Why do you say it is not? "Quote to me from the teachings of Islam why I cannot wear a green turban?" To that, we have no answer because we don't study. So if you want to correct these people you must study your religion. Then you can argue on the same basis. If they quote one *hadith* you have to quote another. You have at least to know same basic things about Islam. But we are too lazy to learn and therefore some of these cranks manage to influence our students. For example, some Malay girls studying medicine in the university were enticed to marry Arqam members. They left their studies and even their parents could not persuade them to come back because they have said it is wrong for them to study medicine. Their duty is to get married and to cover their faces.

I know once they believe this is the religion you cannot change because faith is a very strong thing. It is not easy to change faith. Once they believe this is the right faith it is very difficult to tell them that it is wrong unless you really know how to tell them because you know your religion. But if people who have no knowledge of religion try to correct these people the response is, "What do you know?" You cannot answer and if you cannot answer then you cannot blame those people. It is you who are wrong.

I study my religion not in Arabic but in English and Malay. At least I can argue a little bit with these people but then of course they don't like arguing with anybody who can argue back with them, but there are so many other people who will not argue with them. So they have this influence. And we are living in a society which is inclined towards religion.

We cannot just say close down this thing, close down that thing because you may have a bad reaction. It took us a long time to take a decision to close down Arqam. But that is done only after our learned people have studied and concluded that they are deviationists. It took a long time to decide because they also do not like to say it is wrong because it looks so right. You know what is more right than to see people with turban. He must be a Muslim.

You remember the story of the crusaders, when they reached Jerusalem they killed all the people with turbans. Actually the Arab Christians also wore turbans. So they killed the Arab Christians as well because they identified turbans with Islam. Dress has nothing to do with religion. I mean the fact that you are dressed such a way does not mean you are a Muslim. The problem now is that people like to have a symbol, I mean whether they practice the teachings of Islam or not. It is not that it is not important but they mix up the appearance with the real thing. So there is this problem we face. But we will try to overcome it. The only way to overcome this is for us to learn sufficiently about religion to rebut whatever they say.

For example, they say that Muslims should not accept a non-Muslim as a leader which is fine in a country where 100 or 90 per cent of the people are Muslims but supposing Muslims are a minority, that is, 10 per cent of the total population and the prime minister is a non-Muslim, what do you do? Do you say, I reject the prime minister? You have to accept him as the leader of your country but because these people have brought this kind of teachings in order to gain political advantage, some people accept.

Unfortunately we have a lot of gullible people and they are gullible because they do not know their own religion. I think we have to learn about our own religion and we have to make sure to tell these teachers who are teaching our children what is right. Otherwise they are going to teach all the wrong things about religion. And they will say this world is for the *kafir* [infidel]. Ours is in the next world. I am not so sure because nobody who has gone there has come back. So the government will oversee this. I do not know whether we will be successful but this is one of the problems, this wrong interpretation of Islam. I have complete faith in my religion. I think it is not a hindrance to achieving the worldly achievements but the problem that we have is the wrong interpretation of Islam and that is what we have to tackle. Not Islam itself. Islam is correct as far as I am concerned. I am not asking non-Muslims to accept it as correct, but I accept it as correct. I don't think I need to change the religion or change my religion in order to perform successfully in this world but we need to do something about this extremist and deviationist interpretations of Islam which is definitely holding back the Muslims and the Malays in this country.

Ahmad Sarji Abdul Hamid: You have greatly enriched this seminar with your deep knowledge on many subjects, with your wisdom and visionary views and your articulatory skills which are well known locally and internationally. However, Sir, on *Bangsa Malaysia* and National Unity, I would like to believe that you are reserving most of what you are going to say for the Harvard Club function on January 23.

Sir, the secretariat will be preparing the report of this seminar and participants will be given a copy of the report. The main suggestions of this seminar will be considered by the National Development Planning Committee and I will submit a report to you.

Thank you for your participation. You have displayed a high sense of commitment and discipline and this is what Tan Sri Ghazali Shafie said, leadership by good example, Sir, but I do not know what the opportunity cost is for you for being absent from work.

Sir, with this, thank you very much for your presence and thank you again for your participation.

[December 7, 1991]

2

Statements by Abdul Ghafar Baba, the Deputy Prime Minister of Malaysia

In February 1991, Dr Mahathir Mohamad, outlined the country's vision as a fully developed nation by the year 2020. He explained that Malaysia should be fully developed, in our own mould, without emulating any other nation of the world, least of all the developed West. He stressed that Malaysia should not only be developed economically, but also politically, socially, spiritually, psychologically as well as culturally. What is more important in our efforts towards a developed status is that we should also endeavour to create a united, confident, socially just and politically stable Malaysian society, in which everybody has a place, and takes pride in being a Malaysian.

Dr Mahathir Mohamad also talked about the need to create a united Malaysian nation with an outward-looking Malaysian society, infused with strong moral and ethical values and living in a state that is democratic, liberal, tolerant, caring, economically just and equitable, progressive and prosperous, and in full possession of an economy that is competitive, dynamic, robust and resilient.

The developed country that we envisage for ourselves and future Malaysians must be one that is fully developed beyond the economics. We should be a nation not only of high growth, but one which is equally concerned with the social, political and other aspects of human development. We desire a society, which has confidence in itself and whose members are tolerant of each other's way of life and beliefs, and viewpoints while at the same time imbued with strong ethical and moral qualities and beyond all, a society that is caring. This Malaysian society, as earlier indicated, is to be distinguished by the pursuit of excellence, wary of its capabilities, subservient to none, and able to stand head and shoulders with peoples of other nations.

It is against this backdrop that I wish to share with you some of my views on the economic transformation or changes that we have to face in our efforts towards making Malaysia a developed nation and the role of the public and private sectors in meeting these changes.

Since 1988, the Malaysian economy has been growing from strength to strength, with real Gross Domestic Product (GDP) expanding at a rapid pace of over 9 per cent per annum during the last three years. In fact, the outturn in 1990 was the best since 1976 and has earned Malaysia the distinction of being one of the most dynamic economies in the world. It is worth noting that last year's 10 per cent growth in real GDP has even surpassed the performances of Hong Kong, Singapore, South Korea and Taiwan – as well as our Asean neighbours. Even more encouraging is the fact that rapid growth in 1990 was achieved in a stable environment with low inflation. This outstanding performance was even more impressive when you consider the fact that we had to face all sorts of problems and uncertainties, including the repercussions of the Gulf War, oil price fluctuations and economic recession in some industrial countries.

Latest data suggest that growth in the domestic economy will remain strong in 1991, notwithstanding emerging uncertainties on the international front associated with the political developments in the Soviet Union. Current production indicators show that real GDP growth was maintained at a creditable 8.4 per cent during the first half of the year.

All signs point towards a satisfactory growth performance over the rest of the year. As in previous years, much of the impetus to growth will continue to emanate from the strength of domestic demand, particularly from private sector investment.

The economic outlook in the long run appears just as promising. With the implementation of the Sixth Malaysia Plan and the expected recovery in the world economy, the Malaysian economy is projected to grow at an average rate of 7.5 per cent in real terms over the next five years. Consequently, nominal GNP is expected to reach about RM205 billion by the year 1995, almost double the current level, with per capita income rising to about RM10,200 in 1995. Output growth during the Sixth Malaysia Plan period is expected to be led by the manufacturing sector with an average growth of 11.5 per cent per annum, to be followed by the construction and services sectors, with each growing at 8 per cent per annum.

The agriculture sector, on the other hand, is only expected to record a moderate growth of 3.5 per cent per annum, and mining, a marginal growth of 1.5 per cent per annum. On the demand side, private investment is expected to continue playing the leading role, to be supported by a moderate growth in public investment. Indeed, a similar trend is expected to be holding up well in the next ten years when the Second Outline Perspective Plan (OPP2) projects an average annual growth of 7 per cent for the period 1991-2000. This target is realistic and achievable as it is only marginally higher than the average growth of 6.7 per cent achieved over the last twenty years under the OPP1.

The economic scenario envisaged in the Sixth Malaysia Plan and the Second Outline Perspective Plan suggests a considerable degree of structural transformation of the Malaysian economy by the year 2000. During the same period, the manufacturing sector will see its share rising to 37 per cent from its current level of 27 per cent. In relation to total exports, the share of agriculture is expected to decline to 6 per cent, while that of manufacturing will increase to 82 per cent.

If we think such changes in the structure of the economy are significant, we should try to visualize what would happen in the year 2020. Indeed, we ought to prepare ourselves by anticipating the magnitude of the changes to be brought about by Vision 2020, which will alter almost entirely the economic landscape of this nation. If we are now used to a GDP level of RM115 billion in 1990, it will be a totally new environment when GDP is expected to increase to about RM920 billion (in 1990 prices) in the year 2020. Such an outcome is not unrealistic, and it can be achieved if the economy grows at an average of 7 per cent per annum in real terms over the next thirty years. In the same vein, the level of GNP in nominal terms is likely to increase more rapidly. Consequently, assuming that population will grow slightly lower than the current rate, per capita income in nominal terms is expected to accelerate from RM6,180 in 1990 to about RM80,000 in 2020.

These are only some of the numbers which can be computed quickly, under certain reasonable assumptions, to indicate the extent of possible economic transformation underlying Vision 2020. These figures are enough to indicate the kind of economy we are aiming for in the future, an economy that is entirely different both in size and character, from the one we have today.

These numbers may seem unbelievably high at this juncture. But I am optimistic that if we could harness our investment resources correctly and efficiently from now in this thirty-year march towards economic excellence, then what we perceive today may not appear to be that far-fetched.

To realize this quantum leap in investment requirement, the country must necessarily continue to rely on foreign direct investments (FDIs). These FDIs have provided the basic thrust in the first phase of our industrialization efforts, and I am positive that foreign investments will continue to be an important vehicle in the nation's industrial transformation.

The task of attracting such investments will become more difficult as competition from other less developed countries which have labour cost advantage will become stiffer. However, without a dynamic domestic investment sector, it would be difficult to develop unsustainable national economic resilience. We need therefore to continue to provide the necessary support and incentives to nurture a dynamic and thriving domestic investment sector. We must continue to provide a conducive and supportive environment for domestic investment to grow and modernize through a less restrictive regulatory control and where possible, the proper fiscal and financial back-up facilities.

Savings are a very crucial element in promoting investments as they could directly promote the propensity to invest and to bring about greater capital accumulations. Under the Sixth Malaysia Plan, an average savings rate of approximately 36 per cent is expected. This is creditable by any standard and by 2020, though we expect a slight fall in the savings rate, we should attempt to maintain a level of at least 33 per cent.

To achieve this target, the contributions from both the public and private sectors would be crucially important. The government on its part would try to create the environment that would be conducive to increasing the savings propensity of our people. Where practical, it will try to enhance mobilization of savings by introducing appropriate measures to encourage thrift among our people, enlarge the financial intermediaries in our financial sector, mobilize rural savings and create greater inducements to encourage more locally-based foreign investors to reinvest in the country.

Strategies to mobilize savings, if accompanied by an unchecked wasteful consumerism and extravagant expenditure, would be self-defeating. We have therefore to be continuously vigilant over these wasteful habits and extravagance to ensure that runaway inflation does not rear its destructive presence. It is imperative that price stability be maintained. Equally important too would be the contribution and co-operation of the private sector to complement these government aspirations. While the government could create the mechanism through which greater mobilization of savings could be induced, the private sector should equally strive to enhance their savings propensity.

In terms of our industrialization strategy, the broadening and deepening of our industrial base is important to enhance our industrial competitiveness and sophistication, as well as to keep in tune with changes in the marketplace and new challenges. Where necessary, we would need to re-evaluate our industrial promotion incentives to be consistent with emerging demands of industries. The government would closely monitor these changes and continue to provide the appropriate incentive support.

Public enterprises which mushroomed in the 1970s and 1980s are basically aimed to provide the thrust to the government's industrialization programme. Additionally, they also assist Bumiputera investors in terms of skill development, entrepreneurship training and the holding in trust of projects for eventual Bumiputera participation. While public enterprises should continue to handle these roles, emerging new changes and challenges in the national economy have necessitated a need to redefine their functions.

They should now be made to operate under a highly competitive and highly technological environment managed by highly trained professionals. They should be made to establish linkages with multinational corporations as well as with the numerous SMIs or small- and medium-sized industries within the country. They should also move more in line with international commercial activities and assist local enterprises, especially Bumiputera concerns, in the international marketplace. Finally, and certainly not of any lesser importance, public enterprises should not compete in areas where Bumiputera investments are already present.

An important aspect of our economy that urgently needs to be sorted out is the present precarious state of the labour movement that is in keeping with changing times. Of late, many of its leaders are involved in a tug-of-war on issues of international affiliation. Some leaders holding important positions often go against the majority to enhance their personal international image. Often they collaborate with their international networks working even against the interest of Malaysia. The effects of their work may jeopardize the future well-being of the workers. Instead of playing their part in educating workers towards higher productivity and efficiency, labour leaders are still preoccupied with issues calling for increased allowances, additional benefits and more rest hours. A country with unstable labour movement will certainly hinder the pace of industrialization and this seriously affects the business environment.

While the government will continue to encourage the private sector to play a leading role as the engine of growth of the economy, there is also a need to correct the cultivated myth especially within the private sector about its own efficiency. While we do have some outstanding Malaysian companies, we have to compare the bulk of the private sector performance with that of other countries to know the truth. In this context, many have complained about the poor services they get at the counter contact level of government offices. These counter services are perceived to be generally not satisfactory and regarded by the private sector as unwieldy and inefficient. You have only to examine the number of times you waited in long queues at banks, received poor and delayed services in shops and restaurants, met by unsmiling faces at the counters of departmental stores and supermarkets, and obtained substandard goods and services at above standard prices, in addition to receiving delayed deliveries and broken promises, to know exactly that the private sector is equally inefficient.

The private sector's view of the public sector may not be well founded, at best can be a self-deceiving mirage. While we are not abandoning a winning formula in putting heavy reliance on the private sector to steer the economy, the nation can ill-afford to have a private sector that cannot give its service with a smile and is insensitive to raising efficiency and productivity.

While the private sector is expected to play a leading role in economic development, the public sector must discharge its functions effectively to ensure overall national development. Given this developmental strategy, I envisage a more important role for the public service, as a facilitator and a pacesetter rather than the traditional role of implementor.

The primary responsibility of the public service is to create a conducive environment catalytic for economic growth. The public service has to be ever sensitive and responsive to the heady competition in the global marketplace. The public service needs to be proactive in charting new directions and strategies for growth. This requires an astute and prudent mix of initiatives in administrative and industrial planning, in-depth assessment of industry needs and strategic requirements, offshore market intelligence, evaluation of new technologies and skilful negotiations.

It must also play the pacesetter role in providing the information and directions for trade as well as promote the country's goods and services. The competence of the public service in providing sound administrative guidance to the private sector will ensure the sustenance of the nation's comparative advantage and promote its competitive edge with competing nations.

In the spirit of Malaysia Incorporated, the public service must first of all view the private sector as an equal partner in engineering and managing economic growth. This must be actively cultivated to galvanize the latent energies of both sectors to produce a profitable and potent synergy, for the good of the nation. As such, the existing as well as new mechanisms of developing a consensual relationship must be built on and strengthened.

The public service must continue to place a high premium on supporting the entrepreneurial efforts of the private sector, particularly with respect to the nation's thrust into the competitive international marketplace. The public service must continue relentlessly to establish a culture of excellence. Quality must be the hallmark of the public service. The pressure for better services is on the rise with higher expectations from our increasingly affluent society, not only for wider access to public services but also for better quality of such services. Qualitative improvements must be pursued continually. Only then can the public service play its rightful role in building a fully developed nation as envisaged in Vision 2020.

Privatization which gained credence in Malaysia since 1983 is now in its full gear. Public enterprises which have been privatized in our country, have all shown better financial results, due to increasing inefficiencies. Privatization too has resulted in higher standards and better services to the public. As a result there has been wide acclaim of success on Malaysia's Privatization policy which not only professes the divestiture or sale of government assets but a gradual decline of the interventionist role played by the public sector.

As you are aware, a large number of public enterprises have been privatized or are pipelined for privatization. The privatization of high growth and dynamic sectors like transport, communications, energy and public utilities have and will provide ample opportunities for the private sector to participate. With corporate environment, less governed by bureaucratic rules and procedures, the private sector should now gear these service sectors which are highly essential for industrial development to new heights via increasing the efficiency levels and productivity to keep the cost of production low, and to maintain a competitive edge in the global market.

We are aware that some of the entities privatized or to be privatized enjoy a monopolistic or near monopolistic position in the market, but the private sector should not exploit the situation and instead should keep prices at a competitive level, provide services of quality and reliability by continuously upgrading its technology so that all users will benefit. The government will ensure that the public will not be disadvantaged because of privatization.

I have covered at length the economic agenda of Vision 2020 which will set the pace for private sector involvement. At this juncture another critical factor in our desire to achieve a fully industrialized status is the development of human resources. Many of us think that this mainly means training and educating Malaysians to be skilled and productive operators of technology or equipment, production lines, systems and ideas. I would like to point out that this emphasis is inadequate. It should be complemented by an emphasis on creating, nurturing and increasing the quantity and quality of the following types of Malaysians:

☐ Malaysians who are diligent and resourceful and who can initiate, direct and propel industrial growth, that is, "movers and shakers", risk-takers and organizers. They are crucial in providing the right impetus and dynamism to development.

☐ Malaysians who are inventors and designers of industrial
   and consumer products. We cannot be a real industrialized society if we remain an importer and user of foreign
   inventions. We cannot continue to be the backyard for
   the assembly of foreign inventions and products. We
   need to produce our own to mark our independence in
   industrialization.

Malaysian manufacturers and industrialists who are inculcated and imbued with high standards of morality and social justice. We want honest business people who seek profits through
legal and ethical means, not through fraud and exploitation and
we want business people with a social conscience, who believe in
giving the less advantaged members of society a real chance to
participate in their growth. We need such people because otherwise our path towards industrialization will spawn social and perhaps even political unrest or feelings of deprivation and
estrangement.

The task of producing this multifaceted workforce is a challenge in itself and has to be tackled with vigour and zest so that we
can succeed.

However, in the light of the prevailing tight labour market
situation and anticipation changing demand for skills arising out
of rapid industrialization, the following issues need to be addressed urgently:

☐ How do we cope with the existing demand for skilled
   manpower so that current labour shortages do not put a
   brake on growth?
☐ How do we correct the mismatch between available jobs
   and available skills – how do we retrain the people who
   are presently unemployed or unemployable?
☐ How do we reorientate the education system to provide
   the manpower to meet the demands of industry?

While the government is fully committed to the production of
an efficient, productive, disciplined, educated and highly skilled

workforce with strong moral and ethical values and with determination to excel, it alone cannot address these issues. The cooperation and contribution of the employers and trade unions are essential. If both the public and private sectors can join hands in improving the quality of the workforce, the nation can make significant strides in development. Towards this, the corporate sector must be prepared to allocate a large portion of this budget for training. Each firm or industry should have its own training facilities to prepare its recruits for its particular type of work or to upgrade the capabilities of its workforce.

On the government's part, steps will have to be taken to review and overhaul the educational and training curricula and systems so that the appropriate quantity and quality of industrial manpower is produced. The system must be able to produce young Malaysians who are capable in terms of creative thinking, innovativeness, manipulative skills, technical aptitude, problem solving skills, competitive and yet, at the same time, imbued with high moral and ethical standards.

While we strive to accelerate the process of industrialization, we must not neglect our agricultural sector. We must bear in mind that development of our agricultural sector remains crucial in our effort to develop the rural areas. During the next thirty years, a considerable number of our people will remain involved in agriculture. We need continuing advances in agriculture both as a strategy for income generation and employment as well as poverty eradication of the rural sector. We need progress in agriculture for supply of our food, and inputs for our industries.

The challenge before us is to provide the required stimulant to trigger and sustain the development and transformation of the rural sector towards a more modern and remunerative sector. I believe that the central area of concern would still be towards increasing our productivity both in terms of land as well as labour. We must continue to look for new crops, new clones and new practices and production techniques that will allow us to maximize our production at the lowest cost and remain competitive in the world market. The agriculture sector can never compete for manpower if the labour productivity and thereby wages remain low. Yet, at the same time we cannot continue to rely on cheap migrant labour to reduce our production cost. What we aspire to see is largely organized, market-oriented, capital intensive, private sector-led agricultural sector, that is able not only to provide the needs of the country but also to compete internationally.

There is also the need to intensify research and development in the agricultural sector. We have heard about hydroponics, about farming in buildings and about biotechnology, just to name a few. These could be the future technology directions and that we should take in agriculture, and the private sector is expected to spearhead the development of such technologies.

Greater efforts need to be undertaken to intensify the uses of our agricultural products. We have to industrialize our agriculture sector to increase its value-added. We cannot continue to export raw or unprocessed products because competition from other producing countries that enjoy a much lower cost of production may push us out of competition. The private sector must therefore continue to spearhead the development of agro-based industries, especially in areas where we have comparative advantage such as rubber, oil palm, cocoa and other crops.

We would like to see our rural sector drastically transformed into a modern and highly market-oriented sector interwoven harmoniously into the urban industrialized economy. The government will continue to provide the necessary infrastructure and facilities to ensure that such interdependency prevails for the benefit of both the rural and urban sectors.

The overall thrust of the services sector during the next thirty years is to strive towards the knowledge-based sector to support the Accelerated Industrialization Drive. In line with this the principle impetus for the services sector will come from the emerging subsector of information technology and computer service, professional and consultancy service apart from expanding the more prominent subsectors such as finance, banking, insurance, transportation and communications and tourism.

For us to achieve an advanced and industrialized status it is vital to strategize for an accelerated development of the service sector to be competitive. The best strategy is to utilize information technology and services to equip ourselves with the latest developments so that the services provided can be up to date and will be in demand. Being information-rich we can also gear ourselves from a domestic-oriented service sector by exporting our services.

Other important strategies that need to be taken to improve our services will be upgrading of professionalism in areas of finance such as corporate services, portfolio management, underwriting and international management and specialized risk management in the area of insurance. In areas of freight and shipping services, efforts need to be taken to increase efficiency and competitiveness and also the upgrading of professionals in shipping business.

I have indicated that the only way to go if we want to develop rapidly is through an accelerated industrialization drive. However, we cannot simply ignore the primary sector which has provided this country the resources and more importantly the savings needed for our past development. Neither can we ignore the people who continue to remain in the rural sector to provide the nation with food as well as raw materials and industrial inputs. Thus, our National Development Policy gives much emphasis on "balanced development", not only between growth and equity but also between the major sectors of the economy.

The controversy that arises as to whether to give priority to industry and agriculture is a sham polemic. The answer is not either-or, rather both-and. The industry needs agriculture and vice versa. We need continuing advancement in industry to provide the agriculture and the rural sector with inputs and with markets as much as we need progress in agriculture to provide food, raw materials and also markets.

However, rapid growth always favours dynamic sectors of the economy especially manufacturing and the modern services sectors while the traditional growth sector of agriculture lags behind. Thus priority must be given to a form of industrialization process that is consistent with a strategy of rural transformation so that the rural sector will strive efficiently and will not be a drag to our development effort. There must be effective mechanisms for link-ing sectors to ensure broad-based participation in the gains from growth.

It is through industrialization that we could bring social transformation, social equity, higher level of employment, more equitable distribution of income and well-balanced regional development. The way to industrialization, particularly if it is to fulfill social and economic objectives, involves a complex process and indeed a long one.

In the past, we have built up our national prosperity on the dual track of private sector-led and export-led growth. These twin strategies have brought us a long way. We have nurtured our private sector. We have widened the scale of our limited domestic market by international trade. We have developed our export base from being anchored to primary commodities to a manufactured dominating basket.

As external markets will continue to be important to us, we cannot run from setting an eye on Malaysia's future position in the global picture. We have to seek our own niche.

No doubt we cannot formulate strategies that will provide us with a solid hedge against external shocks, nevertheless, we have to find some means of protecting our economy from the extreme fluctuations. I am confident that with many experts and key thinkers from both the public and private sectors as well as the academia, many distinctive strategies will emerge from the exchange and cross-fertilization of ideas to provide guidance and direction in our stride to be a fully developed nation.

3

Vision 2020's Linkages with the Sixth Malaysia Plan and the Second Outline Perspective Plan

Mohd Sheriff Mohd Kassim

Vision 2020, which was presented by Dr Mahathir Mohamad at the inaugural meeting of the Malaysian Business Council on February 28, 1991, reflects the vision of a fully developed and industrialized Malaysia by the year 2020, in all dimensions: economically, politically, spiritually, psychologically and culturally. It is essentially a long-term vision containing broad policy directions encompassing various aspects.

The Second Outline Perspective Plan (OPP2), 1991-2000, is basically a long-term plan which embodies the new policy called the National Development Policy (NDP) to replace the New Economic Policy (NEP). The main objective of the NDP is to attain a balanced development so as to establish eventually a more united and just society as envisioned in Vision 2020. The OPP2 provides a framework for achieving certain socio-economic targets within a ten-year period.

The Sixth Malaysia Plan, 1991-95, spells out the policies, strategies and programmes to operationalize the OPP2 for the first five years of the OPP2. Apart from outlining detailed macroeconomic and sectoral targets, it provides detailed public sector programmes and development allocation by sector and level of government.

Although the three documents vary in terms of time frame and focus, the objective remains the same, that is, to build a progressive, prosperous and united nation. The ultimate goal of national unity is the core thrust of the three policy documents.

Broad Policy Linkages

The key to the attainment of a fully developed nation as envisaged in Vision 2020 is by overcoming the nine strategic challenges.

First, establishing a united Malaysian nation made up of one Bangsa Malaysia. Second, creating a psychologically liberated, secure and developed Malaysian society. Third, fostering and developing a mature democratic society. Fourth, establishing a fully moral and ethical society. Fifth, establishing a mature, liberal and tolerant society. Sixth, establishing a scientific and progressive society. Seventh, establishing a fully caring society. Eighth, ensuring an economically just society, in which there is a fair and equitable distribution of the wealth of the nation. Ninth, establishing a prosperous society with an economy that is fully competitive, dynamic, robust and resilient.

The sixth, eighth and ninth challenges relate to the economic aspect while the rest of the challenges pertain to socio-political challenges. Thus, these challenges are all-encompassing and cover all the issues that are relevant in building a fully developed Malaysian nation. The question to ask is whether the OPP2 and the Sixth Malaysia Plan address these challenges and if so, how?

The OPP2 and NDP essentially set the pace to enable Malaysia to become a fully developed nation by the year 2020 as envisaged by Dr Mahathir Mohamad. It focuses not only on the economic aspects of development but also on the interrelated aspects such as social justice, quality of life, moral and ethical values, work ethics and the administrative efficiency of the government.

The balanced development which is sought by the NDP to achieve the ultimate goal of national unity encompasses the following critical aspects:

1. Striking an optimum balance between the goals of economic growth and equity;

2. Ensuring a balanced development of the major sectors of the economy to increase their mutual complementaries to optimize growth;

3. Reducing and ultimately eliminating social and economic inequalities and imbalances to promote a fair and more equitable sharing of benefits of growth by all Malaysians;

4. Promoting and strengthening national integration by reducing the wide disparities in economic development between states and between the urban and rural areas in the country;

5. Developing a progressive society in which all citizens enjoy greater welfare, while simultaneously imbued with positive moral and spiritual values, and an increased sense of national consciousness and pride;

6. Promoting human resource development including creating a productive and disciplined workforce and developing the necessary skills to meet the challenges of an industrial society through a culture of merit and excellence without jeopardizing restructuring objectives;

7. Making science and technology integral components of socio-economic planning and development and promoting a science and technology culture compatible with the process of building a modern industrial economy; and

8. Ensuring that in the pursuit of economic development adequate attention is given to the protection of the environment and ecology to maintain the long-term sustainability of the country's development as well as the quality of life.

Figure 3.1

Broad Objectives and Strategies for National Development

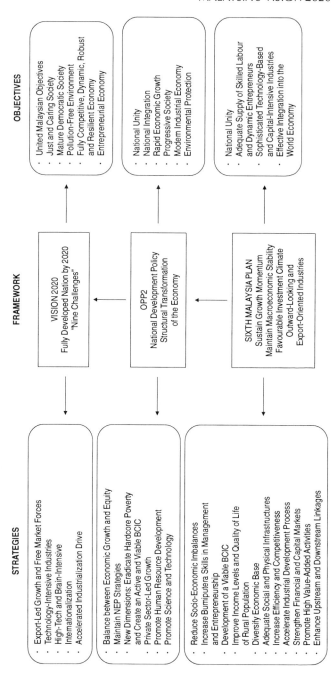

Clearly if one were to compare the nine strategic challenges of Vision 2020 and the eight critical aspects of the NDP, one would find that the two are fully consistent and compatible and are closely linked together. These broad policy linkages between Vision 2020 and the OPP2 as well as the Sixth Malaysia Plan can be conceptually presented as in Figure 3.1.

Economic Issues and Challenges

This section will touch on economic aspects of Vision 2020, especially those related to the ninth challenge. The ninth challenge is establishing a prosperous society with an economy that is fully competitive, dynamic, robust and resilient. In this respect, the vision stated that there is a need for an Accelerated Industrialization Drive and that we must maintain export-led growth strategy, where Malaysians must learn to be competitive through higher productivity and able to withstand the full force of international competition. Dr Mahathir Mohamad stated that we have to be more lean, more resourceful, more productive and generally more competitive and more able to take on the world.

The Vision stated that the establishment of a competitive economy must mean, among other things:

1. A diversified and balanced economy with a mature and widely based industrial sector, a modern and mature agriculture sector and an efficient and productive and an equally mature services sector;

2. An economy that is quick on its feet, able to quickly adapt to changing patterns of supply, demand and competition;

3. An economy that is technologically proficient, fully able to adapt, innovate and invest, that is increasingly technology-intensive, moving in the direction of higher and higher levels of technology;

4. An economy that has strong and cohesive industrial linkages throughout the system;

Table 3.1
Macroeconomic Targets

	1990	1995	2000	2020
Gross Domestic Product (RM Billion)				
In 1978 prices	79	114	156	630
In 1990 prices	115	165	230	920
Manufacturing				
Share of GDP (%)	27.0	32.4	37.2	
Employment ('000)	1,290	1,700	2,144	
% Total Employment	19.3	22.0	24.0	
Unemployment Rate (%)	6.0	4.5	4.0	Full Employment
GNP Per Capita (RM)				
Nominal Terms	6,180	10,200	17,000	80,000
Constant 1978 Prices	4,273	5,400	6,700	17,100
Constant 1990 Prices	6,180	7,860	9,400	26,100
	OPP1	6MP	OPP2	Vision 2020
GDP Growth Rate (% per annum)	6.7	7.5	7.0	7.0
Inflation Rate (%)	4.6	Low	Low	Low

5. An economy driven by brain-power, skills and diligence, in possession of a wealth of information, with the knowledge of what to do and how to do it;

6. An economy with high and escalating productivity with regard to every factor of production;

7. An entrepreneurial economy that is self-reliant, outward-looking and enterprising;

8. An economy characterized by low inflation and a low cost of living and subject to the full discipline and rigour of market forces.

It is not an easy task to realize this vision. It entails structural transformations that need to be undertaken at a stable, manageable and sustainable rate. Towards this end, the policies and strategies of the OPP2 are directed to deal with longer term and structural issues, while the Sixth Malaysia Plan focuses on specific policies and programmes to bring about a structural transformation of the economy.

Growth and Structural Transformation

An important linkage between Vision 2020 and the OPP2 or Sixth Malaysia Plan at the macro level is to achieve a rapid and sustainable growth rate of 7.0 per cent per annum in real terms. Such a rate of growth in the Gross Domestic Product (GDP) will result in the doubling of the output of goods and services in real terms (1978 constant prices) to about RM155 billion by the year 2000, from about RM79 billion in 1990 (see Table 3.1). The Vision 2020 envisaged that by doubling our GDP every ten years, that is, growing at 7.0 per cent per annum, our GDP in 2020 should therefore be about eight times larger.

The OPP2 has also projected a 7 per cent growth rate per annum over the 1990s. It goes further to spell out the policies and strategies that are required to achieve the growth target during the OPP2 period. Given the prevailing strong economic fundamentals and increasing internal strength and resilience of the economy, such a target is within reach. While the prospects for the Malaysian economy will continue to depend on the performance of the major industrial countries and the maintenance of an open and liberal trading regime, domestic policies must be instituted to position the economy to fully tap the opportunities for growth. The emphasis is on managing the success already achieved and enhancing the growth momentum to bring about a better distribution of income opportunities and further improvements in the quality of life.

Under the OPP2 and the Sixth Malaysia Plan, policy measures will focus on maintaining macroeconomic stability, improving factor efficiency, particularly through technological upgrading, increasing labour skills as well as strengthening the infrastructural base. Sectoral strategies will focus on further diversifying the economic base and promoting the development of export-oriented and high value-added activities. The OPP2 allocates an important role for the manufacturing sector as the prime mover of the economy. The manufacturing sector is targeted to grow at 10.5 per cent annually during the OPP2 period and will account for about 37 per cent of GDP in the year 2000 compared with the 27 per cent in 1990. These are significant targets to be achieved and consistent with the Vision 2020 in launching an Accelerated Industrialization Drive to make Malaysia an industrialized nation.

The policies outlined in the OPP2 reflect closely the Accelerated Industrialization Drive in Vision 2020. The policies will aim at widening and deepening the industrial base, leading to higher value-added products, increased linkages with SMIs and lessening dependence on traditional growth subsectors, primarily textiles, electrical and electronics. Towards this end, the primary strategy will be to emphasize the manufacturing sector. In addition, the policy will also focus on removing the identification of new sources of growth to further accelerate the expansion of the constraints and rigidities facing the sector including factor price distortions arising from the prolonged provision of tariff and non-tariff protection so that a more broad-based and diversified growth can take place.

Figure 3.2
Structure of Production

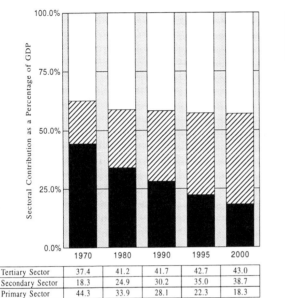

	1970	1980	1990	1995	2000
Tertiary Sector	37.4	41.2	41.7	42.7	43.0
Secondary Sector	18.3	24.9	30.2	35.0	38.7
Primary Sector	44.3	33.9	28.1	22.3	18.3

Although industrialization will form the basis of future growth, the OPP2 has also highlighted the importance of developing the services sector as a generator of growth through policy reforms and other supportive investments that promote the sector as a leading rather than a lagging sector. This sector is expected to assume increasing importance in terms of its potential contribution to GDP growth, employment generation and the reduction of the large services trade deficit. The focus is to absorb the newly emerging technological developments in the various fields of communications, data processing, new educational modes and new forms of foreign investment such as joint-ventures, franchises, management contracts and licensing.

With these structural transformations of the economy, the OPP2 envisages that the share of agriculture will continue to decline from 18.7 per cent in 1990 to 13.4 per cent in 2000. The share of the manufacturing sector which is projected to grow by 10.5 per cent per annum will increase from 27 per cent in 1990 to about 37 per cent in the year 2000 as shown in Figure 3.2. Manufactured exports will account for about 80 per cent of total merchandise exports.

Stabilization Efforts

The concerns of Vision 2020 for stable, non-inflationary growth are also addressed in detail in the Sixth Malaysia Plan. Keeping inflation under effective control has always been accorded high priority as it is seen as a source of uncertainty, instability and inefficiency with its distortionary effects on planning and decision making. There, management of liquidity in the banking system, maintaining interest rates that give a fair return to depositors and reasonably priced funds to investors as well as easing supply bottlenecks by liberalizing imports and increasing domestic production are being given priority.

Another issue on the agenda is to prevent wage increases from falling out of line with productivity gains so that it will not undermine the competitive edge. To increase productivity, the Sixth Malaysia Plan stresses on improving technology, entrepreneurship and the quality of labour and management. Greater emphasis is given to increase the application of science and technology and expanding research and development activities and human resource development. Efficiency in the use of resources will also be enhanced by programmes designed to improve infrastructural and institutional networks and by creating a competitive environment.

An important consideration in maintaining price stability and controlling inflation is to ensure a healthy balance in the government's fiscal position as well as in the external account. The current balance of payments deterioration is seen as a cyclical phenomenon as it is spurred by very high imports of intermediate goods for the manufacturing sector and machinery and equipment which would generate capacity for future periods. However, it has to be kept in check so that it will not be out of control. In this respect, measures will be undertaken to promote exports more vigorously as well as to reduce imports, particularly consumption and intermediate goods through encouraging greater local production. In addition, continued efforts will be made to reduce the large deficit in the services account by further developing the tourism, shipping and insurance industries. At the same time, the government will continue to encourage direct foreign investment, including reinvestment, to sustain the high inflows of corporate capital to maintain a healthy capital account position.

External Sector

In this age of internationalization, greater emphasis will be given towards strengthening Malaysia's foreign trade and international relations. Foreign trade and investment will continue to be a major factor in determining the pace of economic growth. This is in line with the country's outward-looking and export-oriented strategies. As mentioned in Vision 2020, we must persist with export-led growth to expand the frontiers of production, despite the global slowdown, the rise of regional integration or protectionism, trade blocs and managed trade.

In the OPP2, these efforts have been clarified further by identifying the structural changes taking place in the world economy and measures to diversify our export markets. These include our interests in promoting South-South trade, initiatives in the G-15 movement, our active participation in regional organizations like Asean and Apec as well as our role in championing the cause of the East Asia Economic Caucus.

Continued efforts will be made to expand market shares within existing as well as new and non-traditional markets. This includes expansion in regional trade to cover Asean nations and also countries in the Asia-Pacific region. Apart from improving trade practices, product standards and quality, other measures such as active participation in international fora and dialogues with Asean partners will be continued to improve market access of Malaysian products.

Distributional Issues

On the distributional front, and in line with the principle of growth with equity embodied in the NDP, one of the challenges that has to be met in order for Malaysia to be fully developed by the year 2020 is ensuring a sustainable and equitable distribution of the wealth of the nation. Specifically, this entails:

1. The continued creation of employment opportunities to enable income to increase for the lower income group to reduce the gap between the rich and the poor;
2. Development of a viable Bumiputera Commercial and Industrial Community (BCIC) that is at par with the more advanced groups within the non-Bumiputera community;
3. A fair representation of the Malaysian ethnic groups in all the major and important sectors of employment; and
4. An equitable distribution and participation among ethnic communities with regard to the control, management and ownership of productive assets, both in the corporate and non-corporate sector.

The government has emphasized that the attainment of the above distributional objectives is critical towards the establishment of an economically just society, whereby economic advancement or backwardness cannot be identified with any particular ethnic group. There must be a fair balance in the participation and contribution of all ethnic groups in the economy. This is the kind of society that is sought after by Vision 2020.

The NDP, which is the successor to the NEP, will set the pace to enable Malaysia to become a fully developed nation. Although the NEP has made remarkable progress, there is still wide gaps among the various communities which need to be redressed. Thus, the NDP while emphasizing the need for a balanced development, maintains the basic strategies of the NEP to achieve goal of national unity. Its new dimensions are designed to:

1. Shift the focus of the anti-poverty strategy with a view to eradicating hardcore poverty, while at the same time reducing relative poverty;

2. Focus more on the rapid development of an active Bumiputera Commercial and Industrial Community as an essential strategy to increase and render permanent Bumiputera participation in the economy;

3. Rely more on the private sector's involvement in the restructuring process; and

4. Focus more on human resource development, including moral and ethical values, to achieve the objective of growth and distribution.

The implementation of the NDP to reduce poverty particularly will take into account the needs of all communities. Thus, while it is recognized that the majority of the poor in the country are Bumiputeras, there are also non-Bumiputera who live well below the poverty line in both the rural and urban areas. The socio-economic position of certain groups within the Bumiputera community, such as the *orang asli* and the indigenous groups in Sabah and Sarawak, and the Indians within the non-Bumiputera community have lagged behind. In the implementation of the NDP, the needs of these groups will be given due attention to enable them to benefit equitably from the growth of the economy and development programmes.

The restructuring strategy will focus more sharply on the development of a BCIC as a more effective strategy to accelerate Bumiputera participation in modern and expanding sectors of the economy. In line with this, priority attention will be given under the NDP to expand their management capability, skills and entrepreneurial quality. The specific targets with respect to distributional objectives set under OPP2 are:

1. The reduction of the overall incidence of poverty from 17.1 per cent in 1990 to 7.2 per cent by the year 2000. In the process, the incidence of hardcore poverty will be

brought down to around 1.0 per cent by the year 2000,
which means that the hardcore poverty will be
eliminated;

2. Development of an active and resilient BCIC in a competitive environment that offers growing opportunities
for self-initiative and quality improvements in business
management and organizational skills;

3. Further increase in Bumiputera employment, particularly
in the high-paying professional, technical and managerial
job categories in the private sector. The non-Bumiputeras will also be given expanded opportunities for public
sector employment;

4. Maintain the original target of at least 30 per cent share
for Bumiputeras in the ownership of the corporate sector
as a general guide, without any specific time frame for its
achievement, with a view to focusing more on the
qualitative aspects of wealth management, creation and
its retention; and

5. Pursue regional development strategies to reduce the
large imbalances in economic development between
states in the country, and, thereby improve income distribution.

While Vision 2020 provides global targets and OPP2 the
planning framework for the NDP, the Sixth Malaysia Plan seeks
to translate the OPP2 targets into operational plan of action. The
Sixth Malaysia Plan will vigorously pursue the basic philosophy of
growth with equity to further reduce the existing socio-economic
imbalances among the ethnic groups, thus strengthening further
national unity. Strategies and programmes to further eradicate
poverty, restructure society and improve regional balance will be
implemented during the Sixth Malaysia Plan period. Focus will be
made on efforts to improve the quality of achievements rather
than quantity so that the kind of society envisaged by Vision
2020 – progressive, resilient, ethnically integrated, united and
tolerant society – can be realized. In implementing the policies of

poverty eradication, the Sixth Malaysia Plan will take into account
the following considerations:

1. To streamline the implementation of poverty eradication
    programmes to encourage self-reliance, especially
    among the hardcore poor;
2. To enhance the income opportunities of the lower in-
    come group of all races by improving their access to bet-
    ter services and amenities in both rural and urban areas;
    and
3. To concentrate on programmes which are the respon-
    sibility of the public sector such as education and training,
    health care, rural roads, transport and communications,
    housing, water and electricity.

In terms of restructuring society, the Sixth Malaysia Plan will
continue the efforts to increase the share of Bumiputeras in the
economy both in terms of employment as well as in the ownership and control of the economy. The main emphasis is to increase the skills of Bumiputeras in management and entrepreneurship and encourage genuine Bumiputera-non-
Bumiputera partnerships. In line with this, programmes under
the Plan will focus on the following:

1. Provide particular emphasis to improve the quality of
    manpower among Bumiputeras and minority groups
    through the development of marketable skills;
2. As overall employment restructuring can be effected
    through high economic growth priority, attention will be
    given to restructuring of employment at the professional,
    managerial and technical levels;
3. Consolidate and strengthen the BCIC programme with
    emphasis on management and inculcation of positive cul-
    ture of entrepreneurship;
4. Emphasize on the quality of Bumiputera participation as
    well as the ability to maintain or increase their wealth;

5. Encourage active private sector participation in the process of restructuring society; and

6. Diversify the economic base of the less developed states and provide more physical, economic and social infrastructure to upgrade their development standards and to attract more private sector activities to these states.

Human Resource Development

Recognizing that people are our ultimate resource, Dr Mahathir Mohamad stresses in Vision 2020 that Malaysia must give the fullest emphasis towards HRD or human resource development. The main thrust of human resource development is:

1. The development of educated, well-trained and flexible manpower to enable the country to forge ahead and maintain its competitive edge; and

2. The inculcation of positive values and attitudes for the development of an industrialized society and to foster national unity.

The same theme of human resource development is strongly emphasized in the OPP2. With the changing structure of the economy towards greater industrialization, manpower requirements are beginning to change. The expected globalization of the economy, the fast changing technological development taking place here and around the world, as well as the imperative to remain competitive dictate that the manpower of the future will have to be well trained and multi-skilled, flexible and creative. In addition, they have to be fluent not only in technical subjects, but also in languages and with machines. Industrial values such as hard work, punctuality and discipline, are also crucial as we move ahead towards the industrial era.

Thus, the broad thrust of human resource development in the OPP2 is to prepare Malaysians to compete in the global economy. In this connection, the number and quality of Bumiputera professionals, technicians and entrepreneurs will be increased in order that Bumiputeras can play an enhanced role in the national economy. This second thrust is consistent with Vision 2020, where Dr Mahathir Mohamad states that the country cannot afford to achieve progress with only half of its human resources utilized.

With the emergence of a tight labour market, the country cannot continue to depend on its cheap labour as a source of competitive advantage. In the years to come, the quality and productivity of the workforce will enable the country to forge ahead and maintain its competitiveness. To do this, we have to invest in human resource development now so that the workforce of the future can contribute towards the growth of the economy. This essentially is the message both in Vision 2020 and OPP2.

Therefore, the quality of education under the Sixth Malaysia Plan will be enhanced and access to educational and training opportunities to all sections of society will be improved so as to provide educated and trainable workforce with skills, usable across sectors and industries. Under the Sixth Malaysia Plan a sum of RM8.5 billion was allocated for the development of education and training. In addition, the private sector will be encouraged to play a more active role in training and skill development. Apart from encouraging them to set up their industry-specific training centres, they will be allowed to use government facilities during periods when such facilities are available.

Science and Technology

To establish a scientific and progressive society that is not only a consumer of technology but also a contributor to the future civilization of science and technology aspired by Vision 2020, the government will create the necessary conditions under which technology will be built up efficiently.

Apart from increasing the absolute amount of research and development expenditure, special programmes such as venture capital financing as well as direct financial assistance in the form of grants, risk-sharing investment and assistance with soft loans for the purpose of promoting result-oriented and market-driven research and development will be developed.

Strategic focus will be placed on the commercialization of potential research and technology. This will involve downstream related activities such as testing, prototype formulating, designing and redesigning, trial manufacturing and marketing runs as well as licensing and patenting of new products and processes before the basic research and development output can be ultimately transformed into end-use products and processes to suit consumers' needs. This is in line with the theme of Vision 2020 that technology is not the laboratory but the factory floor and the market.

Specifically, the Sixth Malaysia Plan has incorporated programmes that emphasize applied and developmental research and innovation in areas that can contribute significantly to the country's industrial development and competitiveness. Five key technology areas have been identified for building competence. They are automated manufacturing technology, advanced materials, biotechnology, electronics and information technology.

The Environment

In pursuit of development, Vision 2020 also places emphasis on the environment. In addition to having clean and beautiful surrounding, the importance of capability to regenerate forest resources and preservation of natural resources including the fertility of land is stressed.

With this far-sighted direction, the OPP2 incorporates protection of the environment and ecology to maintain long-term sustainability of development as one of its critical aspects. Therefore, development will be pursued in a clean and healthy environment with ecological and climatic stability. Nature and natural resources conservation will also be given priority through a responsible and well-balanced exploitation of natural resources to safeguard the requirements of protection as well as nature and natural resources conservation will be incorporated in all development plans and programmes. The implementation of such strategies will give priority to adopting environmentally sound practices in various sectoral development programmes as well as strategic natural resource management.

Under the Sixth Malaysia Plan, the major environmental issues and concerns that will be addressed include the increasing air and noise pollution in urban areas resulting from the expansion of automobile ownership and vehicular traffic, constraints on the supply of affordable housing and efficient sewerage, sanitation and waste disposal facilities in major towns and encroachment of economic activities on vegetation, forest cover and catchment areas which have serious repercussions on sustained water supply. Environmental consideration will be emphasized in formulating and implementing public sector programmes and projects. Strict enforcement of existing laws will be made to ensure industrial establishments control the production of pollutants and adopt a more effective storage and disposal system. Indiscriminate use of chemicals and uncontrolled discharge of toxic waste from industrial activities will be regulated.

Supportive Role of the Public Sector

Vision 2020 is quite specific on the role of the public sector will continue to be important, especially in providing a stronger foundation for the attainment of our socio-economic objectives. In relative terms, however, its size will be progressively reduced while the share of the private sector will increase further in line with its role as the primary engine of growth.

Public investment in activities that compete directly with the private sector will be reduced and project selection during the OPP2 period will emphasize more on efficiency considerations to further improve the quality of investment. The overall deficit is expected to be reduced further as shown in Figure 3.3. The deficit is expected to be financed mostly from domestic borrowings, in line with the policy to reduce external debt outstanding and to reduce the external debt exposure to vagaries of fluctuating interest and exchange rates in the international financial markets.

Figure 3.3
Public Sector Account

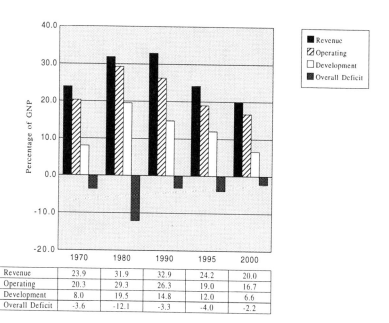

	1970	1980	1990	1995	2000
Revenue	23.9	31.9	32.9	24.2	20.0
Operating	20.3	29.3	26.3	19.0	16.7
Development	8.0	19.5	14.8	12.0	6.6
Overall Deficit	-3.6	-12.1	-3.3	-4.0	-2.2

Apart from privatization, productive deregulation and economic liberalization, the government will continue its effort to foster domestic investment and encourage the inflows of foreign investment. This is essential for Malaysia's accelerated industrialization drive and also making the Malaysia Incorporated Concept a flourishing reality.

Conclusion

The three planning documents will guide our development path to transform our economy into a fully developed nation within a generation. They enhance our planning and decision-making process in clarifying the desirable and realizable state of the economy and society as well as identifying major policy issues and presenting options and approaches to address these issues effectively. They provide a comprehensive framework covering both domestic and external environment which is flexible enough to enable changes and adaptation to circumstances.

4

Inculcating Moral and Ethical Values in Business

Mohamad Noordin Sopiee

There should be no doubt that values are extremely important. They are a core component of culture, which is the software of any society, which determines whether and how a system "ticks" – or does not.

Third, even the more circumscribed subject of moral and ethical values in business in relation to the objectives of Vision 2020 is a huge field. This chapter can only skim the surface. My discussion will certainly be full of over-simplifications and over-generalizations.

Fourth, what is needed is not a *khutbah*. What is necessary is a hard-headed treatment. I hope that I will not be doing any sermonizing or preaching. This entire question should not be addressed from a pulpit.

Since many motherhood statements cannot be avoided, no doubt the necessary quantum of worldly cynicism has to be expressed. Let me express some not. It is clear that many moral and ethical values may be either irrelevant or unproductive in business. Business is an arena where, as in life, there must be the fullest expectation of the conflict of moral and ethical values. Equally clearly, many moral and ethical values that are very important in social or personal life should *not* be inculcated in business if the intention is to maximize the contribution of business to the achievement of the objectives of Vision 2020 – although any thoughtful analysis will reveal that many values that would at first appear to have no relevance in the world of business can actually be extremely productive for business. It should be made clear also that action to forward one objective of Vision 2020 may at times work against the achievement of another objective. The world is a complicated place. And there will always be the need for wisdom and good judgement.

What I shall do is to try to answer only the following four questions: Why? What? Who? and How? In more explicit terms, I will pose the following questions:

1. Why should correct moral and ethical values be inculcated in business to achieve the objectives of Vision 2020?
2. What are some of the key values which should be inculcated?
3. Who should do the inculcating?
4. How can we go about inculcating the correct values?

Why Should Correct Values be Inculcated in Business?

My answer is simple and, I am afraid, uncompromising. First, correct moral and ethical values should be inculcated as an end in itself. Malaysian society should be moral and ethical. Full Stop. It so happens that the fourth central objective of Vision 2020 is the establishment of a "fully moral and ethical society, whose citizens are strong in religious and spiritual values and imbued with the highest of ethical standards." If Vision 2020 did not state this as a central objective, it would have been criticized. And rightly so. Part of the strength of our Vision and generational plan is that it is not narrowly focused only on growth or economic development. It has had the wisdom to recognize that a country cannot be regarded as fully developed unless it is development multi-dimensionally – just as no man is developed if only a part of his being is developed. Just as a man cannot be regarded as developed if he is without "character", the same must be said of a nation.

It is crucial to inculcate moral and ethical values in business if we are interested in developing a society that is fully moral and ethical because business is a big part of society. It is not so much a microcosm of society as a macrocosm of society. What is done in business cannot be held in splendid isolation or in a watertight compartment. A moral and ethical society simply cannot exist if we have an immoral and unethical business sector – any more than a man can be said to be healthy if only the left side of his body is cancerous.

The second basic reason correct moral and ethical values should be inculcated in business is because the business sector cannot avoid being a means for achieving other ends. To be sure, profit is the core purpose of business. It is not a social enterprise as such, or a political enterprise as such or a psychological process as such. But whether the business would want to or not, it cannot avoid being a massive instrument for good – or for harm. Because it is such a central part of our society, the business world cannot avoid its responsibility to contribute to the achievement of non-business objectives, all the other eight central objectives of Vision 2020 – and the other unidentified objectives of Malaysian society. The correct moral and ethical values on the part of business cannot but contribute, as it must.

The first objective of Vision 2020 is national unity. Business must understand that concerning this most fundamental objective, it cannot be and is not a passive bystander. By doing something or nothing, the business would – like the public sector – by its sheer size and impact, contribute to or detract from the establishment of "a nation at peace with itself, territorial and ethnically integrated, living in harmony and full and fair partnership, made up of one *Bangsa Malaysia* with political loyalty and dedication".

It is important that the business world is in possession of the needed national unity ethic, recognition of its role in fostering national unity and actually making a positive contribution to national unity. (Incidentally, it must be clear that all businesses in

Malaysia have vital business interest in our political development as a nation. In the United States, it is no longer clear that what is good for General Motors is good for the Americans. Indisputably what is good for America is good for General Motors. In our case it is clear that what is good for Malaysia is good for Malayan Banking).

Similarly with the second challenge. We cannot be "psychologically liberated", "secure", "justifiably proud" of what we are and what we have accomplished, and become a society that is "distinguished by the pursuit of excellence ... psychologically subservient to none, and respected by the peoples of other nations" if our business morality and ethics are contrary to this objective. Such a society cannot exist if our business enterprises are psychologically unliberated, insecure, ashamed of itself, subservient and characterized by mediocrity. It is almost a contradiction in terms. On the other hand, with the necessary psychological liberation ethic in business, the business world will be a key contributor to the nation's psychological development.

The right democracy ethic within our business world not only makes a direct contribution *ipso facto* to our third strategic objective of establishing a mature consensual democracy. It can be expected to act to contribute to such an end.

Similarly with our objectives on a mature, liberal and tolerant society (Challenge No. 5), and a scientific and progressive society (Challenge No. 6), and a fully caring society with a caring culture (Challenge No. 7), and an economically just society (Challenge No. 8), and a prosperous society, with "an economy that is fully competitive, dynamic, robust and resilient" – our ninth strategic objective.

Just as Malaysia must have the proper ethic of tolerance and liberalism, science and technology, caring, social justice, and competitiveness, growth and resilience, so too must our business world.

The third reason business should have the correct moral and ethical values is that it is generally good for sound business, in terms of the macro picture – the country, the economy and the business world – and in terms of the micro picture – each business enterprise.

We should of course not be naive. Cheating may pay off in the short run. Unfortunately bribery is often expedient. But it is generally true that except for the fly-by-night, short-term thinking enterprise, morality and ethics is productively self-serving.

What are Some Key Values that Should be Inculcated in Business?

In dealing with the first question, part of the answer to question two has been articulated.

First, the business world cannot afford to adopt the ethic of non-involvement. It cannot be a bystander. In conducting the business of business and running the business enterprise, it must accept the fact that it has a national role to play, a key contribution to make. This role it must discharge.

Second, I have mentioned the importance of the correct:

1. National unity ethic;
2. Psychological liberation ethic;
3. Democratic ethic;
4. Tolerance and liberalism ethic;
5. Science and technology ethic;
6. Caring ethic;
7. Social justice ethic; and
8. Competitiveness ethic.

To this list, let me add a few other values:

1. *Integrity.* The importance of integrity is too obvious to state. The challenge to integrity can only be expected to escalate in the years to come. It is not that man has become more corrupt. Rather, the circumstances have become more corrupting.

2. *Discipline.* Much greater discipline is needed in our business world at both the managerial and worker levels.

3. *Industriousness.* The willingness to work hard and diligently is a precious ethic invaluable to the successful enterprise and to the achievement of Vision 2020. No large society in human history has become developed and sustained affluence over any length of time without a very strong work ethic. There are no exceptions.

4. *Excellence.* The desire to excel, to constantly strive for the best, including the stress on quality and perfection, as well as what the Japanese call "kaizen" – the urge to continuously make improvements. We cannot achieve Vision 2020 without a quantum leap in our societal commitment to excellence.

5. *Creativity and Innovation.* It is said that the Japanese lack creativity and innovation. This is a complete misunderstanding.

6. *Competitiveness.* A strong and healthy competitive spirit is another vital prerequisite. It is healthy competition which moves enterprises, the economy and society forward.

7. *Perseverance and Longer-Term Thinking.* Perseverance and longer-term thinking, as opposed to subservience to short-term expediency is another key value which all sectors of Malaysian society need in greater measure.

8. *Self-Reliance.* A quantum leap in the spirit of berdikari must be another key area for the most dramatic value restructuring.

9. *Thrift and a Saving Culture.* A famous Malaysian said that one can predict business success by looking at who have bought Rolls-Royces and who have not. If Malaysia moves too rapidly towards a consumption culture, we can kiss Vision 2020 goodbye.

10. *Commitment to Knowledge, Information and Know-How Acquisition.* The information age puts a premium

upon knowledge, technology and know-how acquisition. The know-how edge will be increasingly important. Increasingly, knowledge will not only be power but also prosperity.

11. *Good Corporate Citizenship.* Gone are the days when business, especially big business, need worship only profit and power and owe a responsibility to none except to itself.

12. *Commitment to Workers' Welfare and Constant Development of Skills.* A country's human resources are its ultimate and most important resource. The constant development of human resource welfare and upgrading must accompany us each step of the way to 2020 or we cannot expect to reach our destination.

13. *The Spirit of Malaysia Incorporated.* Willingness to make a total national effort involving all sectors of society at every level is also a key value which Malaysia will need to put in place – in business as well as in the rest of society – in the coming decades if Vision 2020 is to be achieved.

Who Should do the Inculcating of Values?

Values are inculcated in all societies by the family in the home; the education system, in schools, universities and other educational institutions; the government and public institutions; the private sector; and the society at large.

Here, I would merely take up the point that might be made that we should do nothing, adopt an absolutely *laissez faire* stance and let whatever will be, will be.

First, this is not possible. It is simply not possible to do nothing. Laws are passed in society. Parents pass on values to their children even if they are not aware that they are doing so. Our education system does likewise, etc. The only choice before society is whether we should consciously seek to inculcate certain values and counter others or whether we should unconsciously and undeliberately do so. My view is that we should consciously

propagate productive values and consciously seek to retard unproductive values – although we should do so with care, humility,
wisdom and without going to extremes.

How to Inculcate the Right Values?

Obviously by using all the actors: the family, the educational system, the public sector, the private sector and the society at large.
(Obviously all these institutions are interrelated as instruments for
value structuring and restructuring).

First, the family. There obviously has to be much value
restructuring in the home, which is the most important educational institution in any society. If the child has the right start in
life, it is arguable that much less has to be done further down the
road. Because so much reform has to take place at this level, in
the Malaysian home, the task of value formation and reformation
downstream has to be more effective than otherwise.

Second, the educational system. The building of "character"
has long been recognized as an essential function of any educational system. Obviously much more will have to be done in our
educational institutions, through the curriculum and extracur-
ricular activities in infusing the moral and ethical values of particular relevance to Vision 2020.

Third, the public sector. No doubt there is a danger in a hy-
peractive government. But there is also a danger in an underac-
tive government. As ever, the optimal balance has to be struck.

Clearly, within the context of our correct commitment to a
market economy, where government intervention is necessary, it
must be forthcoming. There should be no "no go" areas.

Among the ideas that have to be examined is the substantial
strengthening of law concerning business crimes, in terms of the
legal provisions and in terms of implementation and implementation machinery. We do not foster the necessary code of morality
and ethics if punishments are out of proportion to the crime and
if business criminals can operate with impunity.

And just as moral and ethical society cannot exist if the business world is neither moral not ethical, the same must be said about the public sector.

All the values that have been suggested for the business sector – and many more – will also have to infuse the public sector.

Fourth, the private sector. Here several ideas might be worth pondering.

First, it might be useful for all business associations to adopt a formal code of conduct for their sectors and to encourage every member to formally adopt an internal code of ethics. This is no panacea, such steps have been taken. But there is virtue in attempting to ensure universal coverage.

Second, there might be some virtue in making it compulsory for every application to set up a company to include a statement of its Code of Ethics.

Thirdly, steps should be taken to review the legal provisions concerning the disclosure of information by companies and more rigorous standards for accounting methods and auditing procedures.

Fourth, steps should be taken to encourage greater involvement of shareholders in the affairs of their company, as in Germany. In Germany, a person representing the workers sits as a member of the Board of Directors.

Fifth, there obviously has to be more training on ethics in practically every Malaysian company.

With regard to society at large, a few suggestions might also be made. I have touched on the central role that law must play in enforcing productive ethical behaviour – because in every society, some people will observe certain norms only under the threat of coercion and punishment. At the same time, it must be recognized that no society, whether in the context of business or not, can work on the basis of such formal compliance alone. The ultimate source of order is not coercion but custom and habit, in other words, culture.

To strengthen the culture of morality and ethics in business, a few small ideas might be worth considering.

We have in the past launched a programme of fostering Leadership by Example. This needs to be resuscitated.

Just as immoral and unethical depravity must be exposed and punished more severely, moral and ethical excellence needs to be given greater exposure, recognition and regard by Malaysian society. In this and other areas, the media has always an important role. But others too must contribute. The system of national honours and recognition, family honour and recognition, school and university honour and recognition, public sector honour and recognition and private sector honour and recognition has to march in step with our commitment to morality and ethics.

I do apologize for so many motherhood statements, for so many generalities and for taking so long. I do hope that some of the remarks are worthy of discussion.

5

Profiteering, Corruption, Misleading Advertising and the Environment

R. Thillainathan

Many have attempted to distinguish between "ethics" and "morals". However, according to William A. Evans, the distinction has never been entirely satisfactory. Both describe rules of conduct and both are concerned with differentiating between right and wrong: "Perhaps we sometimes do intend to convey another meaning if we say that an action is immoral rather than unethical; perhaps the former description connotes some contravention of religious law, some imperative that never changes, while the latter merely indicates a departure from traditional or customary behaviour. But the difference can only be subjective, since the two words, the one Latin (from *moralis*, the adjective of *mos* – custom – and *mores*, morals) and the other Greek (from *ethikos*, the adjective of *ethos* – moral behaviour), are linguistically interdependent and historically synonymous."[1]

Accordingly, in our discussion we do not make a distinction between the two terms. Furthermore, we do not intend to conduct our discussion at the abstract or philosophical level but rather at the practical level in relation to their relevance to busi-

---

[1] William A. Evans, *Management Ethics: An Intercultural Perspective*, p. 7.

ness and economics. Therefore, instead of exploring ethical and moral values and how such values are to be inculcated in business, we will primarily be discussing certain business activities or practices which are perceived to be unethical or immoral and on how best society can deal with such matters.

We do not intend to make an extensive listing of what have come to be regarded as the unethical activities of business.[2] Given the constraints of time and space, we only intend to deal with some of the more glaring examples of such activities and of how to deal with them. Among the unethical activities, alleged or otherwise, that we will explore are profiteering and corrupt practices, pollution of the environment, manufacture of shoddy and dangerous products as well as misleading and manipulatory advertising to cajole customers to buy goods they do not need or want.

In an attempt to ensure the correct behaviour on the part of their employees, some companies have produced elaborate codes on acceptable ethical and moral behaviour. Among the guidelines laid down in such codes are the following: that no bribes should be accepted or offered, that no special favours should be considered and that universally acknowledged moral and ethical standards should not be compromised. In this chapter, we reproduce the code of Gulf & Western, one of the largest corporations in the United States, and the criticisms that have been levelled against such a code.

Profiteering and Corrupt Practices

Profiteering and corrupt practices are catalogued among the worst unethical activities in which a business can engage in. However, the tendency towards profiteering and corrupt behaviour is not something inherent or inevitable among businesses. Such tendencies appear not only to survive but also to thrive in a non-competitive economic order – one in which there are extensive

---

[2]   A more detailed enumeration and discussion of such activities is given in chapter 4 of William A. Evans' *Management Ethics: An Intercultural Perspective.*

controls and interventions. As a result of such controls and interventions there is a search for profits not through genuine production and marketing in a competitive environment, but one where there is a search for returns through lobbying for licences, permits and protection.

The emergence of a non-competitive economic order in many countries around the world as in Latin America, Africa and South Asia has led to a system whereby scarcities are often contrived or created through political means. With these contrived scarcities, rents or captive profits are created and individuals or groups vie with each other to capture these rents by resorting to bribery and corruption. Such an environment is not conducive to entrepreneurship or ethical behaviour. Those who secure licences are invariably those who are good at lobbying and not necessarily those who are the best businessmen. Efficiency and growth will suffer as output is restricted and price is raised from the levels which will prevail under competitive conditions. The greater the number of industries subject to non-competitive production and pricing, the greater the incidence of inefficiency and the bigger the repercussion on the rest of the economy since the output of one industry is often the input of another.

The emergence of the non-competitive economic order can often be attributed to noble aspirations such as the aspiration for fostering rapid industrialization or reducing inequality. But as these aspirations are often founded on an incorrect appreciation of economics, the emergence of a non-competitive economic order can lead to profiteering, inefficiencies and inequities. And the regulator often becomes an easy or willing prey and is liable to capture by the regulated.

There is now mounting evidence that the emergence of a non-competitive economic order can be inimical to economic growth. A non-competitive economy can, at best, hope to grow at a rate at which its labour force is growing and its capital is accumulating. On the other hand, in the case of an economy with a competitive economic order, its actual growth rate has often been found to be one and a half times to twice the underlying natural growth rate.

Furthermore, the opportunities for profiteering and corrupt behaviour are considerably reduced in a competitive economy. However, even under a market-based competitive economic order there is a minimal role for government in public administration, in the dispensing of justice as well as in the provision of internal security and defence. Given this role the opportunities for corruption cannot be eliminated entirely. However, if a government resorts to transparency in the conduct of its affairs, this will reduce opportunities for corruption even further.

Environment

The problem of environmental pollution and the destruction of the ecological balance has become a key issue in recent decades. And business is held out to be the main offender. It has been alleged that in its relentless pursuit of profits business pays scant regard to the need for environmental quality and ecological balance.

In response to the so-called unethical conduct of business with regards to the environment, the environmental movement has been calling for more and more government regulation not only to control but to even eliminate pollution.

From the outset it is important for us to realize what the issues are. The problem is not in eliminating pollution, that is, the choice is not between pollution and no pollution. A world without pollution is only possible if there are no factories and no development. The problem is in fact in identifying measures which will result in the "optimal" amount of pollution – an amount such that the gain from reducing pollution a little more just balances the sacrifice of the other good things – cars, electricity, furniture and so on – that would have to be given up in order to reduce the pollution. If we go further than that, we sacrifice more than we gain.

It is also important for us to realize who is responsible for pollution and who has to ultimately bear the cost of pollution control. It is not the producers, but the consumers who are responsible for pollution. It is the consumers who create a demand for pollution. People who use electricity, for instance, are responsible for the smoke that comes out of generating plants. If we want to have the electricity with less pollution, then we have to pay a higher price to cover the extra costs.

It is also important to realize that the well-off are likely to benefit the most from increased recreational facilities and cleaner air arising from more pollution control measures whereas the less well-off are likely to benefit the most from the provision of cheaper goods and services, arising from less pollution control. The less well-off may prefer cheaper electricity to cleaner air.

Presently, governments have opted to control pollution through specific regulation and supervision. Thus firms are required to erect specific kinds of waste disposal plants or to achieve a specified level of water quality in the water discharged into a lake or river. This has imposed enormous costs on industry. In the United States, for instance, "something between a tenth and a quarter of total net investment in new capital equipment by business now goes for anti-pollution purposes."[3]

It is preferable to control pollution by imposing a tax of a specified amount per unit of the effluent discharged. This will give an incentive to the firm to find the cheapest way of controlling the pollution. It will also give valuable pointers on the cost of reducing pollution. "If a small tax led to a large reduction, that would be a clear indication that there is little to gain from permitting the discharge. On the other hand, if even a high tax left much discharge, that would indicate the reverse, but also would provide substantial sums to compensate the losers or undo the damage. The tax rate itself could be varied as experience yielded information on costs and gains."

"Like regulations, an effluent charge automatically puts the cost on the users of the products responsible for the pollution. Those products for which it is expensive to reduce pollution would go up in price compared to those for which it is cheap, just as now those products on which regulations impose heavy costs go up in price relative to others. The output of the former would go down, of the latter up. The difference between the effluent

---

3   Milton and Rose Friedman, *Free to Choose*, p. 213.

charge and the regulations is that the effluent charge would control pollution more effectively at lower cost and impose fewer burdens on non-pollution activities."[4]

Furthermore, unlike the effluent charge, the specific regulation has the effect of encouraging the regulated to use resources – say, by resorting to bribery and corruption – to influence the regulator to get favourable rulings and not to achieve the declared objective.

If we look at the record of the industrialized countries and not at rhetoric, the air is in general far cleaner and the water safer today than one hundred years ago. Industrialization no doubt has raised new problems but has solved far bigger problems of the past.

Product Quality and Product Safety

It is often alleged by well-meaning and not so well-meaning people that self-interest will induce businessmen to deceive their customers by passing off to them shoddy, adulterated or dangerous products. Given this so-called bias for unethical behaviour, reliance has been advocated for government intervention to protect the interests of consumers. In the United States, for instance, several government agencies have been set up to protect the consumers from being overcharged as well as from unsafe and useless products, including drugs. The two most famous agencies are the Food and Drug Administration and the Consumer Products Safety Commission. It is instructive to examine the actual record of these agencies.

A Food and Drug Administration official entrusted with the responsibility of passing or rejecting a new drug would be led to reject or defer approval of many a good drug – that is capable of saving many lives or relieving great distress and that has no untoward side effects – in order to avoid even a remote possibility of approving a drug that will have unanticipated and newsworthy

---

[4]   Ibid., p. 217.

side effects – which cause the death or serious impairment of a sizeable number of persons.

This inevitable bias is reinforced by the reaction of the pharmaceutical industry. This bias leads to unduly stringent standards. Getting approval becomes more expensive and time-consuming. One estimate has pointed to a hundredfold increase in cost and quadrupling of time, compared with a doubling of prices in general for the period considered. Research on and development of new drugs become less profitable and more risky. Each company has less to fear from the research efforts of its competitors. Existing firms and existing drugs are protected from competition. New entry is discouraged. Research that is done will be concentrated on drugs with high volume sales – and not for rare diseases – and on the least controversial, which means least innovative, of the new possibilities.

The considerable evidence accumulated hitherto shows that the Food and Drug Administration's regulation is counterproductive, that it has done more harm by retarding progress in the production and distribution of valuable drugs than it has done good by preventing the distribution of harmful or ineffective drugs. Safety and caution in one direction has meant death and misery in another.

Let us now turn to the Consumer Products Safety Commission. Its main concern is not with price or cost but with safety. It has conducted tests and issued standards on products ranging from the simple to the most sophisticated. The objective of safer products is obviously a good one, but at what cost and by what or whose standards? In the main, the manufacturers of the products, unlike the civil servants or the consumers, are the only ones who have "sufficient interests and expertise to comment knowledgeably on proposed standards. Indeed, much of the formulation of standards has simply been turned over to trade associations. You may be sure those standards will be formulated in the interest of the members of the association, with a sharp eye to protecting themselves from competition, both from possible new producers at home and from foreign producers. The result will be to strengthen the competitive position of existing domestic manufacturers and to make innovation and the development of new and improved products more expensive and difficult."[5]

Perfection is not of this world. There will always be shoddy products, quacks and con artists. But on the whole, market competition, when it is permitted to work, protects the consumer better than government regulation not because businessmen are more soft-hearted, more altruistic or more competent than the bureaucrats, but only because it is in the self-interest of the businessman to serve the consumer.

But, the advocate of government regulation will say, suppose the Food and Drug Administration were not there, what would prevent business from distributing shoddy, adulterated or dangerous products? It would be very expensive thing to do as indicated by the big damages that the manufacturers of Elixir Sulfanilamide and Thalidomide ended up paying. It is also a very poor business practice, not a way to develop a loyal and faithful clientele. "Of course, mistakes and accidents occur – but as the Tris case illustrates, Government does not prevent them. The difference is that a private firm that makes a serious blunder may go out of business. A government agency is likely to get a bigger budget."[6]

And the advocate of government regulation will say, without the Consumer Products Safety Commission, how can the consumer judge the quality of complex products? The market's answer is that he does not have to be able to judge for himself. He has other bases for choosing. "One is the use of a middleman. The chief economic function of a department store, for example, is to monitor quality on our behalf. None of us is an expert on all of the items we buy even the most trivial like shirts, ties or shoes. If we buy an item that turns out to be defective, we are more likely to return it to the retailer from whom we bought it than to the manufacturer. The retailer is in far better position to judge quality than we are. Sears, Roebuck and Montgomery Ward, like depart-

---

[5]   Ibid., p. 211.

[6]   Ibid., p. 223.

ment stores are effective consumer testing and certifying agency as well as distributors."[7]

Another market device is the brand name. "It is in the self-interest of General Electric or General Motors or Westinghouse or Rolls-Royce to get a reputation for producing dependable, reliable products. That is the source of their 'goodwill' which may well contribute more to their value as a firm than the factories and plants they own."[8]

Advertising

Two main complaints are made against advertising by critics such as Evans. "The first is that it is wasteful and unnecessary and therefore immoral; the second is that it is often untruthful, misleading or in bad taste, which is equally immoral."[9]

The critics claim that advertising is wasteful and unnecessary because it is often "directed at convincing people that there is a difference between products that are totally interchangeable."[10] According to these critics, advertising is a device to attach buyers to one's own brand of a commodity, and it is inevitably manipulatory. In particular, it is argued that there would be no advertising by fully competitive firms or industries. However, George J. Stigler's work on the economics of information has led to a radically different view of advertising. "Consumers require much information. What new products are available, where can new and old products be purchased (since stores come and go), how can one get assurance of quality, who sells at the lowest price, and so on. Advertising proves to be an extremely efficient way of conveying much of this information, and is as essential for competitive firms as for monopolies."[11]

---

[7]   Ibid., p. 223.
[8]   Ibid., pp. 223-4.
[9]   William A. Evans, *Management Ethics: An Intercultural Perspective*, p. 102.
[10] Ibid., p. 103.
[11] George J. Stigler, *Memoirs of an Unregulated Economist*, p. 164.

Philip Nelson, in extending the theory of information to advertising, "has shown that so-called 'institutional advertising' (our firm is the oldest or largest in the industry) conveys to the consumer an assurance of reliability. The firm must have treated customers pretty well or it would not have had so many repeat buyers. The economics profession has become a good deal more discerning in its discussion of advertising than it was a few decades back."[12]

What about the claim of untruthful or misleading advertising? This claim tantamounts to assuming that consumers can be led by the nose by advertising? The obvious answer is that they cannot as numerous expensive advertising fiascoes testify. "One of the greatest duds of all time was the Edsel automobile introduced by Ford Motor Company and promoted by a major advertising campaign. More basically, advertising is a cost of doing business, and the businessman wants to get the most for his money. Is it not more sensible to try to appeal to the real wants or desires of consumers than to try to manufacture artificial wants or desires? Surely it will generally be cheaper to sell them something that meets wants they already have than to create an artificial want."[13]

"A favourite example has been the allegedly artificially created desire for automobile model changes. Yet Ford was unable to make a success of the Edsel despite an enormously expensive advertising campaign. There always have been cars available that did not make frequent model changes – the Superba in the United States (the passenger counterpart of the Checker cab) and many foreign cars. They were never able to attract more than a small fraction of the total custom. If that was what consumers really wanted, the companies that offered that option would have prospered, and the others would have followed suit. The real objection of most critics of advertising is not that advertising manipulates tastes but that the public at large has meretricious tastes – that is tastes that do not agree with the critics." [14]

---

[12] Ibid., p. 81.

[13] Milton and Rose Friedman, *Free to Choose*, p. 224.

[14] Ibid., pp. 224-5.

MALAYSIA'S VISION 2020109

Code of Ethics

In an attempt to ensure correct behaviour on the part of their employees some companies have drawn up a code of ethics for general business behaviour: admonitions to refrain from bribery, immorality and turpitude are obvious examples. An example of the code of ethics of Gulf & Western, a major corporation in the United States, with interests stretching from oil to motion pictures and from construction to paper products, is reprinted from William A. Evans' *Management Ethics: An Intercultural Perspective* and is reproduced as an annexure to this chapter.

As Evans points out, "no statement of this kind can hope to cover all ethical problems, and employees will inevitably have to make decisions not covered by it, such decisions appear to be included under an umbrella instruction to 'do the right thing', but obviously any such document cannot specify what the right thing may be in all cases."[15]

Conclusion

The moral and ethical values that are typically enunciated in a code of conduct for a business enterprise or its employees are hardly ever controversial. Among the guidelines laid down in such a code are the following: that no bribes should be accepted or offered; that no special favours should be considered; that there should be no insider trading; that conflict of interest situations should be avoided; and that accurate books, records and accounts should be maintained.

The problem arises when, based on such moral and ethical considerations or other aspirations, businesses are forced to comply with certain standards with respect to the environment, product quality, product safety and advertising. government agencies are then invariably set up to evolve and enforce these standards.

---

[15] William A. Evans, *Management Ethics: An Intercultural Perspective*, p. 127.

We have highlighted earlier the high costs that have been imposed on industry by these government agencies and regulations. They have prevented some products from being produced or sold. They have required capital to be invested for non-productive purposes. Milton Friedman has argued that the activities of these agencies had led to a considerable slowdown in growth in the United States. "From 1949 to 1969, output per man-hour of all persons employed in private business – a simple and comprehensive measure of productivity – rose more than 3 per cent a year; in the next decade, less than half as fast; and by the end of the decade productivity was actually declining."[16]

It is claimed that self-interest will lead producers and sellers to deceive their customers, that they will take advantage of their customers' innocence and ignorance to overcharge them and pass off to them shoddy products and that they will cajole customers to buy goods they do not want or need.

Those who believe in the market admit that there will always be shoddy products, quacks and con artists. But they contend that "on the whole, market competition, when it is permitted to work, protects the consumer better than do the alternative government mechanisms that have been increasingly superimposed on the market."[17]

To quote Friedman, "competition does not protect the consumer because businessmen are more soft-hearted than the bureaucrats or because they are more altruistic or generous, or even because they are more competent, but only because it is in the self-interest of the businessmen to serve the customer."[18]

We have conducted our discussion of morals and ethics and the strictures they impose on business at a general level. These strictures, especially if they are rigidly interpreted with respect to the environment, product quality and product safety, advertising and such other matters, have led to an escalation in the cost of doing business and to declining growth. They have also tended to

---

[16] Milton and Rose Friedman, *Free to Choose*, p. 191.

[17] Ibid., p. 222.

[18] Ibid., p. 222.

work against new developments, industrial innovations as well as the increased use of natural resources. These consequences, which are dictated by the inexorable forces of economics, are as applicable to Malaysia as any other country in the world. If the ambitious growth targets envisaged by Dr Mahathir Mohamad in his Vision 2020 statement for the country are to be realized and if we are truly to develop into a highly competitive, dynamic and progressive community, then it is absolutely necessary that the economy is not shackled by unnecessary regulations based on some lofty ideals or values. As far as possible the authorities should devote the scarce resources at their disposal in developing competitive markets. This is the best recipe, if not a sure guarantee, for rapid growth as well as for securing the welfare of consumers and workers alike.

A Brain-Teaser for the Non-Believers

Alcohol is a dangerous substance. In the United States, for instance, more lives are lost each year from alcohol than from all the dangerous substances the Food and Drug Administration controls put together. Accordingly, many countries have, at one time or another, imposed prohibition for our own good.

Prohibition was enacted in the United States in a burst of moral righteousness at the end of the First World War. Billy Sunday, a noted evangelist and leading crusader against Demon Rum, greeted the onset of Prohibition in 1920 with this stirring pronouncement: "The reign of tears is over. The slums will be only a memory. We will turn our prisons into factories and our jails into storehouses and corncribs. Men will walk upright now, women will smile, and the children will laugh. Hell will be forever for rent. "[19]

But what was the actual outcome of Prohibition? "New prisons and jails had to be built to house the criminals spawned by converting the drinking of spirits into a crime against the state. Al Capone, Bugs Moran became notorious for their exploits – mur-

---

[19] Ibid., p. 226.

der, extortion, hijacking, bootlegging. Who were their customers? Who bought the liquor they purveyed illegally? Respectable citizens who would never themselves have approved of, or engaged in the activities that Al Capone and his fellow gangsters made infamous. They simply wanted a drink. In order to have a drink, they had to break the law. Prohibition did not stop drinking. It did convert a lot of otherwise law-obedient citizens into lawbreakers. It did confer an aura of glamour and excitement to drinking that attracted many young persons. It did suppress many of the disciplinary forces of the market that ordinarily protect the consumer from shoddy, adulterated and dangerous products. It did corrupt the minions of the law and create a decadent moral climate. It did *not* stop the consumption of alcohol."[20]

Let this episode be a stark reminder of where blind moralizing and blatant interventions in the marketplace can lead to. The market must, it is said, be supplemented by other arrangements in order to protect the consumer from himself and from avaricious sellers and to protect all of us from the spillover effects of market transactions. These criticisms of the market are valid. However, as amply demonstrated by experience and the lessons taught by the University of Hard Knocks, the cure that has been recommended or adopted to meet them is worse than the disease itself.

References

Evans, William A., 1981. *Management Ethics: An Intercultural Perspective*. The Hague: Martinus Nijhoff Publishing.

Friedman, Milton and Rose Friedman, 1980. *Free to Choose*. New York: Harcourt Brace Jovanovich.

Stigler, George J., 1988. *Memoirs of an Unregulated Economist*. New York: Basic Books, Inc.

---

[20] Ibid., pp. 226-7.

Annexure

Resolution of the Gulf & Western Board of Directors' Code of Business Ethics

Whereas it is the desire of the Board of Directors to reconfirm its policy with respect to the ethical conduct of the corporation's business in a format suitable for dissemination throughout the corporation and its subsidiaries, now, therefore, be it resolved that the Board of Directors adopts for and on behalf of the corporation a Code of Business Ethics in the form annexed hereto as Exhibit A; and hereby directs appropriate officers of the corporation to disseminate and implement the aforesaid Code in such manner as to assure compliance with the provisions thereof.

General
Gulf & Western takes pride in a reputation of high moral and ethical standards. Our business is highly competitive, yet we have managed to build a reputation of integrity by adhering to a sound and equitable code of business ethics.

Congress has recently passed an act which (i) prohibits companies and their officers, directors, shareholders and employees from engaging in certain corrupt practices with respect to foreign officials and (ii) requires companies to maintain accurate books, records and accounts and to devise a system of internal accounting controls. This code expresses in general terms the standard of conduct which have always been and continue to be expected by the Corporation and, in some instances, which now are required by law, of all Gulf & Western employees in their relationships with those with whom the Corporation does business, foreign governments and officials, the public and their fellow employees. They constitute a body of principles for guidance in many specific situations, as well as fundamental principles applicable in every situation, whether or not foreseen or specifically provided for. Not only impropriety, but every appearance or suggestion of impropriety, must be avoided.

Policy

Compliance with Law. It is the policy of Gulf & Western to conduct its business on the highest ethical and moral plane, and to comply strictly with all laws and regulations governing its operations. All officers and employees of the Corporation are required to comply with local laws, as well as the laws of foreign nations, in their conduct of corporate business.

Compliance with the law means not only following the letter of the law, but also conducting business so that Gulf & Western will maintain its reputation for integrity and honesty which characterizes its business activity worldwide. Even where the law is not applicable, standards of ethics and morality apply and require the same diligent attention to good conduct and citizenship.

Improper or Questionable Payments. All persons and firms with whom Gulf & Western maintains business relationships will be treated fairly and impartially. The giving or acceptance of gifts, favours, or payments of any sort, either directly or indirectly, which illegally or immorally influence (or would appear to influence) business decisions, is strictly forbidden. Specific guidelines on antitrust, boycotts and other restrictive trade practices, and improper sales aid payments are stated in separate policies and are reaffirmed here.

The use of corporate funds for payments to any government official or government entity for any purpose whatsoever (except in satisfaction of lawful obligations, for reasonable public benefit contributions or for seasonable gifts insubstantial in value) is prohibited. However, it is recognized that in some areas of the world such payments may be required, by custom or practice, to expedite or obtain governmental action to which the corporation is entitled under applicable law. In exceptional circumstances, such payments may be made but only if first approved by the Corporate Legal Department.

The prohibitions against improper payments in this code apply to indirect disbursements of corporate funds or property by an employee, agent or third person as well as direct disbursements of such funds or property.

Act of Hospitality. Acts of hospitality towards any employee or representative of any customer or supplier or government official shall be of such scale of nature as to avoid any impropriety or the appearance of any impropriety or the appearance of any impropriety in connection therewith.

Accounting Records. See Account Policy and Control II-2. The records and books of account of Gulf & Western, each Group, subsidiary and division must accurately reflect each transaction recorded therein. No false or deliberately inaccurate entries shall be made in the Corporation's books and records for any reason. No payment shall be made with the intention or understanding that all or any part of such payment is to used for any purpose other than that prescribed by the documents supporting the payment. The creation and maintenance of any cash fund or other asset for disposition by representatives of the Corporation is prohibited without accurately accounting for such funds and assets, and the disposition thereof, on the books and records of the Corporation. Moreover, no persons shall make, or cause to be made, any false or misleading statement to an accountant in connection with any examination or audit of the Corporation's books and records.

Corporate Political Contributions. Political contributions by, or in the name of, Gulf & Western or any of its Groups, subsidiaries, divisions or operating units are strictly forbidden, as they are illegal in all Federal elections, most state elections and in many foreign countries.

Under no circumstances will a Corporate political contribution of money or anything of value, including loans, contributions or use of either goods, facilities or services, be made either directly or indirectly to individual candidates, political committees, political parties, or political organizations of any kind. The Corporation will not reimburse, directly or indirectly, anyone for his personal contribution or personal participation in political activities.

The policy is not intended to prohibit or in any way deter Gulf & Western employees from personally contributing to or participating in political activities, including contributions and participation in duly authorized employees' political action committees.

Responsibility

There is a Corporate and legal obligation as well as an individual obligation to fulfil the intent of this policy. The Chief Operating Officer of each Group, subsidiary and division, each Gulf & Western Corporation Officer and all managers within Gulf & Western are responsible for the implementation and administration of this policy within their respective organizations. Discovery of events which are in violation of this policy must be reported directly to the Corporate Legal Department.

Furthermore, it is the responsibility of every individual in the Corporation, who in any way may affect the Corporation's compliance with the laws and with standards of ethical and moral conduct to carry out the corporate policy. It is not expected that every employee will be fully versed in the law affecting his responsibilities. However, it is expected that every employee will have a working knowledge of permissible activities involved in his work and will seek guidance from a superior or the Corporate Legal Department concerning any matter on which there is any question.

We expect compliance with the Gulf & Western standard of integrity throughout the organization. Any infraction of recognized ethical business standards or the of the applicable laws will subject an employee to immediate disciplinary action (including the possibility of dismissal).

The Corporate Legal Department is responsible for constant review and interpretation of the law, and should be called upon for guidance and counsel if legal questions arise regarding this policy.

6

Inculcating Moral and Ethical Values in Business

Syed Othman Al-Habshi

Although motivated essentially by profits, business[1] as an activity provides numerous important services to society. It is business activity which brings about all the goods and services, be they for basic or luxurious needs, within society's reach. Business also generates a major portion of the nation's employment, contributes substantially to the country's income and wealth and parts some portion to the government in the form of taxes.[2] Business, to a large extent, is a major impetus to the growth and expansion of the economy apart from drawing in foreign investments and the much needed foreign exchange. It does play a significant role in determining the quality of life arising out of the impacts of the by-products of its legitimate activities on society and on the physical and social environment.

---

[1] "Business" in this chapter refers to all activities undertaken by those other than government and voluntary bodies.

[2] Interestingly, the Fourth Rightly-Guided Caliph of Islam, Sayyidina 'Ali bin Al-Haris Al-Ashtar, specifically reminded the would-be Governor to give special attention to the business people for the same reason. Shafie Hj Mohd Salleh and Mohd Affandi Hassan, 1990.

In the process of rendering such services, society has demanded that business should be responsible for the needs of their employees, particularly in terms of fair wages and other conditions of service, safety of their lives and bodily harms and even their security after retirement. Second, business leaders, by virtue of their power, influence and wealth, are increasingly expected to contribute towards the community's "culture". This includes providing support to the arts, the museums, the opera, and the symphony orchestra; serving as trustees on the boards of educational and religious institutions; and also financial support for philanthropic and other community causes. Third, it is the relationship between private and public ethics. Should a businessman resort to unethical or immoral behaviour in pursuit of his business objectives.[3] This question throws open a very wide area of debate. The related question would be whether such immoral or unethical behaviour incurs any cost to society. The answer would be obvious, especially after the numerous bizarre business practices came to light in recent years which caused the closure of thousands of companies, many more thousands jobless, huge amounts of unrecoverable debts dished out unsecured, unaccountable incomes and many more.[4]

As if the three areas of social responsibilities of business alluded above were insufficient, contemporary discussions on the subject seems to bear a slightly different emphasis. It is on what business should or might do to tackle and solve problems of society.[5] Problems such as the restoration of physical environment, social integration and national unity are being emphasized. The main explanation offered for this new emphasis is the success system itself.

The concern of Dr Mahathir Mohamad, however, is not limited to the business community alone, but that for the whole society should emulate strong moral and ethical values for the achievement of a developed Malaysian nation by the year 2020.

[3]   Peter Drucker, 1974.
[4]   Bruce Nash and Allan Zullo, 1988.
[5]   Op cit., pp. 260-261.

This is noble, ideal yet essential. All human societies have emphasized moral and ethical behaviour based on religion, customs, norms or traditions. We shall therefore confine ourselves, for the purpose of this chapter, to the inculcation of moral and ethical values in business.

Morality and Ethics: Some Comparisons

Ethics[6] is a branch of philosophy that deals with morality. It may be defined as "a systematic inquiry into the beliefs we have and the judgements we make about what is morally right and wrong and morally good and evil." It is an inquiry that attempts to answer the questions, "what kinds of conduct are morally right or wrong?" and "what things are good and what are evil?" [7]

The classical view as represented by Socrates, Plato and even Aristotle settled moral questions by using rational methods or reasons. It is reason that should guide one's morality and not the opinion of many. The ethical standard as propounded by Socrates is good citizenship. In other words, one is ethical if he is loyal to the state. Aristotle, on the other hand, considers "happiness" or *eudaimonia* as the ultimate objective of being ethical. One feels happy after doing good. His definition of "happiness" is not confined to the activity of the soul in accordance with virtue but includes external goods as well. External goods take the form of good appearance, sufficient wealth for a comfortable living, good family life, etc.

The classical ethical theory has been criticized by contemporary moralists who contend that moral right and wrong cannot possibly depend on reason alone. They further argue that such

---

[6]   We do not distinguish between "ethics" and "morality" here to avoid unnecessary confusion. Ethics, however, has two general meanings. The first refers to the code of conduct or the rules by which one should behave, such as medical ethics. The second refers to the systematic inquiry about what is ethical and what is not. It is also referred to as the theory of ethics.

[7]   M. Velasquez and C. Rostankowski, 1985, p. 3.

decisions depend on one's culture. The first view, based on the sociological theory of "cultural relativism" holds that different cultures have different beliefs of morality. The second view is based on the more radical and controversial philosophical theory known as "ethical relativism". This theory holds that an action is considered morally right or wrong if the members of that culture believe the action is morally right or wrong.[8]

The second objection to the classical view that ethics is based on reason is held by those who believe that ethical statements are really expressions of emotions designed to influence people's behaviour. This view, called "emotivism", is due to A.J. Ayer.[9] Both these objections have been refuted and Socrates' view, like Plato's, still holds in the Western conception of ethics which has strong affinity towards positivism.

Islam maintains the integration between the material and spiritual through its concept of Tawhid or unity.[10] The Tawhidic paradigm which determines all actions is the fundamental principle of the Islamic faith. Islamic ethics due to Al-Ghazali[11] is a study of religious beliefs, and of rightness and wrongness of action for the purpose of practice, and not for the sake of knowledge.[12] By the principle of Tawhid, study of action includes those actions which are directed towards God, fellowmen in family and in society, of purification of the soul from vices and of its beautification with virtues. The method of inquiry is not based on reason alone but should be combined with religion or the Syariah or Islamic law, both of which are complementary. Religion provides the truth while reason helps to understand the truth. The

---

[8]   "Ethical relativism" is the view that if the members of a culture believe a certain action is morally right, then it really is morally right to perform it in that culture. By the same token, if the members of another culture believe that the same sort of action is morally wrong, then it really is morally wrong to perform it in that culture. M. Rostankowski, 1985.

[9]   Ibid., p. 7.

[10] A detailed discussion of it can be found in Syed Othman Al-Habshi, 1990.

[11] M. Watt, 1953; Abul Quasem, 1975; Abu Hamid Muhammad Al—Ghazali, 1981.

[12] Abul Quasem, 1975, p. 22.

aim of Islamic ethics is to achieve happiness in this world and more so in the hereafter.

Nature and Scope of Business Ethics

Business ethics may be broadly defined as the code of business conduct or the set of rules which would guide us in undertaking any business activity. By abiding such rules we should be considered ethical or moral in our business dealings. While business aims at making profits through various means, when such rules of conduct are being applied, it does not at all mean that the profit motive is no longer valid. The question is the means of making the profits should not in any way violate such rules. In essence, the general aims of such rules may be listed as to uphold justice and truth, to ensure business system succeeds for the benefit of society and to achieve success in this life as well as in the hereafter.

Contemporary business literature abounds with topics on or related to business ethics. The scope of business ethics includes the responsibility business has to society to what is commonly known as social responsibility. Peter Drucker, the American guru of modern management, maintains that business professionals should not be treated differently from other professionals and for that matter, other individuals.[13] He believes that they should abide by what technically in the academic discipline of ethics is referred to as the "principle of nonmaleficence". Simply put, this principle holds that a chief obligation of professionals is to "do no harm". Milton Friedman[14] argues that the social responsibility of business is to increases its profits. One who spends on solving social problems acts irresponsibly. Konosuke Matsushita, on the other hand, argues that business should make service to society as its objectives, and while serving society profits will automatically be obtained.[15]

---

[13] Peter Drucker, 1975, p. 22.

[14] Peter Madsen and Jay M. Shafritz, eds., 1990.

[15] Konosuke Matsushita, 1984.

Generally, there are four levels of issues in business ethics. The first level which we may call "societal" relates to issues of basic institutions in society. The problem of apartheid in South Africa is a societal-level question. One may ask whether it is ethical to have a social system in which a section, indeed the majority, of the society is deprived of their basic rights. Other examples of societal-level questions are: Should we tolerate gross inequalities in income? Should we spend money on rehabilitating drug addicts? Business leaders, by virtue of their wealth, influence and power may be able to shape debates on issues of societal-level.

The second level concerns stakeholders. These include suppliers, customers, shareholders, bondholders, etc. At this level, issues raised are those relating to how a business concern should deal with the external groups who are affected by its decisions and how the stakeholders should deal with the business concern. Examples of these issues are insider trading, limitation on a company's obligation to inform its customers about the defects or potential dangers of its products, a company's obligations to its suppliers, to the communities where it operates, to its stockholders. How should we decide such matters? These questions relate to policy matters and decisions on them are made daily.

The third level issues relate to "internal policy". At this level, we may ask questions pertaining to employer-employee relationships. What is a fair contract? What are the mutual obligations of managers and other workers? What rights do employees have? How much could they participate in decision making? Do they have any say in layoffs, perks, scheme of service, etc. These questions provide opportunities for the company to be socially responsive to its employees.

Finally, we have the "personal level" of moral issues. The questions here relate to the way people treat one another in the organization. Should we be honest to one another, whatever the consequences? What obligations do we have, both as human beings and as workers who play specific roles in the organization – to the bosses, subordinates and peers? These questions deal with the day-to-day issues of life in any organization.

It is necessary to point out at this juncture that the Islamic business ethics take into consideration not only the values, but also the requirements of the Syariah. In other words, apart from the values, we also have to abide by the dictates of the Syariah for a business transaction to be valid. For example, a transaction is nullified if it contains unlawful elements that arise from the transaction itself – such as *riba*, concealed information, hoarding, etc. – or from what is transacted – such as forbidden goods, goods without complete specifications, etc. – or from those who transact – such as a child who has not come of age and has not been permitted by the guardian, a blind man in the absence of a legal representative, etc.

Before we close this chapter it might be worthwhile to discuss some of the common virtues which we should inculcate and vices which we should avoid or purify ourselves from. These virtues and vices are some of those listed and discussed by Al-Ghazali.[16]

1. *Truthfulness.* Truthfulness is present in speech, intention, resolution, fulfilment of resolution, in action and in all the stations on the path. One is considered most truthful if he acquires truthfulness in all aspects which he acquires. This virtue is most commonly violated in business. Greed for profits seems to be stronger than upholding truthfulness.

2. *Sincerity.* Sincerity in any action is when it is done for the sake of pleasing God and nothing else. Any action that is done for any other motive than to please God is considered insincere. The degree of sincerity therefore is measured by the intention of the doer. Although sincerity is difficult to inculcate, it is a very important virtue which will guarantee long-term success.

3. *Patience.* Patience has two aspects. The first aspect is called mental patience which is restraint on demands of carnal desires and anger. Mental patience is required against excessive desire for food and sex. In misfortune, it

---

[16] Abu Quasem, 1975.

is required against violent outbursts in the form of crying, tearing of clothes, etc. Firmness of mind is required in controlling anger and greed for wealth. The second aspect is called bodily patience which is the endurance of physical pain felt in performing devotional or non-devotional acts and in disease and in injury. Patience is very much required in business because one will somehow encounter something that is disagreeable.

4. *Moderation in Consumption.* Gluttony is one of the worst vices because it is harmful to man. It also prevents one from attaining happiness through knowledge and action. Satiety makes the limbs too heavy, hunger makes one think of food. Moderate intake of food makes one feel from hunger and heaviness of stomach. It is good to train oneself to be moderate in consumption. It will make one active in his business life, but not too active in other "business". Indeed one of the great vices is of course excessive sex.

5. *Keeping Promises.* This is an important virtue in business. However, many business promises seem hard to keep. Keeping our promises all the time will ensure success in business as well. One can win the hearts of many if one is trustworthy, reliable and dependable. Such qualities are necessary for business success.

6. *Avoiding Lies.* Falsehood in speech and in an oath is one of the greater evils of the tongue. It proceeds from the quality of hypocrisy in the soul. To avoid lies is of course virtuous and is definitely an asset in business.

7. *Love of the World.* This is regarded not only as a great vice but the vice from which all other vices proceed. The world is of two kinds. First, the reprehensible world which is sought for the pleasure and enjoyment of the carnal desires only and will cause misery in the next world. The second type is the worldly things that gives enjoyment in this world but is either helpful in the hereafter (knowledge and action) or is an aid to

knowledge and action (legal sexual activity, as much food, clothing and shelter as is necessary to acquire knowledge and action). Love of the reprehensible world will of course bring much mischief to the person.

8. *Love of Wealth.* It is natural for man to love wealth for he is created such. However, it is the excessive love of wealth that will draw one away from doing good or being virtuous and thus encourages him to do the vices instead. This is again the disease of the soul. When business is motivated only by the love of wealth, there can probably be no end to the list of vices one may commit.

9. *Miserliness.* This is one of the greater vices. The proper use of wealth is to spend it when it should be spent and to keep it when it should be kept. Keeping it when it should be spent is miserliness; spending it when it should be kept is extravagance; between these two extremes is the mean which is the virtue of generosity. One should therefore be moderate in the use of wealth.

10. *Love of Influence.* This is even a greater vice than the love of wealth for it causes more evils. Influence means the establishment of a person's status in the minds of others so that they magnify him, gladly obey him and become so submissive that he can use them for all his purposes. Such an influential status is established when people believe that he has a quality of perfection, although this belief may be erroneous. The qualities of influence are knowledge, piety, good character, handsome appearance, bodily strength, or any other attribute usually regarded as perfection, though not so in reality. These are the means by which man influences others. The result of such influence are praise, assistance in his works, respectful salutations, etc. Some measure of influence, however, is necessary in life. For example, one can easily repel enemies if there are others who are ever prepared to come to his aid. It is superfluous influence which causes evil.

11. *Pride.* This is the greatest of all vices; pride can happen
only in the presence of two elements. First is a person
towards whom it is directed, and second is a quality of
perfection in which pride is taken. If a man considers
himself great, while another equal or greater, this is not
pride; nor is it pride if he supposes another as contemptible while he is as contemptible or more. Pride
comes to mind when a man believes that he has worth,
that another man also has worth, but his own worth is
greater than that of the other. These three beliefs will
make him feel a sense of joy, a trust in what he believes, a
sense of his own greatness and contempt for the other.
These constitute pride. This state of the soul, also called
self-esteem and sense of greatness, will produce various
forms of boastful actions. Pride can arise from qualities
such as noble birth, physical beauty or strength, wealth
and followers, friends, relatives and assistants.

Inculcating Moral and Ethical Values in Business

We can hardly dispute the contributions made by business activity
to society. The convenience of obtaining our needs in terms of
goods or services almost at our doorsteps, the creation of
employment which individuals in society can secure, the wealth
creation and accumulation over the years, the economic growth
and expansion that we enjoy and the increasing government
revenue contributed by business through taxes are among the
many contributions made by the business system. However, what
does not figure in our national output or income data are the
"leakages" which occur through business malpractice. First, because such "leakages" are never considered an item in the national accounts. Second, the quantum is not well estimated. Third, it
is probably not ethical to do so. In fact, the amount of money involved in such transactions can be very large, because it happens
daily and in increasing amounts. These transactions can take the

form of bribes, gifts with ulterior motives, "transfer payments" in the form of kickbacks, handsome perks to certain key personnel in the organization even when the business is on the verge of closing down, etc. Perfidy or deliberate breach of trust cases have often reduced share prices of affected or related business organizations in the stock markets of affected or related companies. Thousands of business enterprises have been forced to close down as a result of a variety of malpractices, among which are embezzlement of funds, approval of unsecured and unrecoverable loans, mismanagement, etc. These illegitimate, immoral or unethical practices of the businessmen seem increasingly rampant as though there is no conscience to prick them. While we acknowledge business contributions to society, we cannot ignore or, worse still, condone such unethical behaviour of the relative few.

Suppose these immoral or unethical practices are completely absent in the business community, one can imagine the increase it will undoubtedly bring to the national income figures, the revenue that will be collected by the government, the employment that will be created, the growth rate of the economy and the quality of life that society can enjoy. This is the reason Dr Mahathir Mohamad has enlisted the establishment of a fully moral and ethical society as one of the nine challenges that we have to encounter to become a developed and industrialized nation.

The relevant question here is what kind of specific effects will ethics have on business individuals and therefore on society? Of course it depends on how much of business issues have ethical contents. Unfortunately, ethical issues are everywhere and they occur daily. This is clear from the discussion on the four levels of ethical issues in the preceding section.

The age-old principle of ethical behaviour is "non-maleficence" which simply means "do not harm". But not to harm others may be neutral in the sense that one may not do any good either. So this general principle can be further refined. As

---

[17] Abul Quasem, 1975.

was done by Al-Ghazali,[17] there are three ways of dealing with others. First is to show beneficence to others, that is, by showing them respect and try to fill their hearts with gladness. Second is to refrain from harming others. Harm is not limited to damaging life and property. It even includes looking at someone in a hurtful manner. Not to harm anyone is justice and uprightness, and this is a duty required of everyone. Those who harm others are ir-religious and immoral. Al-Ghazali succinctly expressed these three ways of dealing with others thus: "In respect of other men, too, a man stands in one of three classes: (a) with regard to them he may take the place of just and generous angels, namely, by ex-erting himself for their ends through compassion and the desire to fill their hearts with gladness; (b) with regard to other men he may occupy the position of animals and inanimate objects, name-ly, where they receive neither benefit nor harm from him; or (c) with regard to them he may occupy the position of scorpions, snakes and harmful beasts of prey, from which men expect no good, while fearing the evil they may cause. If you cannot reach the sphere of the angels, at least try not to fall from the level of animals and inanimate things to the ranks of scorpions, snakes or beast of prey. If your soul is content to come down from the highest heights, at least do not let it be content to be hurled into the lowest depths. Perhaps you will be saved by the middle way where you have neither more nor less than what suffices."[18]

A business transaction that is unjust certainly then does harm to others. The harm can be general in nature, that is, where the whole society is affected or specific, which affects only individuals one transacts with. An example of a transaction which brings general harm is monopolistic hoarding of essential foodstuff or *ihtikar*. Such hoarding will definitely increase the price of the es-sential foodstuff since the one who hoards is a monopolist. Ex-amples of transactions which bring specific harm are to hide the defect of the good, giving short measures, concealing informa-tion about the price of the good, etc.

---

[18] Abul Quasem, 1975, p. 210.

We have in recent times read about the throwing of fish into the sea, killing of little chickens by the thousands, marketing of normal drinking water as mineral water, operating unlicensed dangerous factories, not to mention numerous cases of graft charges against people in high office, etc. Another common practice is to charge customers for locally made motorcar spare parts at exorbitant prices of imported parts. Yet another is delaying the completion of contractual works for various reasons, except efficiency. Unfortunately, these are not isolated cases. What we know is probably only the tip of the iceberg.

Conclusion

We have only a short thirty years to become a developed, industrialized and prosperous nation with a people fully committed to strong ethical and moral values. We have to realize that the outward actions are the reflections of the inward qualities of the soul. It is therefore the soul that we have to nurture and develop into good character. It is not impossible, but difficult. It therefore remains, as it were, a great challenge to us all.

References

Drucker, Peter, 1974. *Management: Tasks, Responsibilities, Practices*. London: Heinemann.

Madsen, Peter and Jay M. Shafritz, eds., 1990. *Essentials of Business Ethics*. New York: Meridian.

Matsushita, Konosuke, 1984. *Not For Bread Alone*. Tokyo, Japan: PHP.

Muhammad Abul Quasem, 1975. *The Ethics of Al-Ghazali: A Composite Ethics in Islam*. Kuala Lumpur: Muhammad Abul Quasem.

Nash, Bruce and Allan Zullo, 1988. *The Misfortune 500*. New York: Pocket Books.

Shafie Hj Mohd Salleh and Mohd Affandi Hassan, eds., 1990. *Kecemerlangan Pentadbiran: Dasar dan Amalan Dalam Islam*. Kuala Lumpur: Institut Tadbiran Awam Negara.

Syed Othman Al-Habshi, 1990. "Management Ethics From Islamic Perspective". Paper presented at the National Seminar on Management Ethics jointly organized by Universiti Utara Malaysia and Petronas on March 13 and 14, 1990 at Bangi, Selangor.

Syed Othman Al-Habshi, 1987. "The Role of Ethics in Economics and Business". *Journal of Islamic Economics*, vol. 1, no. 1, pp. 1-55.

Velasquez, M. and C. Rostankowsky, 1985. *Ethics: Theory and Practice*. Englewood Cliffs, New Jersey: Prentice Hall.

Watt, Montgomery, 1953. *The Faith and Practice of Al-Ghazali*. Lahore, Pakistan: Sh. Muhammad Ashraf.

7

Towards a Competitive and Resilient Economy: The External Dimension

Malek Merican

In an effort to design a competitive and resilient Malaysian economy, it is necessary to appreciate our place in the functioning of the world economy that transcends national borders. The impression one gets from the economic point of view is the emergence of a global economy based on the G-7[1] with the United States, Japan and the European Community at its epicentre, and with a majority of the other countries in the world in varying degree of integration having become part of the borderless global economy. There are of course countries not significantly linked with the global economy. These include the USSR and its previous East European allies, Communist China, Myanmar and various African countries, which are not impressive in economic performance. The USSR and some of its component states alongside its previous East European allies are trying to reorganize their economies into market-oriented economies that can be integrated to the interlinked global economy.

---

[1] The Group of 7 largest industrial economies in the world excluding USSR and China, and comprising the United States, Britain, France, Germany, Italy, Canada and Japan.

The sustained growth of the global economy is associated with its emphasis on private enterprise and market-oriented price mechanism. The spectacular collapse of the communist economies led by the USSR with their state-determined resource allocation and maladjusted pricing systems leaves us all applauding the inherent resilience of the private enterprise market-oriented system, as opposed to the communist, feudalistic or crony capitalistic systems.

One will observe by looking closer that the global economy is a system of interlinked economies that is absorbing consumers and corporations without regard to national frontiers. On the demand side are the desires of people who want the best and cheapest products, regardless of where they are made. On the supply side to satisfy these needs we see the emergence of the global firms, initially with head offices in their home countries, but increasingly reorganizing into multinational firms and into global corporations with multi-centred headquarters in different strategic markets of their products. In a world of converging consumer tastes, spreading technologies and in spite of growing protectionism, we see the increasing emergence of global industries and global markets. The market for IBM computers, for example, is defined by the demand and needs they satisfy rather than by political borders.

One gets the impression at this time that the global economy with its multinational corporations and entrepreneurs driven by profit, if not greed, is set to continue, and to grow over time, from strength to strength almost inexorably, even if there may be occasional setbacks. One may not like the capitalist system with its excessive emphasis on profit if not greed, and it has its ugly aspects. But currently there appears to be no obvious alternative to the private enterprise system of globally interlinked economies. Improvements in communication technology and computerization will further strengthen the trends to globalization of the world economy and the interlinked private enterprise system.

One important feature of the global economy is the enormous size and strength of the multinational corporations that are turning into global corporations. The July 1991 issue of *Fortune* magazine's listing of the largest industrial corporations in the world shows that 24 of these mammoth companies have annual sales each larger than the Malaysian GNP of RM110 billion in 1990; and 128 of them have annual sales each larger than the Malaysian government's total revenue of RM29 billion for 1990.

The Malaysian Economic Scene

As Malaysians, we are justifiably proud that the Malaysian economy has grown at the average annual rate of 7.8 per cent during the 1970s and 5.9 per cent during the 1980s. Malaysian GNP per capita at RM6,202 (US$2,283) (1990) is higher than those for Indonesia (US$560) and Thailand (US$1,329). We should be pleased that the proportion of households living below the poverty line in Peninsular Malaysia had declined from 49.3 per cent in 1970 to about 15 per cent in 1990.

At the same time we have to be conscious that the 1990 Malaysian GNP (of RM$110 billion) is only 0.7 per cent of the US GNP of US$5,462 billion and 13.8 per cent of the Japanese GNP of US$2,942 billion. On a per capita basis the Malaysian per capita GNP of RM6,202 (US$2,282) (for 1990) is only 10.5 per cent of the US GNP per capita of US$21,746; and 9.6 per cent of the Japanese per capita figure of US$23,800. And every year in spite of our higher percentage growth rate, the absolute income gaps with these rich countries continue to increase. Even if we allow for currency conversion errors, there is a lot that we should aim to achieve in order to catch up, or to strive to enable Malaysians to enjoy a fuller life.

Before attempting to design a competitive and resilient Malaysian economy, we need to appreciate the international development process, and the forces that propel the continuing growth of the global economy. The open market systems especially in the major countries have led to the emergence of large groups that are efficiently organized and with established research and development capabilities.

Once new products are successfully introduced in particular primary markets, it becomes much easier to export them to the other countries, or to arrange for their subsidiary companies and associates to assemble or manufacture them for the additional markets.

While the very groups dominating the global market compete with each other, their combined business and strength seem to grow, and with advancing technologies, are projected to grow even more dominant. There are scenarios which envisage that over the next twenty years the largest one thousand business groups in the global economy will have sales large than revenues of most governments. Some scenarios speculate at the extent of the concentration of economic power and influence of these big business groups that will have implications on the system of nation states and their governments.

For the purposes of the present discussion, on how to design a competitive and resilient Malaysian economy to meet the challenges of Vision 2020, we need to appreciate the importance of this external dimension. There is the large number of foreign groups that are eager to export their products, to establish their branches had subsidiaries and joint ventures, to assemble and manufacture their products for the Malaysian market or to re-export the products to other markets. The way we encourage or limit their participation in the Malaysian economy will in many ways be the crucial determinant to the growth of the Malaysian economy. If we shut them out, as in the case of Myanmar, economic growth would stall and many even turned negative. The more we shut the leading edge companies and their products and services, the more we deprive ourselves as consumers and reduce our competitiveness and possibly our long-term efficiency as well.

The National Development Policy envisages an open Malaysian economy which will foster local enterprises but will also promote foreign investment and enterprise. "The Way Forward" lists the challenge of establishing a prosperous society, with an economy that is fully competitive, dynamic, robust and resilient as the ninth strategic challenge that must be met. In pondering over the subject assigned to me – on how to design a competitive and resilient economy by the year 2020 – I came across four schools of thought.

One school of thought that I may label as the "Internationalists" argue that the best option for Malaysia is to implement a plan to fully integrate the Malaysian economy into the growing global economy. To our great benefit, we have basically accepted free trade and became a Contracting Party of GATT with its system of Most Favoured Nation (MFN) treatment to all other Contracting Parties. It is argued that Malaysia should throw its weight on the side of freer trade in GATT negotiations on goods and services. While we may wish to retain limited and transitional rights to protect home industries and promote infant industries through tariff and non-tariff barriers, we should limit the use of these protective shelters for limited periods of time to ensure that competition always prevail. The Internationalists would argue that Malaysia should have an aggressive programme to promote not only privatization, but also unrestricted trade in goods and unrestricted entry of services as a means to promote competition to benefit the consumers.

As to queries about risks of domination by foreign enterprises over the Malaysian economy, the response remains that the risks of domination are no greater 20 or 30 years ago than 20 or 30 years in the future; and in the same way that Malaysians have benefited from participation in basically free world trade, we will greatly benefit from integration into the global economy, and will be no more dominated by foreign interests in the increasingly interdependent world of the 2020s than we are now.

The Internationalists also hope that there will be increasing world order that will reduce narrow nationalism. In any case they see the further evolution of the global companies will make them less objectionable and more desirable. They assume that Citibank would cease to be an American bank and become a global bank, managed and owned globally. One third or more of Malaysian managers and employees will probably be working in foreign companies, their subsidiaries and joint ventures which will become increasingly more multinational and global in their organization and outlook. Malaysian companies will also have to attune themselves to international competition not only when they export and participate in business overseas, but even when they engage in domestic trade and provide services in the home market. Malaysian companies will have to aggressively seek out export markets and participation opportunities overseas through the setting up of subsidiaries, joint ventures and strategic alliances. They should try to operate on a global basis and compete for human resources on a worldwide basis.

Another school of thought that we may label as the "Malaysian Nationalists" is very concerned about the domination of foreign interests, and is fearful that further liberalization will give rise to free entry to foreign businesses not only in trade and manufacturing, but also in services. They feel that the principles of "right of establishment" and "national treatment" in the current form proposed by the United States and other developed countries would mean the rapid dismantling of most of our national regulations controlling or restricting foreign service organizations. They feel that acceptance of the United States-type proposals would allow almost total freedom of entry and operation to foreign firms to trade and to provide services and to make and acquire investments. They feel that such a liberalization would be premature and against Malaysian national interest.

The "Bumiputera Nationalists", a sub-school of the Malaysian Nationalists, are even more concerned about the need to promote and safeguard Bumiputera participation in commerce and industry. They would press home the need for restricting entries and opportunities and for affirmative action programmes to elevate Bumiputera control and ownership.

A third school of thought, the "Pragmatists", tries to find a middle ground between the Internationalists and the Nationalists. They do not have problems in supporting affirmative action programmes, for example, the Education and Technology Development programmes to improve Bumiputera and Malaysian participation in economic activities. The establishment of a proficient and practical education programme that will train young Bumiputera and other young Malaysians to be first-rate participants of the global economy is a subject that needs to be systematically debated. Power and wealth will go to nations that wisely invest in their children's education. Similarly, a technology development programme to enhance the effectiveness of Malaysian participation in the emerging global economy should be carefully organized.

Dr Mahathir Mohamad's "The Way Forward" lists the establishment of "a scientific and progressive society, a society that is innovative and forward-looking, one that is not only a consumer of technology but also a contributor to the scientific and technological civilization of the future" as the sixth challenge that should be achieved. How much we are willing to spend and how well we can organize the programmes are issues that have to be taken up.

The Pragmatists would support affirmative action programmes in the form of financial subsidies that would assist the Bumiputera and other Malaysians to become more effective participants in the competitive global economy. They would support the recent proposal to assist Bumiputera entrepreneurs through the setting of Perbadanan Usahawan Nasional Berhad or PUNB to assist the establishment and growth of Bumiputera ventures through the provision of soft loans and technical assistance, and by taking up equity capital and [or] convertible bonds while assisting and allowing Bumiputera entrepreneurs to manage their companies. The hope is to increase the number of Bumiputera entrepreneurs and assist the growth of their companies thereby establishing a strong Bumiputera Industrial and Commercial Community to operate in the competitive and open economy.

The idea of establishing a Bumiputera Development Bank cum Venture Capital Fund has always been a conceptually attractive proposal. It is important to lay out the plan carefully because the risks are in its implementation. The danger is that the effort may result in an accumulation of non-performing loans and loss-making ventures. It may be noted that the earlier MARA efforts were not very successful in spawning Bumiputera entrepreneurs. The Malaysian Industrial Development Finance (MIDF) also tried to fulfill this role and again can be said to achieve only limited success. It is to be hoped that the new PUNB with a comprehensive and ambitious plan will be as successful in its effort as its Amanah Saham Nasional programme.

The Pragmatists would also support the idea that the role and objective of MIDF be reviewed to make it an aggressive and dynamic Development bank to enable greater Malaysian participation in manufacturing and other fields.

In designing the establishment of a competitive Malaysian economy, one may envisage the establishment of the PUNB to assist the Bumiputera, and a reviewed MIDF to assist Malaysian ventures and participations generally. It may also be suggested that a more comprehensive programme to promote a Venture Capital industry be undertaken. The earlier effort to promote a Venture Capital industry has not been successful and none of the very limited number – technically three – of venture capital fund companies that have been established could qualify for the Treasury tax scheme.

The problem for the Pragmatists is to find the middle ground between the Internationalists and the Nationalists. They do not wish to see Malaysian industries or services be overwhelmed by foreigners. They are willing to support foreign participation to extend up to possibly half of the industry, while at the same time wanting to ensure that the local participants are effective and have the capacity to develop rather than be just paid nominees.

Finally there is this school of thought that we may label the "Regionalists". They feel that the way ahead should include a regional grouping as a prelude to the global integration. They feel that there should be a stronger push on Asean economic co-operation. They feel that Asean should also examine possibilities of liberalizing trade in services, rather than concentrate just on liberalization of trade on goods only. The Regionalists argue that one result of the Uruguay Rounds is that trade in services will be subject to liberalization under the GATT. By liberalizing services within Asean now, we will better prepare our companies for competition in the world market later. Among possibilities the "Regionalists" would envisage are the following:

1. Asean banks may not be ready for full international competition but within Asean, they are about the same competitive level. Is it not possible to envisage three to five

banks from each Asean country to be licensed in each of
the other Asean countries?

2. Liberalization in the Asean insurance industry would
   strengthen individual companies by spreading risks.

3. Similarly the maritime shipping industry would benefit
   from greater opportunities within a unified Asean shipping market.

4. A unified Asean aviation market would provide Asean
   countries greater clout in international air services
   negotiation.

5. The produce of Malaysian plantation companies will become increasingly uncompetitive in the world rubber and
   palm oil markets as their labour costs rise far more rapidly than those in Indonesia and Thailand. Should they not
   try to operate in Indonesia and Thailand even though
   they have disposed the few plantations they acquired in
   the Philippines? Can the large Malaysian plantation companies go regional by managing plantations in other
   Asean countries, while trying to diversify their activities in
   Malaysia?

Proposals to Improve the Framework for a Competitive Economy

The Malaysian economy is pretty competitive in many aspects
and it has performed reasonably well. I pondered over what one
may propose to improve its long-term performance. I would include in my list the following suggestions to improve the
framework and the performance of a competitive Malaysian
economy. Some of these proposals may take years to get off the
ground.

There is an urgent and great need to establish a strong
Securities Commission to further develop and supervise the
securities market. The total market value of all the shares listed on
the Kuala Lumpur Stock Exchange is in excess of RM150 billion.
This market capitalization will continue to increase rapidly, with

new listings including shares of companies to be privatized, and from new issues from some of the 300 or so companies that are already listed. If the 7 per cent long-term projected rate of growth of the Malaysian economy is achieved, then the increase in the total market capitalization of the shares listed on the KLSE will be very much higher.

The capital market in a private enterprise economy forms the core of the capitalist system. The capital market is usually divided into two parts: banking and securities. The central bank supervises and fosters the growth of the banking system. In a great majority of countries, they now have Securities Commissions supervising and fostering the growth of the securities markets.

The Malaysian regulatory system governing the securities market is fundamentally fragmented and weak in regulatory terms as well as development terms. The capital market can be a very powerful vehicle for promoting Malaysian development.

Inflows of foreign direct investments are usually associated with direct investment of foreign companies and their subsidiaries to establish plants and operations which they control.

Funds raised through the stock exchange from local and foreign sources would provide finance for the Malaysian as well as foreign companies to undertake expansion. The more efficient in Malaysian capital becomes the cheaper and easier it will be for Malaysian controlled companies to raise fund for operations in Malaysia as well as abroad.

The Securities Commission should supervise the issue of securities by companies as well as by unit trusts – property as well as equity trusts. Currently there is some confusion whether the Kuala Lumpur Options and Financial Futures Exchange or the Kuala Lumpur Commodity Exchange should operate the financial futures and options market for shares and shares indices. In the longer run, it would be desirable to plan for the Securities Commission to be responsible for the supervision and development of the whole securities market, including the option and the financial futures markets as well.

It may be worth emphasizing that to achieve healthy long-term development there should be a clear line drawn between the

Regulator and the private sector participants. It is also important to ensure that the Commission is staffed with capable Commissioners on a full-time basis, since decisions on the some issues need to be made expeditiously. It is desirable to allow the Commission reasonable independence – as in the case of the central bank – from the influence of the Treasury or the political Minister to which it may continue to be answerable on policy issues.

To design a competitive and well-functioning Malaysian economy, we may wish to consider the establishment of two other regulating bodies. We should consider establishing a centralized Utilities Regulatory Commission to approve the pricing policies of privatized utilize to prevent abuse of their natural monopolistic powers, and to promote competition, where practicable. The Utilities Regulatory Commission should organize an effective price surveillance system to cover tariffs charged by Telekom, Tenaga Nasional Berhad, Malaysia Airlines on its domestic airfares, and on water and sewerage rates, road tolls and on port and airport charges. The key regulatory objective is the control of potential monopoly abuse by privatized companies with substantial natural or protected monopoly positions in the market. Rather than have separate and therefore relatively weak surveillance authorities looking into each of these areas, a central authority should be able to perform this function more effectively. A broad approach to deal with questions relating to monopoly economics, measures of reasonable rates of return, formulae to allow tariff adjustments that are linked to general price levels, etc., will require proficient and currently scarce economists, as well as specialized technical experts well versed in each of the fields to be regulated. At the same time the regulatory system should not become more bureaucratic and prevent the managers of the privatized companies from performing their roles and responding to urgent or rapid changes in their production costs or markets. A commission dedicated to the whole field of monopoly pricing that may also forge out retail price related formulae to allow price adjustments to be made, should be more effective in the long run than a system where each proposed price changes has to be approved by the relevant Ministers or by the Cabinet, which will then be criticized for agreeing to price increases. It may be noted that the idea of a centralized regulatory authority for privatized monopolies was considered and also proposed in the Privatization Masterplan Report. While conscious that an efficient private enterprise economy should not be burdened by regulations and commissions, it may still be desirable to consider the establishment of a Commission on Restrictive Trade Practices. If we are to ensure the well-functioning of the open and liberal Malaysian economy, it is desirable to establish a machinery to prohibit restrictive trade practices and reduce collusion among oligopolistic manufacturers and traders. The aim is not to control or fix prices but to ensure the effective working of the price determination system in a private enterprise market-oriented economy. The Commission should try to eliminate collusion and price fixing and find ways to promote effective competition.

The Commission should also be charged with responsibility to review restrictive practices in the services sector which should include the professions as well as the financial fields that are not supervised by the central bank. It may be noted that the "Big Bang", that is, the deregulation of the stockbroking industry, in the United Kingdom resulted from anti-monopoly investigations on the services sector.

Role of the Employees Provident Fund

Among the most important redesigning of the framework to promote a competitive Malaysian economy is the urgent need to revise the investment policies of the Employees Provident Fund, and to restructure its role in the emerging capital market that has to support the private sector companies to become the primary engines for economic growth.

An open market economy dependent on private sector drive requires a well functioning capital market. The Employees Provident Fund is a powerful vehicle to effect compulsory savings from the salaried population and to provide funds to finance government expenditure.

In the earlier years, the Employees Provident Fund served as a powerful vehicle to provide non-inflationary funds to finance not only development expenditure but also public sector deficits that were enlarged by an over extended public sector programme. Now with the current downsizing of Federal government deficits and the implementation of its Privatization programmes, the government does not need to issue government securities to the Employees Provident Fund to the same extent as before. With the new policies of relying more on the private sector as the primary engine of national growth, it is crucial that we ensure sufficient funds are mobilized to meet the investment needs of public-listed companies. A vital part of this re-channelling of funds rests on the revision of Employees Provident Fund investment policies.

In a model developed economy, private savings flow into private provident funds and insurance companies, which then invest more than half of such savings in equities, the balance in government and corporate bonds. In Malaysia a substantial portion of private savings emerge in the form of compulsory contributions to the Employees Provident Fund which was then invested almost wholly in government securities. Contributors' outstanding balances at the Employees Provident Fund amount to some RM45 billion as at the end of 1990, and is expected to increase to almost RM100 billion by the year 2000. How we re-channel these funds over the coming years will have a strong bearing on our national growth.

As at the end of 1990 only about RM1 billion (or 2 per cent) of Employees Provident Fund's total investment of about RM45 billion was invested in Malaysian equities. At the same time Malaysian insurance companies and private provident funds are starved of funds by the compulsory Employees Provident Fund levy. As a result the Malaysian equity market is unbalanced by the relatively small investment portfolios managed by insurance companies and private provident funds. The percentage of Employees Provident Fund funds to be invested in Malaysian equities should be steadily and substantially increased. In the long run it should be increased to possibly around 20 per cent. How this is to be done should be carefully planned. If the percentage of Employees Provident Fund assets to be invested in equities is to be substantially increased, and the Employees Provident Fund Manager is to undertake the investment directly, his dominance in the market will give rise to many problems. Beliefs and rumours about his intentions and investment strategies may move share market prices. The position may be alleviated by the Employees Provident Fund using professional fund managers such as merchant bankers and others so that management of the Employees Provident Fund portfolio is fragmented, and the Employees Provident Fund manager's dominance is somewhat reduced.

But if we are to design a healthier equity capital market, we should aim to promote the emergence of 20 to 30 substantial Malaysian funds which should be managed by professional fund managers. We need to foster the growth of a more professional fund management industry with good market research capabilities that is attuned to support long-term growth potential of public-listed companies.

Currently we have only a very limited number of substantial local funds that invest in the Malaysian equity market. The list includes Perbadanan Nasional Berhad, Lembaga Tabung Angkatan Tentera, the Employees Provident Fund, the Social Security Organization and Tabung Haji. The other funds including those of the insurance companies and the private provident funds are relatively small. Hence the equity market is often subject to market rumours created by market manipulators and to pressures caused by movements of foreign equity funds.

One may propose at least three different ways of downsizing the Employees Provident Fund dominance and create competition in fund management to provide higher returns to contributors. It is easy to be complacent in accepting the current 8 per cent dividend return paid to Employees Provident Fund contributors. A carefully managed provident fund can provide significantly higher return per annum and when this return is cumulated over a lifespan of 25 to 30 years, the larger return can make a considerable difference to the salaried individual contributors. In any case, we need to re-channel a substantial portion of the new funds flowing into the Employees Provident Fund to investment in shares of public-listed Malaysian companies to enable these private sector entities to become the primary engines of national growth.

One option is to urge ten or more of the largest employers of labour to set up Supplementary Provident Funds. The selection of employers may be subject to each having not less than RM200 million of shareholders' funds and employing more than a thousand employees with well established businesses with good track records. It is envisaged that the Employees Provident Fund would allow employees of the company sponsoring a Supplementary Provident Fund to opt to join such a scheme, in which case a portion of the 20 per cent (that is, 9 per cent from the employee and 11 per cent from the employer) contribution currently payable to the Employees Provident Fund, (let us say 10 per cent of the employee's salary), to be credited to the Supplementary Provident Fund. In addition an employee with a stated minimum balance with the Employees Provident Fund may also opt to transfer up to a percentage of the employee's excess balance to the Supplementary Provident Fund. The sponsoring company will have to arrange for Trustees and Fund Managers to hold and invest the funds in equities and bonds so as to yield a favourable return to the employees.

The second option is to allow the establishment of Employees Provident Fund Approved Unit Trust Funds to be managed by selected private sector fund managers. Employees Provident Fund contributors with balances of not less than a certain amount may opt to invest up to a certain percentage of the excess in the Approved Unit Trust Funds.

In the case of the Supplementary Provident Fund as well as the Approved Unit Trust Fund, and Employees Provident Fund contributor wishing to withdraw from these schemes will have to transfer whatever their outstanding balances back to the provident fund.

The third option is to place an absolute ceiling on the combined employee and employer monthly contribution to the

Employees Provident Fund, on the argument that such an employee should be able to look after his own interest. Alternatively he may be allowed to pay the excess over a stated amount of his combined monthly contribution to a licensed life insurance company by participating in a life insurance scheme the contributor considers to be more favourable.

There have been proposals that a portion of the Employees Provident Fund funds should be invested overseas. However it would seem to be a terrible waste of opportunity not to recycle the long-term savings that the salaried population has been compelled to contribute to the Employees Provident Fund, back into the local capital market, to promote Malaysian development.

Unless we redesign our investment policies and the role of the Employees Provident Fund, the Malaysian capital market will remain unbalanced and will not be very efficient in funding Malaysian companies to become primary engines of national growth. If we adopt the proposed options, we would also be injecting a greater degree of competition into the fund management industry to the benefit of the salaried population.

In its present form and with inappropriate investment policies, the Employees Provident Fund threatens to be a major obstruction to the growth of a competitive market-oriented economy that Malaysia should be trying to establish. Urgent national discussion to redesign the Employees Provident Fund should be embarked upon.

Designing a Resilient Economy

On the question of how to design a resilient economy I can only come up with a list of issues for consideration. My list of issues basically is to ensure appropriate and rapid response to a changing economic situation.

I would put up at the top of the list the establishment of an effective macroeconomic monitoring and management capability. Relevant data need to be rapidly collected to show what is happening to the Malaysian economy in the context of the global economy. This is done by Bank Negara Malaysia, the Statistics

Department, the Treasury and the Economic Planning Unit. Their adequacy and timeliness may be reviewed. The government agencies should be able to make competent assessments and propose appropriate responses or options for decisions by the relevant authorities. At the same time sufficient and timely information should be able to comment and provide a feedback of their views on proposed remedial measures or new ideas. The careful building up of a strong capability on the public sector side as well as on the private sector side are important matters for consideration if good responses are to be made. Without a good macroeconomic monitoring and management capability, correct responses may be delayed or not adopted at all, and the cost to the nation may be considerable.

The second general issue I would list is to emphasize that prices and wages should be adjustable both ways to provide resilience. The price determination mechanism should be decontrolled and the authorities at various levels should resist the temptation to fix what should be market determined prices.

In the same way we should adopt a flexible wage system focused on productivity increases. And preferably with generous bonuses in good times which can be cut back during unfavourable times for the economy and also for the firm to adjust.

If we are to have a resilient market-oriented economy, I believe that we should also allow interest rates to be determined by the capital market and the banks. Bank Negara Malaysia may influence market liquidity but neither the central bank nor the Treasury should fix interest in the market.

Given that Malaysia is a relatively small economy, Bank Negara Malaysia should continue to allow the exchange value of the ringgit to float in the exchange market. It is of course desirable that the exchange value of the ringgit should be relatively stable. It is up to the central bank and the Treasury to pursue macro management policies which will minimize inflation and generally stabilize the exchange value of the ringgit.

In the context of such a monetary and market framework, it will be much easier for the national economy to be resilient enough to respond to unexpected and especially adverse developments.

Conclusion

I would like to emphasize the importance of increasing the competitiveness of the Malaysian economy by recalling the times when Sri Lanka and Myanmar had per capita incomes higher than that of Malaysia. And among Asean countries, the Philippines previously also had per capita income higher than that of Malaysia. Wrong economic policies lead to slow growth and even stagnation. If Malaysia is to achieve the 10.3 per cent per annum increase in per capita income to RM17,000 by the year 2000 from about RM6,200 in 1990 as envisaged in the Second Outline Perspective Plan, and more so if it is to aim at the quadrupling (4.7 per cent increase per annum) in real per capita income to about RM25,000 by the year 2020 as stated in "The Way Forward" it can only plan to do so by integrating itself to the growing global economy. We have to forge competitive Malaysian controlled firms that are able to provide not only the home market but can also export their goods and services to the global market. They may even have to locate part of their operations overseas. We have to welcome foreign investments and work with these foreign and global firms to produce competitive goods and services for the Malaysian market as well as markets abroad.

We should improve the functioning of the Malaysian capital market by establishing an effective Securities Commission and other regulatory authorities usually regarded as necessary to improve the functioning of a competitive market-oriented economy. We need to modify the investment policies and role of the Employees Provident Fund.

To improve the resilience of the Malaysian economy we should plan to further improve Malaysia's macroeconomic monitoring and management capability. Now that we operate at full employment – if not actual labour shortage – inflation will become a chronic problem that needs to be contained through careful macroeconomic management.

8

Creating a Viable Economic Base for Malaysia Towards 2020

Ali Abul Hassan Sulaiman

ONE of the challenges Malaysia has to face in its effort to become a fully developed country by the year 2020 is the creation of a competitive, dynamic, robust and resilient economy. Although this challenge is entered last in the list of nine challenges outlined in the Vision 2020 agenda, it is nevertheless one of the most crucial because the achievements of many of the other challenges rest on the existence of a viable economic base for the country.

The rapid economic development that we have achieved since independence has progressively brought the vision of a fully developed economy by the year 2020 within our reach. Among the strengths that we now have include a high domestic savings rate, a relatively well-developed physical, social and institutional infrastructure, political, economic and financial stability as well as a relatively developed private sector-driven manufacturing and industrial base. In the last two decades we have achieved a sustained rate of growth averaging 6.7 per cent per annum. Vision 2020 requires the achievement of a sustain growth of output which is only slightly higher, at 7 per cent per annum, combined with appropriate policies to achieve the qualitative aspects of the vision.

Likely World Scenario
Till the Year 2020

Forecasting the rate of growth of a single country over a period of thirty years is a risky business. Forecasting "megatrends" for the world over thirty years is riskier still. In building up the world scenarios described in this chapter we have examined past trends and sought guidance from various medium- and long-term forecasts produced by others about the probable scenarios in the decades ahead. In addition, the structure of the economy of present-day developed countries as well as their growth trajectories served as useful guidance on what is achievable and the probable structural transformation that is likely to occur in our own case.

The rate of change that can occur in our case is, however, likely to be more rapid. The prospects for achieving better quality growth is more favorable due to the possibility of leap-frogging by importing the latest technology and know-how as well as by avoiding known pitfalls based on the experiences of others.

Megatrends

The following "megatrends", the seeds of which are already visible today, is expected to characterize the next few decades:

1. Increased globalization of the world economy as the world becomes more "linked" or "enmeshed" through increased trade, investment and capital flows complemented by technology, knowledge and information flows as well as labour movements. Such linkages will be supported by rapid improvements in communications and transport, increased trade resulting from economic growth and increasing per capita incomes, the appearance of new "growth poles" particularly in the Asia-Pacific region, further globalization of output and the opening up of "closed" economies like Eastern Europe, India and perhaps Indochina. Trends over the last six

years, where growth of world trade has exceeded the rate of world output may thus continue in the future.

2. Despite the above, weaker counter-trends towards protectionism is likely to persist but are expected to lose ground. Unable to prevent free trade in its totality, interest groups are expected to support the formation of large trading blocs, wherein they can survive under a certain degree of protection. A large part of international trade will thus be "intra-bloc". Trade between regions is, however, expected to continue its present growth trend (see Table 8.1).

3. The emergence and progressive maturing of Free Market Socialism and increasing trade, investment and other links between them and the rest of the world.

4. The end of the "cold war" in global relationships, replaced by relatively open and largely co-operative economic relationships between various regional blocs. The major players are possibly EC, Nafta and EAEC or some other Asian union.

5. The privatization of the welfare state and the "denationalization" of state enterprises. Reduced role of the government will follow current trends towards increasing economic liberalization and deregulation. In developed countries and some less developed countries like Malaysia where tax effort is presently very high this trend may be paralleled by "tax reform" involving reduced tax rates.

6. The continued rise of the Pacific Rim with an increasingly market-led China and Vietnam playing an increasingly important role, while Japan, the Asian NICs and Asean will continue to remain robust. The Pacific's increasing dominance will be spurred by rapid growth in output and a large and increasingly wealthy population base.

7. The continuing, but in relative terms slightly declining, importance of North American and European economies.

Table 8.1

Recent Trends in "Intra-Bloc" and Inter-Regional World Trade

A. Intra-Bloc to Total Bloc Trade – %

Region	1980	1988	1980-1988 Growth (%)
EEC	53.6	59.8	1.4
United States, Canada	26.7	35.3	3.6
ANZAC	6.1	7.6	2.8
Eastern Europe, USSR	50.1	55.7	1.3
Latin American Integration Association	13.8	9.5	– 4.6

B. Inter-Regional Trade as % of World Trade

Region	US$ Bil.	%	US$ Bil.	%	Growth (%)
North America-Asia	49.7	2.5	90.6	3.2	7.8
Western Europe-Asia	30.1	1.5	70.8	2.5	11.2
North America-Western Europe	75.3	3.8	90.1	3.2	2.3

Source: World Development Bank.

8. Recovery and sustained growth in a large part of Latin America as many countries successfully restructure themselves from present balance of payments and other economic problems.

9. Continuing slow growth in Africa, compounded by problems caused by its relatively high rate of population growth.

10. Stable population in much of the developed world and sharply declining population growth rates elsewhere.

11. The "information era" which at present is rapidly replacing the industrial era in present-day developed countries will make way for the age of "biotechnology".

12. Re-ascendancy of the arts, spiritualism, ethics and religion, following existing trends towards an increased consideration for the environment and quality of life.

With regard to the world competitive environment affecting Malaysia, the following trends are likely to become increasingly important:

1. Continuing reduction in the relative requirements for raw materials due to miniaturization, replacement by synthetics made from freely available materials and higher energy efficiency. This is reflected in lower cost of materials and direct labour per unit value of manufacturing and industrial output. For example, OECD consumption of energy fell 120 per cent since 1974 despite increasing output. As a result, existing trends where an increasing proportion of world trade is made up of manufacturers can be expected to continue. Raw material exports will, on the other hand, continue to decline in relative importance (see Table 8.2).

2. Emergence of an Asian consumer boom following rapidly rising per capita incomes and continuing population growth.

Table 8.2

Recent Trends in the Composition of Trade

A. World Trade	%	%
Year	1980	1988
Manufactured Goods	58	75
Agricultural Products	15	14
Petrochemicals	25	10
Minerals	2	2
Total Value	US$2,000 Billion	US$2,829 Billion
B. LDC Trade		
Manufactured Goods	42	68
Agricultural Products	30	20
Petrochemicals	23	9
Minerals	5	3
Total Value	US$250 Billion	US$458 Billion

Source: World Development Report.

3. Higher wages as employment shifts from simple opera-
    tions and low skilled jobs to technical, managerial,
    professional and higher crafts. The middle class in most
    countries will expand as will the number of women work-
    ing.

4. As more LDCs enter the industrial age, access to abun-
    dant factors such as land, cheap labour and raw materials
    will become less important to achieve competitiveness
    and will be replaced by the possession of technology and
    skills as well as the ability to process output efficiently.
    Each new entrance will attempt to exploit their materials
    and labour endowments as an industrialization strategy
    so that, for Malaysia, competitive advantage based on the
    possession of such natural attributes becomes "less
    durable" and more difficult to depend on. The impor-
    tance of skills and technology is enhanced by the fact that
    as the production structure goes into higher value-added
    activities, materials and direct labour content as a per-
    centage of value-added will become smaller so that pos-
    session of these inputs become less decisive as a strategy
    advantage.

5. The possession of physical, social and institutional in-
    frastructure will increasingly be equalized between na-
    tions as rapid progress is made by many of the more
    successful developing countries, and as old infrastructure
    and technology become obsolete and require fresh in-
    vestments by present-day developed countries. To be in
    the forefront and not be left behind, Malaysia must there-
    fore invest heavily in such infrastructure.

6. Many more industries will become global in nature. The
    location of multinational headquarters where research
    and development, strategic planning, and where the
    most valuable and high value-added activities take place
    will greatly influence the wealth of the nations so that suc-
    cessful nations are those which have become the home
    base of successful multinational corporations.

Probable External Environment to the Year 2020

Guided by the "megatrends" noted previously, we have attempted to forecast broad trends affecting world population, output and trade. These are summarized in Tables 8.3, 8.5, 8.7 and 8.8.

Relative Economic Size

Analysing the future growth in output in terms of trade groupings and regions, we find that the Asia-Pacific area will continue to be the most populated group (see Table 8.3). At the same time its economic size as measured by expected total output, at US$12.5 trillion will by then slightly exceed that of North America and roughly equal that of Nafta. In fact, the inclusion of Oceania in EAEC by adding a further US$700 billion to the region's output would firmly tip the balance in its favour. The EEC's economic size at US$10.5 trillion will, however, not lag far behind these two giants (see Table 8.5 and Figure 8.1). The tri-polar nature of the world economy will thus be firmly in place by 2020.

Purchasing Power

In terms of purchasing power, Table 8.7 shows that the EAEC region will also be much wealthier than at present, with an average per capita income of around US$5,600. Nafta and EEC would, however, be much wealthier still with incomes averaging around US$26,000 and US$28,000 respectively. The income gap will, however, narrow significantly if China is excluded from the EAEC average. Within EAEC, Japan and Asian NICs will be very high income economies. Japan is in fact expected to be much wealthier than even North America or Europe. Asean's expected average income at around US$2,700 would firmly fit it into the upper-middle income category while China will have progressed to a similar position as present-day Thailand. The economic "mix" of EAEC will thus be more varied than that of Europe or Nafta.

Figure 8.1

Population and Economic Size by Region, 1990-2020

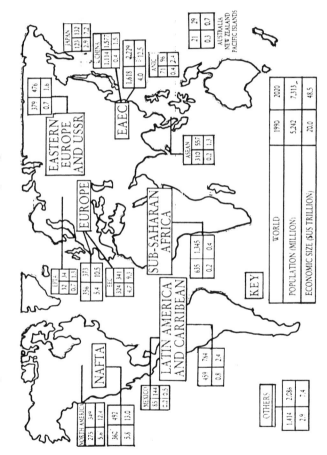

Table 8.3

Population by Region, 1980-2020

Region	1980	1990	2000	2010	2020	2020/1990
			Million			
Nafta	321	360	403	448	492	1.4
North America	252	275	301	326	349	1.3
Mexico	70	85	102	122	143	1.7
EUROPE	348	356	363	369	373	1.0
European Community	316	324	331	336	339	1.0
EFTA	31	32	33	33	34	1.1
EAEC	1,419	1,618	1,831	2,036	2,229	1.4
Japan	118	123	128	131	132	1.1
China	977	1,114	1,255	1,386	1,501	1.3

Asian NICs	63	71	80	89	96	1.3
Asean	262	310	367	430	499	1.6
Eastern Europe and USSR	349	379	412	444	476	1.3
Latin America & Caribbean	364	459	560	669	784	1.7
Sub-Saharan Africa	470	635	845	1,082	1,345	2.1
Australia, New Zealand & Pacific Islands	19	21	24	27	29	1.4
Others	1,142	1,414	1,681	1,914	2,086	1.5
WORLD	4,432	5,242	6,119	6,988	7,813	1.5
Malaysia	14	18	23	27	32	1.8

Notes:
1. World Development Report for 1980 and 1990 figures.
2. See Table 8.5 for growth assumptions.
3. Asean excludes Singapore which is included in Asian NICs.

Table 8.4
**Growth Rate Assumptions Used
in Forecasting World Population to 2020**

Region	1981-1990	1991-2000	2001-2010	2011-2020
Nafta	1.1	1.1	1.1	1.1
North America	0.9	0,9	0.8	0.7
Mexico	1.9	1.9	1.8	1.6
EUROPE	0.2	0.2	0.1	0.1
European Community	0.2	0.2	0.1	0.1
EFTA	0.2	0.2	0.2	0.1
EAEC	1.3	1.2	1.1	0.9
Japan	0.5	0.4	0.2	0.1

China	1.3	1.2	1.0	0.8
Asian NICs	1.2	1.2	1.0	0.8
Asean	1.7	1.7	1.6	1.5
Eastern Europe and USSR	0.8	0.8	0.8	0.7
Latin America	2.3	2.0	1.8	1.6
Sub-Saharan Africa	3.1	2.9	2.5	2.2
Australia, New Zealand and Pacific Island	1.3	1.3	1.1	0.9
Others	2.2	1.7	1.3	0.9
World	1.7	1.6	1.3	1.1
Malaysia	2.6	2.3	1.9	1.5

Source:
1. World Development Report.
2. United Nations, Population Reports, 1990.

Table 8.5

Economic Size by Region, 1980-2020 in constant 1990 prices (US\$ Billion)

Region	1980	1990	2000	2010	2020	2020/1990
Nafta	4,413	5,846	7,860	10,090	12,970	2.2
North America	4,224	5,645	7,590	9,710	12,430	2.2
Mexico	189	201	270	380	540	2.7
EUROPE	4,404	5,354	7,090	8,650	10,540	2.0
European Community	3,864	4,690	6,240	7,610	9,280	2.0
EFTA	540	664	850	1,040	1,260	1.9
EAEC	2,601	3,916	5,870	8,600	12,530	3.2
Japan	1,980	2,819	3,980	5,340	7,180	2.5
China	254	418	650	1,060	1,640	3.9
Asian NICs	191	434	820	1,460	2,380	5.5

Asean	176	245	420	740	1,330	5.4
Eastern Europe and USSR	646	680	830	1,120	1,570	2.3
Latin America and Caribbean	702	809	1,200	1,690	2,380	2.9
Sub-Saharan Africa	134	162	210	270	360	2.2
Australia, New Zealand and Pacific Islands	241	323	430	560	710	2.2
Others	2,040	2,892	3,910	5,470	7,430	2.6
World	15,181	19,982	27,400	36,450	48,490	2.4
Malaysia US$	24	43	90	172	340	8.0
RM	65	115	230	474	920	8.0

Notes:
1. World Development Report for 1980 and 1990 figures.
2. Asean excludes Singapore which is included in Asian NICs.
3. "Economic Size" is estimated by applyoing projected GDP or GNP growth rates to 1990 base figures.
4. See Table 8.6 for growth assumptions.

Table 8.6

**Growth Rate Assumptions Used
in Forecasting Economic Size by Region to 2020**

Region	1981-1990	1991-2000	2001-2010	2011-2020
Nafta	2.9	3.0	2.5	2.5
North America	2.9	3.0	2.5	2.5
Mexico	0.6	3.0	3.5	3.5
EUROPE	2.0	2.9	2.0	2.0
European	2.0	2.9	2.0	2.0
EFTA	2.1	2.5	2.0	2.0
EAEC	4.2	4.1	3.9	3.8
Japan	3.6	3.5	3.0	3.0
China	5.1	4.5	5.0	4.5

Asian NICs	8.6	6.5	6.0	5.0
Asean	3.4	5.4	6.0	6.0
Eastern Europe and USSR	0.5	2.0	3.0	3.5
Latin America and Caribbean	1.4	4.0	3.5	3.5
Sub-Saharan Africa	1.9	2.5	2.7	3.0
Australia, New Zealand and Pacific Islands	3.0	3.0	2.5	2.5
Others	3.5	3.1	3.4	3.1
World	2.8	3.2	2.9	2.9
Malaysia	2.8	3.2	2.9	2.9

Source:
1. World Development Report.
2. World Bank's *Long-Term Outlook for the World Economy*, 1990.
3. United Nations' *Project Link World Outlook*, 1990.

Table 8.7
**Per Capita Incomes by Region, 1980-2020
in 1990 constant prices**

Region	US$					
	1980	1990	2000	2010	2020	2020/1990
Nafta	13,731	16,257	19,500	22,540	26,340	1.6
North America	16,789	20,527	25,220	29,810	35,590	1.7
Mexico	2,708	2,376	2,640	3,120	3,750	1.6
EUROPE	12,670	15,039	19,520	23,440	28,290	1.9
European Community	12,216	14,475	18,880	22,680	27,370	1.9
EFTA	17,256	20,750	25,900	31,100	37,540	1.8
EAEC	1,833	2,420	3,200	4,230	5,620	2.3
Japan	16,832	22,900	31,030	40,880	54,400	2.4
China	260	375	520	760	1,090	2.9

Asian NICs	3,022	6,087	10,140	16,440	24,730	4.1
Asean	673	790	1,130	1,730	2,670	3.4
East European and USSR	1,850	1,795	2,010	2,510	3,300	1.8
Latin America and Caribbean	1,927	1,763	2,140	2,530	3,040	1.7
Sub-Saharan Africa	286	255	250	250	270	1.1
Australia, New Zealand & Pacific Islands	13,006	15,395	18,180	20,860	24,420	1.6
Others	1,786	2,045	2,330	2,860	3,560	1.7
WORLD	3,425	3,812	4,480	5,220	6,210	1.6
Malaysia US$	2,080	2,248	3,420	6,380	9,500	4.2
RM	4,520	6,182	9,400	17,560	26,100	4.2

Notes:
1. World Development Report for 1980 and 1990 figures.
2. See Table 8.6 for growth assumptions.
3. Asean excludes Singapore which is included in Asian NICs.
4. Per capita figures are estimated from Tables 6.3 and 6.4.

Table 8.8

Regional Economic Size as Proportion to World

Region	1980	1990	2000	2010	2020
			%		
Nafta	29.1	29.3	28.7	27.7	26.7
North America	27.8	28.3	27.7	26.7	25.6
Mexico	1.2	1.0	1.0	1.0	1.1
EUROPE	29.0	26.8	25.9	23.7	21.7
European Community	25.5	23.5	22.8	20.9	19.1
EFTA	3.6	3.3	3.1	2.8	2.6
EAEC	17.1	19.6	21.4	23.6	25.8

Japan	13.0	14.1	14.5	14.7	14.8
China	1.7	2.1	2.4	2.9	3.4
Asian NICs	1.3	2.2	3.0	4.0	4.9
Asean	1.2	1.2	1.5	2.0	2.7
East European and USSR	4.3	3.4	3.0	3.1	3.2
Latin America and Caribbean	4.6	4.0	4.4	4.6	4.9
Sub-Saharan Africa	0.9	0.8	0.8	0.7	0.7
Australia, New Zealand and Pacific Islands	1.6	1.6	1.6	1.5	1.5
Others	13.4	14.5	14.3	15.0	15.3
Malaysia	0.2	0.2	0.3	0.5	0.7

Note: Calculated from Table 8.5.

Trade Patterns

The link between growth in output and trade has in the past been mixed – trade sometimes exceeding and sometimes lagging behind output (see Table 8.9). A high, medium and low scenario is thus built to take into account this variable relationship. The "megatrends" noted earlier, however, favours the high trade growth scenario. Applying these growth rates to current imports of the regions analysed, the probable trade patterns in 2020 is obtained. The result is summarized in Table 8.10.

World trade would increase four-fold from present levels under the low trade growth scenario to eight-fold under the high growth scenario. Trading patterns in terms of the relative size of trade accounted by particular regions, however, do not differ significantly under the various scenarios. The EEC is expected to retain its present status as the largest trading bloc. EAEC, will, however, overtake and surpass Nafta as the next largest. The other regions of Latin America, Eastern Europe, Africa and Oceania will remain as relatively minor players. Much of trade can, however, be expected to be "intra-bloc" in nature. This may be particularly true for EEC.

Vision of the Malaysian Economy in 2020

Based on the targeted output growth rate of 7 per cent per annum, the Malaysian GDP or gross domestic product would have increased from RM115 billion in 1990 to RM920 billion (in constant 1990 prices) by 2020, about eight-fold increase. The population would have by then reached a level of around 32 million having grown at the average rate of 1.9 per cent per annum during the thirty-year period.

The expected increase in output and slower projected growth in population will result in per capita incomes steadily rising from RM6,180 in 1990 to RM26,100 (in constant terms) or US$9,500 by 2020 – sufficient to qualify us as a high income country. In addition, continuing application of the philosophy of growth with equity is expected to result in almost complete eradication of poverty and a distribution of wealth which closely

Table 8.9

Comparison of Rate of Growth of World Output and Trade

Period	1965-1980	1980-1989	1989-1994
WORLD			
Output	4.1	3.1	3.0
Exports	6.7	4.1	10.2
Imports	4.7	4.3	10.2
DCs			
Output	3.8	3.0	3.0
Exports	7.4	3.9	10.5
Imports	4.6	4.9	10.5
LDs			
Output	5.8	3.8	4.5
Exports	3.3	5.4	10.4
Imports	5.0	1.4	10.7

Source: World Development Report, 1991 and World Bank Project Link, 1990. .

Table 8.10

World Trade Scenario, 1990-2020

Region	Growth Scenario			Value 2020				Share 2020			
	High	Med	Low	Base Value	High	Med	Low	Base Value	High	Med	Low
		(%)				US$				(%)	
Nafta	6.9	5.8	4.0	662	4,955	3,555	2,145	19.3	17.4	18.0	16.8
North America	7.0	5.8	4.0	636	4,843	3,455	2,065	18.5	17.0	17.5	16.2
Mexico	5.0	4.6	3.8	26	112	100	80	0.8	0.4	0.5	0.6
EUROPE	7.4	6.0	4.5	1,525	13,095	8,820	5,665	44.4	46.0	44.8	44.5
European Community	7.5	6.0	4.5	1,300	11,382	7,550	4,925	37.9	40.0	38.4	38.7
EFTA	7.0	5.9	4.0	225	1,713	1,270	740	6.5	6.0	6.4	5.8
EAEC	8.3	7.0	5.5	624	6,875	4,710	3,087	18.2	24.0	24.0	24.3
Japan	6.0	4.0	3.0	220	1,265	722	540	6.4	4.4	3.7	4.2

China	10.0	7.2	4.8	60	1,047	488	247	1.8	3.6	2.5	2.0
Asian NICs	9.0	8.0	6.5	264	3,503	2,685	1,765	7.7	12.3	13.6	13.9
Asean	9.0	8.0	6.5	80	1,060	815	535	2.3	3.7	4.2	4.2
Eastern Europe & USSR	7.5	5.4	3.6	188	1,646	920	550	5.5	5.8	4.7	4.3
Latin America & Caribbean	5.0	4.6	3.8	123	532	475	380	3.6	1.9	2.4	3.0
Sub-Saharan Africa	4.5	3.5	2.0	32	120	90	58	0.9	0.4	0.5	0.5
Australia, NZ, Pacific Islands	6.0	5.0	3.5	50	287	220	140	1.5	1.0	1.1	1.1
Others	5.0	4.6	3.8	228	985	890	705	6.6	3.5	4.5	5.5
World	7.3	6.0	4.5	3,432	28,495	19,680	12,730	100	100	100	100

Notes:
1. EPU Forecasts.
2. Base value refers to 1990 figures in US$ billion.
3. Trade figures refer to expected import volumes of the regions, reflecting export opportunities for trading partners.

reflects the population structure so that issues of racial imbalances will recede into the background.

Growth will be primarily led by rapid expansion of the manufacturing sector as well as the modern services sector. Implied trends regarding the structural transformation of the economy are as follows:

1. The share of the primary sector (agriculture and mining) and government services to total output will continue their secular declining trend as the industrial and modern service sectors increase their dominance. For example, by the year 2020 agricultural output which is expected to grow at around 3.2 per cent per annum and thus achieve a 250 per cent increase of real output from present levels, will find its share of total output declining from 18.7 per cent to only 6.3 per cent as a result of much more rapid growth in the other sectors. The nature of agriculture will also change drastically in favour of higher value-added, commercialized and land intensive activities. The share of mining is also expected to decline as exploitation of oil and gas is managed for "sustained" output, while other mineral products, despite success in on-going extensive effort at finding and exploiting other minerals, are not expected to increase output much beyond present levels.

2. The manufacturing sector which is expected to grow rapidly and reach maturity by the year 2020 is expected to account for around 40 per cent of output by the year 2020, compared to its present share of 27 per cent. The Malaysian structure of production is thus expected to be predominantly industrial by the time we reach the year 2020. This sector's share is, however, expected to consolidate thereafter to around 35 per cent by 2030 as Malaysia gets into the post-industrial age.

3. The modern services sector will also grow rapidly over the next thirty years, making up for the decline in the government services subsector, so that this sector as a

whole will increase its share of output from 41.8 per cent in 1990 to around 50 per cent by the year 2020. Rapid growth is expected in all non-governmental services sub-sectors, growing in support of increasing industrialization of the structure of production and increasing strength in tradeable services. Services which are required in their own right such as those related to leisure, health, private education and entertainment will also increase with rising levels of income and improvements in quality of life. This sector is in fact expected to continue to gain in relative size and sophistication even beyond 2020 as Malaysia enters its post-industrial age, possibly reaching 60 per cent by 2030.

Differences in the sectoral rates of growth in favour of the industrial and modern services sector is expected to result in a structure of production which by the year 2020 will be between that of present-day Korea and Japan (see Table 8.11 and Figure 8.2).

The whole production structure, whether primary activities, industries or services, is expected to progressively shift towards higher value-added, higher skill and more knowledge and technology intensive activities. Such qualitative improvements results from expected improvement in the quality of labour and capital following massive efforts in human resource development and research and development. The expected gains in sectoral value-added will occur *parri passu* with reduced reliance on resource rents. Mining, forestry and other extractive activities will thus experience declining importance as would traditional agriculture and low value-added and low skilled manufacturing activities.

Such qualitative gains in the production structure translates into higher returns for factors of production, whether labour or capital, thus supporting the projected trends towards higher level of incomes.

The production structure is also expected to become more integrated as more raw materials and agriculture products are used as manufacturing inputs and as the services sector develops in support of output, trading and consumption activities. Within the

Table 8.11

Malaysia's Structure of Production Compared with the World

Sector	Primary	Industry	Manufacturing	Services
Averages for				
Low Income Economies*	33	28	14	39
Middle Income Economies	19	38	24	43
Developed Economies	3	34	20	63
Industrial Countries				
South Korea	10	44	26	46
Singapore	0	37	26	63
United Kingdom	2	37	20	61

United States	69	17	29	2
Germany	61	32	37	2
Japan	56	30	41	3
Malaysia				
1990	41.8	27.0	30.2	28.0
2000	43.3	37.2	38.7	18.0
2020	49.6	40.0	42.8	7.6
Post Industrial				
2030	58.6	35.0	36.0	5.4

Source: World Development Report and EPU Estimates.
Note: Industry comprise manufacturing, construction and utilities.
* Excluding China and India.

Figure 8.2

Structure of Production, 1989

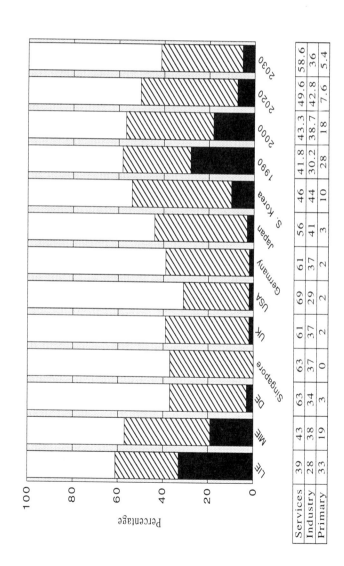

	LIE	MIE	DE	Singapore	UK	USA	Germany	Japan	S. Korea	1990	2000	2020	2030
Services	39	43	63	63	61	69	61	56	46	41.8	43.3	49.6	58.6
Industry	28	38	34	37	37	29	37	41	44	30.2	38.7	42.8	36
Primary	33	19	3	0	2	2	2	3	10	28	18	7.6	5.4

Table 8.12

Structure of Malaysian Exports

	1980	1990	2000	2020
Agriculture and Forestry	44.9	23.4	13.3	4.0
Mining	32.7	16.2	4.9	1.0
Manufacturing	22.4	60.4	81.8	95.0
Total	100	100	100	100
Total Exports M$ Billion	28.0	78.3	254.7	1,480
US$ Billion	10.2	28.5	93.0	538.0
World Trade, US$ Billion	1,808	3,432	6,251	19,680
Malaysian Exports/World Trade (%)	0.56	0.83	1.48	2.73
Malaysian Exports/GDP (%)	54.5	71.3	69.0	53.8

Source: Economic Planning Unit Forecasts.

Assumptions: Forecast for world trade to 2020 is based on "medium scenario" of Table 8.10. Malaysian export forecast for 2000 is based on the OPP2. Export forecast to year 2020 is based on 2.5 per cent for agriculture, 1.5 per cent for mining and 10 per cent for manufacturing. Malaysia's output growth is assumed at 7 per cent per annum in real terms and 11.5 per cent in nominal terms.

sectors, linkages will also be stronger with the development of SMIs and international linkages improved with the development of improved local inputs for FDIs operating in Malaysia and as Malaysia establishes its own FDI activities overseas.

In terms of resource balance, the marginal propensity to consume is expected to remain healthy. Private MPC averaged 0.5 during the OPP1 period but deteriorated slightly to an average of 0.7 in the last three years due to pent-up demand following the recession in the mid-1980s. The figure for 1990 is, however, about 0.6. Assuming that such a low private sector MPC holds and given a secular reduction in relative size of the public sector, the savings rate for the Malaysian economy can thus be expected to improve towards the 35 per cent level over the next few decades. This is expected to be enough to cater for the desired level of domestic and foreign investments by Malaysians. Such funds will, in addition, be supplemented by continuing inflows of "high quality" FDI into Malaysia.

Using export projections till 2000 as contained on the OPP2 and further assuming rapid manufacturing export growth of 10 per cent per annum between 2000 to 2020 compared with much slower growth of 2.5 per cent and 1.5 per cent respectively for agriculture and mining, Malaysia's export is expected to grow at the overall rate of 10.2 per cent per annum in nominal terms between 1990 to 2020. Assuming an inflation rate of around 4.5 per cent (comparable to OPP1 averages) nominal GDP can thus be expected to grow at 11.5 per cent per annum. These projected growth figures would imply that Malaysia's export to GDP ratio will progressively consolidate from 71 per cent as at present to around 54 per cent by 2020 (see Table 8.12). This projection will be in line with increasing internal linkages within the economy and a reduction in Malaysia's relative dependence on the external market. Such a scenario will make the economy more resilient to external shocks.

In addition, the expected differences in their growth rates will result in Malaysia's export basket continuously shifting towards manufactured products, so that by 2020 these would constitute 95 per cent of exports compared with 60.4 per cent as at present. This trend will be in line with the shift in world trade in favour of manufactured products as noted earlier. Such a shift in Malaysia's export basket will also add towards increasing its economic resilience by freeing the country from the dampening effects of the expected secular decline in terms of trade for commodities. This, however, also demands that Malaysia attain competitive status for a reasonable range of manufactured products.

For the balance of payments to remain healthy, import growth will also have to consolidate to a level in line with exports. This will imply higher levels of domestic production of consumption, intermediate and capital goods. These trends will be in line with the aim of increasing the domestic interlinkings within the economy noted earlier. It will also be made more feasible by the creation of a bigger domestic market whether through growth of Malaysia's population and internal output or through the creation of a bigger regional market, say through an Asean Free Trade Area or EAEC. In addition, Malaysia's balance of payments position will be strengthened by the expected improvements in the tradeable services sector.

The Way There

The vision of the Malaysian economy outlined above obviously will not occur on its own, as an inevitable destiny for Malaysia. Rather, they demand that Malaysia pursue the correct policies to achieve a competitive and dynamic industrial structure, supported by a strong modern services sector. The scenarios, in addition, demand that the Malaysian economy continuously progress from low value-added and traditional economic activities to newer and higher value-added activities to support a continuous increase in per capita incomes.

Qualitative Aspects

The possession of the following underlying socio-economic qualities will help ensure that Malaysia is able to develop competitive industries and increase overall economic resilience:

1. The existence of political stability and social justice, operating within a generally accepted institutional framework so that dissensions caused by political, class or ethnic differences do not result in open conflict which disrupts economic activities. The socio-economic policies under the New Economic Policy and the National Development Policy clearly play a crucial role here.

2. The maintenance of economic, financial and price stability so that long-term economic decisions on savings, investments, etc. can be undertaken. This involves the maintenance of a healthy balance of payments and fiscal position, as well as stable prices and exchange rates.

3. The maintenance of non-distorted prices, whether for goods and services, capital or foreign exchange. This will ensure efficient allocation of economic resources between industries and between the tradeable and non-tradeable sectors. Measures include the maintenance of low protective tariffs, avoidance of "financial repression" and the maintenance of a free exchange rate regime. What differentiates successful LDCs from the lagging ones is, in fact, the ability to balance these "efficiency" requirements and to develop appropriate policies for social and economic engineering.

4. The development of a well-integrated production structure through greater intersectoral linkages as well as downstream and upstream linkages within each sector. Such a production structure by reducing external dependency for markets, input materials, components as well as capital goods, help shelter an economy from the effect of external shocks. The globalization of production in many industries, however, may work against greater internal integration. To balance the potential destabilizing effect of this trend, Malaysia needs to increase foreign-domestic linkages through the development of SMIs and ancillary industries and services as well as in-

crease the external integration of its own production by means of outward direct investment.

5. The development of a large domestic or regional market to reduce external uncertainties. Such a regional market also makes it possible for industries with high MES or minimum efficient scales or large "learning curves" to be established at the correct scale of production and thus be efficient enough to export.

Upgrading "Third-Factor" Contribution

One way of becoming competitive in a particular industry is by being the most efficient producer within that industry, producing at a lower cost than the competitors. Thus, in addition to the above "environmental framework", more specific efforts to upgrade factor efficiency will be necessary. These include:

1. The establishment of an adequate physical, social and institutional infrastructure to support an increasing level of economic activities. Such a development prevents bottlenecks and physical constraints from holding up economic activities besides ensuring that "overhead" costs remain low. Such developments also help in ensuring higher "X" efficiency.

2. Ensuring adequate supply of professional, technical, skilled, managerial and research manpower through an effective human resource development programme, complemented by high labour mobility within an efficient labour market. This will help upgrade the efficiency of labour.

3. Increasing production efficiency or improving product quality through better organization, more efficient, advanced productive capital, and ability to produce newer and better quality products. These require the development of an advanced research and development capability and highlight the need for a "critical mass" of inventors, designers, innovators and theoreticians who

are able to produce new ideas, products and processes. These actions help improve the efficiency of capital.

4. The development and the creation of a market-oriented private sector which is able to read market trends and situations, seize market opportunities produced by local research and development capability described previously and respond quickly to market signals.

Required Growth in Labour Productivity

Another important aspect of growth is increasing the efficiency of labour input. Using the output growth target of 7 per cent per annum contained in the Vision 2020 and the implied growth of manufacturing output of 8.4 per cent per annum and matching this with a forecast manufacturing employment growth averaging 3.7 per cent per annum over the same period, we find that productivity per unit labour employed in the manufacturing sector will have to increase, in a sustained manner, by an annual rate of 4.5 per cent (see Table 8.13). This is about one per cent higher than the rate of productivity growth of 3.6 per cent achieved over the last ten years. At this rate of growth, productivity per unit labour will have increased almost fourfold, in real terms, from its existing levels.

Productivity of the non-governmental services sector will also have to register increases of almost the same magnitude. These, combined with productivity growth in other sectors, imply an overall economy-wide average productivity growth of 4.1 per cent per annum between 1991 and 2020 compared with a growth rate of only 2.6 per cent over the past decade. Such a rate of improvement will result in an output figure of about RM40,000 per unit labour by the year 2020, or 3.4 times higher than the level achieved in 1990 (see Figure 8.3).

A significant but achievable quantum leap in efforts to increase labour productivity is thus required. For this, the experiences of industrial countries with respect to productivity improvements provide some broad lessons as follows:

1. Labour productivity can be enhanced by enhancing the amount and quality of capital used by the labour force.

2. Economy-wide productivity can be improved if the whole economy shifts towards activities and industries in which value-added per worker is high, allowing a relative contraction of industries where such value-added is low.

3. Higher productivity is also contributed by improved organization and management of work such as through quality control circles, flexible work schedules, JIT, etc.

4. Productivity growth also comes from investment in firm specific technical skills.

Figure 8.3
GDP Per Worker, 1980-2020

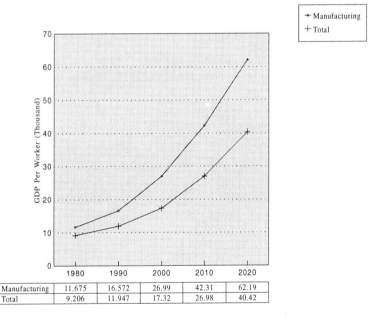

	1980	1990	2000	2010	2020
Manufacturing	11.675	16.572	26.99	42.31	62.19
Total	9.206	11.947	17.32	26.98	40.42

Malaysian firms should thus be encouraged to continue to move towards higher levels of capital intensity and to equip workers with equipments embodying the latest technology. The

Table 8.13

Malaysia: GDP, Employment and Productivity, 1980-2020

	1980	1990	2000	2010	2020
GDP (RM Million)	44,512	79,103	155,650	321,490	601,280
Manufacturing	8,742	21,381	57,860	130,940	240,430
Non-Government Services	13,273	25,025	57,660	135,890	282,720
EMPLOYMENT ('000)	4,835	6,621	8,990	11,910	14,870
Manufacturing	749	1,290	2,140	3,100	3,870
Non-Government Services	1,310	2,177	3,440	5,055	6,820
GDP PER WORKER (RM)	9,206	11,947	17,320	26,980	40,150
Manufacturing	11,657	16,572	26,990	42,310	62,190
Non-Government Services	10,130	11,495	16,760	26,880	41,450

	Average Growth Rate (%)			
	1981-1990	1991-2000	2001-2010	2011-2020
GDP	5.9	7.0	7.5	6.5
Manufacturing	9.4	10.5	8.5	6.3
Non-Government Services	6.5	8.7	9.0	7.6
EMPLOYMENT	3.2	3.1	2.9	2.2
Manufacturing	5.6	5.2	3.7	2.2
Non-Government Services	5.2	4.7	3.9	3.0
GDP PER WORKER	2.6	3.8	4.5	4.3
Manufacturing	3.6	5.0	4.6	3.6
Non-Government Services	1.3	3.8	4.8	4.4

Notes:
1. EPU Forecasts.
2. GDP total in million ringgit.
3. Employment total in thousands.
4. GDP per worker in ringgit.

maintenance of a tight labour market paralleling rapid output growth, high labour mobility and improving the level of skills are necessary to ensure that this continuous transition occurs smoothly.

In line with the required shift in the production structure, Malaysian firms and private individuals should be encouraged to go into higher value-added, higher skilled and more productive activities. As a matter of principle, non-viable or non-competitive activities should thus not be "locked in" or artificially maintained by protection or subsidies, for this will result in a misallocation of labour and capital resources. However, such a policy needs to be pragmatically implemented to reduce potential disruptions and temporary dislocations.

Malaysia must invest heavily in human resource development to upgrade the capability of the labour force and to allow progression into more difficult and more skill-intensive occupations. In the past, development expenditure devoted to education and training represented only between 1 and 1.5 per cent of GDP. A doubling of efforts will still involve only between 2 and 3 per cent of GDP, and is thus well within the government's capability to finance and implement. Greater private sector participation in training and human resource development to meet specific industry needs signify that a large quantum leap in human resource development effort of between 3 and 4 per cent of GDP is quite possible.

Finally, an acceptable and fair "social contract" between labour and capital needs to be established to ensure fair reward to labour, correct incentives for labour to shift skills to areas which are in demand, as well as stable industrial relations. Such a system is likely to be based on:

1. A flexible wage mechanism that rewards productivity.
2. A carefully devised incentive payment system that encourages workers to invest in skill development.
3. Harmonious employer-employee relations based on mutual trust and consensus.

Expected Change in Population and Employment Structure

The Malaysian population in 2020 is forecast to be "youthful". The median age of the population structure in 2020 is expected to be 28 years. By comparison, the median age for North Americans will be 37 and that of Europeans 40. In addition, the "dependency ratio" would progressively improve from around 70 per cent as at present to 53 per cent by 2020, as a result of a relative reduction in the size of the population aged below 15 and above 65. The expected youthfulness and improved dependency ratio of the population by ensuring vibrancy and dynamism of the workforce will facilitate the achievement of the Vision 2020 (see Table 8.14).

The total labour supply is forecast to grow at an average annual growth rate of 2.6 per cent between 1990 and 2020. The size of the labour force will thus increase from 7.0 million to 15.3 million during this period. The demand for labour, based on a sustained growth of GDP of 7 per cent annually during 1990-2020, is envisaged to grow at 2.7 per cent per annum. Employment is thus expected to increase from 6.6 million to around 15 million during this thirty-year period.

The changing structure of production envisaged requires that the largest share of employment comes from the services and manufacturing sectors while employment growth in the relatively slower sectors will stagnate. In addition, rapid technological change which occur as Malaysia gets further into the age of micro-electronics, fibre-optics, information technology, biotechnology and laser technology will require the development of a labour force with the right kind of training.

The manufacturing sector is expected to shift from simple assembly and process type operations to the more advanced, sophisticated and higher value-added and higher skill industries. Similarly, in the modern services sector, productivity gains and the push for competitiveness will demand wider application of the latest technology and more sophisticated method of operations, especially in areas such as banking, finance, insurance and business services. The survival of the agriculture sector too, given low productivity of traditional agricultural activities, depleting land resources and greater environmental consideration, require a steady shift into high value-added, skill- and land-intensive crops and activities using higher technology and greater amount of capital.

Based on the trends described above, the share of professional, technical and related workers is projected to increase sharply from 8.8 per cent in 1990 to 13.5 per cent in the year 2020, while the share of administrative and managerial workers is expected to increase from 2.5 per cent to 4.3 per cent during the same period (see Table 8.15). A projected 2.0 million persons will be employed in professional and technical occupations, representing an increase of 1.4 million from present levels. Many of these will be engineers and engineering assistants especially in the chemical, mechanical, electrical and electronics, and mechatronics fields. Great demand is also expected for multi-skilled craftsmen in tool and die-making, fabrication, machining, electrical and electronics. Both in the cases of manufacturing and services, the demand for managers and supervisors who are technologically oriented will also increase strongly. Education, training and human resource development efforts will thus have to respond accordingly.

Research and Development Requirements

The continuous change into higher value-added activities require not only the ability to import and effectively use high technology embodied in capital goods but also an increased indigenous research and development capability.

At present, Malaysia's research and development effort, as measured by research and development expenditure as a proportion to GNP, is very small and compares unfavourably with that of present-day developed countries (see Table 8.16). Malaysia's research and development expenditure as a proportion of GNP at 0.8 per cent is relatively low. In addition, the bulk of this, that is, around 80 per cent, is undertaken by the public sector, largely focused on agriculture and "upstream" or pure research.

Table 8.14

Malaysia: Population Size and Structure, 1980-2020

	1980	1990	2000	2010	2020
TOTAL ('000)	13,879	18,010	22,660	27,500	32,000
Age Structure					
0 – 14	5,542	6,752	7,890	8,650	8,933
15 – 64	7,846	10,590	13,774	17,375	20,870
65 and above	491	669	997	1,475	2,197
Age Dependency Ratio	77	70	65	58	53

	Average Annual Growth Rate (%)			
	1980-1990	1990-2000	2000-2010	2010-2020
TOTAL	2.6	2.3	1.9	1.5
Age Structure				
0 – 14	2.0	1.6	0.9	0.3
15 – 64	3.0	2.6	2.3	1.8
65 and above	3.1	4.0	4.0	4.0

Notes: 1. EPU Forecasts. 2. The age dependency ratio of dependents to very 100 persons of working age. 3. Dependents refer to those aged below 15 and those 65 and above.

Table 8.15

Employment by Broad Occupational Category

Occupationsal Group	Share of Total Employment (%)					
	1980	1990	2000	2010	2020	
Professional and Technical	6.8	8.8	10.0	11.8	13.5	
Administrative and Managerial	1.8	2.5	2.9	3.6	4.3	
Clerical	8.3	9.8	9.9	10.0	10.1	
Sales	9.2	11.5	13.8	14.5	15.2	
Service	9.8	11.6	12.6	13.6	14.6	
Agricultural	36.4	28.3	20.2	15.5	11.0	
Production	27.6	27.6	30.5	31.0	31.3	
Total	100	100	100	100	100	

Note: Economic Planning Unit estimates.

Table 8.16

Research and Development Expenditure by Country

Country	Unit (Million)	Research Expenditure				Total as % of GNP
		Total	Govt/Inst	University	Private	
Malaysia, 1989	Ringgit Malaysia	765 (100%)	593 (77.6%)	125 (16.4%)	45 (6.0%)	0.8
Korea, 1982	Won	457,689 (100%)	186,077 (40.7%)	66,610 (14.6%)	205,002 (44.7%)	0.95
Japan, 1982	Yen	5,881,539 (100%)	894,310 (15.2%)	948,211 (16.1%)	4,039,018 (68.7%)	2.78
United States, 1980	US Dollar	62,220 (100%)	10,060 (16.0%)	8,284 (11.4%)	43,879 (70.5%)	2.86
United Kingdom, 1975	Pound Sterling	3,622 (100%)	886 (24.4%)	412 (11.4%)	2,324 (64.2%)	2.47 (1978)
West Germany, 1977	Deutsche Mark	41,320 (100%)	7,520 (18.2%)	6,520 (15.8%)	27,280 (66.0%)	3.04 (1981)

Source:
1. Science and Technology Annual, Korea, 1983.
2. White Paper on Science and Technology, Japan, 1983.

Downstream and applied research to meet industrial private sector requirements is thus still limited. The private sector in Malaysia is almost totally dependent on imported technology whether through capital embodied technology or through licensing and other technology contracts.

To be leaders and efficient competitors we need to increase our research and development effort, perhaps focusing on a few areas in which we can quickly develop expertise. For example, our experience in agricultural research and the wealth of gene stock provided by our rich tropical environment, makes the move to a position of eminence if not dominance in biotechnological research an achievable aim over the next few decades. This is a rare chance because most futurists such as John Naisbitt and Patricia Aburdene, 1990 expect that the world will soon progress from the "information age" into the "biotechnological age".

By building dominance here we will easily leap-frog into the forefront of an important area of technological development. The opportunities in the food industry, health care and medicine is expected to be tremendous. Another new area of research which we can focus on is advanced materials technology, for example, ceramics, superconducting materials, etc. Both areas of research, in addition to being at the cutting age of technology, can easily link with the development of our resource-based industries and with the objective of increasing high value-added forms of internal absorption of our mineral and agricultural raw material endowments.

Taking the research and development effort of present-day developed countries as a guide, we should spend at least 2 per cent of our GNP on research by 2010, reaching 2.5 per cent by 2020. The implied level of research and development expenditure is substantial and require a great quantum leap in effort so that in constant 1978 prices, research and development expenditure should reach RM1.6 billion per annum by 2000 rising steeply to RM15 billion by 2020 (see Table 8.17). The number of research and development personnel should also increase accordingly from 300 per 1.0 million population as at present to 2,300 by 2010 and 4,200 by 2020. This level is comparable to

Table 8.17
**Projection of Required
Research and Development Effort for Malaysia**

	1990	2000	2010	2020	1991-2020
R&D as Proportion of GDP	0.8	1.0	2.0	2.5	
R&D Value per Annum (RM Million/1978 prices)	630	1,600	6,200	15,200	11% p.a.
Number of R&D Personnel*	5,500	18,400	62,000	135,000	11% p.a.
R&D Personnel per Million of Population	300	800	2,300	4,200	

* Assuming present dollar to R&D personnel ratios hold, adjusting downwards on account of expected higher efficiencies, sophistication of personnel and higher costs of operations.

that of present-day developed countries (for example, Japan has 6,500 per million, United Kingdom has 3,200 and Germany 3,000. The current figure for South Korea is 1,300 per million). The constant rate of increase between 1991 to 2020 required by this vision is very substantial (but nevertheless achievable) requiring an 11 per cent annual growth for research and development expenditure matched by an 11 per cent annual increase in the number of research and development personnel.

Possible Trajectory of Industrial Development

To be competitive a country must nurture industries in which it has a comparative advantage or be a centre of multinational operations in industries or segments of industry in which it is competitive. Since global production and global operation of services are going to become more widespread in future it also means that a country must nurture its own viable and competitive multinational corporations.

Analysts of factors influencing the competitive advantage of nations (for example, Michael E. Porter's *The Competitive Advantage of Nations*, 1990) observed that countries are usually competitive in particular industries or segments of industries and cannot attempt to be competitive in every industry. It is further observed that where competitive edge is based on technology, quality and product differentiation is more durable and less easily replicated than that which is merely based on abundant resource endowments or the existence of cheap factors of production.

These observations as well as the reality of secular industry life cycles involving the introduction, growth, maturity and eventual decline of industries (for example, Vernon, 1966 and the Boston Consultancy Group) and the imperative of continuously moving from low value-added to higher value-added activities and industries to support a high and rising level of income (Porter, 1990) requires that the Malaysian industrial sector continuously undergo rapid and dynamic changes. These imperatives and the vision contained in the Industrial Master Plan and the Second Outline Perspective Plan are combined to produce a possible scenario of the broad changes and transformation that may affect this key sector. This is summarized in Figure 8.4. The broad implications of these scenarios are summarized below.

During the 1990s the mature or maturing industries ("cash cows" in the Boston Consultancy Group jargon) that will form the backbone of Malaysia's industrial output will be foodstuffs, chemicals, textiles, resource-based industry, electronics and electrical equipment (low-end, assembly-type, components) and certain low or medium technology heavy industries such as cement, iron and steel, automobile and transport equipment.

Without the development of a large regional market, some of these will have to operate under continued protection. These will be the "staples" making up the bulk of manufacturing activity and employment in the 1990s. At the same time, the following industries are expected to be in their ascendant or growth stage ("stars" in the BCG jargon): Modern SMIs, ancillary and support industries and electronics and electrical equipments (high value-added end-products).

Furthermore, given the right policy impetus and direction the following new industries or "babies" may be emerging in the 1990s: Biotechnology, advanced materials including superconducting materials and art-based, design-intensive industries such as fashionwear, accessories, jewellery, quality furniture, etc.

Biotechnology and advanced materials may form the cutting edge of new developments in the traditional resource-based industries, while art-based and design-intensive industries represent a logical development from present consumer goods, apparel as well as traditional crafts and rural industries.

Meanwhile, however, the following industries will have entered their "sunset" or declining stage, being replaced by the newer industries such as assembly-type, labour-intensive, low technology and low skill industries including those operating in free trade zones; traditional crafts and disorganized SMI sector; and non-financial public enterprise subsectors.

The 2000s will see the continuing importance of textile, food and resource-based industries. These will however progressively go upstream into high quality, high value-added and highly differentiated niches and end-products, with the coming into being

Figure 8.4

Malaysia: Probable Industrial Dynamics
of Vision 2020

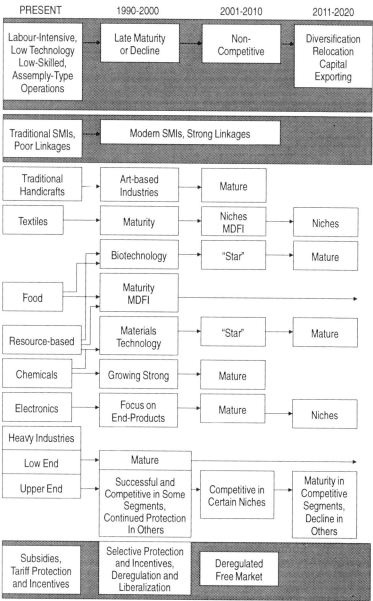

PRESENT	1990-2000	2001-2010	2011-2020
Labour-Intensive, Low Technology Low-Skilled, Assembly-Type Operations	Late Maturity or Decline	Non-Competitive	Diversification Relocation Capital Exporting
Traditional SMIs, Poor Linkages	Modern SMIs, Strong Linkages		
Traditional Handicrafts	Art-based Industries	Mature	
Textiles	Maturity	Niches MDFI	Niches
	Biotechnology	"Star"	Mature
Food	Maturity MDFI		
Resource-based	Materials Technology	"Star"	Mature
Chemicals	Growing Strong	Mature	
Electronics	Focus on End-Products	Mature	Niches
Heavy Industries			
Low End	Mature		
Upper End	Successful and Competitive in Some Segments, Continued Protection In Others	Competitive in Certain Niches	Maturity in Competitive Segments, Decline in Others
Subsidies, Tariff Protection and Incentives	Selective Protection and Incentives, Deregulation and Liberalization	Deregulated Free Market	

of rival production centres in countries who are lagging behind us in industrial development and have a high resource base such as Vietnam and the rest of Indochina, China or even Indonesia, South Asia, Eastern Europe, parts of Latin America and Africa. Manufacturing activities in these industries located in such countries may however be owned by Malaysian corporations, using expertise and cash resources accumulated in the intervening decades.

Other "cash cows" in the 2000s is likely to be food, chemicals, high-end electronics and electrical and mechanical products and the art-based industries. Certain heavy industries producing machinery and some capital goods will have also matured into reliable "cash cows" though a large regional market may however be a crucial precondition. The likely "stars" for this period are biotechnology and advanced materials, assuming sufficient research and development impetus is received from today.

By the last decade of Vision 2020, the "stars" described above would have matured and some of the matured industries of the preceding decade such as electronics will begin to go "up-market" into particular advanced niches and product segments. Many Malaysian corporations in these industries will have also gone overseas where these industries are still at a robust stage of development. The staple industries in Malaysia then may be advanced materials and biotechnology, art-based and design-intensive consumer goods industries and certain segments of heavy and capital goods industries. Food, chemicals, branded consumer goods and ancillary and support industries can however be expected to persist throughout.

Development of Services Sector

The services sector will have to undergo rapid changes in line with industrial development. The relatively declining services sector will be the government and most traditional service subsectors. The government sector's relative decline is in line with its reduced direct role in the economy. Such a reduced role, privatization, combined with increased taxable capacity of the Malaysian public arising from increases in incomes and value-

added activities is expected to enable the government to eventually operate on a strictly balanced budget. Malaysia's external debt
will also have been fully paid by the end of the next decade.

The non-government, modern services sector will however
grow strongly. Services which function in support of industrial
development, namely, financial services, transport, storage, communications, consultancy and advertisement is likely to grow,
both in their level of coverage as well as in their degree of sophistication, with the increasing sophistication of the industrial sector.
New developments in information technology, telecommunications and fibre-optic technology must be mastered together with
the latest developments in financial operations, banking, insurance and transport management. Ancillary support services
will also become important as the manufacturing sector gets into
CAD, CAE, CAM and CNC technology.

At the same time, services which support trade such as shipping, transport, freight and insurance will also have to undergo
similar development. Since much of this is tradeable in nature and
thus open to competition, Malaysian providers of such services
must not only be effective and capable of delivering such services
but must also be competitive. Liberalization of the services sector,
as a result of negotiations under the Group of Negotiations on
Services (GNS), by increasing our exposure to external competition from countries which are well ahead of us in these sectors will
make the development of a viable local capability in this services
subsector a difficult challenge indeed, requiring special effort by
the country. Joint-venture collaboration and strategic alliances
with foreign interests may thus be needed as would special efforts
at developing the relevant services segments through incentives,
human resource development efforts and regional collaboration.

In addition to the above trends, services such as retail trade,
entertainment, leisure, travel and tourism, private health care and
private education will also prosper in line with increasing incomes
and standards of living. These services will also have to move
progressively to higher quality, higher value-added and sophisticated segments in line with the improvements in purchasing
power. Since these basically operate as a "domestic" services sec-

tor where local capability is either adequate or can be easily developed, foreign collaboration is not really required except under special circumstances.

Role of the Public and Private Sectors in Achieving Vision 2020

The achievement of the visions described previously require sustained effort, correct policies and strategies. It also requires our readiness to make significant quantum leaps in certain crucial areas such as research and development and human resource development. It also requires a real understanding of the large dynamic changes in employment structure and in the structure of production and a real readiness to accept the pain and effort necessitated by such changes. The Vision requires the effort of both the public and private sectors or from another perspective, the government and the people.

Role of the Public Sector

The major socio-political, macroeconomic and financial stability conditions and other "qualitative aspects" described previously, required to maintain a healthy environment for investment, has for some time been a trait of macro and socio-economic management in Malaysia. In addition, policies of private sector-led growth, privatization and economic and financial liberalization and deregulation required to move towards a more efficient and competitive economy is already onstream. Much of the "environmental conditions" required by the Vision is thus already in existence. A key role of the government is "simply" to ensure that its fine record in ensuring political and economic stability is maintained and that current efforts at privatization, liberalization and deregulation is sustained. As an agenda for the immediate future, the following should be looked into:

1. Ensure further liberalizations of trade by re-examining existing tariff policies and other trade barriers to further

reduce market distortions and allow Malaysian industries to continue to adjust to a more competitive environment.

2. Fine tuning of current policies with regard to direct foreign investment to ensure movement into higher value-added industries, greater linkages and more meaningful transfer of technology. In addition, for industries requiring global production, special efforts may need to be exercised to identify and attract multinational corporations which are industry leaders to set up their "home base" in Malaysia.

3. Find ways to support the development of viable, home-grown multinational corporations in economic activities in which we are already capable of, especially where potential for internal growth is limited such as plantation, mining and consumer products such as food, textiles and other resource-based industries can benefit by directly investing overseas in markets such as other Asean neighbours, Indochina, China, Latin America and South Asia.

The future will thus be a Malaysia which is efficient, competitive and perhaps a net capital exporter. Policy encouragement, incentives and institutional backing and support are needed to give these efforts the desired impetus.

In addition to the above, bearing in mind the potential strength of the Asia-Pacific region as borne out by the scenario painted previously, and noting the advantages that can be provided by a larger domestic or regional market, especially for capital intensive industries requiring large scale production, current ideas regarding the formation of an EAEC or an Asean Free Trade Area will have to be actively and diligently pursued by the government.

The crucial role of human resource development and research and development requires firm commitment, support and direction from the government. The attention focused on these crucial issues in the Sixth Malaysia Plan and Second Outline Perspective Plan has already put this requirement in its proper perspective. We saw, however, that a significant quantum leap in the efforts and money put towards meeting these objectives is required.

The important public sector roles outlined above imply that while the public sector may experience a relative reduction in its size, its role in economic management, in the socio-economic management and restructuring of society, in providing broad leadership and direction to guide private efforts, in providing social and physical infrastructural support and in developing the institutional framework for development, remains crucial. To support these demanding functions, the public sector while downsizing in physical terms, will have to upgrade itself in terms of skills and professionalism in the relevant areas. Professional skills in economic management, in education and health, and in undertaking pure research and development are among the crucial areas that need to be built up. The system of remuneration, intake and in-service training thus need to be at a level which can attract, develop and retain the right kind of manpower.

Role of the Private Sector

The Malaysian private sector on its part must continue to rise to the challenges implied by the Vision and must be willing to improve and adjust to the much more stringent requirements of the future. To achieve a viable status in its own right, Malaysia's private sector must not only be able to import new technology, compete in a closed market environment or to export overseas on the back of multinational linkages but also must develop their own potential. Thus, in addition to using profits to invest in new technology embodied in modern capital goods, Malaysian companies must also invest in training and human resource development, whether individually or on an industry-wide basis, to meet their specific needs. They must also begin to embark on conducting research and development to find improved and more efficient production methods, new markets, new products and new applications for existing products. Such research and development and human resource development efforts will also facilitate their diversification into newer and higher value-added lines of businesses.

The increasingly liberalized business environment that will characterize the Malaysian as well as the world economy in future implies that the future will no longer be a safe place for businessmen who can only operate in a protected market or survive by tapping the economic values of concessions or licences or by relying on government contracts. Something akin to a "mental revolution" has to occur to ensure that businessmen used to operate in such an easy environment are able to adjust to the new and more challenging competitive environment being created. It is necessary to develop an entrepreneurial class of competitive, resilient people not dependent on government support.

In addition, the industrial dynamics portrayed in the previous section imply that those operating in mature or "sunset" industries must from now on seek out new investment opportunities in newer and growing industries or industry segments. Furthermore, they should be willing to seek and tap investment opportunities overseas so as to remain profitable even when internal production dynamics become increasingly non-favourable.

Last but not least, Malaysians must learn to value effort and creativity. They must also learn to believe in themselves and develop a strong degree of confidence to take in their stride the challenges ahead.

Conclusion

It can be said that the achievement of the status of a developed country by 2020 has been shown to be achievable provided the country is able to sustain rapid growth, shift into higher value-added activities and continuously nurture competitive industries. The efforts required to fulfil these requirements, although significant, are well within the capability of Malaysians. The task ahead is a challenging one, perhaps even more challenging than the phases of development that we have so far achieved. However, the reward in terms of the well-being of our children and future generations and in terms of our integrity as a nation will be substantial.

9

The Savings-Investment Gap, Financing Needs and Capital Market Development

Lin See-Yan

The mobilization of savings is an important prerequisite for capital formation and hence, national development. Economic growth can be sustained only if resources are mobilized efficiently and transformed effectively into productive activities. Historically, Malaysia has managed to sustain a high level of savings. On the whole, the country saved an average of 24 per cent of the gross national product (GNP) a year over the last three decades, a level amongst the highest in the world. In the past five years (1986–1990), the ratio was as high as 31 per cent. Because of the availability of adequate savings for productive long-term investment, Malaysia had consistently achieved a high rate of growth with relative price stability. Growth in the gross domestic product (GDP) at constant prices had accelerated from an average annual rate of about 5 per cent (inflation of less than 1 per cent annually) in the 1960s, to 8 per cent in the 1970s (inflation was higher, averaging about 6 per cent), but slackened to 5.2 per cent during the 1981–1985 period (inflation averaged 4.6 per cent during this period). This reflected the prolonged global recession in the early 1980s. However, the Malaysian economy had since rebounded through the rest of the 1980s with remarkable resilience in terms of performance. Real economic growth picked up to an average of 6.9 per cent per annum during the 1986– 1990 period (9.2 per cent a year in the 1988–1990 period), with inflation averaging 2.8 per cent annually.

Throughout the past three decades, Malaysia had basically relied on the use of realistic five-year economic plans to implement its development strategy, the main aim of which being to ensure that sufficient domestic resources will be forthcoming to meet the goals of national development. However, Malaysia is a small and open economy and, as such, fluctuations in its international terms of trade and their impact on export earnings (and hence, national income) have a significant influence on the rate and level of its domestic and national savings. Consequently, periodic imbalances were reflected in the form of deficits or surpluses in the current account of the balance of payments, which were usually "financed" through sufficient inflows of long-term foreign capital so that overall national external reserves rose significantly even in most of the "lean" years.

This chapter examines the development experience of Malaysia in managing the savings-investment gap to achieve its main objective of sustained rapid growth with price stability. In particular, this chapter attempts to look at the financing needs of the Malaysian economy during the Sixth Malaysia Plan period (1991–1995), including the need to further develop, broaden and deepen the capital market in the country to meet the enlarged financing requirements of private investors in the 1990s. It will present an overview of the savings-investment trends during the period of 1960–1990 and discuss national and domestic savings, the breakdown of public and private savings as well as the comparison of Malaysia's experience with other countries. A systematic flow of funds arrangement tracing the sources and uses of funds in the 1980s with emphasis on the mobilization of savings of the private sector by the financial system is discussed at length. It also focuses on private savings and their decomposition into household and corporate savings. At the same time, growth trends in private investment and its sources of financing are also delved into. This chapter attempts to look at economic growth and the financing needs of the Malaysian economy during the Sixth Malaysia Plan period, including the future for capital market development, while the final section of this chapter summarizes, with concluding observations, on broad policy directions pointing to the way ahead over the next five years.

An Overview of the Savings-Investment Gap

Malaysia had neither a savings-investment gap nor a foreign exchange gap to bridge during the period of 1960–1980 as a whole since there had been, overall, a substantial accumulation of foreign reserves over these years, although there have been periods in between these years where gaps of one type or another had to be bridged on account of poor cyclical international demand for the nation's exports. Essentially, growth in the agriculture and mining sectors provided the surpluses, which were then mobilized by the Government and the financial system to develop the manufacturing and tertiary industries and to expand the basic infrastructure. In the 1970s, plantation agriculture, mineral extraction, and later, oil and gas, yielded significant savings – enough not only to finance reinvestment within these sectors but also pay taxes to finance Government spending. In addition, there was a significant surplus left over to enable the economy to increasingly diversify from being overly dependent on these sectors. Thus, although the level of capital formation had increased rapidly from about 17.5 per cent of GNP in the 1960s to 28.1 per cent of GNP in the 1976–1980 period (see Table 9.1), the nation had been able to finance much of the investment outlays without significant recourse to external financing. Consequently, there had been no large deficits in the current account of the balance of payments, even over short periods, that were not sustainable.

However, this twenty-year trend was not carried into the 1981–1985 period, when the current account in the balance of payments recorded a deficit averaging 8.5 per cent of GNP, with the deficit reaching a high of 14 per cent of GNP in 1982. This reflected the increasing participation of the public sector in national development – the "big-push" – which contributed significantly to a change in the composition of public or private investment. During the 1981–1985 period, public investment rose to reach about the level of private investment's share of 19 per cent of GNP (see Table 9.2). The amount of public investment had increased from RM3.2 billion (or 44.4 per cent of total investment) during the period of 1961–1965 to a high of RM56.5 billion (or 47.9 per cent of total investment) during the period of 1981–1985 (see Table 9.3). As a result, the nation's external debt rose to RM42.3 billion by the end of 1985 (RM10 billion in 1980), with a debt servicing ratio of nearly 16 per cent (4 per cent in 1980). By the end of 1985, through a deliberate policy at structural adjustment, public investment was reduced to 13.8 per cent of GNP, and the current external payments deficit fell to 2.4 per cent of GNP (see Table 9.4). This turnaround within such a short period of time is an achievement by any standard.[1] With continued fiscal restraint in the face of improving commodity prices, the current account of the balance of payments had since turned around to register a surplus of 8.9 per cent of GNP in 1987. However, with rapidly rising investment requirements, a savings-investment gap had emerged once again in the 1989–1990 period. For the period 1986–1990 as a whole, the country still managed to maintain a resource surplus of 1.5 per cent of GNP. The debt service ratio had since continued to improve, to reach a comfortable 7.7 per cent by the end of 1990.

From Tables 9.1 to 9.4, four interesting observations on the savings-investment gap should be noted. First, the gross national savings (GNS) and gross domestic investment (GDI) gap in the 1981–1985 period reached a historic high of 8.5 per cent of GNP, a level that was clearly not sustainable. Recognizing this, the Government implemented major policy changes to narrow

---

[1]   See Lin, See-Yan, 1986 for a chronological account of public policies in the 1980s.

the gap. A vigorous structural adjustment programme was put into place to reorientate the economy back to the path of sustainable growth with price stability.

Table 9.1
Malaysia:
Savings-Investment Gap, 1961–1990

Year	GNS	GDI	BOP Current Account*
	% of GNP		+
1961–1965	17.8	18.9	–1.1
1966–1970	18.2	16.5	1.7
1971–1975	21.1	24.9	–3.8
1976–1980	30.3	28.1	2.2
1981–1985	27.6	36.1	–8.5
1986–1990	31.3	29.8	1.5
1986	27.4	27.8	–0.4
1987	33.6	24.7	8.9
1988	33.0	27.5	5.5
1989	30.7	31.2	–0.5
1990	31.0	35.1	–4.1

* Surplus (+) and deficit (–)

Notes:
GNS: Gross National Savings
GDI: Gross Domestic Investment
BOP: Balance of Payments

Source: Department of Statistics.

Table 9.2

**Malaysia: Expenditure on Gross
National Product at Current Prices**

	1961–1965	1966–1970	1971–1975	1976–1980	1981–1985	1986–1990
	% of GNP					
Consumption	80.5	80.2	77.7	69.5	72.4	69.3
Private	64.5	62.5	60.2	53.1	55.1	53.7
Public	16.0	17.8	17.5	16.4	17.3	15.6
Investment	18.9	16.5	24.9	28.1	36.2	29.3
Private	10.5	9.9	16.9	17.7	18.9	18.6
Public	8.4	6.6	8.0	10.4	17.3	10.7
Net Foreign Trade	0.6	3.3	–2.6	2.4	–8.6	1.4
Gross National Product	100.0	100.0	100.0	100.0	100.0	100.0
Current Account Balance	–1.1	1.7	–3.8	2.2	–8.8	1.9
Gross National Savings	17.8	18.2	21.1	30.3	27.4	31.2
Gross Domestic Savings	22.6	22.1	25.5	34.7	33.7	36.4

Source: Bank Negara Malaysia.

Table 9.3

Malaysia: Savings and Investment, 1961–1990

	1961–65	1966–70	1971–75	1976–80	1981–85	1986–90
				RM Billion		
Public Gross Domestic Capital Formation	3.2	3.4	7.0	19.9	56.5	48.5
Public Savings	0.6	0.6	2.2	14.7	38.8	39.6
Deficit or Surplus	−2.6	−2.8	−4.8	−5.2	−17.7	−8.9
Private Gross Domestic Capital Formation	4.0	5.1	14.9	33.6	61.5	81.0
Private Savings	6.2	8.8	16.4	43.0	51.6	96.0
Deficit or Surplus	2.2	3.7	1.5	9.4	−9.9	15.0
Gross Domestic Capital Formation	7.2	8.5	21.9	53.5	118.0	129.4
Gross National Savings	6.8	9.4	18.6	57.7	90.4	135.6
Balance on Current Account	−0.4	0.9	−3.3	4.2	−27.6	6.2
Gross Domestic Savings	8.6	11.4	22.4	65.9	110.1	158.1

Source: Bank Negara Malaysia.

Table 9.4

Malaysia: Savings and Investment, 1961–1990

	1961–65	1966–70	1971–75	1976–80	1981–85	1986–90
			% of GNP			
Public Gross Domestic Capital Formation	8.4	6.6	8.0	10.4	17.3	11.2
Public Savings	1.5	1.1	2.5	7.7	11.7	8.8
Deficit or Surplus	–6.9	–5.5	–5.5	–2.7	–5.6	–2.4
Private Gross Domestic Capital Formation	10.5	9.9	16.9	17.7	18.9	18.1
Private Savings	16.3	17.1	18.6	22.6	15.8	22.4
Deficit or Surplus	5.8	7.2	1.7	4.9	–3.1	4.3
Gross Domestic Capital Formation	18.9	16.5	24.9	28.1	36.2	29.3
Gross National Savings	17.8	18.2	21.1	30.3	27.4	31.2
Balance on Current Account	–1.1	1.7	–3.8	2.2	–8.8	1.9
Gross Domestic Savings	22.6	22.1	25.5	34.7	33.7	36.4

Source: Bank Negara Malaysia.

Second, with the discipline of continuing fiscal restraint in the face of improving commodity prices, the GNS-GDI gap narrowed; and by 1987, it turned to a surplus equivalent to nearly 9 per cent of GNP. However, with rising investment requirements and increasing consumption, a savings-investment gap had emerged once again in the 1989–1990 period.

Third, traditionally, public savings would be insufficient to finance public investment. In the 1960s and 1970s, this gap was readily bridged from non-inflationary sources, without any significant resort to external borrowing. By the first-half of the 1980s, the absolute size of this gap (at nearly RM18 billion) was about twice that in the 1970s. This gap had since narrowed considerably (RM9.2 billion in 1990), mainly because of higher public savings which reflects better economic performance.

Fourth, unlike the public sector, the private sector had been consistently a significant net saver in the 1960s and 1970s. In the first-half of the 1980s, however, this surplus in savings turned negative (–RM9.9 billion), reflecting primarily lower private savings (especially corporate savings), following the recession and poor commodity prices. Since 1986, the situation had reverted to a surplus (average of RM4.8 billion annually over the period of 1986–1989), before turning to a deficit of RM4.1 billion in 1990 due to the sharp rise in both private consumption and investment on account of the sustained buoyant economic performance.

Based on the structure and resource endowment of the economy, Malaysia's high savings rate was a function essentially of factors that are not unlike those found in most commodity producing economies. In Malaysia's case, the importance of commodities, the role of public sector expenditure and demographic patterns had been important structural factors which determined the savings pattern. In addition, on the institutional side, the mandatory contribution by 80 per cent of the workforce to the Employees Provident Fund (EPF) was also important in explaining the savings behaviour.

Traditionally, Malaysia has had high aggregate savings. Throughout the 1970s, the gross domestic savings (GDS) rose to levels that were comparable with those in Japan and Singapore, and ahead of Thailand and Korea (see Table 9.5) and, significantly above those of the major OECD nations. For 1989, Malaysia's GDS:GNP ratio of 33 per cent was higher than Canada (22 per cent), France (21 per cent), West Germany (26 per cent), Italy (21 per cent), the United Kingdom (16 per cent) and the United States (14 per cent). In 1979, it was as high as 35 per cent of GNP. However, this share fell to 25 per cent of GNP in 1982, before recovering to 37.3 per cent of GNP in 1987.

Table 9.5
Gross Domestic Savings:
Selected Asian Countries

	Japan	Singapore	Korea	Malaysia	Thailand
Year	% of GNP				+
1971–1975	36.8	26.4	19.3	25.7	23.3
1976–1980	32.5 •	33.3	25.8	34.7	24.0
1981–1985	31.2	45.7	29.0	33.6	19.5
1986–1989	33.4	40.2	37.7	37.0	27.3

Source: *International Financial Statistics,* International Monetary Fund.

Subsequently, the share fell to 33 per cent again in 1990. Being a primary producing country, Malaysia is not unlike other resource-rich countries, such as Algeria, Venezuela and Indonesia, which also have rather high GDS:GNP ratios (see Table 9.6). Since an important part of the capital used for developing much of the basic and other industries were imported, net foreign payments abroad (NFPA) had become increasingly important.

It is not surprising that Malaysia's GNS has consistently remained lower than its GDS (see Table 9.7). On a comparative basis, they were lower than Japan and Singapore, and somewhat higher than Thailand and Korea (see Table 9.8).

Table 9.6
Gross Domestic Savings:
Selected Oil Exporting Countries

	Indonesia	Venezuela	Malaysia	Algeria
Year	% of GNP			+
1971–1975	19.5	40.6	25.7	32.0
1976–1980	27.0	33.2	34.7	41.7
1981–1985	31.7	25.8	33.6	39.5
1986–1989	35.1	25.0	37.0	31.8

Source: *International Financial Statistics,* International Monetary Fund.

Table 9.7
Malaysia: Gross
Domestic and National Savings

	GDS	GNS	NFPA
Year	% of GNP		+
1961–1965	22.6	17.8	−2.9
1966–1970	22.1	18.3	−1.9
1971–1975	25.7	20.8	−3.5
1976–1980	34.7	30.0	−4.3
1981–1985	33.6	27.4	−6.2
1986–1990	36.6	31.1	−5.7
1986	32.1	27.4	−7.2
1987	37.3	33.6	−6.6
1988	36.3	33.0	−5.9
1989	33.9	30.7	−5.3
1990	33.0	31.0	−4.4

Source: *International Financial Statistics,* International Monetary Fund.

Table 9.8

Gross National Savings:
Selected Asian Countries

	Japan	Singapore	Korea	Malaysia	Thailand
Year		% of GNP			+
1971–1975	36.6	25.2	20.0	20.8	25.7
1976–1980	32.4	31.3	26.7	30.0	24.8
1981–1985	31.3	43.2	25.2	27.4	18.5
1986–1989	34.0	41.2	36.6	31.2	25.8

Source: *International Financial Statistics,* International Monetary Fund.

The gap between GNS and GDS is expected to remain in the future, reflecting Malaysia's continued dependence on foreign direct investments (FDIs). It is unlikely that this trend to pay abroad (annually about 6 per cent of GNP) in terms of profits and dividends on FDIs will be reversed in any significant manner.

Essentially, the nation's high level of savings reflected both high average and marginal rates of savings over a long period. These rates are high by any standard (see Table 9.9).

Table 9.9

Annual Savings Rate

	Average	Marginal
Period	%	+
1965–1970	18.1	22.9
1971–1975	21.2	25.6
1976–1980	30.4	38.7
1981–1985	27.6	20.6
1986–1990	31.2	37.6

Source: Bank Negara Malaysia.

The Flow of Funds

The figures on flow of capital funds in the 1980s are presented in Tables 9.10 and 9.11. They identify the three major sources of funds, namely, private savings, long-term capital from abroad and public savings, and show how these funds are used to finance public and private investment or placed abroad, including for portfolio investment purposes. These flow of funds tables are also presented in chart form (see Figures 9.1 to 9.4), providing additional information of how private savings are mobilized through the organized financial system, including the banks. While these tables and charts contain a wealth of information, the following salient points are worth noting.

First, the annual flow of capital funds, which rose rapidly from nearly RM18 billion to RM29 billion between 1980 and 1984, had since slackened to only RM25 billion in 1988 before rising again to RM41 billion in 1990. The decline reflected mainly the deliberate policy move to rely less on foreign sources of finance (especially bank borrowings) to reduce the Government's external debt burden (hence, significant repayments and prepayments) and reverse the trend of declining public savings.

Second, since peaking in the 1983–1984 period, private investment and public capital outlays had downward trends until 1987, when they started to pick up again, in consonance with the significant improvement in savings.

Third, by 1988, private savings had re-established its pre-eminent role as the single most important source of capital funds.

Fourth, with the implementation of cutbacks in public expenditures in the 1982–1983 period, the resorting to external borrowing had slowed down significantly. By 1987, official foreign borrowing had turned negative and a net outflow of RM5.1 billion was recorded in 1988, reflecting in particular significant early loan prepayments. Although the net inflow of foreign direct investments (FDIs) had also slackened since 1983, following the recession, the annual rate of inflows had remained healthy and substantial. During the period of 1981–1985, the net inflow of corporate FDIs amounted to RM12.7 billion, double the amount

Table 9.10

Malaysia: Flow of Capital Funds

	RM Billion										
	1980	1981	1982	1983	1984	1985	1986	1987	1988	1989	1990
SOURCES OF FUNDS:											
Private Sector Savings	10.5	8.7	9.2	10.3	13.3	10.1	13.8	20.2	21.0	19.3	21.5
Monetary System	6.0	4.8	5.3	3.6	4.7	2.6	5.5	3.2	3.9	9.3	10.8
Provident and Life Assurance Funds	2.5	2.1	3.4	3.9	3.5	4.0	4.2	5.2	4.9	6.4	7.3
Savings and Other Financial Institutions	0.5	0.2	0.5	3.1	2.9	3.2	−0.6	0.1	1.3	5.4	5.7
(Other Funds *minus* Foreign Direct Investment)	1.5	1.6	0.0	−0.3	2.2	0.3	4.7	11.7	10.9	−1.8	−2.3
Inflow of Long-Term Funds	2.2	5.9	8.4	9.2	6.6	4.2	3.4	−1.4	−3.2	3.2	7.1
Foreign Direct Investment	2.0	2.9	3.2	2.9	1.9	1.7	1.3	1.1	1.9	5.0	8.0

Official Foreign Loans	0.2	3.0	5.2	6.3	4.7	2.5	2.1	-2.5	-5.1	-1.8	-0.9
Public Sector Savings	5.1	5.8	5.8	8.0	9.5	9.7	4.5	4.9	7.3	10.3	12.6
Public Sector Surplus	3.5	2.0	3.4	6.6	8.1	7.2	1.5	3.4	5.4	7.8	10.1
Transfers to Private Sector	1.6	3.8	2.4	1.4	1.4	2.5	3.0	1.5	1.9	2.5	2.5
Total Flow of Capital Funds	**17.8**	**20.4**	**23.4**	**27.5**	**29.4**	**24.0**	**21.7**	**23.7**	**25.1**	**32.8**	**41.2**
USES OF FUNDS:											
Private Investment	10.1	11.1	11.7	13.3	14.0	11.3	10.1	11.1	15.0	19.0	26.1
Accumulation of											
International Reserves	1.0	-1.1	-0.6	-0.1	0.3	3.2	4.1	2.9	-1.1	3.3	5.4
Unidentified Private											
Payments Abroad	0.6	1.4	0.6	1.2	2.4	-0.5	-1.0	2.4	2.7	-0.5	-3.0
Public Investment	6.1	9.0	11.7	13.1	12.7	10.0	8.5	7.3	8.5	11.0	12.7

Source: Bank Negara Malaysia.

Table 9.11
Malaysia: Flow of Capital Funds

	% Composition										
	1980	1981	1982	1983	1984	1985	1986	1987	1988	1989	1990
Sources of Funds:											
Private Sector Savings	59.0	42.7	39.3	37.5	45.3	42.1	63.6	85.2	83.6	58.8	52.1
Monetary System	33.7	23.5	22.7	13.1	16.0	10.8	25.3	13.5	15.5	28.3	26.2
Provident and Life											
Assurance Funds	14.1	10.3	14.5	14.2	11.9	16.7	19.4	21.9	19.5	19.5	17.7
Savings and Other											
Financial Institutions	2.8	1.0	2.1	11.3	9.9	13.3	−2.8	0.4	5.2	16.5	13.8
(Other Funds *minus* Foreign											
Direct Investment)	8.4	7.9	0.0	−1.1	7.5	1.3	21.7	49.4	43.4	−5.5	−5.6
Inflow of Long-Term Funds	12.3	28.9	35.9	33.4	22.4	17.5	15.7	−5.9	−12.7	9.8	17.2
Foreign Direct Investment	11.2	14.2	13.7	10.5	6.4	7.1	6.0	4.6	7.6	15.3	19.4

Official Foreign Loans	1.1	14.7	22.2	22.9	16.0	10.4	9.7	-10.5	-20.3	-5.5	-2.2
Public Sector Savings	28.7	28.4	24.8	29.1	32.3	40.4	20.7	20.7	29.1	31.4	30.7
Public Sector Surplus	19.7	9.8	14.5	24.0	27.5	30.0	6.9	14.4	21.5	23.8	24.6
Transfers to Private Sector	9.0	18.6	10.3	5.1	4.8	10.4	13.8	6.3	7.6	7.6	6.1
Total Flow of Capital Funds	100	100	100	100	100	100	100	100	100	100	100
Uses of Funds:											
Private Investment	56.7	54.4	50.0	48.4	47.6	47.1	46.5	46.9	59.8	57.9	63.4
Accumulation of International Reserves	5.6	-5.4	-2.6	-0.4	1.0	13.3	18.9	12.2	-4.4	10.1	13.1
Unidentified Private Payments Abroad	3.4	6.9	2.6	4.4	8.2	-2.1	-4.6	10.1	10.7	-1.5	-7.3
Public Investment	34.3	44.1	50.0	47.6	43.2	41.7	39.2	30.8	33.9	33.5	30.8

Source: Bank Negara Malaysia.

Figure 9.1
Flow of Capital Funds, 1980 (RM Billion)

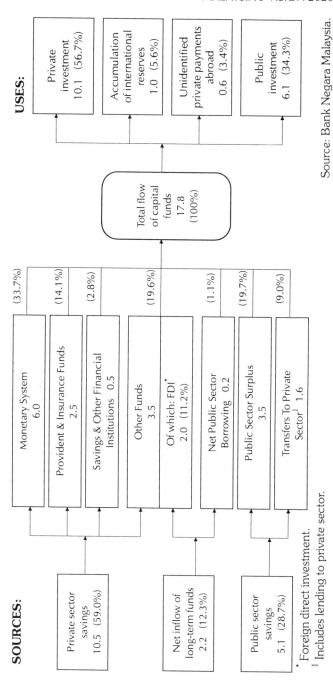

Source: Bank Negara Malaysia.

* Foreign direct investment.
[1] Includes lending to private sector.

Figure 9.2
Flow of Capital Funds, 1981-1985 (RM Billion)

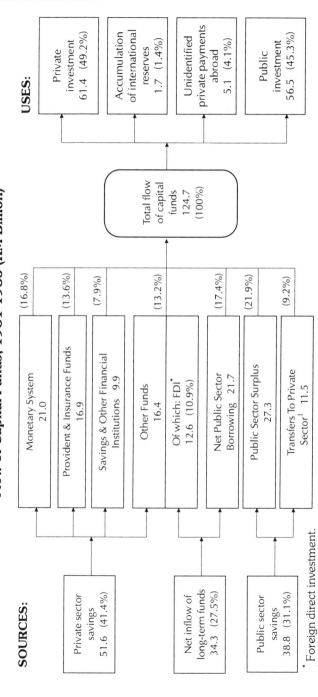

USES:

Private investment 61.4 (49.2%)

Accumulation of international reserves 1.7 (1.4%)

Unidentified private payments abroad 5.1 (4.1%)

Public investment 56.5 (45.3%)

Total flow of capital funds 124.7 (100%)

Monetary System 21.0 (16.8%)

Provident & Insurance Funds 16.9 (13.6%)

Savings & Other Financial Institutions 9.9 (7.9%)

Other Funds 16.4 (13.2%)

Of which: FDI* 12.6 (10.9%)

Net Public Sector Borrowing 21.7 (17.4%)

Public Sector Surplus 27.3 (21.9%)

Transfers To Private Sector[1] 11.5 (9.2%)

SOURCES:

Private sector savings 51.6 (41.4%)

Net inflow of long-term funds 34.3 (27.5%)

Public sector savings 38.8 (31.1%)

* Foreign direct investment.
[1] Includes lending to private sector.

Figure 9.3
Flow of Capital Funds, 1986-1990 (RM Billion)

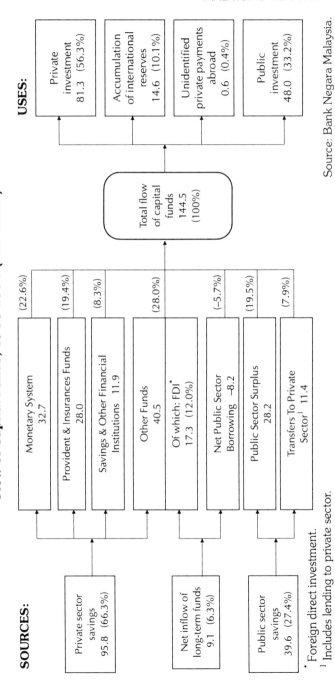

Source: Bank Negara Malaysia.

* Foreign direct investment.
[1] Includes lending to private sector.

Figure 9.4
Flow of Capital Funds, 1990 (RM Billion)

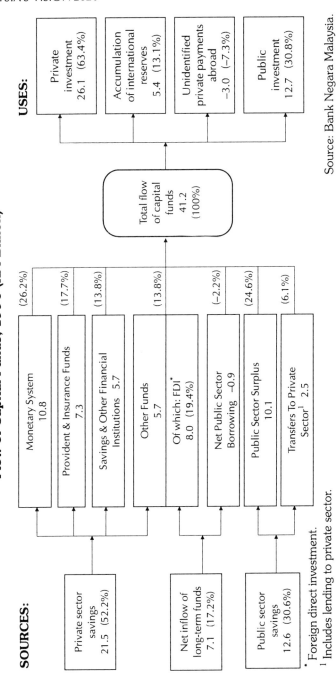

Source: Bank Negara Malaysia.

* Foreign direct investment.
[1] Includes lending to private sector.

invested during the 1976–1980 period. Since then, the Government had actively promoted and encouraged foreign investment into the country. As a result, the real inflows had since increased to RM16.6 billion during the 1986–1990 period (see Table 9.12).

Fifth, reflecting the substantial prepayments, the external reserves of Bank Negara Malaysia, the central bank, declined by RM1.1 billion in 1988 despite a strong trade and current payments position. The reserves had since picked up significantly to increase by RM5.4 billion in 1990, following the sustained buoyant economic performance.

Sixth, in 1980, the banking system mobilized close to one-half of private savings. This share had fallen to nearly 40 per cent during the period of 1981–1985. By 1988, it fell further to about 20 per cent, reflecting the steady growth of the capital market. Capital market institutions, including the unit trusts, accounted for about one-half of private savings in 1988 (28 per cent in 1980). However, with the rise in interest rates, the share of private savings mobilized by the banking system had since increased to more than 50 per cent during the 1989–1990 period.

Tables 9.13 and 9.14 show the sources and uses of funds within the financial system. They attempt to highlight the major sources of funds, as represented by the range of financial instruments such as currency, deposits, loans and provident and pension claims, etc., issued to the surplus units of the economy. At the same time, they also indicate the direction in which funds were used by the financial system, namely, the assets which the institutions hold, in terms of the primary debt and securities of deficit units, as well as the financial instruments of the institutions within the system.

During the 1980s, the major sources of new funds of the financial system continued to be derived from the various forms of deposits and from contractual savings. Of the total new resources of RM246.3 billion raised during the period 1981–1990, deposits mobilized accounted for 43.4 per cent or RM106.9 billion, while contractual savings with the life assurance and provident funds represented about one-fifth of the new resources

(RM48.1 billion). The balance came from increases in capital and reserves and other liabilities. The new resources mobilized were channelled back to the public and private sectors mainly in the form of loans and advances, which accounted for about 43.5 per cent or RM107.1 billion. The other major uses of the new resources were investment in Government securities, including Treasury bills (17.4 per cent or RM42.9 billion), placements within the system (16.7 per cent or RM41 billion), investments in gold and foreign exchange reserves by the central bank (5 per cent or RM12.4 billion) and funding for the corporate sector through the investment in stocks and shares (8.4 per cent or RM20.7 billion).

Table 9.12
Malaysia:
Direct Foreign Investment

Period	Corporate	Banks	Net	Corporate	Net
	RM Million			% of GNP	+
1961–65	1,000	57	1,057	2.7	2.8
1966–70	925	176	1,101	1.8	2.1
1971–75	3,259	339	3,598	3.7	4.1
1976–80	6,414	−2,406	4,008	3.4	2.1
1981–85	12,697	742	13,439	3.9	4.1
1986–90	16,579	−2,203	14,376	3.8	3.3
1986	1,262	−47	1,215	1.9	1.8
1987	1,065	−2,491	−1,426	1.4	−1.9
1988	1,884	−2,914	−1,030	2.2	−1.2
1989	4,518	1,635	6,153	4.7	6.4
1990	7,850	1,614	9,464	7.1	8.6

Table 9.13

Sources and Uses of Funds of the Financial System

	1980	1981–85	Annual Change					
			1986	1987	1988	1989	1990
			RM Billion				
SOURCES:							
Capital and Reserves	0.5	10.2	1.6	0.5	1.0	1.0	3.1
Currency	0.7	1.7	0.4	0.8	1.1	0.9	1.1
Demand Deposits	0.8	3.9	–0.6	1.4	1.5	2.5	6.3
Other Deposits	6.6	40.9	5.1	2.5	4.9	22.3	15.9
Borrowings	0.6	2.2	0.4	0.7	1.0	0.6	0.8
Funds from Other Financial Institutions	1.0	6.9	–	–0.4	–	–0.2	5.8
Life Assurance and Provident Funds	2.5	16.8	4.2	5.2	5.1	5.9	7.3
Other Liabilities	2.3	12.2	5.6	6.6	8.3	12.1	8.1
Total	**15.0**	**94.8**	**16.7**	**17.3**	**22.9**	**45.1**	**48.4**

USES:							
Currency	0.2	0.2	–	–	0.2	0.1	0.5
Deposits with Other Financial Institutions	1.7	17.0	2.8	0.7	3.3	11.0	7.3
Bills							
Treasury Bills	–	1.4	0.2	1.0	0.3	–0.5	0.4
Commercial Bills	0.9	3.2	–	–0.2	–	0.5	1.2
Loans and Advances	7.4	42.9	4.7	0.4	9.6	18.9	25.6
Securities							
Malaysian Government Securities	2.2	16.9	3.3	7.2	4.7	5.6	2.3
Corporate Securities	0.5	4.5	1.1	1.5	0.7	5.2	7.4
Gold and Foreign Exchange Reserves	0.9	2.1	3.9	3.1	–1.3	3.3	1.5
Other Assets	1.2	6.6	0.7	3.6	5.4	1.0	2.2

Table 9.14 [a]
Sources of Funds of the Financial System

SOURCES:	1970 RM Mil.	1970 % Share	1975 RM Mil.	1975 % Share	1980 RM Mil.	1980 % Share	1985 RM Mil.	1985 % Share
Capital and reserves	960	8.3	1,771	6.6	3,894	5.3	14,051	8.3
Currency	1,132	9.7	2,425	9.1	5,104	6.9	6,773	4.0
Demand deposits	1,068	9.2	2,198	8.2	5,326	7.2	9,272	5.5
Other deposits	3,984	34.3	10,714	40.2	34,374	46.4	75,288	44.6
Public sector	1,222	10.5	1,662	6.2	6,777	9.1	8,349	4.9
Other financial institutions	292	2.5	1,678	6.3	5,832	7.9	15,709	9.3
Private sector	2,470	21.3	7,374	27.6	21,765	29.4	51,230	30.3
Borrowings	250	2.2	528	2.0	1,668	2.2	3,848	2.3

Domestic	230	2.0	495	1.9	1,649	2.2	3,807	2.3
Foreign	20	0.2	33	0.1	19	0.0	41	0.0
Funds from other financial institutions	679	5.8	1,384	5.2	3,915	5.3	10,864	6.4
Domestic	426	3.7	573	2.1	1,189	1.6	5,182	3.1
Foreign	253	2.2	811	3.0	2,726	3.7	5,682	3.4
Life Assurance and Provident Funds	2,882	24.8	5,388	20.2	12,218	16.5	29,042	17.2
Other Liabilities	667	5.7	2,270	8.5	7,656	10.3	19,817	11.7
Domestic	533	4.6	1,991	7.5	7,128	9.6	19,124	11.3
Foreign	134	1.2	279	1.0	528	0.7	693	0.4
TOTAL	11,622	100.0	26,678	100.0	74,155	100.0	168,955	100.0

Table 9.14 [a]—continued

Sources of Funds of the Financial System

SOURCES:	1987		1988		1989		1990	
	RM Mil.	% Share	RM Mil.	% Share	RM Mil.	% Share	RM Mil.	% Share
Capital and reserves	12,907	6.3	13,934	6.1	14,923	5.5	18,038	5.6
Currency	7,965	3.9	9,031	4.0	9,904	3.6	10,975	3.4
Demand deposits	10,123	5.0	11,623	5.1	14,112	5.2	20,427	6.4
Other deposits	82,995	40.7	87,951	38.8	110,305	40.6	126,181	39.4
Public sector	8,598	4.2	10,381	4.6	9,916	3.6	7,405	2.3
Other financial institutions	25,498	12.5	24,837	11.0	23,741	8.7	29,573	9.2
Private sector	48,899	24.0	52,733	23.3	76,648	28.2	89,203	27.8
Borrowings	4,833	2.4	5,739	2.5	6,320	2.3	7,176	2.2

	Value	%	Value	%	Value	%	Value	%
Domestic	4,494	2.2	5,484	2.4	6,127	2.3	6,733	2.1
Foreign	339	0.2	255	0.1	193	0.1	443	0.1
Funds from other financial institutions	10,572	5.2	10,635	4.7	10,458	3.8	16,275	5.1
Domestic	6,000	2.9	5,991	2.6	5,024	1.8	9,072	2.8
Foreign	4,572	2.2	4,644	2.0	5,434	2.0	7,203	2.2
Life Assurance and Provident Funds	42,024	20.6	47,101	20.8	53,037	19.5	60,336	18.8
Other Liabilities	32,401	15.9	40,726	18.0	52,878	19.4	61,015	19.0
Domestic	31,822	15.6	40,344	17.8	52,468	19.3	60,745	19.0
Foreign	579	0.3	382	0.2	410	0.2	270	0.1
TOTAL	203,820	100.0	226,740	100.0	271,937	100.0	320,423	100.0

Source: Bank Negara Malaysia.

Table 9.14 [b]—continued
Uses of Funds of the Financial System

USES:	1970		1975		1980		1985	
	RM Mil.	% Share	RM Mil.	% Share	RM Mil.	% Share	RM Mil.	% Share
Currency	97	0.8	155	0.6	420	0.6	598	0.4
Deposits with other								
financial institutions	972	8.4	2,334	8.7	6,910	9.3	23,872	14.1
Domestic	783	6.7	2,117	7.9	5,682	7.7	22,147	13.1
Foreign	189	1.6	217	0.8	1,228	1.7	1,725	1.0
Bills	663	5.7	1,372	5.1	3,790	5.1	8,383	5.0
Treasury	545	4.7	1,007	3.8	1,416	1.9	2,777	1.6
Commercial	118	1.0	365	1.4	2,374	3.2	5,606	3.3
Loans and Advances	3,437	29.6	9,296	34.8	29,892	40.3	72,786	43.1
Public sector	18	0.2	287	1.1	796	1.1	1,136	0.7

Other financial institutions	425	3.7	858	3.2	938	1.3	5,525	3.3
Private sector	2,790	24.0	7,691	28.8	27,485	37.1	66,088	39.1
Foreign	204	1.8	460	1.7	673	0.9	37	0.0
Securities	3,641	31.3	7,887	29.6	17,991	24.3	39,451	23.4
M'sian Government	3,091	26.6	6,896	25.8	15,959	21.5	32,904	19.5
Foreign Government	195	1.7	126	0.5	31	0.0	44	0.0
Corporate	355	3.1	865	3.2	2,001	2.7	6,503	3.8
Gold and foreign exchange reserve	2,229	19.2	3,989	15.0	9,709	13.1	11,773	7.0
Other assets	583	5.0	1,645	6.2	5,443	7.3	12,092	7.2
Domestic	561	4.8	1,596	6.0	4,788	6.5	10,616	6.3
Foreign	22	0.2	49	0.2	655	0.9	1,476	0.9
TOTAL	11,622	100.0	26,678	100.0	74,155	100.0	168,955	100.0

Table 9.14 [b]—continued
Uses of Funds of the Financial System

USES:	1987 RM Mil.	1987 % Share	1988 RM Mil.	1988 % Share	1989 RM Mil.	1989 % Share	1990 RM Mil.	1990 % Share
Currency	739	0.4	882	0.4	929	0.3	1,409	0.4
Deposits with other								
financial institutions	26,382	12.9	29,696	13.1	40,673	15.0	47,943	15.0
Domestic	23,281	11.4	24,639	10.9	35,382	13.0	42,936	13.4
Foreign	3,101	1.5	5,057	2.2	5,291	1.9	5,007	1.6
Bills	4,782	2.3	5,090	2.2	5,121	1.9	6,768	2.1
Treasury	3,942	1.9	4,281	1.9	3,784	1.4	4,217	1.3
Commercial	840	0.4	809	0.4	1,337	0.5	2,550	0.8
Loans and Advances	82,832	40.6	92,432	40.8	111,335	40.9	136,975	42.7
Public sector	1,142	0.6	748	0.3	2,040	0.8	2,325	0.7
Other financial								

institutions								
Private sector	5,886	2.9	5,982	2.6	3,247	1.2	1,845	0.6
Foreign	75,769	37.2	85,685	37.8	104,927	38.6	131,795	41.1
Securities	35	0.0	17	0.0	1,121	0.4	1,010	0.3
M'sian Government	52,688	25.9	58,153	25.6	69,010	25.4	78,718	24.6
Foreign Government	43,383	21.3	48,101	21.2	53,749	19.8	56,032	17.5
Corporate	3	0.0	27	0.0	2	0.0	2	0.0
Gold and foreign	9,302	4.6	10,025	4.4	15,259	5.6	22,684	7.1
exchange reserve								
Other assets	18,568	9.1	17,274	7.6	20,619	7.6	22,135	6.9
Domestic	17,829	8.7	23,213	10.2	24,250	8.9	26,475	8.3
Foreign	15,744	7.7	20,858	9.2	21,689	8.0	23,853	7.4
TOTAL	2,085	1.0	2,355	1.0	2,561	0.9	2,622	0.8
	203,820	100.0	226,740	100.0	271,937	100.0	320,423	100.0

Source: Bank Negara Malaysia.

Table 9.15

Public and Private Savings, 1961–1990

	1961–1965	1966–1970	1971–1975	1976–1980	1981–1985	1986–1990
RM Billion						
Public Savings	0.6	0.6	2.2	14.7	38.8	39.6
Private Savings	6.2	8.8	16.4	43.0	51.6	96.0
GNS	**6.8**	**9.4**	**18.6**	**57.7**	**90.4**	**135.6**
% Share						
Public Savings	8.8	6.4	11.8	25.5	42.9	29.2
Private Savings	91.2	93.6	88.2	74.5	57.1	70.8
% of GNP						
Public Savings	1.5	1.1	2.5	7.7	11.7	8.8
Private Savings	16.3	17.1	18.6	22.6	15.8	22.4
GNS	**17.8**	**18.2**	**21.1**	**30.3**	**27.5**	**31.2**

Source: Bank Negara Malaysia.

Resources of the financial system rose at an average annual rate of 12.6 per cent in the 1960s and accelerated to 20.4 per cent in the 1970s to a total of RM74.2 billion at the end of 1980. However, this pace of growth slackened to 15.5 per cent per annum during the period 1981–1987, reflecting mainly the slow-down in the growth of deposits from an average annual rate of 21.6 per cent to 13 per cent. However, the slowdown in the growth of total resources was moderated to some extent by the continuing growth in the contributions to the life assurance and provident funds. Given the lower growth of total resources, loans extended by the financial system also moderated, from 24.1 per cent in the 1970s to 15.7 per cent during the 1981–1987 period. Faced with ample liquidity, a significant part of these funds were invested in the securities of both the Government and the corporate sector. However, since 1988, growth of deposits and loans of the financial system had started to pick up to 16.3 per cent and 18.3 per cent per annum respectively on the average during the 1988–1990 period. This was basically due to four consecutive years of sustained buoyant economic growth and rising incomes. As a result, the flow of resources increased further to RM38.9 billion annually during this period.

Private Savings and Investment

In Malaysia, the data on savings at the subsectoral level are scan-ty. A breakdown of the gross national savings (GNS) into public and private savings (see Table 9.15) showed that since peaking in 1979, private savings (as a percentage of GNP) has been on a sig-nificant downward trend in the first half of the 1980s. In 1987, it picked up again to a high of 27.1 per cent of GNP, reflecting bet-ter terms of trade (see Table 9.16), but it has since moved down to 19.6 per cent of GNP by the end of 1990. The declining trend in private savings has been a matter of concern for public policy for rather obvious reasons.

Table 9.16
International Terms of Trade

	61–65	66–70	71–75	76–80	81–85	1987	86–90
	Average Annual % Change						
Exports	−3.6	−1.5	7.2	13.8	−0.3	10.1	1.9
Imports	−1.4	0.8	10.1	7.4	0.9	1.6	3.1
TOT*	−2.2	−2.3	−2.9	6.4	−1.2	8.4	−1.3

* Terms of Trade
Source: Department of Statistics.

It is worth noting that a significant part of private savings was held in the form of bank deposits, mainly with the three major deposit taking institutions, or MDTIs, that is, the commercial banks, finance companies and merchant banks (see Table 9.17). Indeed, a substantial part of GNS was held as deposits and in provident, pension and insurance funds. Savings in capital market instruments (especially in equities) are a rather recent phenomenon, becoming increasingly important only since the late 1970s. More recent are investments in private sector securities.

A sectoral breakdown of private savings into household and corporate savings indicated that, as a share of total private savings, household savings had increased significantly over the 1981–1988 period. During this period, the absolute fall in private savings reflected mainly the recession and the consequent deflation of incomes (GNP fell absolutely for the first time ever in 1985) as well as the decline in corporate savings, which was affected by falling profits. The savings of the corporate sector fell from RM3.1 billion in 1980 to dissavings of as much as RM5.5 billion in 1985 (see Table 9.18). Household savings had continued to increase until 1986 (that is, from RM7.4 billion in 1980 to RM15.9 billion in 1986), reflecting continuing high forced savings and income levels (of employees) that were sticky downwards. Since 1987, household savings had declined to

RM13.5 billion and subsequently stabilized at around RM13 to 15 billion level, accounting for about two-thirds of private savings. In contrast, the corporate sector had turned around from dissavings totalling on the average RM3.8 billion annually over the 1985–1986 period to register savings of RM6.7 billion annually on the average over the 1987–1990 period.

The corporate savings shown in Table 9.18 were derived after deducting estimates of household savings from total private sector savings. However, corporate savings can also be compiled as the aggregate of post-tax retained earnings plus depreciation of private domestic corporations. Estimates of these factors are available (with limitations) from the reports of the Financial Survey of Limited Companies conducted annually by the Department of Statistics. From the gross profit data reported in the survey, adjustments would need to be made to deduct direct corporate income taxes and dividends paid to domestic residents before adding back depreciation to get the estimate of corporate savings. The estimate for corporate savings would still have to be adjusted to exclude the operational surplus of the non-financial public enterprises (which are regarded in the national accounts as part of public savings) to get the estimate of private corporate savings. Because of definition, coverage and timing problems, the derived estimates of private corporate savings using this methodology, however, were somewhat (significantly, at times) lower compared with the estimates shown on Table 9.18. The differences are not easy to reconcile.

Consistent with the behaviour of private savings until the mid-1980s, gross investment in Malaysia had softened considerably in 1984, especially private investment outlays (which fell to as low as 15 per cent of GNP in 1987, before picking up again to 23.3 per cent in 1990). Nevertheless, despite the "big push"[2] in

---

[2]   "Big Push" refers to the Keynesian strategy of accelerating growth and modernization by pressing ahead with industrial, social and infrastructural investments despite falling revenues as a result of the recession and falling commodity prices.

Table 9.17

Forms of Gross Private Savings

	1961–65	1966–70	1971–75	1976–80	1981–85	1986–90
Gross Private Savings in RM Billion	5.7	7.7	16.4	42.9	51.6	96.0
In deposits	2.5	3.4	6.4	15.8	28.5	35.0
(with MDTIs)	(1.7)	(2.5)	(5.4)	(12.6)	(24.9)	(31.3)
In provident pension						
and insurance funds	0.5	0.8	2.4	6.5	18.4	28.5
In other forms	2.7	3.5	7.6	20.6	4.7	32.5
As % of GPS						
In deposits	43.9	44.2	39.0	36.8	55.2	36.5
(with MDTIs)	(29.8)	(32.5)	(32.9)	(29.4)	(48.3)	(32.6)
In provident pension						
and insurance funds	8.8	10.4	14.6	15.2	35.7	29.7
In other forms	47.3	45.4	46.4	48.0	9.1	33.8

Source: Bank Negara Malaysia.

Table 9.18

Components of Gross Private Savings

| | | | | | | RM Billion | | | | |
	1980	1983	1985	1986	1987	1988	1989	1990
Gross Private Savings	10.5	10.3	10.1	13.8	20.2	21.0	19.3	21.6
Corporations (I)	3.1	-0.4	-5.5	-2.1	6.7	6.4	6.6	7.0
Households (II)	7.4	10.7	15.6	15.9	13.5	14.6	12.7	14.6
Of which Deposits (D) in:								
Banking System (III)	2.5	3.3	3.5	3.2	1.9	2.0	5.7	7.3
Provident Funds (IV)	1.9	3.7	4.6	4.6	5.0	5.3	6.2	7.3
Currency (V)	0.6	0.3	0.2	0.4	0.8	1.0	0.8	0.9
D = III+IV+V	5.0	7.3	8.3	8.2	7.7	8.3	12.7	15.5
II [as % of GPS]	70.5	103.9	154.5	115.2	66.8	69.5	65.8	67.6
D [as % of II]	67.6	68.2	53.2	51.6	57.0	56.8	100.0	106.2

the early 1980s, the impact on Malaysia's growth as a result of the high rate of capital accumulation had been rather modest. As a result, the capital intensity of production in Malaysia had been rising since 1971. The incremental capital output ratio, ICOR,[3] in 1984 was about 60 per cent higher (see Table 9.19) than in the Second and Third Malaysia Plans periods (1971–1980). The rising ICOR reflected sharp increases in investment in social capital and in lumpy industrial projects (with long gestation periods) by the public sector, and a concentration in construction and property-related projects. Since 1986, the ICOR had been reduced substantially to 3.4 in the 1988–1990 period, reflecting the changing pattern of private investment towards more productive investments in mining and broad-based manufacturing.

Table 9.19
Public and Private Investment

ICOR	1971–75	1976–80	1981–85	1986–90
	In Constant Prices			
	3.1	3.1	7.2	7.1
% Change				
Private Investment	3.5	12.9	–0.7	14.6
(excluding oil & gas)	(1.1)	(8.6)	(1.6)	(15.2)
Public Investment	16.0	12.6	12.7	2.9
(including oil & gas)	(18.5)	(17.7)	(8.2)	(4.2)

On private investment, the following salient points are worth noting. First, reflecting the drive to push private activity to lead growth arising from cutbacks in public spending since 1983, private investment had recovered despite its sluggishness in 1985–1986. In 1981, private investment accounted for 55 per cent of GDI. This share fell to 54.2 per cent in 1986, but had since increased significantly to 66.4 per cent in 1990.

---

[3] ICOR is calculated by dividing total investment by the change in gross domestic product.

Second, the composition of GDI is rather revealing; in 1985, about 50 per cent (worth RM11.5 billion) was in building and construction. For the period of 1981–1985, the average share was 48 per cent. This trend also helps to explain the high ICOR.

Third, in the first-half of the 1980s, there had been a growing predominance within GDI in the utilities and services (mainly office buildings and housing) sectors – from a combined share of 50 per cent in 1981 to 52 per cent in 1985. GDI in manufacturing and mining had tended to decline until 1987/1988.

Fourth, there had been a preponderance of new private investment in the services sector, mainly in building and construction in the period 1981–1985 (see Table 9.20). By 1988, new private investment in agriculture and utilities had continued to remain moderate, while that in mining and manufacturing had increased significantly.

The increase in investments in the mining and manufacturing sectors reflected the success of the Government's policy to orientate its investment strategy to foster the growth of private initiative and entrepreneurship, and to enlarge the private sector's productive base in the manufacturing and mining sectors.

Fifth, the role of the private sector in the key areas of investment diminished in the 1981–1985 period. Reflecting this, the size and share of new private investment in the major areas of mining and manufacturing declined (see Table 9.21). By 1990, the trend for the manufacturing sector had reversed, as can be seen from the significant rise in private investments in manufacturing.

Financing Needs and Capital Market Development under the Sixth Malaysia Plan

Under the Sixth Malaysia Plan (1991–1995), the Malaysian economy is expected to continue to remain robust, with an average annual growth of 7.5 per cent. To achieve this targeted rate of growth, over RM155 billion in real investment outlays (RM107 billion for the private sector and RM48 billion for the public sector) will be required during the Sixth Malaysia Plan

Table 9.20
Flow of Private Investment by Sectors

Sector	1981	1983	1984	1985	1986	1987	1988	1989	1990
				Nominal, RM Billion					
Agriculture	0.5	0.8	0.7	0.8	0.8	0.8	1.1	1.1	1.8
Mining	2.2	1.6	1.0	1.0	0.9	0.9	1.4	2.6	3.9
Manufacturing	3.3	1.6	2.5	4.1	3.1	4.8	3.2	3.9	8.1
Construction	1.4	1.8	2.0	1.8	1.5	1.4	3.5	4.1	3.7
Utilities	1.7	1.1	1.5	1.7	1.4	0.8	1.9	3.9	2.5
Services	2.4	4.9	5.6	2.9	2.6	2.4	2.6	4.0	6.2
Total	11.5	11.8	13.3	12.3	10.3	11.1	13.7	19.6	26.2

Table 9.21

Share of Private Investment in Gross Domestic Investment by Sectors

Sector	1981		1985		1990	
	RM Billion	% of GDI* in Each Sector	RM Billion	% of GDI* in Each Sector	RM Billion	% of GDI* in Each Sector
Agriculture	0.5	28	0.8	35	1.8	40
Mining	2.2	67	1.0	60	3.9	55
Manufacturing	3.3	87	4.1	60	8.1	91
Construction	1.4	90	1.8	80	3.7	85
Utilities	1.7	41	1.7	45	2.5	60
Services	2.4	39	2.9	49	6.2	65
Total	11.5	55	12.3	53	26.2	66

* GDI—Gross Domestic Investment

Source: Bank Negara Malaysia.

Table 9.22
Savings-Investment Gap, 1985–1995

Sector	1985	1990	% of GNP 1995	Cumulative Fifth M'sia Plan	Cumulative Sixth M'sia Plan
Public Sector					
Savings	13.6	11.4	7.5	9.1	8.9
Investment	13.9	11.6	9.5	11.1	10.6
Resource Gap	–0.3	–0.2	–2.0	–2.0	–1.7
Private Sector					
Savings	14.0	18.9	28.4	21.9	25.2
Investment	15.8	23.5	25.3	18.7	24.3
Resource Gap	–1.8	–4.6	3.1	3.2	0.9
Total					
Savings	27.6	30.3	35.9	31.0	34.1
Investment	29.7	35.1	34.8	29.8	34.9
Resource Gap	–2.1	–4.8	1.1	1.2	–0.8

Source: Sixth Malaysia Plan, 1991–1995.

period. This large amount of investment would have to be financed largely from domestic savings, with prudent recourse to foreign sources of financing. Although Malaysia's GNS is projected to increase from 31 per cent of GNP during the Fifth Malaysia Plan to 34.1 per cent of GNP over the Sixth Malaysia Plan, gross investment is expected to expand to 34.9 per cent, thus leaving a resource gap of 0.8 per cent of GNP, as shown in Table 9.22.

As in the past, the public sector resource balance will continue to be in deficit during the Sixth Malaysia Plan, with a modest gap of 1.7 per cent of GNP. Although the private sector resource balance will show a surplus of 0.9 per cent of GNP (and 3.2 per cent by 1995), this will not be sufficient to finance the savings-investment gap of the public sector. This gap will have to be met by inflows of foreign capital, which is likely to be forthcoming. However, there is always an inherent "danger", more a source of future instability, in relying unduly on overseas financing of economic development, especially in an international environment of continuing uncertainty, the prospective burden of external debt servicing and the unreliability of foreign capital in the face of difficult economic conditions.

The importance of promoting high private savings, especially household savings, in order to be in a position to effectively finance sustained rapid growth with monetary stability cannot be over-emphasized. This can be seen from Table 9.23, which shows the changing pattern of intersectoral flows among the public, foreign, corporate and household sectors. From this table, it is clear that, as in many East Asian countries, households in Malaysia provide the "anchor" to sustain the high national savings rate. Indeed, the household sector has been a consistent net lender to both the corporate and public sectors throughout the 1980s. This net lending rose from 6.7 per cent of GNP in 1981 to a high of 18.9 per cent of GNP in 1986, before declining to stabilize at 10.2 per cent of GNP in the 1989–1990 period.

On the other hand, the corporate sector is a consistent net dissaver in the country and has been relying on household and

Table 9.23

Intersectoral Flow of Funds

SECTOR	% of GNP										
	1980	1981	1982	1983	1984	1985	1986	1987	1988	1989	1990
Households											
Investment[1]	5.6	4.3	4.3	3.3	3.6	4.8	5.0	3.6	3.2	3.0	3.0
Savings	14.5	11.0	13.8	16.2	21.4	21.7	23.9	18.1	17.0	13.2	13.2
Net Lending	8.9	6.7	9.5	12.9	17.8	16.9	18.9	14.5	13.8	10.2	10.2
Corporations											
Investment	10.2	10.6	9.7	12.5	12.8	8.6	8.3	9.9	12.1	11.6	13.2
Savings	6.0	4.7	1.5	-0.6	-3.5	-7.6	-3.1	9.0	7.5	6.8	6.4
Net Lending	-4.2	-5.9	-8.2	-13.1	-16.3	-16.2	-11.4	-0.9	-4.6	-4.8	-6.8
Public Sector											
Investment	11.8	16.2	19.6	19.9	17.1	13.9	12.7	9.8	10.0	11.4	11.8

Savings	9.9	10.5	9.7	12.2	12.8	13.5	6.6	6.5	8.6	10.7	11.4
Net Lending	-1.9	-5.7	-9.9	-7.7	-4.3	-0.4	-6.1	-3.3	-1.4	-0.7	-0.4
Foreign Sector											
Investment	4.0	5.2	5.5	4.4	2.5	2.4	1.9	1.4	2.2	5.2	7.1
Savings	1.2	10.1	14.1	12.3	5.3	2.1	0.5	-8.9	-5.6	0.5	4.1
Net Lending	-2.8	4.9	8.6	7.9	2.8	-0.3	-1.4	-10.3	-7.8	-4.7	-3.0
Total											
Investment	31.6	36.3	39.1	40.1	36.0	29.7	27.9	24.7	27.5	31.2	35.1
Domestic Savings	30.4	26.2	25.0	27.8	30.7	27.6	27.4	33.6	33.1	30.7	31.0
Foreign Savings	1.2	10.1	14.1	12.3	5.3	2.1	0.5	-8.9	-5.6	0.5	4.1

[1] For the household sector, investment is assumed to be equal to the value of residential construction for the year.

Source: Bank Negara Malaysia.

foreign savings (inflows of foreign direct investment in particular) to fund its investment needs. The corporate sector relied on as much as 16.3 per cent of GNP to fund its investment needs in the 1984–1985 period, when the corporate sector as a whole experienced dissavings during this period. However, as the economy recovered from the severe recession in the mid-1980s, corporate savings began to improve and the net lending ratio declined to an average of 4.3 per cent of GNP during the period of 1987–1990.

Since consistently large flows of household savings are crucial in the financing of private investment in Malaysia, stable growth requires that this key source of savings be actively promoted to ensure that they will indeed be forthcoming. As already indicated in Table 9.18, a significant part of household savings takes the form of savings with the major deposit-taking institutions (MDTIs), contributions to the EPF, and lately, investment in equities. While the MDTIs will remain aggressive in, at least, maintaining their market share, the dynamism of the EPF in funding private investment outlays offers a new challenge, since traditionally, the EPF has been acting merely as a non-inflationary source of reliable finance for the Government. Household savings through the EPF have consistently accounted for about 4 to 5 per cent of GNP during the 1981–1990 period. On the other hand, the residual "voluntary" part of private sector savings had been on a declining trend, reflecting to some extent rising consumption.

Since peaking at 22.6 per cent of GNP in 1979, "voluntary" private sector savings had declined to as low as 9 per cent of GNP in 1985 due to the prolonged global recession. Although it had since recovered to 21.9 per cent of GNP in 1987, the ratio had started to decline again during the subsequent years to 14.5 per cent of GNP in 1990.

Under the Sixth Malaysia Plan, the role of the public sector will be reduced gradually to allow the private sector to continue to lead in stimulating economic expansion. Concomitantly, the overall deficit of the Federal Government is estimated to decline from 6.5 per cent of GNP during the Fifth Malaysia Plan period

(1986–1990) to 5.5 per cent in the Sixth Malaysia Plan (RM44.6 billion). This deficit will be financed mainly from domestic borrowing, particularly from the EPF, and, rather insignificantly, from foreign borrowing. Since the Government will continue to downsize its operations, the private sector has been entrusted with a much bigger role to play in generating growth in the years ahead. To achieve the targeted growth of 7.5 per cent per annum, an estimated RM107 billion in real private investment outlays will be required during the Sixth Malaysia Plan period. In order to promote the private sector as the main engine of growth, the financial system will have the job to fund these private sector investments, together with foreign direct investments.

How was the RM57 billion of real private investment (RM80 billion in nominal terms) financed under the Fifth Malaysia Plan (1986–1990)? Data on this are not available as of this moment. As such, a complete picture cannot be put together. However, we can get a "feel" of what could have happened from the results of recent sample Surveys of Private Investment in Malaysia conducted by Bank Negara Malaysia. But, these provide no more than a likely "scenario" regarding financing since the survey results were rather aggregative in nature. These surveys covered only 377 firms and they could provide, at best, fragmented information of the whole since the methods of financing could differ depending on whether the firms were: big or small; domestic, foreign or joint-ventures; new or matured; engaged in "what" type of activity (surely, the financing of oil exploration would differ vastly from plantation agriculture); and so on. That is why the financing of the RM107 billion in real private investment outlays has not been spelt out in the Sixth Malaysia Plan. As in previous plans, the financial markets are expected to "sort this out". Nevertheless, the Plan clearly stated that the GNS would have to rise to 36 per cent by 1995, or an average of 34.1 per cent over the 1991–1995 period. Furthermore, the Bank Negara Malaysia survey data do indicate, and may even provide, a broad indication of future financing trends, as shown in Table 9.24. For the Fifth Malaysia Plan period (1986–1990), overall, the firms surveyed funded 56 per cent of their investments from their own internally-generated funds, comprising depreciation allowances, retained profits, reserves and provisions; among these firms, such financing could range from one-half to two-thirds. Moreover, it would appear that this source of funding had declined over time – indeed, could well fall below 50 per cent over the Sixth Malaysia Plan period. Related to this is the next significant source – inter-company loans; for Malaysian firms, this would mean borrowings within the group; for foreign direct investments (FDIs) firms, this usually meant borrowing from head office, subsidiaries or associates abroad. This source accounted for 18 per cent, with a range of 12 to 29 per cent. Next, comes bank financing – 12.5 per cent with a range of 10 to 14 per cent. This is not surprising considering that banks continue to focus on working capital financing, although project financing should assume increasing importance over the Sixth Malaysia Plan period. Borrowing from abroad would not be all that significant – 6.2 per cent, ranging from as low as 1 per cent to a high of 17 per cent. Access to the capital market, mainly through the issue of common stock, accounted for 4.4 per cent, ranging from 1 to 8 per cent. This source could be expected to be much more important under the Sixth Malaysia Plan. The remainder came from the sale of assets – a rather insignificant portion of 2.3 per cent.

Using Bank Negara Malaysia data (see Table 9.24), it would appear that private investment of some RM80 billion under the Fifth Malaysia Plan could have been financed as shown in Table 9.25.

For the Sixth Malaysia Plan, Bank Negara Malaysia data provide the basis for two possible scenarios of financing: one, using the 1990 position as a reasonable approximation, and the other, adjusting for a reduced role for internally-generated funds (which are already falling), made-up to some extent by higher inter-company loans (because of much larger projects involving direct foreign investments) and higher recourse to bank financing, with access to the capital market as residual, as shown in Table 9.26.

Table 9.24

Bank Negara Malaysia's Survey of Private Investment in Malaysia: Financing of Capital Expenditure, 1986–1990[1]

Sources of financing	1986	1987	1988	1989	1990[1]	1986–1990
	% of Total Private Investment					
Internally-generated funds[2]	52.0	64.2	53.3	65.8	50.1	56.4
Share issue or Share premium	1.6	6.1	1.3	2.3	8.3	4.4
Proceeds from the sale of property or investment	5.8	1.8	0.9	1.3	2.2	2.3
Inter-company loans	13.5	12.1	28.8	15.8	19.2	18.2
Loans from financial institutions	27.1	15.8	15.7	14.8	20.2	18.7
In Malaysia	10.3	10.5	11.0	13.9	14.3	12.5
Abroad	16.8	5.3	4.7	0.9	5.9	6.2
Total	100.0	100.0	100.0	100.0	100.0	100.0

[1] Forecast.
[2] Comprising utilization of depreciation charges, retained profits, reserves and provisions.
Source: Bank Negara Malaysia.

Table 9.25
Financing of Private Investment under
the Fifth Malaysia Plan, 1986–1990

Sources of financing	% Share	RM Billion
Internally-generated funds	56.4	45
Share issue or premium	4.4	3
Proceeds of sale of property or investment	2.3	2
Inter-company loans	18.2	15
Loans from private institutions	18.7	15
In Malaysia	**12.5**	**10**
Abroad	**6.2**	**5**
Total	100.0	80

Source: Bank Negara Malaysia.

Table 9.26
Two Possible Scenarios of Financing

Scenario	% Share		RM Bil.	+
	I	II	I	II
Internally-generated funds	50	40	95	76
Inter-company loans	19	20	36	38
Bank financing:	21	24	40	46
Domestic	**15**	**17**	**29**	**33**
Foreign	**6**	**7**	**11**	**13**
Access to capital market	8	16	19	30
Sales of investment, etc.	2			
Total	100	100	190	190

Source: Bank Negara Malaysia.

In order to realize the real private investment outlays of about RM107 billion over the 1991–1995 period, actual spending on capital formation in the private sector in nominal terms would be significantly larger – about RM190 billion over the five-year period compared to RM80 billion in 1986–1990. This implies that, possibly, at least RM19 billion (10 per cent of the total) would need to be tapped from the capital market. This amount could be as much as RM30 billion (16 per cent) in the event that the availability of internally generated funds is significantly reduced (40 per cent of total instead of 50 per cent as in 1990). This "ball-park" volume of financing from the capital market (RM19 to 30 billion) over the 1991–1995 period is very large, that is, 6 to 10 times that was raised during the period of 1986–1990. Realistically, this target range of financing can only be met through an urgent and significant programme to strengthen, widen, deepen and liberalize the capital market, including the introduction of new instruments and derivative products in the context of well-administered markets that place a premium on the integrity of contracts and on prudential regulation. Funds raised under the Fifth Malaysia Plan through this market are shown in Table 9.27. It should be noted that not all funds raised in the capital market are necessarily used to finance capital formation. Many firms, including the newly-privatized Government enterprises, use the capital market to manage their liabilities more effectively, as well as to raise working capital. Of the RM20 billion raised in the 1986–1990 period, it is estimated that only about RM3.5 billion (or less than 20 per cent of the total) were raised to finance real capital formation under the Fifth Malaysia Plan.

Furthermore, financing through the capital market does have important implications not only on the traditional banking system but also on other institutions which mobilize substantial savings, particularly the Employees Provident Fund (EPF). Under the Sixth Malaysia Plan period, total net investible funds of the EPF have been projected to total RM37.7 billion, based on existing rates of contribution. Assuming that the EPF would invest only 50 per cent of these funds in Malaysian Government securities

(MGS) annually, the excess investible funds would still be sizeable, ranging from RM3 billion to RM4 billion annually over the Sixth Malaysia Plan, as shown in Table 9.28.

Table 9.27
Net Funds Raised in the Capital Market

Sector	1988	1989	1990	1986–90
	RM Million			
Public Sector	**7,534**	**2,459**	**3,798**	**26,204**
Government securities	7,034	2,459	3,898	25,504
Investment certificates	500	–	–100	700
Private Sector	**2,826**	**4,651**	**10,895**	**20,341**
Ordinary shares[1]	967	2,874	9,124	14,609
Cagamas bonds[2]	1,250	1,250	400	3,000
Promissory notes	609	527	1,371	2,732
Total	**10,360**	**7,110**	**14,693**	**46,545**

[1] Includes loan stocks.
[2] Includes MIDF bonds.

Source: Bank Negara Malaysia.

Table 9.28
**Excess Investible Funds of the
Employees Provident Fund**

	1991	1992	1993	1994	1995	Total
	RM Billion					
Net investible funds	6.0	6.7	7.5	8.3	9.2	37.7
MGS	3.0	3.4	3.9	4.7	5.2	20.2
"Others"	3.0	3.3	3.6	3.6	4.0	17.5

Source: Bank Negara Malaysia.

As such, there is an urgent need to find prudent alternative avenues of investment in the private sector for the EPF's "excess" investible funds. In view of this and to further support the development of the corporate securities market, the new Employees Provident Fund Act came into force on June 1, 1991, widening the investment opportunities of the EPF, which had so far been highly concentrated in Malaysian Government securities (MGS). Under the new Act, the EPF will only have to invest 50 per cent of its funds in MGS during any one year, compared with the previous requirement of 70 per cent, thereby enhancing the ability of the EPF to diversify its investment portfolio. This will also imply the availability of new resources (that is, the EPF "excess" funds) to be tapped by the private sector through the capital market. It should be observed that the effective use of the EPF's surplus investible funds (that is, RM17.5 billion over the period of 1991–1995) in the capital market, in the context of competition, is crucial if the private sector's substantial investments over the Sixth Malaysia Plan period are to find ready access to the broadest possible spectrum of financing at reasonable cost.

To a large extent, the development of the capital market holds the key to assisting the private sector in the financing of its capital formation over the Sixth Malaysia Plan period. Hence, the urgent need to strengthen, deepen and broaden the capital market, especially the corporate securities market, as a reliable source of finance for the private sector. During the Fifth Malaysia Plan period, new funds raised from the capital market for the public and private sectors' development amounted to RM26 billion and RM20 billion respectively (see Table 9.27). However, these amounts will need to increase manifold during the Sixth Malaysia Plan, given that the financing requirements of both the public and private sectors are much larger (RM48 billion and RM107 billion in real terms respectively, compared with RM34 billion and RM57 billion during the Fifth Malaysia Plan), and larger still in nominal terms. The equity market in particular must continue to expand rapidly to meet the needs of investors and savers. This is by far the most popular and liquid market and has rather enormous potential for development. In this regard, efforts are being undertaken to further develop the Kuala Lumpur Stock Exchange (KLSE) into a sophisticated international stock exchange. To meet the demand from an increasingly sophisticated securities industry and to strengthen the supervision of the capital market, the Government is considering the establishment of a single regulatory body in the form of a securities commission to promote and ensure the orderly development of the capital market.

Equally important is the development of the private debt securities or bond market. The term "private debt securities" or PDS describes debt instruments issued by corporations and other non-Government entities. Such debt instruments are basically bonds and commercial papers, although they sometimes tend to have exotic names such as RUFs, NIFs, SNIFs, and Flip Flops. Commercial papers are short-term debt instruments with maturities of less than one year, while bonds are issued on a longer-term basis. The private debt instruments can be issued on the basis of conventional principles as well as on the basis of Islamic principles. They may be convertible into some other type of securities, usually ordinary shares, at the end of the maturity period or earlier. Currently, there is no definition of the term "private debt securities" in any legislation. In comparison, the term "debenture" is defined in the Companies Act, 1965, while the Bills of Exchange Act, 1949 provides for the definition of "bills of exchange" and "promissory notes", which are also debt instruments. There is a need to give a legal definition to the term "private debt securities" to facilitate regulatory functions.

An active private debt securities market is one of the missing links in the Malaysian capital market. An integrated modern securities market should have the following:

1. Capital market securities which encompasses the equities market, the Government bond market (including the bonds of Government agencies), and corporate bond market; and

2. Money market securities which is a market for short-term debt instruments issued by the Government (including its agencies), and corporate commercial papers.

The equities market is already relatively well developed. The market system and infrastructure of the Government bond market and short-term Treasury bills market are already in place. To complement these more established markets, the private debt securities market should be developed to be on par with the others. The need to develop the private debt securities market is rather urgent due to the following factors:

1. The Malaysian Government bond market is already developed, with a group of market makers and a large volume of papers with varied maturities. A principal dealer network for Government securities, comprising 23 principal dealers, is already well in place;

2. The volume of MGS is not expected to increase significantly during the 1990s, since the Government would be downsizing its operations and, therefore, reducing its domestic borrowing requirements in the context of the consolidation of Government activities and the intensification of privatization;

3. The investment needs of the economy will expand and the increasing demand for more avenues for investment in a wide range of financial assets will continue to grow, in the context of a rising level of savings and a high savings rate; and

4. To meet the increased sophistication of Malaysian corporate and institutional borrowers, the financial system would be forced to focus on the provision of sophisticated alternatives to bank borrowing, in all their varied forms and complexities, including different types of bond and equity financing.

The first move to deepen the financial system through the development of the private debt securities market was the establishment of Cagamas Berhad in 1986. Since its establishment, Cagamas Berhad has issued RM2.9 billion of unsecured bearer bonds to finance its purchase of housing loans from the banking industry. The development of the secondary market in Cagamas bonds has been successful. At present, Cagamas bonds are traded through the Scripless Securities Trading System (SSTS), just like Government papers. In December 1988, Bank Negara Malaysia published the *Guidelines on the Issue of Private Debt Securities,* basically to encourage creditworthy corporations to finance their productive activities through the issue of bonds. At the same time, the Minister of Finance granted an exemption from stamp duty for the issue of, and trading in, private debt securities effective from January 1989. Following these moves, a significant increase in issues of private debt securities ensued, as can be seen in Table 9.29.

Table 9.29
Issues of Private Debt Securities

Securities	1988	1989	1990	Total
	RM Million			
Straight bonds	509	337	1,353	2,199
Convertible bonds	–	49	516	565
Commercial papers	100	240	140	480
Islamic papers	–	–	379	379
Total	609	626	2,388	3,623

Source: Bank Negara Malaysia.

Since one of the prerequisites of a viable private debt securities market with many issuers is the ready availability of credit ratings, a credit rating agency called the Rating Agency of Malaysia was incorporated in November 1990. Nevertheless, there is a need to further intensify efforts to develop the private debt securities market, in view of the following factors:

1. Although the volume of debt papers issued since 1989 has increased significantly, the momentum is not sustainable in the longer-term as considerable hurdles to the issuance of and investment in private debt securities still exist;

2. Secondary market trading in the bulk of the private debt securities issued so far cannot as yet be considered as active due to a lack of interested players; and

3. The feasibility of a financial futures market would be limited without a developed underlying securities market. In this regard, eventually the Government will need to establish a financial futures market to further enhance the development of a modern and efficient financial system in the country.

The Way Ahead

Under the Sixth Malaysia Plan (1991–1995) and the Second Outline Perspective Plan (OPP2), 1991–2000, it has been declared as a matter of public policy that the savings-investment gap generated since the end of the Fifth Malaysia Plan (1986–1990) must be bridged by raising gross national savings (GNS) to 36 per cent of GNP and stabilizing gross domestic investments (GDI) at about the 35 per cent level. In this context, despite the continuing process of downsizing Government operations and privatization, the public sector will remain a net user of savings until the year 2000, albeit rather modestly. The net saver will continue to be the private sector, principally the household sector augmented by significant inflows of foreign direct investments since the corporate sector will remain a net user of savings.

For 35 years until the end of 1990, the financial system was systematically built up and efficiently organized under the leadership of Bank Negara Malaysia, to ensure that the GNS were kept high and effectively mobilized to finance dynamic public sector development programmes (which acted as the main stimuli to growth) without inflation. Since the mid-1980s, the private sector has been called upon to take over from the Government as the main engine of growth. Since then, private sector capital outlays (led by substantial inflows of foreign direct investments and mounting domestic private initiatives) indeed have become the driving force in the growth process. Given that the Government no longer needs sizeable flows of long-term financing, the entire financial infrastructure and apparatus will need to be (and indeed, already in the process of being) restructured and reorganized to meet rapidly mounting private sector needs. The banking industry is already consolidating and repositioning itself to meet new challenges, including a new emphasis on liability and asset management, project evaluation and risks management, and venture capital initiatives. The banking system is expected to do more, indeed much more if it is to adequately fulfil its role over the Sixth Malaysia Plan period. Attitudes, approaches, techniques, and instruments will have to be changed, so will the conduct of banking and banking practices. But, the key lies in dynamic capital market development, for it is here that the new demands will be most obvious and intense since traditionally, bank financing was the order of the day.

Given the sheer size of private investment outlays (RM190 billion) to be financed over the Sixth Malaysia Plan period, and indeed until the year 2000, the capital market, in all its facets, needs to be strengthened, broadened, deepened and liberalized (consistent with prudence) as a dependable and non-inflationary source of financing for private sector expansion. In particular, private investors would need to tap this market not only to meet corporate expansion aims (for example, mergers and acquisitions, restructuring and rationalization, etc.) and privatization exercises, but more importantly, to finance – much more than before – their capital expansion programmes and new ventures. On the latter alone, some RM19 billion to RM30 billion are likely to be expended over the Sixth Malaysia Plan period (that is, 6 to 10 times the amount raised for the purpose over the period of 1986–1990). The demands on the capital market will be very, very large indeed. To be successful, it will have to do so in association with the EPF, which will need to be much more dynamic in outlook and in its presence since it will command significant "excess" investible funds for purposeful investment in the broad capital market (even based on existing rates of contribution). In particular, the KLSE's prospects for future growth is rather good – to take full advantage of this potential, its regulatory framework will need to be strengthened (in the prudential sense) and its products and instruments offered diversified; the market also needs to be deepened and made more liquid.

Equally promising, if not more so, is the largely underdeveloped private debt securities or bonds market. It is quite clear that a dynamic and viable private debt securities market needs the following basic characteristics:

1. Genuine issuers are permitted to bring new issues of securities to the market on a timely basis;
2. There is a sufficiently active secondary market to provide liquidity and an indication of market prices to guide prospective new issues; and
3. There is a comprehensive legal and administrative framework in place to provide a conducive environment for encouraging *bona fide* new issues and healthy secondary market activities.

These three basic characteristics are interrelated. Without the liquidity provided by the secondary market, the primary or new issues market would be seriously hampered in its function of helping productive entities acquire new capital. If there is no investors' confidence in the market, due to lack of or inadequate regulatory safeguards, the secondary market would not be able to garner a sufficient number of players to provide the necessary breadth and depth required of a liquid market. On the other hand, the primary market, and consequently the secondary market, can also be stifled if there is over-regulation. Obviously, the key to the future development of the private debt securities market is to have in place a legal and administrative framework that will reflect a fine balancing of the conflicting concerns for investor protection and unbridled market dynamism.

The way ahead is long and difficult, but challenging. The banking system, being the more mature, should have little difficulty in adjusting to and profiting from the new realities and the new competition. The capital market, however, has the more difficult task – certainly the more challenging one. Given effective demand from the private sector and the Government's commitment to move, and move quickly, the administrators of markets should promptly liberalize and expand, while the market makers should respond positively to the call for new business initiatives. Most certainly, the presence of Bank Negara Malaysia will continue to be there, providing the leadership and acting as the catalyst to see to it that viable and responsible markets with integrity do emerge and are efficiently managed.

References

Bank Negara Malaysia, 1959–1991. *Annual Reports, Quarterly Bulletins and Monthly Statistical Bulletins,* Kuala Lumpur: Bank Negara Malaysia.

Bank Negara Malaysia, 1989. *Money and Banking in Malaysia,* Kuala Lumpur: Bank Negara Malaysia.

Lin, See-Yan, 1977. "Malaysia: Money and Monetary Management since Independence, 1957–1976", unpublished Ph.D. Thesis, Harvard University, Cambridge.

Lin, See-Yan, 1986. "Prospects for the Malaysian Economy", Paper presented at A Chatham House Conference on: *Malaysia as a Commercial Partner,* Royal Institute of International Affairs, London, November 1986.

Lin, See-Yan, 1986. "ASEAN: Financial Development and Interdependence" in: Augustine H.H. Tan and Basant Kapur, eds., *Pacific Growth and Financial Interdependence,* Sydney: Allen and Unwin.

Lin, See-Yan, 1987. "Malaysian Capital Market: Current Situation and Prospects" in: K.L. Koh, H.H.M. Chan, P.K. Ho and P.N. Pillai, eds., *Current Developments in International Securities, Commodities and Financial Futures Markets,* London: Butterworths.

Lin, See-Yan, 1988. "The Flow of Funds for National Development: Savings, Investment and the Mobilization of Resources in Malaysia" in: Dahlan Sutalaksana, ed., *Development Issues in the Current International Monetary System,* Singapore: Addison-Wesley.

Lin, See-Yan, 1989. "Malaysia: Developing Securities Markets", Paper presented at the Roundtable on: *Innovations in Foreign Financing: Country and Debt Conversion Funds, Venture Capital Funds and Limited Recourse Financing,* Stratford-upon-Avon, United Kingdom, June 1989.

Lin, See-Yan, 1989. "The Savings and Investment Gap – The Case of Malaysia", Paper presented at the Tokyo Symposium on: *The Present and Future of the Pacific Basin Economy – A Comparison of Asia and Latin America,* Institute of Developing Economies, July 1989.

Lin, See-Yan, 1990. "The Money Market in Malaysia", Paper presented at the Conference on: *The Study of Money Markets in Asia,* Japan Centre for Economic Research, June 1990.

Lin, See-Yan, 1991. "Malaysia: Issues in Capital Market Development", in: K.H. Lee and Shyamala Nagaraj, eds., *The Malaysian Economy Beyond 1990: An International and Domestic Perspective,* Kuala Lumpur: Malaysian Economic Association.

Lin, See-Yan, 1991. "Malaysian Financial Markets", Paper presented at the Third Annual Pacific Basin Finance Conference on: *The Internationalization of Capital Markets in Asia,* Seoul, South Korea, June 1991.

10

Industrial Targets of Vision 2020: The Science and Technology Perspective

Omar Abdul Rahman

The mission statement of Vision 2020 states that, "By the year 2020, Malaysia is to be a united nation, with a confident Malaysian Society, infused by strong moral and ethical values, living in a society that is democratic, liberal and tolerant, caring, economically just and equitable, progressive and prosperous, and in full possession of an economy that is competitive, dynamic, robust and resilient." The 30-year perspective provides a long-term focus for our national development effort. It augments the existing long-term planning of the Outline Perspective Plans and the medium-term five-year development plans.

Vision 2020 has also added a new sense of urgency to the tasks that lie ahead, required a reappraisal of the current situation and a prospective assessment of the needs of the future. It demands a new approach to planning, aligning socio-political objectives to growth targets and bringing into play all the major factors of production. It is without doubt that the demand on S&T in the attainment of the targets will be tremendous. This chapter will outline this demand and discuss an innovative approach for policy planning and the S&T development strategies that can become a major driving force in economic growth.

S&T and the Objectives of Vision 2020

The socio-political objectives of Vision 2020 are listed below:

1. To have sufficient food and shelter with easy access to health care and essentials.
2. To eradicate poverty.
3. To remove the identification of race with major economic functions and to have a fair distribution in the control, management and ownership of the modern economy.
4. To maintain a population growth rate of 2.5 per cent annually.
5. To double our real GDP every ten years between 1990 and 2020.
6. To have a balanced growth in all sectors, namely, industry, agro-forestry, energy, transport, tourism, communications and banking, that is technologically proficient, fully able to adapt, innovate and invent, with a view to always moving to higher levels of technology.

From the S&T perspective four groups of technologies would be required to meet these socio-political objectives. They are:

1. Technologies for satisfying basic needs such as food and shelter.
2. Technologies for a better quality of life such as health care, communication and transport, protection of the environment and stabilization of population size, etc.
3. Technologies for wealth creation and maintenance of industrial competitiveness.
4. Technologies for governance appropriate for the need of government in the high-technology age.

The demand for S&T is therefore wide-ranging. For the purpose of this chapter, however, attention will be given mainly to the S&T perspective for wealth creation. Sustained economic growth will provide the necessary means to meet the overall socio-political objectives of Vision 2020. Furthermore, the need for some group of technologies – for example, basic needs – is no longer critical for Malaysia. Indeed, this particular group, especially in the area of food processing, can be harnessed for wealth creation.

Industrial Targets of Vision 2020

A sustained economic growth is the key to the attainment of the objectives of Vision 2020, requiring an average GDP growth of 7.0 per cent per annum for the next 30 years. For the time-frame of the Second Outline Perspective Plan (OPP2), this growth target is to be met largely from manufacturing and services, as agriculture, the erstwhile mainstay of the economy, is expected to play a smaller role. The GDP share of manufacturing and services are projected at 37.2 per cent and 45.4 per cent respectively in the year 2000 compared to the figures of 27 per cent and 42.3 per cent for 1990, whereas agriculture will decline from 18.7 per cent to 13.7 per cent.

To achieve the above targets the manufacturing sector must grow at an average rate of 10.5 per cent per annum for the period 1991-2000. There is also a high expectation for manufacturing to be the main export earner, rising to 81.3 per cent in 2000 from 27.0 per cent in 1990. Clearly therefore the combined public and private sector effort in the coming years must focus on transforming Malaysia into a truly industrial economy, committed to wider application of S&T in the productive sectors, to strengthening and widening the industrial base and to maintaining competitiveness of our manufactured products in the world market.

Dynamics of Industrial Development and Wealth Creation

An industrial economy is committed not only to change but to an accelerating rate of change through the following processes.

First, generating wealth by the recurrent application of knowledge; knowledge being the source of the constant increases in productivity that underpins and guarantees long-term economic success. Second, persistent change in occupational structure which in turn demands the institutionalization of education and training. And third, accepting recurrent obsolescence of existing institutions, products, processes and jobs.

The source of wealth creation is innovation which is the exploitation of market needs by means of a sequence of technological paradigms. The mechanism of wealth creation is competition. Competition is a discovery process and it is through competition that the key technologies which fix and create customer needs are identified and developed. Competition takes place not only directly between products in the marketplace but also indirectly and perhaps, more importantly, between different technologies.

Therefore, to sustain wealth creation, nations or firms must have the ability to meet increasingly sophisticated consumer requirements by drawing upon the complete array of opportunities provided by knowledge, in particular S&T knowledge. As nations and companies compete, there will be winners and losers. This is because both technological opportunities and market needs are fraught with uncertainty, and the products produced are subject to imitations, or different technologies can meet customer requirements better and more cheaply.

The successful route to sustained wealth creation has always been built upon making use of existing knowledge as the base and making use of that knowledge to launch new technological trajectories in which distinctive competencies are exploited for national comparative advantage.

The Basis of Industrial Competitiveness

Old theories on national competitiveness have become inadequate due to the changing nature of international competition such as the rise of multinational corporations that not only export but compete abroad through offshore subsidiaries. Thus explanation of national competitiveness based on favourable exchange rates, interest rates, government deficits, or on the function of abundant cheap labour, or on possession of bountiful natural resources, or on government intervention or on different management practices are not completely valid. There are ample contradictions to all the rules.

Furthermore, the concept of comparative advantage based on favourable factor endowments of land, labour, natural resources and capital, has to be reexamined. The standard theory assumes that there are no economies of scale, that technologies everywhere are identical, that products are undifferentiated and that the pool of natural factors are fixed. The theory also assumes that factors such as skilled labour and capital do not move among nations. These assumptions no longer hold especially in industries which involve sophisticated technology and "highly skilled" employees. Furthermore, new factors for comparative advantage such as basic infrastructure of telecommunication, road systems, ports and airports have assumed greater importance.

Access to abundant factors is less important in many industries than the technology and skill to process them effectively and efficiently. In other words, technology gives firms the power to circumvent scarce factors. Technology also changes the rules of business. For example, flexible automation which allows for small lot size and easy model changes, is reducing the labour content of products in many industries. And access to state-of-the-art technologies is becoming more important than low local wage rates.

Central to the question of competitive advantage is therefore technology. Theories have been put forward on the differing labour productivity being based on technology differences and of "technology gaps" in which nations will export in industries in which their firms gain a lead in technology and that exports will fall as technology inevitably diffuses and the gap closes. This emphasizes the linkage of technology to competitiveness and therefore to sustained wealth creation through export of manufactured goods, and that underlying all these is the need for continuous improvements and innovations in methods and products.

No nation can be competitive in every field. A nation's pool of human, technological and other resources are limited. The ideal is to develop these resources in the most competitive industries or industry segments, thus the previously mentioned need for developing specific technological trajectories based on position of existing strength. The essential competitive advantage must be created and sustained through concentration on specific market segments, differentiated products, technology superiority, special skills and economies of scale.

The competitiveness of a nation is the result of the competitiveness of the nation's firms, because firms, not the nation, compete in the international marketplace. Commitment to increasing productivity and to innovation must therefore be at the firm's level. This must translate into sustained investment in research, physical capital and human resources by firms.

New Ways of Creating Wealth

Analysts are now talking about the Third Wave of industrial revolution where knowledge-based technologies are replacing the "brute muscle technologies" of the Second Wave, and about the new wealth creating system. The following conclusions have been made:

1. The new accelerated system of wealth creation is increasingly dependent on the exchange of data, information, and knowledge. It is "super symbolic". No knowledge exchanged, no new wealth created.

2. The new system goes beyond mass production to flexible, customized, or "demassified" production. Because of the information technologies, it is able to turn out short runs of highly varied, even customized products at costs approaching those of mass production.

3. Conventional factors of production – land, labour, raw materials and capital – become less important as symbolic knowledge is substituted for them.

4. Instead of metallic or paper money, electronic information becomes the true medium of exchange. Capital becomes extremely fluid so that high pools of it can be assembled and dispersed overnight. Despite today's huge concentrations, the number of sources of capital multiply.

5. Goods and services are modularized and configured into systems which require a multiplication and constant revision of standards. This leads to struggles for control of the information on which standards are based.

6. Slow-moving bureaucracies are replaced by small, demassified, work units, temporary or "ad hocratic" teams, increasingly complex business alliances and consortia. Hierarchy is flattened or eliminated to accelerate decision-making. The bureaucratic organization of knowledge is replaced by free-flow information systems.

7. The variety of organizational units multiply. The more such units, the more transactions among them, and the more information must be generated and communicated.

8. Workers become less and less interchangeable. Industrial workers own few of the tools of production. Today the most powerful wealth amplifying tools are the symbols inside workers' heads. Workers, therefore, own a critical, often irreplaceable, share of the "means of production".

9. The new "hero" is no longer a blue-collar worker, a financier or a manager, but the innovator (whether inside or outside a large organization) who combines imaginative knowledge with action.

10. Wealth creation is increasingly recognized to be a cyclical process with wastes recycled into inputs for the next cycle of production. The method presupposes computerized monitoring and deeper levels of scientific and environmental knowledge.

11. Producer and consumer, divorced by the industrial revolution and reunited in the cycle of wealth creation,

with the consumer contributing not just money but market and design information vital for the production process. Buyer and supplier share data, information and knowledge. Someday customers may also push buttons that activate remote production processes. Customer and producer fuse into a "prosumer".

12. The new wealth creation system is both local and global. Powerful microtechnologies make it possible to do locally what previously could be done economically only on a national scale. Simultaneously, many functions spill over national boundaries, integrating activities in many nations into a single productive effort.

The above again points to the central role of technology and reinforces the concept of the new basis of competitiveness based on factor endowment centred on knowledge-based technologies.

Science and Technology Strategies

Clearly bold strategies are required in accelerating and intensifying the application of technology in the various sectors of the Malaysian economy. The following are suggested:

Past Exploitative, Future Innovative

We have passed the stage of natural resource exploitation as a means of maintaining national prosperity. The share of the GDP from mining and quarrying, for example, was only 9.7 per cent in 1990 compared to manufacturing at 27.0 per cent.

The future lies in value-added activities even in the resource-based sector and for this the industrial structure must be technology-intensive (see Figure 10.1). The strategy should be on building long-term competitiveness based on technology-driven quality, investments in skilled manpower and government policies conducive to business freedom in a growth asserted economy. This strategy calls for wider use of technology in all sectors of the economy and nurturing the growth of domestic tech-

Figure 10.1
Route to National Prosperity

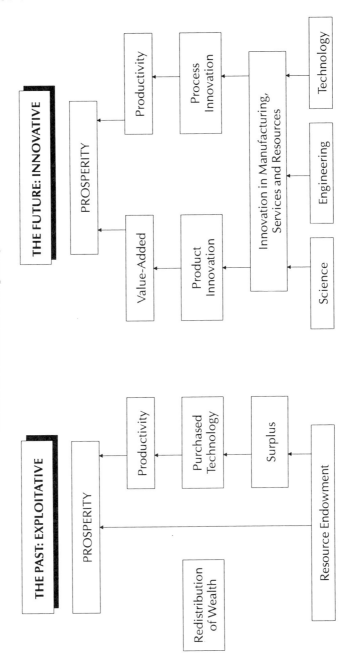

nology-based small- and medium-sized industries (SMIs). Foreign
investment should also be encouraged in the areas that bring in
new technologies and expertise.

Buy-Some, Make-Some

In technology acquisition, the national thrust should be through a
mixture of import and local development. In both instances careful selection is necessary. Buying technology wisely requires accurate and up-to-date information about trends in global
technology, the capacity to select and to absorb, that is, a complete technology transfer capability of search, assess, use, maintain, improve and create (see Figure 10.2).

Generating technology locally must be based on national attractiveness in terms of the potential benefits (maximum returns,
ability to capture the benefits) and feasibility (capacity to realize
the R&D potential in a timely way). A mechanism must be put in
place that can transfer the R&D results to the marketplace.

Be World Leader, Not Mere Follower

World leaders who derive the most economic benefits from their
businesses remain so on the basis of competitive advantage
which is maintained through various means. Of particular importance are proprietary process technology, product differentiation
based on unique products or services, coupled with advanced
skills and capabilities embodied in specialized and highly trained
personnel and internal technical capability. Competitive advantage with the above characteristics are not easily eroded; furthermore it is also associated with high level of productivity.

It should be the strategy for Malaysia, therefore, to achieve
world leadership position with the above characteristics in targeted sectors (for instance, latex products, oleochemicals, etc.)
where we have existing strength either in knowledge (technology), resources or skills. A national effort, involving both the
public and private sectors, must then be mounted to achieve the
goals of these technological trajectories or national technology
supremacy targets, with transnational collaboration as necessary.

Figure 10.2
**Schematic Representation of
the "Make-Some, Buy-Some" Strategy**

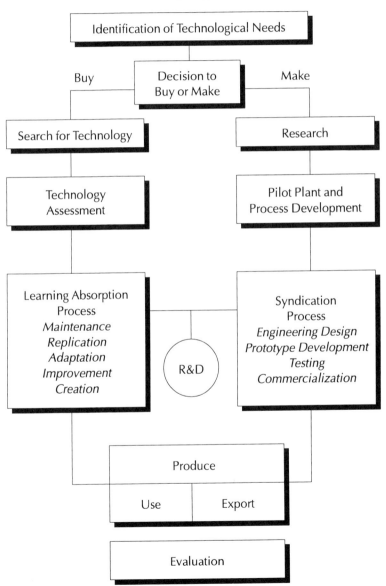

Figure 10.3
S&T Information Flow in Development Planning

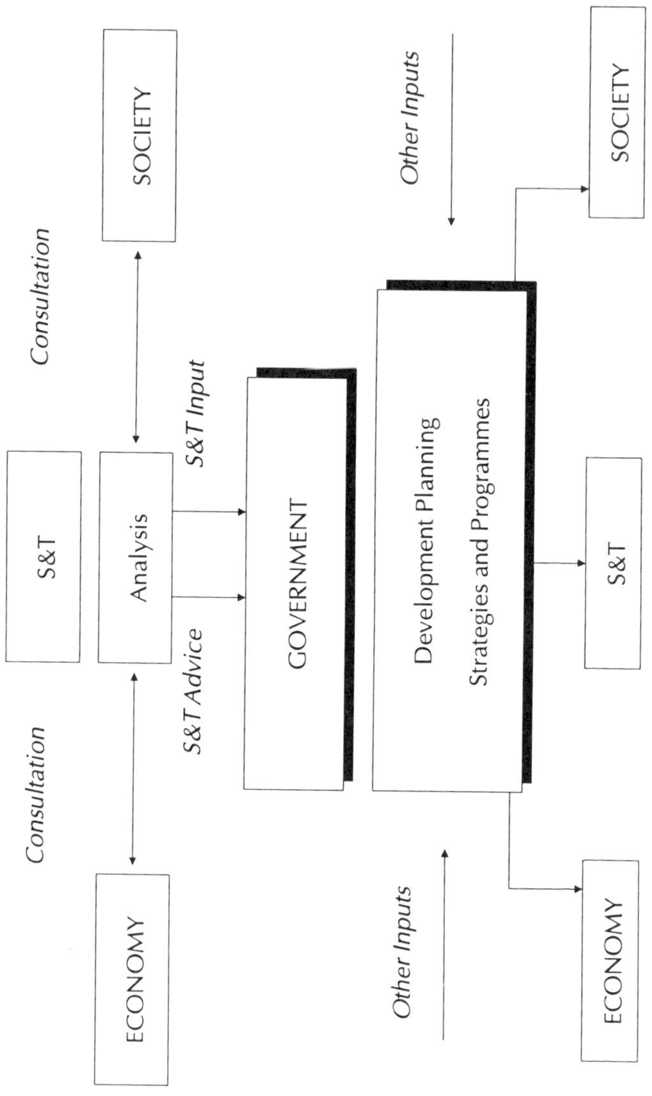

Work Hard, Work Smart

You may recall that the "Third Wave" industrial revolution is characterized by knowledge-intensive and technology-intensive processes where wealth creation is dependent on the exchange of data, information and knowledge. Production is becoming less materials-intensive and less energy-intensive, shifting from mass to batch systems and to automated flexible manufacturing and Just-In-Time sourcing. Under these circumstances, the labour force is no longer the limited-skill operator but a multi-skilled worker, using CAD-CAM systems and robotics. He is a technician, no longer a "brute-force" labourer.

The strategy is therefore to embark on a comprehensive programme towards creating a "work hard, work smart" workforce through increasing quality awareness and quality management know-how in manufacturing, and acquiring skills to reduce design-to-market cycles rather than mere production-to-market time.

An Agenda for Action

One of the eight "critical aspects" of the new National Development Policy spelled out in the OPP2 is: "Making science and technology an integral component of socio-economic planning and development, which entails building competency in strategic and knowledge-based technologies and promoting a science and technology culture in the process of building a modern industrial economy."

The above new role for S&T and the demand for the strategies described earlier would require a strengthening of the mechanisms and processes of S&T elements into the national development planning process. To be effective and efficient, channels of communication and advice must be established between the S&T, the Economy and Society components on the one hand, and between the S&T and the Government components, on the other (see Figure 10.3). Additionally mechanism for prospecting and consultation and a capacity for information gathering and analysis must also be put in place so that the process of S&T advice will bring in strategic implications of S&T in the long term taking into consideration intersectoral, inter-departmental and other horizontal linkages.

In addition actions are needed to enhance the R&D system, innovation and commercialization processes and the human resource development programmes.

S&T Planning and Management Process

There is clear evidence that nations succeed in industries where their national culture and environment support innovation and at-tainment of technological supremacy. Indeed the government has a role in factor creation and government policies can in-fluence the improvement of factors such as human resources, scientific knowledge, economic information and infrastructure. This leads to two imperatives – first, a strengthening of the na-tional S&T enterprise and therefore the need for a transparent policy for S&T; and second, defining the role of science and tech-nology in the socio-economic infrastructure and therefore the need for S&T in national policies.

A policy for S&T deals largely with matters internal to the S&T system such as science education, infrastructure for S&T services and budgetary allocation to basic and applied research. It provides the baseline data and framework for the S&T planning process (see Figure 10.4).

S&T for policy on the other hand deals with policies largely outside the S&T system and, in the context of this chapter, largely those that impact the economy and the comparativeness of in-dustries. Science and Technology cannot be decoupled from its commercial application in seeking to enhance national ad-vantage. Policy to stimulate commercial innovation must look not only at S&T, but also policy towards competition and regulation.

Science and Technology Advice to government which is part and parcel of the S&T Management System must take into con-sideration the need for both Policy for S&T and S&T for Policy. Broadly speaking there are three main systems involved (see Fig-ure 10.5) and within the context of the exploitation of research

Figure 10.4
The S&T Planning Process

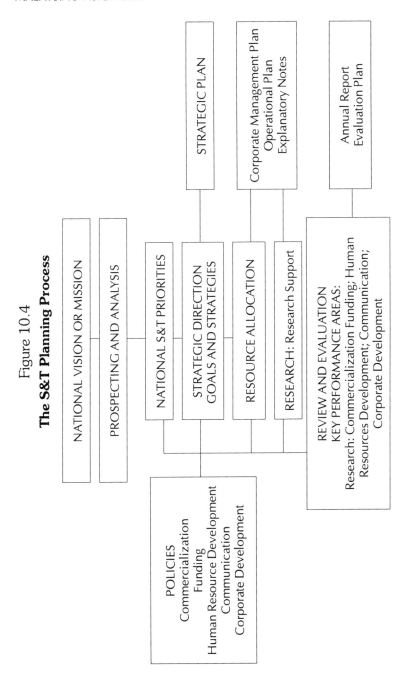

Figure 10.5

Information Flow Between Systems – Policy For S&T For Policy

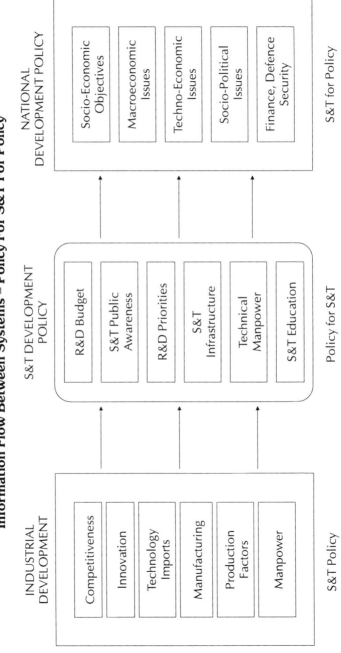

and development for technology, these are the S&T system, the national development planning system and the industrial development system. The S&T advice process is concerned with information flow between these systems for optimal results, namely that the planning process, the development of strategies and the management of programmes can be better served through informed judgement based on better understanding for the technical content. The S&T advisory process consists of several components:

1. The process of prospecting for S&T which is looking beyond the S&T parameter, for demand, opportunities and role for S&T in meeting long-term socio-economic objectives. This includes a capacity to analyse and to provide wider options for strategies and programmes and therefore enhances the development planning process itself.
2. A mechanism for consultation to provide a platform for exchange of information and views of the various stakeholders to improve decision-making.
3. Channels for information flow for advice and for the interpretive and co-ordinative interfacing to achieved integration at all levels.

Prospecting is especially important because it enables planners to "choose" a future instead of being totally controlled by "destiny". Prospecting, which is a mixture of forecasting, projection, anticipation and speculation, will therefore enhance the planning process and the subsequent decision-making for the "rational creative action" (see Figures 10.6 and 10.7). Prospecting is also necessary at the firm level.

The current situation in Malaysia is represented in Figure 10.8. The primary mechanism for consultation within the S&T system is the National Council for Scientific Research and Development (MPKSN), with the channels for information flow and for interphasing between the S&T system and the govern-

Figure 10.6
**The Role of Prospecting
in the Rational Creative Action**

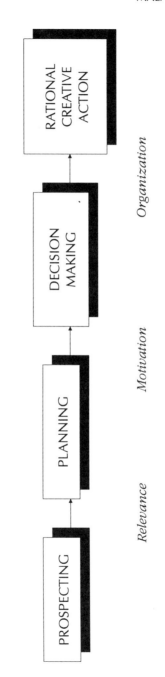

Figure 10.7
**Rational Creative Action
For Technology Supremacy Targets**

PROSPECTING
Assess current strengths
Build future scenario
Determine target segments

PLANNING
Plan R&D activities
Estimate budget and other resource requirements
Identify local participants and foreign collaborators

DECISION MAKING
Choose key players
Finalize R&D programmes and budget

RATIONAL CREATIVE ACTION
Establish infrastructure, instrumentalities and operational procedures

Figure 10.8

The S&T Planning System and the National Development Planning System in Malaysia

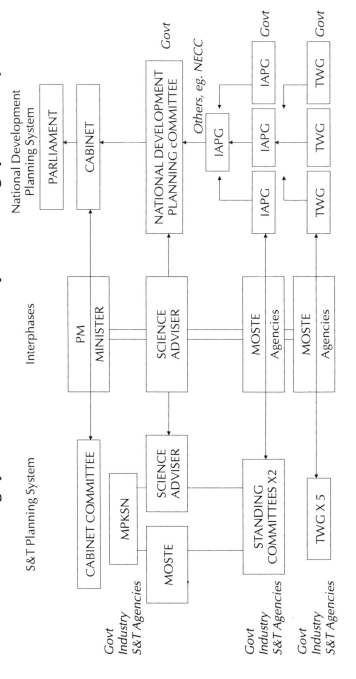

ment planning system occurring at several levels: the Cabinet, National Development Planning Committee (NDPC), Inter-Agency Planning Groups (IAPG) and the Technical Working Groups (TWG).

The organization and process has been very useful thus far. However, there are considerable constraints. Firstly the mechanism for prospecting is absent and for information analysis is inadequate and both need to be enhanced. Whereas a similar mechanism for economic matters are found in the Treasury, Bank Negara Malaysia, Ministry of International Trade and Industry, Malaysian Industrial Development Authority, Economic Planning Unit, Malaysia Institute of Economic Research and Institute of Strategic and International Studies, not to mention those in commercial banks, etc. a limited capacity to gather and analyse data and information in S&T and related issues resides only in the MOSTE. In view of the complex nature of the relationship between S&T and the economy and other aspects of S&T for policy and the rapidity of change within the S&T system itself globally, the present situation needs substantial rectification.

The consultative mechanism also needs to be more agile to enable frequent interaction. It should be more transparent and be able to accommodate views from non-government sectors.

There are adequate points for interfacing between the S&T system and the government planning system. However, the frequency of interfacing is restricted, because the IAPGs and the TWGs are active only during the "planning season".

The action plan is to improve the S&T planning and management process including the channels for science advice in all sectors and at all levels and to establish a strong capacity for prospecting both in the government and private enterprises.

Research and Development

The first attempt at priority determination and co-ordination of public sector R&D activities was made during the Fifth Malaysia Plan (FMP) period by the introduction of the R&D Vote and the mechanism for Intensification of Research in Priority Areas

(IRPA). The S&T Vote received an allocation of RM400 million in the FMP and this has been increased to RM600 million in the Sixth Malaysia Plan (SMP). The original priority areas in agriculture, industry, medical and strategic R&D have been extended to include socio-economic R&D.

IRPA is intended to strengthen R&D management and to rationalize resource allocation R&D, providing greater sensitivity to national development needs. Through upgrading "basic research in exploitable areas of science and applied research in sectoral areas for economic growth", IRPA was designed to be a strategic tool for S&T development in targeted areas. It has brought some measure of focus and purpose into the national R&D effort and is now ready to be taken a step further.

The current bottom-up or supply-push approach should be shifted to a stricter competitive bidding based on top-down and demand-driven approach. The driving force is the priorities which are determined by the needs of industry and the declared national technology supremacy targets.

Making IRPA more demand-driven would require a reorientation not just of the IRPA process itself but that of the public sector research institutions themselves. A mechanism must be established to allow for greater interaction with the industry and for R&D planning to take full consideration of market factors.

R&D for the achievement of the national technology supremacy targets must be seen as a total national effort involving both the public and private sector research organizations, the domestic conglomerates and the SMIs. The effort should be supported where appropriate by transnational collaboration in R&D. This effort should be accompanied by an investment policy tailored to hasten technology acquisition in the target areas.

Determining the national technology supremacy targets would require a high degree of capability in prospecting and identifying existing national technological strengths. Establishing collaborative R&D with the right multinational partner is one way of achieving the national technology supremacy targets, and is a more realistic way of attracting R&D investment by multinationals in Malaysia. The key would be to make our self-interest into mutual interest with the collaborator.

The action plan is to restructure IRPA to be more demand-driven by the needs of industry; facilitate interaction between government R&D institutions and industry; and utilize IRPA as a means of achieving national technology supremacy targets bringing in transnational co-operation and multinational collaboration as appropriate.

Innovation and Commercialization

National efforts in R&D are frequently science-driven with emphasis on the "R" and not on the "D". Consequently public sector investment is largely on research infrastructure without being complemented by investment in pilot-plant or upscaling, prototype development, industrial design and packaging facilities or capabilities.

A large commercialization gap thus exists between the laboratory and the marketplace (see Figure 10.9). This gap is also made up of an absence of facilities for commercialization such as market assessment (both local and global), marketing channels, business management and venture capital.

To derive full economic benefits from R&D, this activity must be treated as a continuous process of research, innovation and commercialization. It must be product-oriented and technology-driven (see Figure 10.10).

Our past effort in R&D through IRPA was to take science through to technology. The new thrust is to focus on products and the marketplace and, using IRPA, to develop the necessary technologies through to the innovation and commercialization stages. In this demand-driven approach, science will take care of itself.

S&T initiatives under the Sixth Malaysia Plan include measures to encourage the commercialization of research and technology including the establishment of appropriate institutional, legal and administrative framework. Measures also include quality and design enhancement programmes and supporting in-

Figure 10.9
Elements of the Commercialization Gap

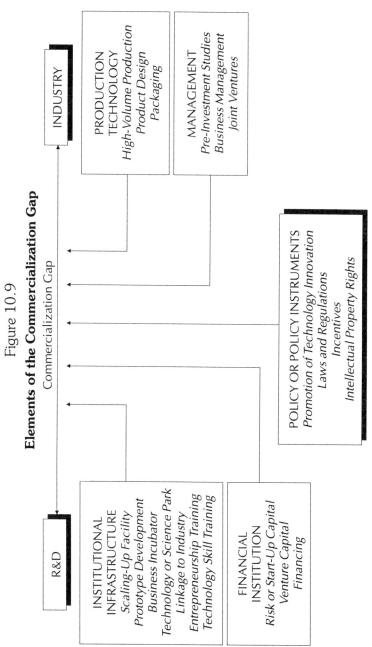

Figure 10.10
**The Research, Innovation
and Commercialization Sequence**

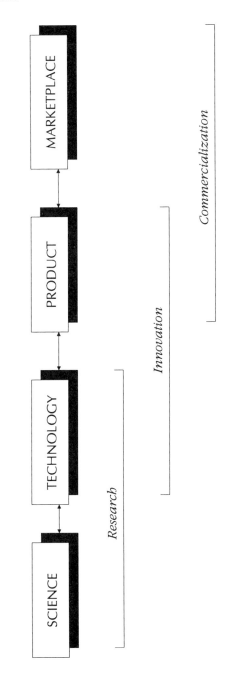

frastructure for patent and management of intellectual property. Actual programmes and projects should now be put in place.

The action plan is to develop the capacity for innovation and commercialization of research results to complement IRPA and establish the necessary institutions and mechanisms to support the above as well as for global market analysis and international marketing channels.

Human Resource Development

The key factor in the successful application of S&T to meet the targets of Vision 2020 is the development of human resources to man and manage the national S&T enterprise and to run industry productively and competitively.

There is currently a shortage of high-level scientific manpower both at the management and operational levels. Since the presence of a strong scientific community is crucial for the country to keep abreast of global technological advancement and to develop endogenous capability, increased efforts must be made to enlarge the pool of scientists and technologists with the appropriate environment and reward structure for full career development. Opportunity for knowledge acquisition and skills upgrading or transformation must be made available.

Although curricular reform is a slow process, educational institutions must have the capacity to harmonize their activities with the changing global S&T scene and the local industrial structure as well as with government priorities. This will require reform in organizational structure, decision-making process and learning teaching methodology. Universities will need to embark on strategic planning to be more responsive to short- and long-term industry needs because industry will increasingly become the major employer.

The establishment of an industrial society that is innovative, forward-looking and able to contribute to national development also requires a highly motivated and skilled workforce. The responsibility of keeping the workforce skilled and productive should be shared by both the government and the private sector employers. Training should then be a collaborative effort through the harmonization of the activities of the government, universities, R&D institutions, private sector institutions and employers.

Training should be used to provide the "quantum leap" in the acquisition of skills and competencies particularly in selected strategic key industries. International co-operation and transnational collaboration should be utilized for upgrading competence in the selected critical skills.

The action plan is to provide the necessary tools and resources to enable educational institutions to play a full role in scientific and technological manpower development in support of national or industrial objectives; identify critical skill areas and mount concerted effort in upgrading competence in these areas; and create a national culture of continuous education, training and skill development.

Conclusion

Attainment of Vision 2020 is dependent on sustained economic growth based largely on the export of manufactured goods. Malaysia's competitiveness in the world market is therefore a crucial factor.

Industrial competitiveness depends on technology and innovation. Strategic considerations to maintain industrial competitiveness would require bold measures to enhance the existing processes and mechanisms in S&T planning and management, the R&D delivery system (incorporating the innovation and commercialization processes) and human resource development programmes. Four strategies have been put forward: past exploitative, future innovative; buy-some, make-some; be world leader, not mere follower; and work hard and work smart.

The main point is to stage a concerted public and private sector effort in making Malaysia a truly industrialized economy, with wide application of research and technology in all the productive sectors; in attaining supremacy in national technology target areas; in having a large pool of highly productive, multi-skilled workforce; and in fostering a culture of continuous learning and innovation.

Several actions are suggested, all being hinged on our having a high capacity in prospecting for choosing a future and working towards that future. Prospecting is a prerequisite to planning and decision-making in all sectors which would then drive the necessary institutional and attitudinal reorganizations, the final steps in building a comprehensive commitment to ensuring the relevance and effectiveness of S&T strategies in contributing to Vision 2020.

References

Economic and Social Commission for Asia and the Pacific (ESCAP), 1988. *Technology Atlas*, Vol. 6, Bangalore, India: APCTT.

W.T. Golden, *Worldwide Science and Technology Advice*, Pergamon, 1990.

Government of Malaysia, 1991. *The Second Outline Perspective Plan, 1991-2000*, Kuala Lumpur: Government Printers.

Government of Malaysia, 1991. *The Sixth Malaysia Plan, 1991-1995*, Kuala Lumpur: Government Printers.

E. Jantsch, "From Forecasting to Planning to Policy Sciences", *Policy Science*, 1, 31-47, 1970.

Omar A.R., "Generation of Technological Innovation for Commercialization of Research". CSC/Nigeria Workshop on Commercialization of R&D, 24-28 April, 1989, Lagos, Nigeria.

Omar A.R. and Michael Y. Smith, "IRPA as a Strategy for S&T Development in Malaysia." CSC/Malaysia Seminar on Strategic R&D Planning and Management, 8-11 August 1988, Kuala Lumpur, Malaysia.

Porter, M., 1990. *The Competitive Advantage of Nations*, New York: Macmillan Inc.

Schumpeter, J.A., 1950. *Capitalism, Socialism and Democracy*, 3rd Edition, New York: Harper & Row.

Toffler, Alvin, 1990. *Power Shift: Knowledge, Wealth and Violence at the Edge of the 21st Century*, New York: Bantam.

11

Achieving the Industrial Targets of Vision 2020: The Science and Technology Perspective

Yukio Shohtoku

With the launching of the National Development Policy (NDP) and the Sixth Malaysia Plan, it is indeed an opportune time to review and discuss the role of science and technology and their impact upon Malaysia's march towards Vision 2020.

It has widely been discussed in many circles, both in Malaysia and overseas, that the recent developments in science and technology, especially in the field of electronics, has created such a magnitude of change and evolution as the Industrial Revolution of nineteenth-century England. The fruits of research and development in electronics, especially semiconductors, have given birth to what we know of as the age of Information Technology, where all dimensions of politics, economics and culture not only in Malaysia but in the rest of the world are highly subject to and dependent upon knowledge and information. Computers and communications are the main driving force for shifting our society in such directions. In discussing science and technology and their impact upon our future, the role of electronics and its applications in computers and communications cannot be overemphasized.

However, I shall not take this macro-socio-economic approach to the subject here as I do not think that I am qualified for the task and I believe that it should be expounded by experts in this field.

In this chapter, I shall take a more focused and realistic approach to five areas of the subject in an attempt to submit my proposals. My proposals in these areas are based upon my four and a half years of working experience in Malaysia and from the inputs of my Malaysian colleagues at Matsushita Electric.

Education in Science and Technology

Malaysia already has a highly advanced education system that provides a reasonably high level of elementary education as well as the opportunity for higher education of international standards and quality. However, it is important that Malaysia addresses the following points in order to establish a more internationally competitive economy.

Emphasis on Mathematics and Science in Elementary and Middle Schools

At the risk of over-generalizing, I might explain that "economy is technologically proficient, fully able to adapt, innovate and invest, that is increasingly technologically-intensive, moving in the direction to higher levels of technology", especially in those countries where mathematics and science are taught as "high priority" subjects in the course of compulsory education.

The education of boys and girls in mathematics and science at an early stage has a strong impact upon their aptitude for and interest in their choice of engineering and technology-related subjects at higher stages of education. A declining level of education, especially in mathematics in certain countries, is causing a great deal of constraint in their efforts to enhance international competitiveness and, in some cases, deterioration of industrial strength and research and development.

Although emphasis in mathematics and science takes many years of continued efforts in school before fruition, it is certainly a task to be implemented in the context of Vision 2020.

Vocational Training for Better Fit Between Industries and Institutes

Malaysia can be justly proud of a great number of good quality technicians and craftsmen that various vocational training institutes have turned out to the various industries and trades.

However, recent changes in technology have created different basic needs for vocational training and, in some cases, caused mismatches between vocational training programmes and industries' current and future needs.

It is, therefore, proposed that various federal government ministries co-ordinate their respective institutes and review and bring their programmes of various industries for Vision 2020. Such areas as die and mould engineering and mechatronics should be looked into in connection with the review of current vocational training.

Polytechnic and University Education

While Malaysia must diversify her manufacturing base to help reduce overdependence on electric and electronics industries as her main drive for growth and export, emphasis on electronics in higher education should not be discussed in the same category of diversification of her narrow manufacturing base. Electronic knowledge and technology are not only utilized in the traditional electric or electronic areas but they have wide applications in abroad spectrum of industries and research and development activities.

Today, we see application of electronics in furniture design, apparel fashion styling, architectural design for bridges or car maintenance as digital technology has found its way into devices, instruments and systems in professional equipment in these industries and trades. This trend of widening horizons in electronics applications in human life will continue to accelerate, as many breakthroughs are in the making in many industrialized countries.

The quality of electrical and electronics engineers or technicians from the polytechnics and universities in Malaysia is highly competitive but the current level of supply from such higher education institutes should be increased. There must be continuous efforts to motivate parents to emphasize on science and cultivate interest in technical subjects among their children. A motivating factor to encourage such a move will be the higher monetary and non-monetary rewards when they graduate.

It is also proposed that universities and industries enter into joint-study projects to initiate live linkage between the academic and private sectors. This linkage will further be strengthened as the private sector expands research and development activities in Malaysia with increasing participation by Malaysian engineers and technicians. Such linkage is very common in Japan and the United States.

Computer Technology and Software Development

Dr Mahathir Mohamad mentioned that "Already Malaysians are among the biggest users of computers in the region. Computer literacy is essential if we want to progress and develop." Malaysia is certainly to be highly credited not only for a high usage of computers and terminals but also for a very high level of computer literacy.

By the year 2020, Malaysia should start preparing itself for the research and development, production and application of information technology or computer software and technologists who are able to integrate, interface, and apply such technology into the nation's needs. The issue here is how we can use computer hardware to develop Malaysia into an information-rich and knowledge-intensive country. While progress and even breakthroughs are being achieved in efficiency, cost, performance, size and weight of hardware, the know-how of utilizing the hardware, that is, software, does not synchronize.

The development of softwares cannot be achieved by simply transplanting systems developed by other countries into the Malaysian climate. The software must be custom-tailored in each country according to their different operating systems, customs and culture.

Our society which is information-hungry will require high volume storage, super high speed real-time digital transmission and processing with high reliability and confidentiality. Then, we would also require all kinds of software technology to interface the various dimensions of requirements.

Therefore, Malaysia should possess the capability of developing such softwares or systems, high-speed digital communication networking as Malaysians will find it most efficient and effective to utilize in their efforts to enhance international competitiveness.

Currently, there is a worldwide shortage of software engineers and analysts. This trend is not likely to change in the short term as needs for utilizing hardware will intensify in many different and new areas both in the public and private sectors. It is, therefore, proposed that more emphasis be placed upon producing more software engineers in universities and other higher institutes of learning, as Malaysians cannot rely upon the constant import of softwares from overseas to meet increasing demand. Refer to Figure 11.1 for various stages of applications of computers in manufacturing industries.

Industrial Standards

Many industrialized countries have established industrial standards under the leadership of the public sector. In Japan, both public and private sectors have joined hands to create industrial quality and performance criteria, and have enhanced the standards to the level of encompassing a wide range of products in almost all industries. The administration of the standards system and procedures are being implemented by the Ministry of International Trade and Industry.

South Korea and Taiwan have successfully installed a comparable system and agency for enforcing approval and certification programmes. It is suggested, therefore, that the Federal Government examine various international standards and systems, obtain input from the private sector in Malaysia and take the initiative in developing a Malaysian industrial standards system, industry by industry and in defining a level of criteria for quality and performance for a broad spectrum of industrial goods and in enforcing compliance with the state-designated standards with the co-operation of the private sector. This will help enhance the quality and therefore, the reputation of products made in Malaysia in the export market as well as instil in the consumers' mind more confidence and trust in locally-made products.

Role of the Government

The United States and Japan have proved to be strong in technologies that have received heavy federal backing. In the case of the United States, the Department of Defence provided essential support for the computer and aerospace industries. Heavy investment in biological science by the National Institute for Health has contributed substantially to the United States' lead in biotechnology. But the States is trailing badly in engineering and production technologies, materials and electronic components which were the main areas of government support in the case of Japan.

Similarly here in Malaysia, it is recommended that the federal and state governments, through their respective departments, identify specific areas with specific targets where funds would be channelled to. Private sector roles could also be identified in such an exercise.

Culture, Work Ethics, Work Attitude for Blue-Collar Workers

Malaysia's economy has managed to emerge from its primary industries stage rapidly and is making great strides into the next stage of secondary industries such as mining and manufacturing.

In fact, her development out of the age of primary industries has been so rapid and forceful that her economy is, in fact, leapfrogging into third industries, namely, service industries.

While service industries deserve the respect and recognition due to them, we must also be aware of mounting tendency, especially among younger people, to look down upon blue-collar jobs, and choose employment where they perceive there will be less "sweating on the forehead".

We have seen some cases in certain countries where blue-collar workers are not given "First-Class Citizenship" and as a result the quality of their work has been on a constant decline and this decline has further been aggravated by labour unions making excessive demands for pay-hikes.

The bottom-line of this trend is that not only manufacturing industries have weakened, given way to imports, or shifted overseas, but there has also been tremendous erosion in the development of science and technology, especially in high-technology research and development.

Dr Mahathir Mohamad has rightly said that, "Technology is not for the laboratory but the factory floor and the market." Research and development without a matching manufacturing base will not be as effective or efficient as when there is a strong interface between the factory floor and laboratory in manufacturing. It is therefore very important and necessary for us to continue to inculcate in the minds of our younger generations the values and significant role of blue-collar jobs in Malaysia's stride towards a science and technology-driven society as envisaged in Vision 2020.

Finally, let me discuss the role of the private sector in the context of the Malaysia Incorporated Concept as, thus far, I have been focusing upon public sector's involvement in Vision 2020. The private sector has its share of the burden for Malaysia to achieve Vision 2020. While there are a number of areas where the private sector's involvement is important, let me deal with two issues as may subject is related to the industrial targets of science and technology.

Table 11.1
Research and Development Expenditure
– Consolidated Basis

	1988	1989	1990	1991	FCST
	(88/4 89/3)	(89/4 90/3)	(90/4 91/3)	(91/4 92/3)	–
R&D Expenditure (RM Million, Yen Billion)	2,263 319	$2,451 346	$2,718 383	$3,064 432	–
(Billion Ringgit based on 3.9.91 rates)	$6.49	$7.04	$7.80	$8.79	–
Percentage of Previous Year	114%	108%	111%	113%	–
Percentage of Sales	5.8%	5.8%	5.8%	6.1%	–

Research and Development

While there could be few exceptions, most manufacturing industries have focused on manufacturing only. In this field, both local and foreign manufacturers have achieved good results by producing at high quality and reasonable cost and lead-time.

However, Malaysia's international competitiveness must be enhanced in order to promote exports because exports are important for Malaysia to achieve Vision 2020. To make that happen, the manufacturing subsection should seriously address the role of research and development as it holds the key to a leading edge in competitiveness in terms of cost, quality and delivery. Combining research and development with manufacturing will be the most important tool to enhance the competitiveness of products manufactured in Malaysia.

In the case of Matsushita Electric Industrial Co. Ltd. Japan under the motto "all research is for the happiness of mankind", the Matsushita Electric R&D department has been committed to the improvement of a broad spectrum of technologies.

In the future, Matsushita's R&D will focus on the development of system equipment to improve people's lifestyle towards an advanced, information-oriented society and the creation of a smooth relationship between such equipment and human beings. Matsushita Electric ultimately aims at developing products and technology that meet user needs in terms of function and quality, as well as bring emotional satisfaction through further improvements, energy and labour savings. The Matsushita group currently has more than sixty R&D laboratories around the world which employ some 23,600 engineers and scientists.

Research and Development Areas

Table 11.1 is an overall view of the research and development areas of Matsushita Electric.

Industrial Property

The amount of industrial property, including patents and utility models, is a yardstick for successful research and development activities. Matsushita Electric is one of the corporations that owns a large amount of industrial property in Japan. In addition, it has been granted more and more foreign patents by 72 countries such as the United States, United Kingdom, Germany and Canada.

Table 11.2
Industrial Properties:
Patents and Utility Models
(As of April 1991)

Japan	40,400
Overseas	11,890
Total	52,290

In carrying out research and development activities, the private sector should fully tap the Malaysian resources and talents as the quality of engineers or technicians from local institutes of higher learning is internationally competitive.

In-House Human Resource Development

While the public sector has important roles to play in school education, the private sector should take over the responsibility once it recruits graduates. The private sector should provide on-the-job as well as off-the-job training within and outside the industry so that young graduates joining the private sector after graduation would further enhance their skills, knowledge and business sense on the basis of what they have acquired in school. Practices of pinching staff from other companies without giving back due share to the responsibility of human resource development should be discouraged.

The private sector should also initiate joint-study projects with institutes of higher learning to create an interactive relationship between the academic and industrial circles. The private sector should therefore co-operate and co-ordinate its efforts with the public sector to produce synergy for Malaysia's march towards Vision 2020.

Development of Computer Technology

The systematic development of computer technology and information technology becomes apparently more important and necessary to move the manufacturing industries from labour-intensive to computer-aided manufacturing and eventually to high technology manufacturing industries. The following engineering disciplines are needed:

1. Computer software development: Systems analysts, computer programmers.
2. Computer hardware development: Computer designers, computer maintenance and repairs, manufacturers and designers of chips.
3. Computer-aided manufacturing: Engineering designers using computer-aided design or CAD – dies and moulds; engineering personnel using computer-aided manufacturing or CAM – manufacturing machines using computers; and computer-aided design and manufacturing or CADAM.
4. Material technologist: Material – its properties and applications (research and development).
5. Industrial designers.
6. Robotic engineering: Robotic designers, robotic repairs and maintenance, robotic applications.
7. Industrial engineers.
8. Science and Technology awards: Recognition of excellent achievement in the field of engineering, that is, research and development, new innovations such as National Science Award, Young Scientist Award (which is already in existence) and National Innovation Award, etc.; and recognition through state awards.

Figure 11.1
Engineering Development
in Manufacturing Industries

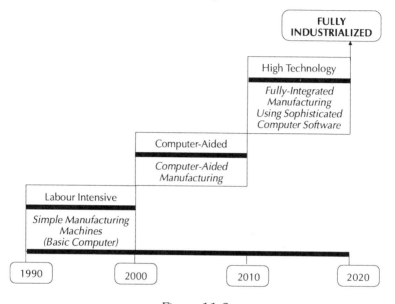

Figure 11.2
Development of
Engineering Technology

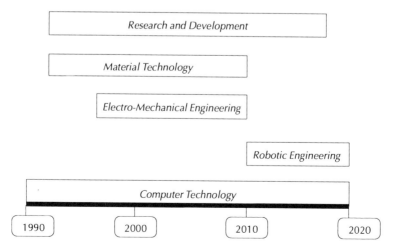

Figure 11.2
Overall View of R&D Areas

Semiconductors. Solid-state image sensors, laser diodes, opto-electronic integrated circuits, microprocessors, memories, gate arrays.
Production Systems. Computer-integrated manufacturing, FA systems, tape automated bonding, insert machines, robots, welding robots, welding machines, measuring equipment.
Materials or Components. Circuitry components, mechanical components, unit parts, optical devices, printed circuit boards, memory devices, sensors, display and printing devices.
Batteries. Solar batteries, secondary batteries, primary batteries, special batteries.
Motors. Compact motors, servo motors, ultrasonic motors.
Lighting. Lighting sources, photometry and colourmetry, vision and colour, designing of lighting installation.
Office Machines. Document files, desktop publishing systems, word processors, colour copiers, printers.
Electrical or Household Appliances. Hot water supply systems, air-conditioning systems, system kitchens, washing machines, vacuum cleaners, cooking appliances, refrigerators.
Information or Communications Systems. Telephones, facsimiles, TV telephones, mobile communications, satellite communication systems, integrated services digital networks, personal computers, workstations, neurocomputers.
Audiovideo. Liquid crystal TV, high definition TV (HD TV), enhanced definition TV (ED TV), digital TV, broadcasting systems, satellite systems.
Automobile-Related Products. Automobile AV systems, mobile telephones, navigation systems, engine control systems, suspension control systems, sensors-activators, automobile air-conditioning systems, automobile batteries.
Audiovideo. Digital VTR, electronic still cameras, video movie cameras, video disc players, videotape recorders, digital audio tape recorders, CD players.
Networks. Home automation, CAPTAIN systems, CATV systems, local area networks.

Applied Research and Development Areas

Signal Processing Technology. Digital technology, image processing technology, natural language processing technology.
Software Technology. Computer software technology, communication software technology.
Systems Technology.
Semiconductor Technology. Device technology, opto-electronics technology, ultra-fine pattern formation technology.
Materials technology. Thin-film technology, material machining technology, material analysis technology.
CAD-CAM Technology.
Electro-Mechanical Technology.
Printing Process Technology.
Manufacturing Technology. Computer-integrated manufacturing technology.
Lighting Technology.
Energy-Related Technology.
Biotechnology.
Life science, Human science. Man-machine interface, ergonomics.

Basic Research and Development Areas

12

Human Resource Development: The Key to a Developed Society

Othman Yeop Abdullah

History has taught us that the character and strength of a nation is invariably tied up with the quality and attributes of its citizenry. Ancient Greek civilizations flourished by the strength and military skills of the Spartans and the culture and spirit of the Athenians. Islam, born in the scorching desert of Saudi Arabia, spread into an enduring civilization, with an empire that lasted for almost eight hundred years. It laid the genesis for modern science, medicine, law, architecture, mathematics and cosmology. This was achieved by a community that was once backward but subsequently propelled by the pursuit of knowledge with complete adherence and devotion to the Quran and the teachings of the Prophet Muhammad.

Industrialized countries like Japan, Switzerland and South Korea have risen despite limited natural endowments. They have no minerals and the climate, land structure and soil are not conducive to agriculture. Yet these countries have achieved spectacular economic growth on the strength and ingenuity of their human resources.

On the other hand, there are countries that are well endowed with natural resources such as minerals or oil and yet failed to capitalize on their given wealth. They remain observers, not partaking in the exploitation of their resources. They choose by their own default to remain on the fringes of progress. They are content to oscillate between developing and under-developed status, utterly dependent on foreign technology and expertise to exploit their dwindling resources. These countries have failed to effectively develop their human resources to capitalize on their natural wealth and to steer their own destiny.

At the industry level, human resource development is not only essential but critical to a company's survival. There is an intrinsic impermanence in modern industry where market and technology are so volatile that any failure to proact to change and be innovative will result in a company being driven out of business. A company that is short on capital can borrow money but a company that is short of the required human resources has little chance of survival either in the short or long term.

Human resource development has currently emerged as a serious field of study, seeking answers to strategic questions that conventional wisdom has not satisfactorily provided. If economics is concerned primarily with economic equilibrium and related problems, it does not have much to offer in determining a realistic strategy for the effective utilization of human resources.

"Human Resource Development"

The concept of "human resource development" is a fairly substantive and complex field. It embraces three levels of strategic planning and analysis of which are the aggregate, sectoral and the industry levels. The primary objective of human resource development is to effectively utilize scarce or abundant human resources towards achieving both broad and specific objectives of the nation as well as the industry, business and the individual employee. In its broadest sense, it is the development of plans of action to meet the manpower requirements in anticipation of the changing conditions of the social, economic, industrial and business environment. It is part of manpower planning where the manpower requirements are first identified in broad categories according to sectors – agriculture, manufacturing, construction, trade and banking, government services and others. The labour force is further broken down to broad classifications, defined in terms of professional and technical, administrative and managerial, clerical, sales, service, agricultural and production.

Realistic plans for the development and utilization of manpower resources are made after consideration of the external and internal factors affecting the manpower objectives of each industry and organizational unit.

Global trends, market and technological changes and the time span of the human resource development projection are factors that influence human resource development plans. At the same time national priorities and company objectives are essential ingredients that determine the thrust and shape of human resource development.

The integration of macro with the micro perspectives is therefore vital to maintain focus and relevance. In view of the dynamic nature of the environment the bottom-up process of providing periodic feedback needs to be maintained to ensure relevance of the plan to changing situations. The absence of a constant bottom-up process for plan refinement would result in a mismatch between supply and demand.

Global Trends and the Human Resource Development Environment

It is almost axiomatic that human resource development is the key towards a developed and industrialized society. The process of developing a human resource development plan for Vision 2020 involves projections and reviews of three consecutive outline perspective plans and six five-year plans. Based on what transpired during the past 30 years it is apparent that the next 30 years will witness more rapid and volatile changes in the environment. To minimize any dislocation from the changes that are impacting externally, it is essential that strategic plan for human resource development with systematic linkages among the players and the constituencies involved be developed. At the same time a rigorous monitoring and evaluation mechanism is vital to provide feedback for adjustments in the plan. Periodic review and fine-tuning of the objectives and the operational plan of human resource development are essential to ensure relevance and to avoid wastage of resources which may disrupt the industrialization goals.

In planning for human resource development, particularly for skills and expertise that require long gestation period, changes in technology for targeted industries need to be closely monitored. This role, known as "boundary spanning", is vital as changes in technology and market structure have broad implications on human resource requirements and job behaviour. The following are some pertinent changes in the environment that must be taken into consideration in planning for human resource development either in the short or long term:

1. Compared to the 1970s and 1980s, the next three decades will witness formidable technological explosion facilitated by the advancement of information technology, modern medicine and biotechnology. The technological explosion may render most scientists technically obsolete ten years from graduation from a technical school. They would lack the latest skills and knowledge in their own field. Most scientists would be unfamiliar with ten or fifteen new sciences which may spring up meanwhile. In terms of human resource development, the implication would be to develop team player skills to enable scientists to work as a multi-disciplinary team or to have continuous training programmes.

2. The next thirty years will also witness a tremendous communication explosion with faster and shortened distances for travel. There will be a substantial increase in productivity for those nations that have the capacity to acquire relevant knowledge and new technology.

3. New knowledge and technology will affect power relationship and facilitate decentralization in government or in industry.

4. Economic activities will be more global than they are today. This would mean that ownership of firms would be very much internationalized. These trends have the following implications on human resource development: first, every employable person has a choice of more than one place to work; second, there will be a universal fraternity of specialists and a tremendous demand for excellence and professionalism; third, the nature of work changes with new technologies and new culture; routine jobs will be performed by robots; and finally, labour trans-migration may take place on a greater scale from developing to developed countries, attracted by higher salaries and other incentives.

5. There will be shorter product life. Every four to five years a company may change 50 per cent of its products. Marketing knowledge and skills would be a great asset.

6. There will be a tremendous expansion of the service sector, in particular the information-related industry.

7. Information replaces energy as the main transforming resource. It adds value to products and services by increasing the efficiency of labour, materials and capital used. Information speeds the discovery of minerals and reduces the cost of their recovery. It facilitates the discovery of new materials, the development of new equipment and new processes.

The changes in the environment may accelerate to such an extent that countries which do not have the absorptive capacity for technology transfer and diffusion or the creativity and technology to undertake research and development may never establish any competitive edge in a global market. Monitoring the changes, adapting and introducing new innovations will require knowledge and skills. According to Dr Mahathir Mohamad,[1] "It is blindingly clear that the most important resource of any nation must be the talents, skills, creativity and will of its people". An effective and

---

[1] Mahathir Mohamad, "Malaysia: The Way Forward".

realistic human resource development plan may be able to absorb the shocks and ride with the rapid changes taking place.

Human Resource Development Approaches

I would like to discuss three general approaches to human resource development. They are the ad hoc approach, the incremental model and the comprehensive approach.

The Ad Hoc Approach

Under this approach the human resource development plan is short term and localized. It is often a reaction to specific problems faced by an industry or an agency. for example, as a response to acute shortage of system analysts a crash training programme for one to three years is developed. This approach has very limited utility as it is reactive and where the trained manpower has a long gestation period, the immediate requirements cannot be met. More often than not an agency limps along without the support staff.

Incremental Model

This approach has some elements of "ad hocism" but it has a wider perspective of time and focus. It is utilized where manpower demand is unclear and erratic. To be useful and effective this model requires a smoothing out process over a period of time of the human resource development plan. This approach may achieve the objective of human resource development plan if the following requirements are met:

1. There is clear identification of the skills required for specific jobs in specific industries for the short and long term.
2. An internalized feedback and evaluation system is built in to improve and adjust the operational plan.
3. There is continuous data update of technology and product change for the targeted industries.

4. Continuity of ownership and support of the plan at the micro level.

A Comprehensive HRD Plan

This approach has the following elements as inputs into its human resource development plan:

1. Information on global trends of the industries targeted as priority. The information covers the rate of growth, the market structure, manpower demands and the various relevant technological innovations either current or in the pipeline.
2. It integrates the manpower needs of all the players, namely, the industry, the government and the training institutions.
3. The approach mobilizes the commitment and support of the critical constituencies.
4. The human resource development goals are clear and various critical milestones are identified for purposes of evaluation.
5. The plan draws some reference points from the priority or targeted industries in selected countries. This is used to stimulate and measure the human resource development requirement and monitor the changes accordingly.
6. Incentive package for staff development and succession plans are integrated within the human resource development plan.
7. There is a strong commitment to training. Formal and informal training for each category of staff is catered for over his entire career with the company or institution.

The most effective human resource development plan is based on the comprehensive approach as its perspective is more extensive and global. It uses detailed indicators from model countries as reference points in developing and reviewing its own human resource development plan. The involvement of various players with its implementation plan makes the human resource development relevant and useful.

Industrialization and Structural Transformation

It is recognized that for any case of industrialization the major categories of human resources required are:

1. The various disciplines of engineering – mechanical, electrical, electronic, civil and telecommunications.
2. Support technical staff – chargemen, electronic technicians, etc.
3. Scientists and technologists for research and development.
4. System analysts, computer science programmers for information technology and data processing.
5. Teachers and trainers in various fields.
6. Managers and administrators.
7. Accountants and lawyers.
8. Entrepreneurs.

Industrialization in a highly competitive global environment influences the manpower utilization structure and affects the qualification requirements and the mental aptitude of workers. This is obvious since there is close interrelation and mutual interaction between job structure, educational attainments and technical training on the one hand, and economic and technological progress, on the other. The road to industrialization in the next 30 years may involve the following incremental changes:

1. Demand for simple and heavy manual labour diminishes and jobs involving non-manual efforts rise.

2. The development of robotics for routine and structure or dangerous tasks. The range of individual occupation expands with new types of jobs and locations.

3. The development of science and technology and the increasing dependence on knowledge worker and information technology.

4. The importance of positive values, ethics and a sense of commitment as a driving force towards higher productivity and resilience.

It is imperative that the contents of modern education at tertiary levels will have to be changed to include the various elements necessary to balance technology, social and natural sciences, engineering with ethics, morality and leadership training.

Education, technical and vocational training plays important social and economic roles. First, it provides the vehicle for social mobility to realize the restructuring objective of the New Development Policy. Second, it meets the demands for the appropriate labour force to propel the industrialization process. Third, it assists in developing the human resources in skills, knowledge and spiritual value according to the Malaysian mould and values.

The most vital ingredients required in achieving the objectives of Vision 2020 through human resource development are:

1. Adequate places and facilities in tertiary education to meet demand.

2. Relevance and quality of curricula and facilities.

3. Flexible and adaptive structures within training institutions to meet rapid changes and new demands.

4. Periodic industry feedbacks on needs and performance to enable change and adjustments either in content or in direction of training and education.

5. Industry participation in forecasting global trends in technology and manpower.

6. Industry participation in training at organization and tertiary levels.

Entrepreneurship training and broad-based education to foster an entrepreneurial spirit is therefore important. The training may cover such areas as business start-ups, appreciation of technology for small-scale enterprises and some practical training on self-employment.

At present, the process and the administrative arrangements are not sufficiently robust to absorb the changes taking place in the labour market. This lack of robustness in the administrative arrangements is the result of the non-integrative nature of both sectors, it is necessary to discuss the current process and administrative arrangements involved.

In the public sector, forecasting industry needs is undertaken by the Ministry of Human Resources. This is done on the basis of sample surveys carried out by the Statistics Department and the intermittent requests by employers for specific skills. On the other hand, forecasting government sector needs is done by another agency, that is, the PSD or Public Services Department. This is internally undertaken based on the projects made by the PSD. This Economic Planning Unit is responsible for integrating both the industry and the government sectors.

In the case of the private sector, forecasting of industry needs is almost absent. Staff development in the form of in-house training is undertaken by individual firms and organizations. A comprehensive plan of action based on national and regional or global trends is never developed.

The gap between planning and real needs has to some extent hampered effective manpower development for industrialization, especially in the high-technology sector.

The other serious flaw in Malaysia's manpower development is the insular projection of manpower requirements in its plans. In Japan, for example, the Ministry of Trade and Industries, in planning the manpower requirements for Information Technology starts by examining the global trends of the IT industry, the manpower situation and from there examines the Japanese situation. This process enables the Japanese to have both a global and a regional perspective of situations to enable it to plan the appropriate strategy accordingly.

Conclusion

The forward and backward linkages in the administrative arrangements for human resource development are still very fragmented. The relationship between the aggregate and the industry levels in carrying out manpower auditing and predicting human resource requirements in the medium and long terms needs to be strengthened.

For a start, a clear forecasting format on manpower requirements, utilized at the macro levels needs to be introduced. Precise demand patterns at the micro level and fine tuned according to priority industries and specific jobs must be undertaken. The industry's growth rates in short and medium terms need to be worked out not just for the purpose of capital formation but also for human resource development.

Current patterns of human resource development appears to be aggregative, static and often off tangent to economic and industry trends.

The policy impetus through incentives and venture capitals given to small and medium scale industries have not been adequately matched by human resource development. Consequently, while the government provides the necessary infrastructure and climate for the growth of small- and medium-sized industries, the absence of a sufficient number of entrepreneurs hampers the smooth take-off of this segment of the industrialization plan.

It is recognized that universities and formal training institutions need a more flexible system of operation. Currently, they are less responsive to change. If change is desirable, institutions require long lead time to recruit the required faculty and adjust the curriculum to new demands.

Human resource development has emerged as a vehicle towards realizing the goals of Vision 2020. Industrialization and economic growth depends principally on the development of people – of their potentials, skills, capabilities, resourcefulness and commitment. They are the carriers and the guardian of the nation.

References

Abu Daud Sulong and Hanifah Nordin, 1989. *Pembangunan Sumber Tenaga Manusia Ke Arah Gunatenaga Mahir dan Profesional*, Kuala Lumpur: Biro Ekonomi Pergerakan Pemuda UMNO Malaysia.

Hee, T.J. and Seng Y.P., (ed.), 1987. *Developing Managers in Asia*, London: Addison-Wesley.

Malaysia, 1985. *Mid-Term Review of Fifth Malaysia Plan, 1986-1990*, Kuala Lumpur: Government Printers Malaysia.

Tsuru, Shegeto, (ed.), 1983. *Human Resources, Employment and Development*. London: Macmillan Press Ltd.

United Nations Industrial Development Organization, 1985. *Medium and Long Term Industrial Master Plan Malaysia, 1986-1995*.

Malaysia, 1991. *The Second Outline Perspective Plan, 1991-2000*, Kuala Lumpur: Government Printers.

Hamzah Ismail. *Relevance of Current Industrial Training, Institutional Framework and Policy Making Process for Malaysia's Industrialization Goals: Overview and Assessment*, Kuala Lumpur: Institute of Strategic and International Studies.

Mahathir Mohamad, 1991. "Malaysia: The Way Forward", Kuala Lumpur: Prime Minister's Department.

Lynch, James L., *Making Manpower More Effective: A Systematic Approach to Personnel Planning*.

Naisbitt, John, 1984. *Megatrends*, New York: Warner Books.

Naisbitt, John, 1990. *Megatrends 2000*, New York: Avon Books.

13

Human Resource Development: The Education and Training Aspect

Ungku A. Aziz

We will now discuss how human resource development can contribute towards the creation of a developed and industrialized society. Dr Mahathir Mohamad's working paper delivered at the inaugural meeting of the Malaysian Business Council on February 28, 1991 sets out the nine challenges which are taken as given and are not discussed *per se*. This chapter concentrates on the education and training implications of these challenges as far as the objectives of Vision 2020 are to be realized.

Clarifications and Definitions

As often happens in the social sciences, there are no universally accepted definitions. Therefore, to avoid misunderstanding and confusion I am stating the definitions which I believe to be acceptable to a fairly wide readership.

"Human Resource Development"

There are four elements in human resource development. It includes all forms of education and training and embraces the whole spectrum of dissemination of knowledge and skills to learners of all ages.

Education implies the transfer of knowledge and the expansion of the learner's mind while training involves imparting skills in all manner of operations from the manipulation of tools to the use of information technology. I shall use the term "education and training" rather than "human resource development".

"Society"

In the context of this chapter, "society" includes all who describe themselves as Malaysians. It connotes people of all races, creeds, genders and ages. I understand that there are categories of society such as rural society and urban society or Malay, Chinese and Indian communities who may be identified by certain common characteristics.

"A Developed and Industrialized Society"

It is relatively simple to describe a developed society or an industrialized society or even a developed and industrialized society. However, it is not so simple to indicate the point at which a society that has been described as "developing" or "less developed" or "under-developed" enters the stage of being "developed".

In much of the literature, including reports by the agencies of the United Nations or the World Bank, a simple dichotomy has been used to differentiate between the developing and developed countries. Other dichotomies include developing and advanced countries with the so-called "newly industrialized countries" or NICs being applied to intermediate societies such as Singapore and Taiwan. Another set of labels is "North and South" which can be as confusing geographically as the pre-Perestroika "East and West".

Although it may be somewhat tautological, the purpose of this discussion is to consider a developed society which is described as one that has an acceptable level of prosperity and an equitable degree of distribution of opportunities for owning wealth and earning income.

In the matter of human resource development, a developed society implies a sufficiently sophisticated system of education and training that will disseminate knowledge and skills throughout the society. It is one that has become the learning society.

All modern nations that can be unequivocally described as developed have a substantial industrial sector that is not only technologically advanced but benefits from research and development or innovation that continuously increases its rate of industrial sophistication.

Issues Facing the Nine Challenges from the Education and Training Perspective

For purposes of discussion, the nine challenges may be divided into two groups which are interactive and cumulative both within and between the groups.

Group 1 includes challenges where education and training can have a direct impact as well as long-term indirect impacts.

1. Challenges that concern the mind: Challenge No. 2, attitude formation; Challenge No. 5, creation of a tolerant and liberal atmosphere; Challenge No. 6, developing a scientific and progressive worldview; and Challenge No. 7, infusing the caring culture.
2. Challenges that involve the spirit: Challenge No. 4, spiritual enhancement.

Group 2 challenges include challenges where the influence rather than the impact of education and training will be more noticeable in the medium-term and long-term.

1. Economic Challenges: Challenge No. 8, proceeding towards a more equitable society; and Challenge No. 9, achieving economic prosperity.

2. Political Challenges: Challenge No. 3, fostering a mature democracy; and Challenge No. 1, strengthening national unity.

All challenges are ranked according to the order in Dr Mahathir Mohamad's paper except for challenge 1, that is, the arrangement does not indicate any order of priority. Education and training programmes should be implemented in such a way that they involve all the nine challenges. The impact of each programme may be realized at different times. Some programmes will take longer than others. Some programmes will have impacts that help to overcome several challenges while other programmes may be concerned with rather specific challenges.

Challenges that Concern the Mind

In Group 1, in the first sub-group education and training programmes should be concerned with the infusion of new attitudes as well as the alteration of existing attitudes. This involves the expansion of the learners' minds as well as the acquisition of knowledge and skills.

Specific education programmes, curricula or methodologies will not be discussed in this chapter. To do so would require considerably more time and the chapter would become a book by itself.

Challenge No. 2 involves the creation of a psychologically liberated, secure and developed Malaysian Society with faith and confidence in itself, sufficiently robust to face all manner of adversity, while it pursues excellence.

Education programmes will have to be redesigned to promote self-confidence and minimize tendencies towards inferiority complex. Learners will strive for perfection. A robust mind will be better able to confront adversity if it is well trained to cope with stress. It should also have the operating skill to initiate alternative ways of solving problems or overcoming difficulties.

The essential approach in education is to teach all learners at all levels the ways to expand their minds. If teachers have the right attitudes they will be sufficiently "psychologically liberated" to explore fresh perspectives.

Although the pursuit of excellence is something that belongs more directly to the higher or tertiary and post-tertiary levels of the education system, it is equally important to instil the notion of striving for the best rather than the third best or, worse still, being satisfied with just a pass level among students and creative people, including the media community.

The formation of the right attitudes in the mind lies at the base of the way to overcome the other challenges such as Challenge No. 6 where a progressive scientific outlook goes with being proactive and innovative.

Tolerance towards cultural, religious, political and ethnic differences constitutes the liberal attitude. The caring culture (Challenge No. 7) is built up by compassion towards others who appear to be less fortunate than oneself.

Challenge No. 5 involves the establishment of a mature, liberal and tolerant society in which Malaysians of all colours and creeds are free to practice their customs, cultures and religious beliefs and yet feeling that they belong to one nation. In this context there are two sets of attitudes that need to be fostered by education. There is the external perspective that is conducive towards toleration of the religions and cultures of others. Then there is the internal perspective that fosters a sense of nationalism, in the better sense of the word, or a sense of belonging to a particular nation.

The education system should contain designs for both perspectives. Externally understanding promotes tolerance and appreciation especially in the area of cultural activities.

One of the major difficulties that people in Malaysia face in the field of religion is the issue of exclusiveness. While some religions and beliefs accept individuals who continue to profess other beliefs, other religions are exclusive and do not tolerate followers who want to follow other systems of belief.

The continued juxtaposition of theistic and non-theistic religious systems for hundreds of years is evidence of a miraculous degree of toleration. Historically, the relative peace that has prevailed in Malaysia must be attributed more to the rather relaxed way of life than to any specific education program- mes. However, in this age of instant global information systems there are perceptible tendencies for groups to form hard attitudes of orthodoxy and extremism, and occasionally resorting to violence.

This is where the national philosophy has to be emphasized within the education system. The three key concepts to be intro- duced at each level of the system are understanding, tolerance and appreciation of cultural presentations.

Some guidance will be necessary for those designing economic programmes as to the boundaries of toleration. There is also an issue where there are likely to be confrontations be- tween religious values and the cosmopolitan culture that is in- sidiously spreading among urban youth. While the forces of the free market and individual freedom of choice should be respected, a country that plans to proceed rapidly towards a rela- tively high degree of economic prosperity will need to place some curbs on the dissemination of so-called Western values of youth culture that advocate anti-establishment, selfish individualism or sexual promiscuity which in any case would contradict the values inherent in Challenge No. 4.

Challenge No. 6 involves the establishment of a scientific society that is innovative and forward-looking, one that is not only a consumer of technology, but also contributes to the scien- tific and technological civilization of the future. We are consider- ing a set of attitudes that reflect not only the views of individuals who constitute the society but the collective mind of that society taken as a whole.

In history there are examples of societies that are not scien- tific or progressive since they are primitive. Or they have systems of belief that are antagonistic to science. Or they are lost in awe of other ways of trying to manage the universe.

Although I am not advocating a digression in this discussion, regarding which particular brand of science we have in mind, I would be failing in my academic responsibility if I did not refer to this aspect at least, *en passant*.

I shall assume that we are referring to western science that has enabled man to change the face of the earth; to provide some nations with unimaginable levels of living and others with inconceivable means of destroying the environment and ultimately mankind itself. To achieve a scientific society with sufficient attention to numeracy and literacy as well as Information Technology operacy, the education system has to foster scientific attitudes such as to question what is, to seek something better and to consistently proceed according to the scientific method. Innovations, discoveries and inventions come when these attitudes become an integral part of the minds of scientists, managers, administrators and politicians.

There need to be institutions that discover, foster and reward budding scientists so that an increasing flow of talent is maintained.

A footnote to the establishment of a scientific and progressive society is the reminder that man cannot live by science alone. He needs cultural nourishment for his mind. The education system and society generally has to be connected to the literary and aesthetic heritage of mankind. The mind of the educated person needs cultural nourishment just as much as the body needs physical nourishment. We have examples of advanced nations where scientific achievement is balanced by an education system that encourages learners to appreciate the great works of the past and present and to be familiar with at least a portion of the creative works and discourses of mankind through time and across the globe.

Challenge No. 7 is the challenge of establishing a caring society and a caring culture, a social system in which the welfare of the people will revolve not around the state or the individual but around a strong and resilient family system.

The strengthening of the family system so that it will care for its members is an integral part of Islamic, Confucian and Hindu values. In certain developed economies it can be seen that rising standards of material advancement has led to the fragmentation of families.

Education will have to emphasize the importance of the extended family that is currently a prominent feature of Malaysian society. Incidentally, architecture may play a subtle negative influence.

If we accept some elements of the belief that society comes before self then the case of vulnerable groups such as the aged, the blind and the others will become the object of caring projects that are organized by voluntary associations which are increasingly supported in money and manpower by all levels of society. Education projects which give primary school children the direct experience of caring activities such as decorating an old folks' home can be effective in the long term.

The concept of caring includes concern for nature, the environment and the locality of domicile. The notion that no living creature should be made extinct by human activities is also a form of caring. Similarly, caring citizens do not unthinkingly scatter waste products along the road or at places which are part of the public domain.

Certain cultures are extremely careful in the handling of books. The love of books for what they contain begins with the loving and careful handling of the physical document itself.

A caring culture is composed of a set of attitudes towards the objects that are thought to be worthy of care. Patterns of behaviour are fostered and sustained by example and reinforcement. Parents or leaders in society should set examples that are rarely forsaken.

In Malaysia, trans-ethnic or inter-social caring attitudes and activities are more difficult to achieve. That is a good reason for such activities to be made an integral part of the education system at every level.

Challenges that Involve the Spirit

We now come to the challenge that involves the highest degree of abstraction. This is the challenge that involves moral and ethical values. The object is the establishment of a fully moral and ethical society whose citizens are strong in religious and spiritual values and imbued with the highest ethical standards.

So that we may be clear as to the contribution that education can make for the overcoming of this challenge, the concepts involved need to be examined in some detail. Whenever possible, for the sake of this chapter and indeed for this book, we should try to avoid becoming embroiled in philosophical dialogues regarding definitions or the comparative merits of different value systems.

The fact that the term "religious and spiritual" values is used encourages one to believe that those who do not profess any particular religion but who accept certain systems of moral and ethical values are included.

The design of appropriate education programmes will be helped by the preparation of clear statements of the moral and ethical values that those concerned uphold. It will be ineffectual and uninspiring to seek for the lowest common denominator of ethical values for the whole society. Perhaps this rather provocative statement may be made the focus of some discussion.

As has been mentioned in discussing Challenge No. 5, toleration is the *sine qua non* for approaching values and religions. Toleration is linked to understanding and interest. Therefore the role of education is clear.

For the sake of record and with trepidation and modesty, spiritual affairs could be approached from four directions in Malaysia. First, there are the theistic religions where belief in a single omniscient being is an absolute condition. This includes Islam and Christianity. Second, non-theistic religions, including Hinduism and Buddhism, have their own systems of beliefs for life and death as well as for this world and the other world. Third, the Chinese who do not profess either of the above categories have an elaborate pantheon of gods, spirits and other ethereal beings. Besides this, many of them, especially entrepreneurs, are guided by the precepts of *feng shui* and the I-Ching. Finally, many of the tribal peoples who live outside the urban and rural areas practise sophisticated forms of animism.

In all the above groups, ideas about eschatology are the driving forces behind the observance of the highest ethical standards. Whether a person cheats or tries to bribe another depends partly on the risks he sees of getting caught by the authorities of this world such as the Anti-Corruption Agency, as well as how far he believes that punishment in the other world or the next will be intolerable.

If education is to play a role in fostering high ethical values in Malaysian society then these values need to be clearly stated. They should be taught by precept as well as practice. Neither teachers, parents, administrators, businessmen nor leaders should practise double standards which lead to an utter loss of credibility. If we hope to drink the purest water we must know how to measure the levels of purity and then we can find satisfactory sources of such pure water.

Although it could have been put at the beginning of this section, I have deliberately left the subject of the spirit to the end. It is a subjective matter and depends on one's knowledge, experience and worldview. What I am suggesting is that Challenge No. 4 deals with the spirit while other sections which can be influenced by education programmes belong to the realm of the mind. Besides having a physical body and a central nervous system which includes a brain, man also has a mind and a spirit which are real although they have no physical manifestation. Any plan that expects to change attitudes and values will have to take a position on these issues.

Group 2 challenges are challenges where the influence rather than the impact of education and training will be more noticeable in the medium and long term. This does not imply that although the impact of education and training will be more indirect it is less essential. It could be claimed that without the effective implementation of appropriate education and training programmes, some challenges such as Challenges No. 8, 9, 1 and 3 may not be overcome. It that were to happen for any or all of those challenges, then the objectives envisaged in the statements may not be realized within the time frame of 2020.

The essential difference between economic challenges and political challenges is that while the former concentrates on the production and distribution of wealth the latter is concerned with the nature and strength of the national polity.

Although Dr Mahathir Mohamad's "Malaysia: The Way Forward" states that "economic development must not become the be-all and the end-all of our national endeavour", he nevertheless, in the following paragraph, describes the issues of economic development and economic social justice as vital objectives in the perception of the central strategic challenges.

Economic Challenges

Challenge No. 8 involves securing an economically just society. This means a fair and equitable distribution of the nation's wealth as well as a full partnership in economic progress. An economically just society cannot emerge as long as there is a perceptible identification of race with economic function and identification of economic backwardness with race.

Before the contribution of education and training can be discussed it is necessary to make some clarification. If race is no longer identified with economic function, that is, all major economic functions are participated in by significant proportions of all races and no race is mainly concentrated in certain economic activities, then two other requirements will have to be met. Not only should the distribution of wealth be equitable between the races but opportunities for participation in employment in important economic sectors should be opened to those communities who have not been able to gain entrance because of lack of knowledge, skill or experience or obstacles to access.

At this juncture the concept of "positive discrimination" may be introduced. For example, unless a deliberate plan supported by clear policies and adequate resources is made available, a situation where there are a small proportion of engineers of one race may never be corrected. Scholarships, administrative selection policies and academic preparation programmes can be designed and implemented so that in one or two decades a fairer distribution in the proportion of engineers of different races in the country will be obtained. This can be accomplished without lowering standards of education or graduation.

Education and training are the most effective ways to overcome the challenge of achieving an economically just society.

While it is outside the province of education and training, if entry into certain sectors of commerce and industry are deliberately restricted by those who are already there, then all that will happen will be the production of unemployed graduates. That is why institutional and structural changes may be needed to match the output of education and training programmes.

A significant example of the relationship between the dissemination of knowledge and skills and obstacles to institutional change can be found in some parts of the rural economy. Farmers and fishermen need to be taught new techniques of production. However, if the existing exploitative systems of moneylending, landlordism and lack of protection for rural labour are not changed at the same time, the new technologies will ultimately exacerbate the degree of rural poverty. Rural developers, at all levels, need to be educated to realize that education and training or extension programmes are closely linked to systems of marketing and institutions for saving and borrowing so that schemes will be more successful than many of those that have been launched over the last three decades.

Education programmes, especially at the secondary and tertiary levels, need to be more tailor-made to suit the needs for overcoming the challenges of achieving an economically just society.

The design and implementation of education and training programmes should be practical and pragmatic. It sometimes happens that graduates or trainees who return from overseas are unable to adapt what they have learnt overseas for effective local application. Partly, this is the result of their being given the main task of passing examinations to secure academic qualifications. They are not provided with opportunities to gain relevant experience either in the advanced countries where they have studied or in some developing country where the approaches that they have learnt are being successfully applied.

An example is the Japanese programme based on the Japan Centre at the University of Malaya in Kuala Lumpur. Students are given a two-year training in Malaysia in the use of the Japanese language at tertiary level and then they follow a normal Japanese

University degree course for four years in Japan. After graduation, they are encouraged to seek employment in a Japanese company and to enter the firm with fresh Japanese graduates so that they have a year's experience of working in a Japanese company in Japan. Then they return to Malaysia to serve the company which has trained them.

Challenge No. 9 is in the establishment of a prosperous society with an economy that is fully competitive, dynamic, robust and resilient. As was recognized in the twenty-year New Economic Policy, positive discrimination is needed to achieve certain objectives. Until an economically just society is achieved, Challenge No. 9 may have to be modified in the face of Challenge No. 8. One of the basic tenets of the prevailing philosophy of developing economies is that competition is the most effective way to prosperity. An economy where the competitive forces of the market determine the prices of products and resources through the free interplay of supply and demand must be resilient, robust and dynamic if it is to survive and progress. It may be assumed that internal competition is to be matched by external competitiveness. This is particularly significant because Malaysia is such an open economy. In any conceivable future, certainly through to 2020, its prosperity will be rather dependent on the competitiveness of its exports in the world market and on the extent to which it can attract foreign investments and the transfer of technology.

Since reference to the role of the co-operative movement will be made further on, it may be useful to note at this point that many attempts by the government to temper the effects of exploitation by monopolists and monopsonists in the markets for rural produce have not always been effective in reducing rural poverty. This point is mentioned so that readers may not hold the naive belief that all private enterprise are competitive. Furthermore, state-run monopolies are not always benign.

In the run-up to the level that will enable Malaysian society to be described as one that enjoys a good measure of prosperity, education and training will have an important role to play. There are three aspects to this issue that deserve attention:

1. Education and training that will increase the productivity of labour and other resources and that will enhance the capabilities of management;
2. Education that will make Malaysians more rational consumers and more skilled savers and investors, less inclined to gamble on the stock market; and
3. Education that will spread knowledge and skills increasingly and widely to all levels of Malaysian society so that as many people as possible will become involved in the network of production and consumption that is called the modern industrial sector.

The structures and methodologies for these three aspects of education and training will be discussed later.

Political Challenges

The order of discussion is so structured that political challenges come last. This have no significance from the point of view of ranking in importance or priority of implementation. All programmes for overcoming the challenges should proceed simultaneously. I believe that it is more productive to discuss political matters after changes in the mind and economic changes have been clarified. In that sense, therefore, political changes represent the apex of the discussion concerning the nine challenges that have to be overcome.

Therefore, in this spirit, Challenge No. 3 takes precedence over Challenge No. 1. Challenge No. 3 is the challenge of fostering and developing a mature democratic society, practising a form of mature consensual, community-oriented Malaysian democracy that can be made a model for any developing country.

We can only hope that if our way of democracy survives to the year 2020 then it will have three quarters of a century of experience. By 2057 we shall celebrate our first centenary. By then the mere fact of survival should earn us the accolade of maturity.

The consensual approach has been known to those who have genuinely practised *adat perpatih* for a long time. It is basic to decision making in Japanese society. To a significant extent, it is a characteristic of industrial relations in Germany. Nevertheless, in Malaysia, one would have to cross certain roads and turn certain corners, if we were to try to converge on consensual modes while we move away from adversarial or confrontational modes. We could teach future citizens and current leaders that conflict resolution need not be seen solely as a zero-sum game.

Education can contribute not only by giving learners a grounding in history but also by teaching them the philosophy as well as the practice of the democratic way. This implication of community-oriented approaches has already been discussed in Challenge No. 7 of a caring society. The nature of values has been touched in the discussion of spiritual strength in Challenge No. 4.

It is worth pausing to sum up by noting that two vital ingredients for a democratic polity are a measure of material affluence and a modicum of economic justice.

Challenge No. 1, quite appropriately the ninth challenge to be considered is the first one listed in Dr Mahathir Mohamad's working paper. Indeed this is the apogee of the challenges; the establishment of a united Malaysian nation with a sense of common or shared destiny. The characteristics of a united Malaysian nation are well spelt out: it is at peace with itself; it is territorially and ethnically integrated; its nationals live harmoniously in fair partnership; and political loyalty is dedicated to the nation.

Among Third World countries, including those that are yet to be classified as advanced or developed, there are those that face bleak prospects of rapid economic advancement because of insecurity. Civil wars, frequent riots, oppressive dictatorships or military regimes are not the stuff that democracies can easily be built on.

While internal peace can be purchased by increasing affluence, equity and expanding learning opportunities, ultimately in a developing country eternal vigilance is needed. All tendencies towards violence, extensive dissatisfaction, sudden loss of credibility of the leadership or any attempts to resort to violence as a means to influence the power structure need to be promptly and effectively dealt with.

The most direct contribution of education and training is to include all communities in the system at all levels. At the secondary and tertiary levels there is a need to help students understand our form of economic justice, that is, Challenge No. 8. Territorial integration can best be achieved by insuring a judicious mixture of learners from all territories in fully residential schools and universities.

Ethnic integration is a more sensitive issue. The less sophisticated – in the modern industrialized sense – a people are, the more resistant they will be towards integration through changes in the place where they live or in their respective cultures. On the other hand, it can be seen that in the large urban connurbations and industrial centres, young people easily merge into lifestyles that are somewhat cosmopolitan and conducive towards integration even though the comparative quality of such living may be questionable.

The way in which Challenge No. 4 is overcome and the velocity of its success will have considerable impact on the emergence of national harmony coupled with strong political loyalty. Dedication is the other side of the coin of a caring society. This is the challenge where education has an important role to play both directly and indirectly. And this is the challenge where all forms of education, at all levels, from pre-school to distance education and life-long learning can contribute the greatest impact, especially in the long run.

Methodologies and Strategies for Implementation

In the course of analysing the nature of the nine challenges, I have indicated areas where education and training programmes can be effective. I shall now try to consider the forms and contents of appropriate education and training programmes in the light of the previous discussion.

Seven common aspects of education and training programmes need to be stated and accepted. First, financial resources and skilled manpower are rather limited and since they have alternative uses their diversion to education needs to be rationally planned and unwaveringly carried out.

Second, the effects of changes in education and training are only perceptible in the long run. It takes several years to design programmes and plans that are realistic and integrated. It would take several more years to train the administrators and trainers and to give them some hands-on experience in comparable situations. It takes more than a dozen years for the first batch of learners to go through the newly designed system. Four to six more years will be needed to allow for tertiary graduates. Even if the first steps were taken in 1992 the initial stream of graduates would come out just in time to celebrate the year 2020.

I mentioned these time factors to give readers some idea of the dimension within which changes in education and training operate. Fortunately Malaysia already has an education system that has been in existence since the declaration of independence. Nevertheless, parts of the system have been subject to comprehensive or partial changes during the last three decades. To the extent that alterations can be successfully made at various points in the system the total time needed to educate and train the right kind of graduates can be shortened.

I would suggest that in monitoring the quality and quantity of graduates is as important as monitoring the quality of education and training that is being delivered.

Third, since duration or time is imperative because education and training design has to be teleological or tendentious therefore free choice can only be allowed on a limited scale to educators, learners and parents. Philosophies of education that were in vogue when some of the current senior educators and professors were writing their doctorates in the United States and the United Kingdom are rapidly becoming obsolete in those countries. We should design a Malaysian philosophy education that is utterly consonant with the objectives of Vision 2020.

Fourth, education and training should be conceived as a fully co-ordinated infrastructure that offers ordinary Malaysians life-long education opportunities wherever they may live. All education and training programmes should be co-ordinated and planned by the Ministry of Education which should have transferred to it the necessary budgetary provisions. Currently there are several training programmes sponsored by public sector agencies which are outside the purview of the Ministry of Education. Distance education at all levels and in all studies should be the responsibility of the Ministry of Education. Post-secondary non-university education should also be made the responsibility of the Ministry of Education.

Fifth, strategic issues: content and delivery. Malaysians need to be made competent in three basic skills: literacy, numeracy and operacy in thinking.

Literacy

We have decided to use the National language as the main medium of instruction in education. Therefore learners must achieve a high degree of competency in reading, speaking and writing skills in that language. At the same time because of the open nature of the Malaysian economy and because of our policy of trying to attract foreign investment especially sophisticated technologies, our learners must be trained to communicate in significant foreign languages. While a competency in reading and speaking English is essential, an increasing number of graduates from other language systems will be needed. We may need to have at least half as many students in Japan as we have in the United States. This would involve about 10,000 students at any one time in good universities in Japan through the next two decades. We should need smaller numbers of equally competent graduates from universities in Germany and France. A constant flow of several hundreds of graduates will be needed who can cope with the Korean language and business culture besides a number of Malays and non-Malays who could cope with the Chinese and Arabic languages and their respective commercial cultures.

Since the learning of languages should become part of the learning culture it should not only be confined to school or university teaching. Direct methods should be developed so that learners could conveniently learn Japanese or German through Malay and not through English.

Literacy programmes should include some introduction to literature. More efforts need to be devoted towards teaching the aesthetics of classical Malay prose and poetry besides exposing learners to modern Malay literature.

Dewan Bahasa dan Pustaka has pioneered a substantial programme of translation of good literature of other languages. This could be focused more specifically so that those who read good works in Malay translation may be able to develop aesthetic standards by comparing our works with those that have a universal acceptance. The private sector could be encouraged to translate and publish approved works by giving tax incentives or even subsidies. Malaysia should consider the possibility of gaining greater access to translations and original works that are published in bahasa Indonesia. This is one of the shortcuts that could have a substantial marginal effect on the volume of reading materials available.

Numeracy

As vice-chancellor and chairman of the Malaysian Examinations Council, I had an excellent opportunity to observe the academic performance of a wide variety of Malaysian students. Involvement in the teaching of economics at the university level as well as the design of a new syllabus for the STPM economics papers left me with the impression that generally numeracy is one area where rural students are particularly weak. There may be many reasons for this state of affairs. Perhaps because of historical reasons a large proportion of primary school teachers were not sufficiently trained in the techniques of teaching mathematics and they have left a kind of phobia of numbers and quantitative relationships in the minds of generations of rural students. In the age of Information Technology it may seem strange to advocate the need for strengthening learner's capability to cope with numbers. All the complex statistical parameters that I had to work out using logarithm tables and slide rules can now be instantly obtained on a hand calculator.

What is not understood by planners and others is that numerical thinking is possible because of neuronal networks in the brain. Numeracy and literacy are thought out in different parts of the brain. If young learners are thoroughly exposed to numeracy exercises, their brain systems will become more complex and they will be better able to think in quantitative terms. The memorization of numbers, timetables or formulae is less significant in this context. It is the skill of grasping the meaning of numerical relationships such as ratios, sets or functions that is important. Modern managerial decision-making frequently requires an ability to grasp not only a mass of numerical data which is set out in a table or a chart but to catch the implications of trends that could have alternative projections.

Operacy

This is a technical term in the theory of lateral thinking which means, "thinking skill". The fact that managers and directors in Southeast Asia are prepared to pay substantial sums to learn lateral thinking should encourage the sceptical reader to accept that there might be something useful in it. Indeed several schools and universities in Malaysia are already offering courses in thinking skills. It is fallacious to believe that competence in numeracy or literacy can simultaneously enable one to be competent in thinking skills. It may be clearer to some readers if I were to suggest that learning to swim or play golf will not teach one tennis.

Sixth, knowledge. All our, traditional general education systems have placed great emphasis on rote learning. Learners are required to memorize long extracts of the relevant literature. It is therefore not surprising that this trend has seeped through the system. In the modern world where information half way across the globe can be accessed almost instantly, the memory no longer needs to be stuffed with data or texts. What is needed is to teach the learners how to find information when they need it and how to use it in their thinking.

Even so I believe that there is value in teaching learners the art of memorization as a way of developing their brains and minds. In reality the art of memorization is rarely taught in our system.

During the learning years from primary to the end of secondary school, students need to be taught knowledge of the world in which they live. In Vision 2020, since they will be expected to become involved with increasingly sophisticated technologies they should be given a good grounding in the fundamentals of technology. As they specialize vocationally or professionally they will need to be taught specific skills and provided with sufficient opportunities for hands-on experience. Equally important is the need to teach Malaysian teenagers how to cope with change in their working environment. Since the rate of advancement in technology is increasing, the realization of Vision 2020 will create an even greater velocity of change. This need should be incorporated into the education system as an essential ingredient.

Seventh, skills. The mind seems able to store an infinite amount of knowledge. This stored knowledge can be linked to newly acquired knowledge by appropriate thinking skills. However, a skill that is learnt can only be improved and refined. Additional skills are only learned if there are new training opportunities.

The education system needs to be designed in such a way that while the dissemination of knowledge can be organized on some structured incremental system, the training of skills needs to be regularly updated to meet changing circumstances. Those responsible for planning education and training institutions need to be alert to the needs that are likely to be required in the near future. They should also be bold enough to terminate programmes that are merely producing square pegs when all the holes are round. The unemployed graduate who may be the victim of a transitional recession is a different kind of problem from the unemployable graduate whose skills have become obsolete.

We have seen that much of the function of education involves the fostering of right attitudes. To carry out this particular task, teachers have to be competent and committed. Any sign of a credibility gap between what is advocated and what is practised by those responsible for running the education system will have serious negative results.

We have discussed the need for the acceptance of high ethical values. This is one of the most delicate areas in education. The teachers, the teaching materials and the practices need to be harmonized and disseminated to the learners in packages that they can understand and adopt.

Designs for a Developed and Industrialized Society

Education and training strategies for the achievement of the aims of Vision 2020 require exploration of alternative designs of structures and methodologies. In the beginning of this chapter, clarifications and definitions were set out. Then, each of the nine challenges were examined in the light of the contributions that education and training could make towards overcoming them. Later, the broad strategies and methodologies that could be applied were examined. Now implementation will be the main focus. I shall examine the delivery of education and training programmes in the formal sectors which include all educational institutions directly administered and mainly financed by the Ministry of Education and certain official agencies. I shall also examine the so-called informal sector which is generally organized by voluntary associations who may receive financial assistance from the government.

I shall devote some attention to five specific topics that are not always considered when human resource development is discussed:

1. Distance education;
2. The role of the private sector in education;

3. The role of the co-operative movement in education;
4. The special needs of the *orang asli;* and
5. Health, sports and recreation in human resource development.

In Malaysia, by any measurement, the bulk of education and training is provided by the government. Therefore government planning and implementation will be the most influential factor in meeting the challenges of Vision 2020.

I have noted that educational plans involve rather long-term planning. There are few useful results that can be obtained from short-term changes in education. Instead of being a sign of pragmatism and flexibility, frequent short-term twists and changes in implementation often demonstrate impatience, uncertainty and lack of vision. The design of plans has to be visionary, foresighted and comprehensive. Extreme patience is needed to wait for the first results to appear a decade or more later.

At this point in Malaysian history it may be timely to examine the possibility of appointing a Royal Commission that would examine the whole structure of education and training in all sectors and make recommendations in the light of the achievement of the aims of Vision 2020.

It is not that our system has many weaknesses or that too many resources are being used uneconomically or that the objects of education and training are inadequately co-ordinated or harmonized. It is the fact that with the announcement of Vision 2020, Malaysia is confronted with a new map and is expected to travel at a faster speed. Therefore it seems apposite to make a thorough reexamination of the whole system and to change the existing system into a new system with additions where necessary.

Several excellent studies have been made on the primary education system. The only concern that I have is the percentage of primary school-leavers who do not continue in the secondary stream and who appear to regress into illiteracy and anumeracy – if that is the word. This point reinforces the need for some form of continued education that could be provided by distance education techniques.

The planning of secondary education and research about its results have mostly been carried out by officials. It would be better if the universities and other social science research institutions were encouraged and facilitated to give attention to aspects of the aims, execution and results of secondary education.

One subject that needs to be included as a specific topic is the skills of thinking. This should include not only elements of lateral thinking, problem-solving and decision-making but also the art of caring for the mind and the spirit.

There may be a case for re-examining the methodologies of teaching English and other languages in the light of the need for a greater ability to comprehend written instructions in English as well as being able to understand spoken English and other selected languages.

Vocational education tends to be seen as a stream that is pursued by those who are less successful in other streams. This is a pity. In future the blue-collar and hardhat workers should be able to earn comparable if not better wages than white-collar workers. The ranks of management should be opened to vocational graduates who are able to study management courses while they are working in their technical jobs. Here we can appreciate the contribution that a well-designed distance education system could offer.

In the distant past, the *guru* was one of the most respected members of society. Today few able young persons would have the ambition of becoming a professional teacher and making a career of it. This is indeed regrettable.

The implementation of caring attitudes in the minds of learners will depend on the dedication and credibility of all the teachers in the education system.

Any discussion about the ways our universities can help overcome the nine challenges could easily fill more pages than this whole chapter. Soon the government and the public will have to make an unequivocal choice between a uniform standard for all public universities and a hierarchy of quality that candidates for admission as well as employers will know and select accordingly. An independent commission could be established to make regular objective assessments so that performance and weaknesses of universities could be known. This idea is different from the Committee of Vice-Chancellors and Principals that exists in the United Kingdom. This commission should only be concerned with the assessment of academic quality in terms of teaching, research and examination results. It should not have any responsibilities for the disbursement of funds.

With regard to research there is a noticeable tendency for research institutes in the social sciences as well as in science and technology to be established outside the universities. This may be a progressive trend in affluent countries like the United States or Japan. However, in a relatively limited academic community such as in Malaysia, where universities are frequently under-financed for their research programmes, it may have negative effects in the long term. Two factors are worth thinking about in this respect. First, each institute tends to be built around one or two star performers who are attracted by the freedom to run their own domain with better prospects for income and promotion as well as perks which are irrationally distributed in universities according to the Buggins turn principle. Each of these institutes requires administrative and technical infrastructure which will be a further call on scarce resources.

More importantly is the fact that most real problems encountered in this technological age require a multi-disciplinary approach. For example, left to their own devices and because of the lack of leadership, a problem such as the design and construction of slopes along highways might be studied separately by a geologist or an engineer. Actually, the nature of slopes and the solution to the problem of maintaining stability requires close collaboration between geologists, soil scientists, climatologists, hydrologists, botanists and road engineers. The best results will be achieved when all these scientists work together and regularly interact with each other. They will also work better if they are provided with adequate finance, laboratory facilities and other resources. It goes without saying that by working with firms that are directly responsible for design and construction, it is more likely that their work will result in the resolution of real problems in the real world.

Research and consultancy is the interface where capable university scholars meet and work with the private sector and the public sector. A new attitude will be necessary among university administrators and councillors to encourage capable academics to serve the nation as researchers and consultants while they fulfill their required academic tasks.

I shall now consider the five specific topics. The list is not exclusive. There are many other equally important subjects that should be discussed. However imperatives of time and space limit the scope of this chapter.

Distance Education

Distance education is not always fully understood by many key decision makers in Malaysia. Distance education would operate in the following way. Learners who are given admission would study at home at their own pace. They would receive printed teaching materials, including specially prepared lessons, workbooks and text books. In certain centres they would have access to designated public or university libraries. They would receive lectures and demonstration through radio and television. They would communicate with their teachers through the post or by telephone tutorial as well as study schools at universities for a few weeks when university students are on vacation. Standards of examinations would be of the same level as that of residential institutions of higher education.

It may be superfluous to make the point that Malaysia already has all the necessary technology for providing a distance education system. All it lacks is the software and the political will to realize it. I envisage distance education in Malaysia to be organized at three levels:

1. Courses that disseminate knowledge and skills at all levels equivalent to higher technical schools, technical colleges and universities;

2. Courses that provide continuing education for learners who may be employed but who intend to improve their knowledge and skills such as management or accounting students at various levels; and

3. Adult education for those who wish to continue learning as part of the ideal of life-long learning such as literature, including creative writing, languages, agricultural techniques, etc.

Thailand, Indonesia and India's experiences in distance education proves that widespread delivery of quality education in a national language is possible.

And if the distance education system is provided with financial support on the scale of a single university it should be able to survive as a viable organization.

It is important to be aware that this is one of the education and training systems that can be disseminated throughout the country. This is one system that can transcend space, race or occupation. Several of the challenges that require the inculcation of new understanding and new attitudes can be provided to a wide audience through a distance education system.

Private Sector's Role

There are at least three ways, among many possibilities, how the private sector can contribute towards the achievement of Vision 2020 in the field of education and training:

1. The establishment of privately funded and managed institutions of education and training;

2. The provision of in-house or collaborative education and training programmes by firms; and

3. Direct support in the form of grants and scholarships to institutions of higher education by the private sector.

Initially the Malaysian Business Council could develop programmes to make its members increasingly aware of these possibilities. Every association of enterprises and entrepreneurs should be encouraged to plan and implement programmes that will contribute positively on all the above three fronts.

Leaders in the private sector should be encouraged to change such attitudes as "we are paying taxes and making donations and providing training to our own employees therefore we do not need to do more." They should seek a new perspective where they continuously try to promote programmes that will meet the needs of the three ways mentioned above.

Co-Operative Movement's Role

For reasons that are outside the scope of this chapter, the co-operative movement has not projected an image of an institution that can make a substantial contribution towards the development of education and training in Malaysia.

Actually the adumbration of the nine challenges that lie in the way of achieving Vision 2020 confront the co-operative movement with a unique opportunity to play an important role in contributing towards national development while it simultaneously metamorphoses into a new dimension where it can leave behind its colonial philosophy.

If for no other reason, rather more space is given to the co-operative movement because I am presenting this chapter in my capacity as the President of Angkasa, the National Apex organization of the Malaysian co-operative movement.

There are three specific areas where the co-operative movement can contribute towards overcoming many of the challenges that stand in the way of realizing Vision 2020.

First, the co-operative movement is founded on the system of values that were recognized in Europe by the German co-operator, F.W. Raiffeisen and the Rochdale pioneers of Manchester. In Asia these values were found to be compatible with the national aspirations of the Republic of Indonesia by Doctor Mohammed Hatta. In Japan, half a century before the Japanese had heard of European co-operation, Ninomiya Sontoku had been promoting self-reliance and mutual aid for the alleviation of rural poverty.

In Malaysia, if the leaders and members of the co-operative movement are really serious about contributing towards the realization of Vision 2020 then they will have to learn the real meaning of these values and practise those that are advocated in Challenges No. 3, 4, 7 and 8. This means that the Ministry responsible for co-operative development, the department of co-operative development as well as all the institutions for co-operative development under the aegis of the Ministry such as the Co-operative College and the Co-operative Education Trust Fund should be mobilized for the realization of Vision 2020.

Second, through the school co-operatives, direct experience of democracy and entrepreneurship can be obtained by students. Malaysia is a leading country in the formation of school co-operatives. More that 90 per cent of secondary schools and most universities have co-operatives. The Ministry of Education should have a policy of encouraging teachers and headmasters to guide school co-operatives which should be managed as much as possible by students. The teachers' burden should be given due recognition.

In Japan, savings groups begin in primary schools. Perhaps that is one reason why the Japanese habitually save 15 to 20 per cent of their personal incomes. In France, school co-operatives encourage their members to carry out social projects such as redecorating old folks' homes or cleaning up the gardens of welfare homes.

School co-operatives should be encouraged to become involved in internal tourism. While the slogan "to know Malaysia is to love Malaysia" may be a cliché it can become a powerful influence in the development of civic consciousness. School co-operatives under the guidance of Angkasa are already organizing tours to visit each other during vacations. Each host co-operative provides its guests with data about the geographical and economic characteristics of its area, significant historical information besides demonstrations of cultural performances.

Where conditions are favourable and uninformed resistance is not excessive, university co-operatives have been able to provide students and libraries with cheaper books that are efficiently delivered.

Third, there are a number of organizations that are dedicated to the enhancement of the economic and social position of women. As a developing country, Malaysia's record of providing opportunities for women to enter all sectors of employment and other activities is relatively good. In the co-operative movement considerable attention is given towards the formation of women's co-operatives as well as the greater participation of women in leadership roles. One area that deserves special attention is the formation of co-operatives for women factory workers especially in the electronics industry. These workers need an organization to provide them with self-managed facilities for savings, credit and consumption.

The Special Needs of the Orang Asli

I am referring specifically to the *orang asli* in Peninsular Malaysia. I am certain that some of the tribal communities living outside the large and small urban centres in Sabah and Sarawak also have special needs but I am unable to discuss them here.

If we accept the main objective of *orang asli* development policy is to bring them into the mainstream of Malaysian life then this objective can now be better designed in the light of Vision 2020. Education and training is of special significance because it would be a contradiction of the values expressed in the nine challenges to transfer physically whole communities out of their present location into areas of rural land adjacent to settlements or into the fringes of small urban areas which would rapidly degenerate into debilitating slums.

For those *orang asli* communities that indicate they want modernization, plans should be implemented in education and training so that the process will harmonize with the cycle of the generations.

For their own health and for the growth of their children, mothers should be provided with day-care centres and adequate health education. Primary schools should be located as near as possible to *orang asli* settlements. Primary school programmes should include opportunities for pupils to become familiar with their natural habitat. Parents could help teachers.

Fully residential secondary schools for *orang asli* learners should be set up at nodal points not too distant from their settlements. Some of the teachers should be selected from their own communities so that the children can be helped in their passage towards modern living. There should be an adequate number of scholarships for qualified *orang asli* candidates to enter institutions of higher learning.

In the meanwhile, suitable learning programmes could be developed to enable adult *orang asli* to earn a better living. Their expertise in the jungle should be utilized so that they can produce rattan, timber and natural products that have medicinal or industrial uses. These commercial activities should be organized cooperatively so that the *orang asli* can learn to manage their own affairs and not be exploited.

Who shall implement these programmes? The best model would be to create an agency similar to MARA. This agency has achieved considerable success in dealing with the education and training of Bumiputera and providing them with business opportunities. MARA has now evolved into a more sophisticated commercial organization. It seems unlikely that it could develop the right attitudes for dealing with the economic and social development of the *orang asli*. A new agency would have to initiate new programmes which would start well behind MARA's initial benchmark.

Health, Sports and Recreation's Role

One of the basic requirements for the realization of Vision 2020 is a society that not only becomes increasingly healthy but is also becoming increasingly health-conscious.

Improvements in the general state of health are measured by declining morbidity rates, increases in life expectancy as well as increases in average height and weight of young people. Education and training can contribute towards such improvements by teaching the learners and their parents better health habits, nutrition and exercise. Health is not something that necessarily comes with modernization. Indeed some of the unhealthy eating habits generated by relentless advertising and marketing strategies will induce diseases in populations that hitherto have had a minimal acquaintance with them.

The concept of the caring society involves the protection of vulnerable groups from the influences of unhealthy habits. This includes protection from the spread of drug addiction and AIDS, the latest scourge. Education and training programmes for all can contribute towards the improvement of the nations's wealth.

The growth of increasingly sophisticated and cheaper media technologies creates a tendency for people to become increasingly vicarious participants in sports. To counter this trend, facilities for mass participation in athletics and games need to be constructed at as many urban and rural centres as possible. A corps of instructors needs to be created. It is likely that once the necessary seeding has been done this will be taken over by private enterprises and co-operatives.

If these suggestions are thought to be expensive or impractical, then it might be a useful exercise along the lines of the equitable society, to compare sums spent by public and private organizations on the construction of golf courses with the amounts spent on the provision of playing fields in the rural areas.

This chapter does not examine the needs and ways for the training of sports stars. Nevertheless, it is realized that if Malaysia could produce some international stars it might contribute towards the strengthening of national unity.

Recreation facilities can be seen as part of general education and life-long learning. The enjoyment of nature can lead not only to a love of the country but it can nurture feelings that strengthen attitudes leading towards a caring society.

Conclusion

The purpose of this chapter is to explore the alternative ways by which education and training could contribute towards overcoming the nine challenges, severally and together, so as to achieve

Vision 2020. Approaches, perceptions and strategies may differ but they should all be designed to be appropriate for each of the challenges.

Some new ideas have been put forward such as the use of distance education and a MARA-like agency for the development of the *orang asli*. Some existing institutions may be reoriented. These include more focused teaching of literacy, numeracy and thinking operacy in schools and universities.

The co-operative movement has been specially mentioned for its contribution towards the enhancement of loyalty, civic-consciousness, a caring society and entrepreneurship. Radical policy reforms by government and the co-operative movement need to be carried out to eliminate such negative values as selfish individualism, ignorance by leaders and arrogance of certain officials.

The private sector can innovate and support education and training programmes that could positively help overcome many of the challenges. We should not forget that public and private enterprise can become malignant if the correct values are not accepted and practised.

The broad details of the issues have been presented both from the point of view of vertical as well as lateral thinking in the hope that new approaches will be designed for the realization of Vision 2020.

It is not only the macro-view of the nine challenges that have to be overcome but it is also the micro-view of the nature of each challenge that must be carefully thought out. The time frame involved that may be feasible should be borne in mind.

14

Human Resource Development: The Key Towards a Developed and Industrialized Society

Charles D. Roxburgh

Very few countries have a vision – and I can assure you, none, with a perfect 2020! I can only say how privileged and proud I feel to be a part of Malaysia country during this very momentous phase of its development.

Vision 2020 is not just any vision. It is a vision of the march of a country's development in its totality – its economy, the quality of life; the value of its people; and the resilience, competence and discipline of its workforce. And as our Prime Minister has expressed, some of our characteristics of our Vision 2020, will include among other things a society that is united and confident, liberal and tolerant; a society that is robust and resilient, competent and at home with the latest scientific and technological advancements; a society that is caring and just, proud of its own traditions and heritage; a society that is economically and spiritually prosperous, flourishing in a clean and healthy environment within a system that is democratic and uniquely Malaysian. It will be such a society that our human resource development efforts will have to yield.

Human Resource Strategy

Attempting to map out the strategy for such an effort would be daunting under any circumstance. For me, being less than adequately competent in the values, aspirations, priorities and some of the basic systems in the country, it will be that much more challenging. I might add, however, that this same disadvantage might, on the other hand, help provide a more detached and global perspective.

Let me restate what I think should be the very broad concept of our human resource strategy towards Vision 2020. It is one based on the effective inculcation and strengthening of core values in the society as a whole and the satisfactory development of an adequately qualified workforce capable of fully meeting the country's commercial and industrial needs and beyond. It is a two-pronged strategy – requiring value strengthening and workforce development.

Value Strengthening

Let me start with the first prong and, in my mind, the hardest part – strengthening of values in the society. This should be a global and all-encompassing effort involving the whole nation and would, in the main, centre on the inculcation of basic values. Dr Mahathir Mohamad spoke of the need to change our way of life in the context of Vision 2020 – "*Mengubah cara hidup*". This is what this first prong is designed to achieve – to bring about this change.

How do we bring about such a change? To succeed, we will need a national effort – national in the sense that the whole nation is fully galvanized into undertaking a sincere commitment to this change. Every individual in the country will have to undertake a self-appraisal of his or her values against the set of values that we are determined, as a nation, to live by. Without such an undertaking, the result will be meaningless repetition of slogans and hollow exhortations.

So, as a first step in this first prong, we need a total national commitment to "*mengubah* our *cara hidup*". To help realize this commitment, we also need an all-embracing national plan for "value strengthening". For this purpose, the population can be divided into two target groups – adults and children.

Adults

This separation is significant if we accept that values such as discipline, honesty, caring and a desire for learning are mainly developed during our formative years. We must consider however that while adults may readily endorse and support certain new ways and values, they may not necessarily change their old values and habits. Herein lies the first obstacle – the very group that is supposed to set the value orientation pace for the younger group might itself have problems in making the transition. It does seem, therefore, that these adults will first have to come to terms with the full significance of Vision 2020 – that it does not only promise the glory at the end of the rainbow but also requires the sacrifice, grit and commitment of everyone.

The adult population – parents, guardians, elder relatives and teachers – will be directly responsible for the value strengthening of the younger generation. They may need a further understanding of their responsibilities as the direct programmers to their wards' values system. Maybe some formal programme to help this adult group could be developed to ensure all such direct children value models are truly effective in grooming this next generation towards the vision we sought.

Children

Let me now turn to the second group – our children. Children can be divided into four groups – pre-schoolers, primary pupils, secondary pupils and post-secondary youths. The opportunity for value development in these four groups will, of course, decrease progressively with the older groups. Therefore the appeal in value strengthening will have to be different with each group.

For pre-schoolers, those below the age of six, the parents will have to be fully responsible for undertaking their value development. However, a two-to three-year nationwide programme could also be developed covering ages four to six on a supplementary basis to assist parents in this development. This would call for a standardization of all kindergarten and playschool syllabus geared towards making them more effective value and attitude development – a move that, perhaps, has already been considered for some time.

For those who are in school we need to effectively incorporate all the desired values into their everyday development – both formal and informal. The formal will include the structured subjects while the informal will be the learning environment, the actual conduct of those teachers interacting with and leading them, as well as the approach to learning itself. For example, initiative and ways for acquiring, appreciating and using knowledge may be given more emphasis.

Thus through planned and focused pre-school value development which is strengthened through formal and informal curriculum in school, we will be able to develop in our children those values and qualities that we wish for our future society.

It is always much easier to suggest what to do rather than how to do it. It will not be easy but, I would hasten to add, that it can be done. Let me just give a very small but perhaps telling illustration at this point. I come from Texas in the United States. During the Fourth of July, the United States' Independence Day, almost every single house would be decked with the "Stars and Stripes" of the United States flag. In my four years here in Malaysia, I have always been surprised that August 31 does not seem to produce this same effect. This, to my mind, is opportunity lost – a great opportunity to get everyone, especially the younger ones, to effectively participate and create a symbolic gesture of loyalty and patriotism for the country.

Over ten million of our population, or about 60 per cent, are 20 years and below. In the year 2020 they will be 29 to 50 years old. They will be running the country. If we can all commit ourselves to the values of Vision 2020, believe in them, practise them, and get our children to believe in and practise them too, the society of Vision 2020 will only be a matter of time.

Workforce Development

Let me now move on to the second prong and the one I think is easier to achieve – workforce development. This involves identifying, forecasting and developing the required skills to meet the nation's needs. This would include industrial and commercial, research and development as well as public sector needs.

Identification of the required skills is a key first step. This would call for as accurate as possible a database of our current and forecasted longer term skills requirements based on our total projected economic and social needs up to the year 2020.

Accurate Database

Getting an accurate fix of our immediate skilled manpower needs is often difficult. Making a projection of this need over the next 30 years is doubly difficult. Nevertheless, both the public and private sectors must have a common understanding of what is needed, a common objective to work towards based on a common database that both are comfortable with.

Private Sector-Public Sector Co-Operation

And this brings me to the next point – public-private sector co-operation. Establishing and making this co-operation really work is vital. Otherwise our efforts will dissipate and little will be achieved. What can we do to foster this all-vital co-operation so that the two groups will really be working as one?

The groundwork for this co-operation was laid some years ago when the Malaysia Incorporated concept was introduced. There is no doubt in anyone's mind of the necessity of this co-operation or the sincerity behind the government's effort in working towards this objective. Some encouraging progress has been made since then and what remains is to further build on this concept to make the co-operation complete and fully effective.

Structured Communication Forums

A fundamental aspect of effective co-operation is effective communication. There must be ongoing dialogues between the public and private sectors. Joint consultative committees covering appropriate ministries, departments or functions could be created to provide the structure of such communication interchange.

Such structured channels would lead to the effective pooling of ideas and experience between the public and private sectors. Additionally, the private sector would have a greater sense of ownership of decisions taken by the government, thus, increasing private sector commitment to national development plans and programmes.

Once such communication channels are institutionalized, further concrete joint efforts could be made to give more depth to this understanding and co-operation. Let us discuss a few of such possibilities. One is the cross-posting of staff between government departments and selected private sector companies whenever such postings are possible and beneficial. Another possibility is to encourage managers and professionals from the private sector to teach in colleges and universities or be guest lecturers at such institutions.

Identification of Needed Skills

I mentioned earlier that this second prong involves the identification, forecasting and development of required skills to effectively meet the nation's continuing need. Let me go back briefly to the identification and forecasting of required skills.

Studies need to be made to determine the extent of guidance and realignment required to bring our future skilled workforce output in line with our forecasted need. Some reorientation of our society with regards to skills preference and bias might need to be made where necessary.

Today, for example, there is a shortfall of technical support staff like technicians, welders, chargemen, etc. The government has recognized this and is appropriately embarking not only in training more people in these areas, but also attempting to elevate the standing of these skills as a profession in the eyes of society. This is the kind of structural correction that should be taken in realigning our skills distribution to needs.

Once the manpower needs for the various stages leading to the year 2020 has been firmly identified along various skills and professions, the qualifications for each group could be determined. Subsequent training and development leading to the required level of competence could then be programmed.

All these could only be done with maximum effectiveness if the plan is not subject to excessive changes and modifications as a result of faulty identification of need, either in terms of the required skills or number, or both.

Development

Development itself should cover three areas. First, specific industry skills; second, general skills; and third, work or business ethics and discipline.

The first, specific industry skills, is the easiest to develop. It covers technical and professional development geared towards a specific industry or profession. The petroleum industry, for example, would need engineers and geologists, while the banking industry would need mainly accountants and financial people.

In the second area, general skills, emphasis should be placed on equipping our workforce with better supporting skills including management, negotiation, entrepreneurship, communication, public relations skills, etc. In the area of communication, mastery of a second language is essential. The government has emphasized this point repeatedly and is already taking steps to strengthen English as a second language in the country. I think this is an excellent move.

The third development area, business and work ethics, is dependent largely on the value system of the society. Thus, if our value strengthening, as discussed earlier, were successful, a sound work culture and business ethics would be easily developed and assimilated by the workforce.

Conclusion

I am sure many things can, and will be undertaken, to prepare us for Vision 2020. The government has taken many steps that fit into the jigsaw puzzle of this vision. There may be a few pieces still missing but so few that they should not stop us from seeing and recognizing the picture in the puzzle, thus making identification of the missing pieces easier. No doubt all the pieces will fully come together before long. I have been in this beautiful country for more than four years. I have learned a little of its language and participated in its activities. I have watched with respect its progress and have learned to admire its people.

I began earlier by saying how privileged I feel to be a part of this country during this very momentous phase of its development. In your history, 1511, the Melaka Sultanate, was very momentous. It signalled the twilight of a glorious Melaka. I believe, 1991 is equally momentous in heralding the dawn of a glorious Malaysia. Vision 2020, unveiled in 1991, symbolizes the final phase of the nation's 500-year march back into the sun. Let not the next generation blame you for failing to successfully complete this march.

15

Malaysia Incorporated: Private Sector-Public Sector Collaboration

Abdullah Abdul Rahman

Vision 2020 is a declaration of the strategic intent of the Malaysian government in its 30-year quest for an industrialized country. The reiteration of Dr Mahathir Mohamad at the inaugural meeting of the Malaysian Business Council on February 28, 1991 of " ... the necessity of making Malaysia Incorporated a reality ... " emphasized the importance of the policy as one of the desired strategies to achieve the objective of Vision 2020.

The Malaysia Incorporated Policy is a strategy for the attainment of a competitive, dynamic, robust and resilient economy. It stresses the need to define, develop and operationalize a new pattern of behaviour, thinking and interaction *vis-à-vis* the private sector-public sector relationship. The identification of the critical approaches within the private sector-public sector productive partnership will ensure the sustenance of the nation's comparative advantages in an increasingly competitive global economic environment. The pursuit to improve Malaysia's competitive advantage to match competing nations in the international marketplace must necessarily be the strategic intention of the Malaysia Incorporated Policy.

Malaysia Incorporated

The concept of Malaysia Incorporated was propounded by Dr Mahathir Mohamad in 1983 as one of the fundamental bases of national development. While the concept has been accepted into the framework for development, its operational reality on the other hand is less evident, and indeed little understood by our society. Dr Mahathir Mohamad has broadly defined the concept of Malaysia Incorporated to mean a system of co-operation between the government and the private sector towards the creation of a Malaysian company to achieve progress and where the profits accrued will be shared by all. The government is a shareholder in this company, and if the company progresses and makes profit, a portion will accrue to the government and subsequently to the people as a whole. Dr Mahathir Mohamad has on various occasions underlined the relationship between the respective roles of the public and private sectors under this concept. In this symbiotic relationship, the public sector is expected to function efficiently to support the efforts of the private sector as the main engine of growth of the national economy.

Unlike other policies for national development, Malaysia Incorporated is behavioural in nature, encompassing shared values and a sense of common purpose. Consequently the policy must be viewed within the spectrum of the "software" of societal relationships. Its manifestations in this sense are less tangible and visible, thus rendering it more difficult to quantify or measure.

Nevertheless, the relationship envisaged represents an ethos within a society which transcends the dichotomies distinguishing the domains of the public and private sectors. In its ideal state, the polarities between the public and private sectors should exist. There is a synergy between these two sectors which not only reinforces their respective roles but is also mutually supportive. What is the thrust therefore of this relationship towards the goal of Vision 2020? The directions for private sector-public sector collaborations are clearly spelt out in Dr Mahathir Mohamad's "Malaysia: The Way Forward", namely:

1. The liberalization of the Malaysian economy in order to ensure dynamic growth;
2. Pursuing export-led growth in spite of the rise of protectionism, trade blocs and managed trade;
3. The expansion and improvement to the value-added and quality of our manufactured products to support the Accelerated Industrialization Drive;
4. Strategizing to carve out a market niche for Malaysian products in the global marketplace; and
5. The restructuring of the private sectors towards increasing Malaysian ownership in the market economy through the development and expansion of small- and medium-sized industries.

It is evident from the above that both the public and private sectors have their respective roles to play individually and jointly towards achieving the goals of Vision 2020. This can be pursued within the ambit of the Malaysia Incorporated concept.

Role of the Public Sector

The public sector is responsible for ensuring that all subsystem within the national policy respond to the goals set in Vision 2020. While the private sector has been entrusted with the leading role in spearheading economic development, the public sector has to play its role as an equal and productive partner in ensuring overall national development. Given the national agenda to establish a competitive, dynamic and resilient economy, the public sector must of necessity play its role as the pacesetter and facilitator in addition to its traditional role of implementor.

Facilitator

The public sector's primary responsibility is to create a conducive environment that would be catalytic in providing the right impetus for rapid economic growth. It is the duty of the public sector to ensure that economic growth is facilitated within given legal and regulatory parameters. The public service must constantly review and improve upon its systems, procedures and processes to facilitate the private sector to achieve its desired goals and targets. In supporting the entrepreneurial efforts of the private sector, particularly with respect to ensuring the competitiveness of Malaysian exports in the international marketplace, the need for deregulation and an improved delivery system must be met. This is to facilitate the conduct of businesses and improve further the investment climate.

Pacesetter

The public sector must increasingly focus in its role as a pacesetter in the nation's socio-economic development. Contingent to this role, the public sector has to be ever sensitive and responsive to changes in the global environment in setting the pace and charting new directions and strategies for growth. It needs to be proactive to the demands of the international marketplace. The onus is on the public sector to charter new markets for our manufactured exports and new areas for entrepreneurial ventures. Here the public service must play the role of pacesetter by not only providing the right kind of information, but also actively promoting the country's goods and services overseas through the strengthening of its overseas institutions and personnel. The public sector requires the knowledge, skill and prudence in business and industrial planning, in-depth assessment of industry needs and strategic requirements, commercial and market intelligence, evaluation of new technologies and skilful negotiations to enable it to provide sound administrative guidance to the private sector. These new requirements of the public sector will contribute to our competitive advantage with competing nations.

Implementor

The public sector's traditional role as the custodian of the public good and as implementor of socio-economic development programmes remains equally important. In the context of the national agenda it must play this role effectively in order to provide the essential social services to the people and to protect the public interest at large. In addition there is a greater demand for better services with higher expectations from our increasingly affluent society not only for wider access to public services but also for better standards of such services.

Facilitating Private Sector-Public Sector Collaboration

Consultative Panels

Since 1983, Consultative Panels have been established in most government agencies comprising representatives from both the public and private sectors. In 1990, the Sub-Committee of the Panel on Administrative Improvements was established with the view to stimulate the implementation of the Malaysia Incorporated concept. Chaired by the chief secretary to the government and comprising leaders in the private sector, this Sub-Committee is expected to identify those areas of co-operation for improving the delivery of services from the public to the private sectors and to work towards improving public administration in so far as it concerns the operations of the private sector in the area of economic development.

Deregulation

Efforts at deregulation to improve public administration have been introduced through the implementation of six strategies, namely:

1. The use of composite application forms;
2. The issue of composite licences;
3. The extension of the validity period of licences from one to five years;
4. The establishment of licensing centres in the local authorities;
5. The abolition of licences or licence fees; and

6. The improvement to the systems and procedures for licensing.

In addition, Section 107 of the Local Government Act 1976 has been amended to allow all Local Authorities to implement the composite application forms, composite licences and the extension of the validity period of licences.

Administrative Improvements

Arising from the discussions in the Consultative Panels at various ministries and departments, numerous administrative improvements in the delivery of services from the public to the private sector have been introduced. Among these were:

1. The setting up and increase in the number of one-stop centres for licensing of industries, business activities, housing projects, etc. at the state level. These one-stop centres also deal with land matters, infrastructure, taxes, local rates, utilities and other facilities;
2. Reduction of procedures for processing export licences for GSP, Asean-PTA and textiles;
3. Delegation of powers to enable licensing to be done at lower levels, at state and district offices, to expedite work processes and reduce waiting time;
4. Provision of guidebooks on procedures for licences and permits and on rules and regulations pertaining to the conduct of industrial or business activities;
5. Setting up of service counters to assist the private sector on queries and problems;
6. Computerization of work processes to expedite delivery of services; and
7. Installation of modern telecommunication systems at most agencies such as facsimile, telephone system with better facilities, additional lines, etc. to upgrade communications with government agencies.

Efforts at improvement of administrative procedures were largely agency-specific. The aggregated improvements across the entire public administration however were substantial. Administrative improvements were carried out incrementally but continuously to ensure efficient delivery of public sector services to the private sector.

New Directives on Malaysia Incorporated

In view of the critical importance of the Malaysia Incorporated concept in the development of the nation in line with the Second Outline Perspective Plan and Vision 2020, the government has issued Development Administration Circular No. 9 of 1991 entitled "Guide on the Implementation of the Malaysia Incorporated Policy".

This circular requires Consultative Panels comprising members from both the public and private sectors to be established in each ministry, department or office at the Federal, State and district levels. The Panels should focus discussions on the streamlining of rules, regulations and procedures which will facilitate the private sector. Ministries and departments should also hold annual dialogue sessions with the private sector to discuss policies and programmes which involve the private sector. In order to encourage closer relationship through the sharing of information and knowledge between the two sectors, government officers are allowed to take part in seminars, workshops and open forums sponsored by the private sector. Social interactions are also encouraged through jointly sponsored sporting activities. The circular also allows for ministries, departments or offices to receive tokens of appreciation or recognition for efficient service from private sector associations though not from individual companies.

Role of the Private Sector

The strategic directions of Vision 2020 and their substantive elaborations expressed in the programmes of the Second Outline Perspective Plan and the National Development Policy placed the private sector with the major task of generating economic growth. In the recent past, this strategy of private sector-led growth has pushed the nation to a higher level of economic success.

As the primary engine of growth, the private sector cannot afford to be inefficient and lethargic. The direction for an export-led growth demands the private sector to be strong, dynamic, robust, self-reliant, competent and resilient to match rivals in the competitive global markets. The private sector must seek to maintain the competitiveness of its products in order to get a fair share of the congested marketplace. Local exporters must diversify their products so as to reach diverse markets. They must pool their resources and strive to penetrate non-traditional markets of the developing Asian, African and Latin American countries.

The challenges before the private sector demands dynamism, boldness and willingness to take bigger risks and the application of sophisticated market intelligence. The colossal task of beating the trading blocs of the developed countries requires resourcefulness, efficiency, innovation, cost-effectiveness, productivity and the injection of competitiveness among our entrepreneurs. There need to be new approaches to revitalize corporate performance.

Towards a Competitive Private Sector

Companies must recognize that to be successful they have to compete in the global marketplace. They need to take advantage of the changes taking place in these environments. Fundamental to this is the identification of new market opportunities, evaluating international manufacturing and sourcing alternatives and analysing the profitability of sub-business units. They need to match the competitive advantage of their global rivals, rationalize product lines to capture global scale economies, institute quality circles and Just-In-Time production, and adopt effective human resource practices. I would like to elaborate on the seven criteria for a competitive and successful company with a future. These are:

1. Strategic intent;
2. Competitive marketing;
3. Quality products;
4. Competitive innovations;
5. Competitive human resource management;
6. Sense of national pride; and
7. Professionalism.

Strategic Intent

Just as the strategic intent of the nation has been set, companies must set about determining their own strategic intents. The concept of strategic intent describes the ambitions of companies that have risen to global leadership over the past 20 years. While their ambitions were out of proportion to their resources and capabilities, they created an obsession with winning at all levels of the organization and then sustained that obsession over the last 10 to 20 year quest for global leadership. Strategic intent envisions a desired leadership position and establishes the criterion the organization will use to chart out its progress. Examples of expressions of strategic intent are "Encircle Caterpillar" set out by Komatsu and "Beat Xerox" sought by Canon. According to Gary Hamel and C.K. Prahalad: "Strategic intent is more than simply unfettered ambition ... The concept encompasses an active management process that includes: focusing the organization's attention on the essence of winning; motivating people by communicating the value of the targets; leaving room for individual and team contributions; sustaining enthusiasm by providing new operational definitions as circumstances change; and using intent consistently to guide resource allocations ..."[1]

Strategic intent is about purpose. Everything begins with this. Organizations may formulate goals and objectives with sound ideas and intentions, yet lack overall purpose. Strategic intent provides the purpose and captures the essence of winning.

---

[1]   Gary Hamel and C.K. Prahalad, "Strategic Intent", *Harvard Business Review*, May–June 1989, pp. 63–76.

Competitive Marketing

Competitive marketing is propelled by a will to win, where competitors are seen as the enemy to be defeated. A key ingredient for success in marketing warfare is the establishment of competition-centred strategies and not just customer-centred strategies. This global perspective of the marketplace as a battleground must be internationalized by not only foreign-owned multinationals but also by local manufacturers seeking to export their products. Competitive global marketing requires that Malaysian exporters consolidate their resources and specify product advantages in order to ensure product marketability. They must undertake competitor analysis to anticipate the moves of their global competitors. It is also essential that global marketing networks be established whereby products are marketed through traditional and non-traditional outlets as well as private-label merchandisers.

In the competitive marketplace, the entrepreneur has to create and sustain competitive advantage through the outmanoeuvring and defeat of his competitors. Products must distinguish themselves in the eyes of the customer who must be given reason to discriminate in their favour. Quality, functionality, service, image and pricing are factors which differentiate products and it is the clever mix of these factors which will provide companies with the competitive advantage.

Quality Products

The importance of quality products is nothing new. Companies competing in the international marketplace must ensure product credibility. Quality continues to grow in importance as a factor for success in the marketplace. It continues to be a competitive weapon for competing companies. To enter and remain in the global marketplace, quality must never be sacrificed. Products must be sensitive to discriminating customer demands. Quality demands having the right products at the right time, at the right place and at the right price.

Competitive Innovations

Continual innovation in the kind of products and production processes are essential to maintain and enhance competitive advantage of our products. Innovations must be targeted to achieve specific market segments. We cannot afford innovation for innovation sake. Research and development efforts therefore should be stepped up and directed towards improving the competitive advantage of products.

Competitive Human Resource Management

Competitiveness in the marketplace demands competitive human resources. Management strategies must give due attention and adequate resource allocation to training, upgrading and retraining of skills and expertise within companies. Companies have a role and responsibility to equip their own manpower for changing tasks that accompany changing technology. Human resource management must also give due attention to the interest and well-being of the employees and reward them for their contributions. They must be well managed. A skilled, innovative and satisfied pool of workers provide the winning edge and competitive advantage for the company.

Sense of National Pride

Companies must be imbued with a sense of pride for the products and services that they produce. Pride in the company's product is a motivating factor that induces the company to produce quality results and propels the company to achieve greater success. Companies must see beyond success to realize that each achievement cumulatively contributes towards the nation. This culture of high performance is a commitment to achieving national aspirations. The concern for the nation, its progress, its economic survival and its recognition in the global marketplace should be the underlying ethos for private sector entrepreneurial ventures. This sense of national pride must be imbued at all levels of private sector companies where the label "Made in Malaysia" is held in high esteem. To be winners at the global marketplace, we must have a sense of national pride.

Professionalism

Malaysian businessmen need to advance the image of Corporate Malaysia. A Corporate Malaysian projects such characteristics as reliability, credibility, honesty, integrity and trustworthiness. His word is his bond. He must subscribe and adhere to a code of business ethics. The hallmarks of his business posture are delivery on time, meeting specifications, abiding to agreements, conforming to legitimate procedures and providing accurate information. Professionalism on the job will also help him gain the respect of his business partners. Up-to-date knowledge, expertise, entrepreneurship, business acumen and foresight are some attributes of professionalism on the job that will ensure his success. In all these, he must be one step ahead of his competitor. The Corporate Malaysian must project a winner.

New Thrust for Malaysia Incorporated

The SMIs: New Focus for Collaboration

There must be a conviction that Malaysia Incorporated is a key strategy for achieving the goals of Vision 2020. With this conviction will come the commitment of translating this policy into reality. Today, the concept is merely operationalized among organized segments of the business community. The SMIs, or small- and medium-sized industries, which comprise a large component of the business sector is still largely under-represented in Consultative Panels and committees within the Malaysian Incorporated fora. SMIs contribute 40 per cent to employment and 30 per cent of value-added products segment. In view of this, the future of Malaysia Incorporated will depend on how this subsector is drawn into the mainstream of private sector-public sector collaboration.

It is clear from our achievements to date that the Malaysia Incorporated Policy needs to be targeted to the SMIs for implementation. SMIs have a crucial role to play in generating employment opportunities, in strengthening industrial linkages, in penetrating markets and generating export earnings. This sector will be the birthplace of future entrepreneurs. The government has slated this sector to be the primary foundation for our future industrial thrust.

SMIs must be assisted to grow bigger and stronger. The government's role is to provide SMIs with promotional and advisory administrative guidance. Modernization programmes must be introduced to upgrade their technological base. Their ability to participate in export-led growth requires that their products meet international standards and may effectively compete globally. Towards this end the government must execute an industrial policy which includes:

1. The prudent protection of potentially viable domestic industries;
2. Phasing out less productive industries and channelling resources to more productive segments of the economy;
3. Positive discrimination in favour of SMIs with strategic content;
4. Merging of SMIs in similar product lines to consolidate their individual comparative advantages to enable their venture into the global market;
5. Facilitating linkages between interdependent SMIs;
6. Providing entrepreneurial development and skills training;
7. Easy access to credit and banking facilities; and
8. Administrative guidance for their effective participation in the mainstream of the national economy.

Institutional Framework

The establishment of the Malaysian Business Council sets the pace for the development of new institutions for consensus building within the Malaysia Incorporated Policy at the highest level.

Consequential development of an institutional network should be developed through all levels of the national economy. This collaborative mechanism must extend across and within sectors and subsectors. The development of this network will provide the cohesiveness in the pursuit of the goals of Vision 2020 collectively and interdependently within the components of the economy. This will contribute towards reducing the fragmentation and diversity of interests which characterizes our private sector. Through the network of institutions there will be an aggregation of interests which will facilitate communication between the government and the private sector which will ensure that no significant segment will be left out of our development effort.

Conclusion

Malaysia Incorporated is a pervasive policy for the success of the nation as aspired in Vision 2020. The effective collaboration between the public and private sectors is crucial to the development of the nation's competitiveness in the global marketplace. The role of the public and private sectors have been clearly identified for the immediate response and consequent initiative by both sectors. This is the challenge that lies before us. The measure by which we achieve our goals is determined by the measure of our commitment and conviction of the value of Malaysia Incorporated policy as the key strategy in the development of the nation.

16

The Malaysia Incorporated Concept

Robert Kuok

Dr Mahathir Mohamad has set for us Malaysia's specific growth targets for the next three decades – an average annual growth rate of 7 per cent, leading to a gross domestic product in 2020 that is eight times larger than in 1990. Are these attainable? I would say Yes; but it will be a long and difficult road ahead – with pitfalls along the way. The three parties undertaking the journey together – the government, the private sector, and the common citizens of Malaysia – need to know clearly what we want to achieve and the best way to get there. The fastest route is not necessarily always the best – an apparent "shortcut" could actually throw us back a few paces. A long-term view is needed for all three.

An Analogy of Travellers

When travellers set out on a journey, what are the factors that determine their success? Both external and internal factors.

External Factors

External factors include the weather, the mode of transport and those things that would facilitate their journey, for example, modern roads, good signposts, resthouses, etc.

Internal Factors

Internal factors include the mental and physical health of the
travellers.

Let us apply this to the context of Vision 2020. First, the
"weather" would be unexpected changes in global environment
or developments that have impact on our strategy and its success
– largely beyond our control.

Second, the "mode of transport" is the strategy of the
Malaysia Incorporated Concept – the right balance of co-operation between the public and private sectors and a common will to
succeed.

Third, the "help" along the journey would be the type of system that needs to be in place for any economic development to
take off.

Examples include an adequate infrastructure (transport and
telecommunications), healthy fiscal and monetary policies, the
right amount of government regulation and also the ability to
deregulate when the need arises, a skilled labour force with opportunities for training, an environment that encourages
entrepreneurship, joint ventures (that help technology transfer)
and a diversified economy, and diversified markets.

Malaysia is strong on some of these while others need improving. I would like to focus on the internal factors of success.
The health of the travellers, applied to Vision 2020, would cor-
respond with the right frame of mind and values to be inculcated
among all Malaysians, whether in the government, the private
sector or the ordinary citizen.

The Practice of Discipline

My own experience and observations of the most successful
economies in the Asia-Pacific all point to one basic ingredient for
success – discipline. Let us look at how the three parties can apply
discipline in the strategies they adopt for Vision 2020.

The government should have a strong sense of social responsibility, ensure that quick pursuit of profit by big businesses does

not lead to destruction of our national fabric nor our natural environment and eliminate or minimize corruption at all levels – corruption is the cancer of society.

The private sector should display civic-consciousness, patriotism and a zeal for nation-building. It should engage in competition but also recognize complementation, exercise a strong sense of corporate duty towards its workers – training them, managing them with fairness and regarding their creativity and productivity and aim for those types of industries that create stronger industrial linkage.

The common citizen should inculcate qualities such as competence, hard work and pursuit of excellence, should in good times be disciplined in his spending habits – to keep inflation in check and go beyond the petty confines of race and begin to think of himself as Malaysian, rather than as Malay, Indian or Chinese.

Discipline also implies that those in power should clearly identify which policies work and which doesn't and have the courage and conviction to reject the latter – even if they make themselves unpopular with certain sections of society. They should also be self-critical and learn from past mistakes.

The Role of the Malaysian Chinese in Malaysia Incorporated

I would now like to touch on a strategy that can lock in the Chinese elements of our society to the successful implementation of Vision 2020.

The migrant Chinese is essentially a product of his culture – traditional values such as hard work, thrift, respect for elders, placing importance on education, pragmatism, "nose for profits" lie deep within him. If these innate qualities are allowed to express themselves in the societies he resides in, they will have a yeast-like effect on that country's economic development.

Look at the fast-growing economies of the Asia-Pacific and you see this happening in Indonesia, Thailand, Philippines, Singapore and Malaysia – they all have one common thread, namely, an economically-active overseas Chinese community. They have been described in the international press as the new "Third Wave" in Southeast Asia, after the Americans and Japanese, and the countries touched by this wave are showing increasingly vigorous economies. They number approximately 50 million spread throughout the Asia-Pacific region, operating in a "borderless economy" long before the so-called multinationals envisaged the concept. Because of the size of their investment flow in the region, even Japanese conglomerates now recognize that they are a force to be reckoned with, and are seeking business links with them. The Bank of Tokyo recently established an Expatriate Chinese Affairs Desk to deal with twenty-seven of the most powerful overseas Chinese companies.

Of course, like any other group they also have their negative points, for example, corrupt businessmen, links with underworld societies, etc. These criminal elements should be tightly controlled by the host country by strengthening its law enforcement to minimize their adverse influences. But the government should not confuse a few rotten apples with the majority of the Chinese community.

Some of the positive traits of overseas Chinese outlined by Washington Sycip, Chairman, SGV Group of Manila, in a speech he made to the Third Pacific Rim Forum last year include:

1. The ability to smell profits quickly and to make quick decisions.
2. A penchant for eating well – preferring round tables for quicker exchange of information.
3. Generally avoiding politics but maintaining good relations with the government.
4. Being good citizens in their host countries.

In fact the way I see it, the Malaysian government should assist Chinese Malaysians to retain and maintain the traits as mentioned above and values inherited from their migrant forefathers as these have proved to be great contributors to the economic progress in this country as well as in the surrounding region.

How can they do this? One way is to allow the continued existence of Chinese education in schools and opportunities for learning the Chinese language. This way, children going to these schools would also learn the Malay language – so they should not be considered any less Malaysian than their counterparts going to national schools. After all, the best values of any culture repose in its written and spoken language.

The Malaysian Chinese, once convinced that the government is not trying to strip them of their Chinese roots, will give their wholehearted support to the economic development of the nation, thus giving added momentum to the drive to achieve the goals of Vision 2020.

Conclusion

I believe Vision 2020 can be achieved, but only with the unstinting co-operation and strong discipline of the three parties – the government, the private sector and the people – working hand in hand towards this common goal. The rest can be left to the magic-like workings of a free enterprise society in which each individual is free and encouraged to exert all his genius and his sense of drive, within the reasonable confines of a fair and just legal system, thereby bringing Malaysia to the level of a "developed" economy by the decade commencing 2010.

17

The Malaysia Incorporated Concept: A Key Strategy in Achieving Vision 2020

Ernest Zulliger

I am often asked by new members of the Malaysian International Chamber of Commerce and Industry to define the concept of Malaysia Incorporated. I respond by stating that this is the Malaysian government policy which encourages "the active co-operation between the government and the private sector in formulating policies for the development of the country, and then implementing those policies".

We have seen the policy being implemented to an increasingly effective degree over the past five years, and I have a strong suspicion that it is not a coincidence that we have also witnessed extremely strong economic growth in the country over the same period.

Eighty per cent of the 630 or so member organizations of the Malaysian International Chamber of Commerce and Industry have a substantial foreign shareholding. As foreigners we are honoured, impressed and appreciative of the fact that we are involved in the dialogue process with the government, and I can promise you that this message is passed to our head offices overseas who generally view the Malaysia Incorporated Concept as a major plus point towards investing in Malaysia. This is because it is a clear reflection of the government's support for free enterprise and the private sector.

I was interviewed recently by *World Link*, the magazine of the Davos World Economic Forum, and was quoted as saying "I have rarely come across an environment as open and supportive of the private sector as we have here today in Malaysia. Efficient communication from the private sector right to the top echelons of the government, the government's determination to take action, its pragmatic attitude, and the ability to correct what may hinder investment and growth, without any doubt go to make up the cornerstone of Malaysia's success story."

I believe that it would be difficult to contradict that statement. I have recently spent a considerable amount of time visiting other countries, and I can assure you that although in many places increasingly conducive policies are being introduced to promote investment, few have generated the sort of working relationship which we find here in Malaysia.

Vision 2020, OPP2 and Sixth Malaysia Plan

I will now comment briefly on the concept of Vision 2020. If I had to condense the twenty-seven pages describing the concept into one paragraph, I think I would do it as follows:

"Malaysia will become a fully developed country by the year 2020. It will attain this goal by:

1. Maintaining stability by concentrating on national unity and old-fashioned values such as thrift, honesty, family responsibility, fairness, tolerance, etc. In simple terms stability is the foundation for growth; growth is the raw material for stability.
2. Actively maintaining a consensus democracy.

3. Facilitating a 7 per cent average annual economic growth while keeping inflation under control.

4. Promoting free enterprise and the private sector as the engine of growth.

5. Developing the government-private sector dialogue process.

6. Giving priority to education and training.

7. Nurturing the environment.

8. Facilitating Malaysian business to be internationally competitive."

I can confidently state that there is no member of the Malaysian International Chamber of Commerce and Industry who is likely to take issue with any of these aims.

I mentioned earlier that Malaysia Incorporated is something unique to Malaysia. I believe also unique to Malaysia is the fact that to my knowledge there is no other country in the world that has published at the same time a thirty-year, a ten-year and a five-year plan, all three of which have a considerable degree of credibility. As far as Chamber members are concerned, for all investors, foreign and domestic, a prime requirement is stability, and as far as we can see the above long-term plans look like being a blueprint for stability.

I believe that because of the good things going for Malaysia one of our biggest dangers will be complacency; and in this context I would like to raise under six headings certain matters which I believe the government and the private sector should address carefully at an early stage if the credibility of various sections of the Plans is not to be put under pressure.

First, the necessity for Malaysia to continue aggressively expanding its export base both geographically and in terms of product diversification, and to be competitive in overseas markets. Under this heading I would comment on two areas, firstly that of skilled manpower and managerial staff. The Chamber's recent survey conducted in association with the Federation of Malaysian Manufacturers, the Malaysian Employers Federation, the Economic Planning Unit and Universiti Kebangsaan Malaysia has indicated the serious shortages that can be expected in the next ten years in skilled and managerial manpower. The short-term solution is to radically relax and promptly the present regulations on the employment of expatriates at all levels, from unskilled to professional. In this context we look forward to learning the detail of the measures that have recently been announced. The long-term solution lies in the setting-up of an adequate number of regional training facilities, with local public sector-private sector committees established to ensure that the facilities, the syllabuses and the teachers are appropriate for the needs of commerce and industry in the area.

Second, in the context of the nation's competitiveness is the requirement for the Malaysian services sector also to be able to provide services of an international standard. Services such as banking, insurance, engineering, design, marketing, public relations, advertising, inspection, transport, distribution, warehousing, communications, tourism and general consultancy must be competitive in quality and price.

Early consideration must be given to ensure that the Malaysian services sector receives the same encouragement from the government as the manufacturing sector, particularly in the context of foreign equity regulations and the employment of expatriates. Apart from the impact on competitiveness, a dynamic and effective domestic services sector will have a major beneficial effect on the balance of payments situation.

The second area of concern I would like to mention is tourism. The benefits that tourism can bring to Malaysia are enormous, and conversely Malaysia as a tourist destination I believe could be unparalleled. It is my view that the number of tourists from Europe and America visiting Southeast Asia in the coming decade will far exceed the figures currently being forecast. Tourism can benefit a country greatly, not only as a money spinner, but also indirectly as a promoter of trade and investment; tourism can also utterly ruin the attractive characteristics of a country. The need for meticulous government planning for the macro scene in this area is essential, and I am pleased to understand that a Master Plan for Tourism is to be completed at the end of 1991. The Malaysian International Chamber of Commerce and Industry would be more than happy to assist wherever possible in its preparation.

My third aspect for concern is the environment; environmental considerations from now on must become a factor in every government and business decision, just as are quality, service, productivity, etc. On the other hand, the role of government in the area of policy making and effective enforcement is equally crucial. The lack of early firm action will lead to a rapid deterioration of essential resources such as air, water and land, and to massive cleaning-up expenditure in the future. Malaysia has still a chance to learn the lessons from other countries in East Asia and Eastern Europe. For example, the staggering build-up of traffic in Kuala Lumpur in the past two years, what appears to be the haphazard development of condominiums regardless of consideration for traffic circulation and services, and what would appear to be the lack of any Master Plan for a public transport system provide real cause for worry. The Malaysian International Chamber of Commerce and Industry is a strong promoter of Kuala Lumpur as a centre for regional offices, but this promotion work becomes daily more of a challenge as the traffic congestion grows from bad to worse.

Also in the context of traffic, I should comment on the vehicle exhaust smoke problem. This I hope and believe is an instance where positive government action will produce quick results. Earlier this year, in two short months the Chamber's Secretariat made 856 reports of vehicles emitting excessive exhaust smoke. These reports stopped when in August the Ministry of Transport announced draconian measures to overcome the problem. The recent announcements on the conversion to unleaded petrol are indeed most encouraging. Let us hope that similar decisive steps are taken in other problem areas of the environment.

My third example on the subject of the environment is timber extraction. This subject is unfortunately receiving poor international press and this in my view may be partly understandable. I say this because if – as it would appear – many Malaysians themselves do not fully understand the government's timber extraction policy, and how it is enforced, then it is not surprising that the international press should be so inquisitive.

It is recommended that the policy should be transparent and be widely know, so that all Malaysians and the international business community can be good ambassadors on the subject. The Malaysian International Chamber of Commerce and Industry's main concern is that if international condemnation increase, export markets for other Malaysian products may be affected, and not just markets for timber and timber products.

My fourth area of worry concerns the law courts. Malaysian International Chamber of Commerce and Industry members have become increasingly concerned at the long delays and inefficiency of the disposal of civil claims in court in particular regard to debt collection, real property and employment matters. Mindful of the fact that justice delayed is in many cases justice denied, it is hoped that major attention is given to this problem area. Apart from radical improvement to the procedures used in court, adequate attention should also be directed towards means of reducing already overwhelming workloads and the resulting backlogs.

The fifth concern is in the area of licensing and bureaucratic red tape. The Panel on Improving Government Administration appears to be doing an excellent job in this field. Its goals, as has been made known, seem to be not only to simplify the licensing system, but also to improve the overall quality and productivity of Government, and the streamlining of the whole apparatus of government which by international standards seems to be oversized. Much still remains to be done and the Malaysian International Chamber of Commerce and Industry would wish to assist wherever possible in the vital tasks of this panel.

The final area which I would like to cover is that of industrial relations. To achieve the targets of the Sixth Malaysia Plan, let alone those of the OPP2 and Vision 2020, manpower relations must remain at the present very satisfactory level. We must keep in mind the lessons of other countries where poor industrial relations have seriously affected economic development.

Conclusion

I would end as I began by praising the Malaysia Incorporated Concept. One of the reasons that the OPP2 document received virtually no negative criticism was the fact that so much of it had been discussed by interested parties for months beforehand. The constant dialogue and consultation between the government and the private sector is crucial to the efficient development of a country in ensuring that the use of resources is optimized and that mistakes can be avoided at an early stage. Now reverting to the title of this chapter, I would like to close by stating my firm belief that the Malaysia Incorporated Concept is indeed a key strategy towards achieving Vision 2020.

Appendix 1

Inauguration Speech of the Malaysian Business Council

Dr Mahathir Mohamad

It is a great pleasure for me to be here today for the inauguration of the Malaysian Business Council, and as its Chairman I thank you for your presence here this morning.

We are meeting at the beginning of the decade of the Nineties – a time of great challenge for our nation as well as for the region. As a nation we are almost thirty-four years old. That is not very old as nations go but for a developing country which has been able to control its own destiny only after independence it is a very meaningful period of time.

In the first three decades of nationhood we have moved rapidly from being a low-income, undeveloped economy, relying merely on rubber and tin as our economic mainstay, to a nation that has diversified into the services and the industrial sector, backed by a sophisticated financial system. Yet far from neglecting the primary produce, we have enhanced our competitiveness and diversified into many new commodities which earn us a lot of foreign exchange.

By any standard we have done well but there is no time to rest on our laurels. We must aim to become a developed country at par with those of Europe and North America. It may not happen tomorrow or next year or even by the end of this millennium but we must not be discouraged. Everything must have a beginning.

We have gone beyond the first step. Now we must continue at a quickened pace.

To expedite the attainment of our goal we must set new standards and make quantum leaps – in terms of all the key institutions of our country, in terms of our economic culture, adjustments and innovations. Above all, we must understand our goal and the road towards it. We, here, means all of us – the government, the private sector, workers, management and all the institutions which are directly or indirectly involved in the development of this nation.

This national aspiration must be shared by all, at every level. It is not a grandiose dream that we are targeting at. It is an achievable vision, provided of course that we all pull together.

The government has already espoused the Malaysia Incorporated concept, a concept that is based on a partnership between the government and the private sector, a concept of a nation as a giant corporation in which the public and private sectors are together tasked with ensuring its success and are entitled to share the benefits. Despite initial scepticism, the idea has caught on. Today, government officers are more helpful towards the private sector and they are constantly improving their service through innovative ways. Gone are the days when the success or otherwise of the private sector are of no concern to government officers. They now accept and appreciate that the private sector does not only make profits for itself but contributes towards economic growth and therefore towards the betterment of all, including themselves. The private sector which welcomed the concept of Malaysian Incorporated must not only expect better service from the government but must also contribute towards its realization. They must make it easier for the government to serve them by understanding the regulatory role of government and its concern for social and economic justice for all.

Let us all be perfectly clear. By no means can it be argued that all collaboration between the public and private sectors is justifiable or necessary. There is co-operation that is productive; and there is collaboration that is unproductive. Collaboration that results in negative social consequences, in frustrating the achievement of national values and aspirations, must be fought against. In many areas there must be more than an arms-length relationship. On many issues there must be productive regulation. What is good for the business sector may not always be good for the people as a whole. But in many areas we do need to work closer. This Council is one of the mechanisms intended to contribute further to this relationship.

No doubt that many of you are already on a host of councils but the government regards the establishment of this Council as an important step in bringing bring the public and private sectors together at the highest level to discuss issues of mutual interest to the nation. It is a small Council – consisting of ten Ministers, eight leaders from the public service and forty-four leaders from the private sector. It is small because this is essential in order that we can discuss in an atmosphere of candour and intimacy. Your membership is a responsibility to this country and to the people.

This Council shall have four primary objectives:

☐ First, to facilitate a free flow of information and ideas between the public and private sectors;

☐ Second, to address problems pertaining to industrial and commercial development and to remove impediments to economic growth;

☐ Third, to create better understanding and to enhance the relationship between the public and private sectors; and

☐ Fourth, to identify and promote areas of co-operation and collaboration between the public and the private sectors.

In order to fulfill these objectives, the terms of reference of the Council will be as follows:

☐ First, to examine domestic and international business and economic developments central to Malaysia's aspirations;

☐ Second, to discuss current and emerging issues and problems;

☐ Third, to examine and provide practical options and strategies;

☐ Fourth, to provide feedback on policy issues and developments with regard to industrialization;

☐ Fifth, to remove misunderstandings and barriers to productive co-operation between the public and private sectors; and

☐ Sixth, to generate consensus on national economic directions and strategies.

As a Council member, I shall speak frankly. As Council members, I expect you to speak frankly too. There can be no in-depth examination or discussion if there is not this commitment to candour. We cannot remove misunderstanding and roadblocks to productive co-operation if we fail to communicate clearly. If practical options and strategies are to come forth there must be a free and frank exchange of information and ideas. I hope every Council member will speak and listen intently, with an open heart and an open mind.

It is important that you give priority to meetings of the Council. In order to ensure the necessary administrative back-up the government has set up a Centre for Economic Research and Services to be located at ISIS [Institute of Strategic and International Studies] Malaysia, with adequate staffing. This centre will be responsible for research, secretarial, organizational and administrative services for the Malaysian Business Council. The government has allocated an annual sum for the operational costs of the Malaysian Business Council Centre. There is no compulsion on the private sector as a whole to make financial contributions to the Council and its work. But provision has been made for all private sector donations to the council to be tax exempted.

At this juncture I think it is appropriate if I do a quick review of the current economic scene at home and worldwide. Since the recessionary years of 1985–1986 we have recovered strongly to achieve record rates of growth. We have become highly industrialized and we now export more manufactured goods than primary commodities. Where before growth was based on expansionary public expenditure, now most of the economic growth is due to private sector activities.

Our growth is still largely based on exports and export-related activities. Our domestic market is still too small to become an engine of growth. Per capita income is one-fifth of that of developed countries. Accordingly what happens to the world economy and to free trade is crucial for us.

Despite the Gulf War, Malaysia as a net oil exporter is able to balance somewhat the effect on oil supply and oil prices. But we are not totally insulated. Already we are feeling the effects of reduced air travel, diversion of ships for war purposes, increase in transportation and insurance costs, reduced economic growth and possible recession among our principal trading partners. Our exports to the warring states in the Gulf have been reduced due to war risks, logistical problems and inaccessibility. The predicted rise in oil prices has not materialized. Indeed there are prospects for a glut both during and after the war.

Clearly Malaysia is not going to achieve the growth rates of the three previous years, if we sit back and do nothing. The government has done a comprehensive study of the effects and possible effects of the Gulf War on us. If we are to ensure minimum harm to our economy due to the war, we must make adjustments and we must act. We must be prepared to move away from the beaten path. We must be prepared to take risks, reasonable risks.

The government is ready to make these adjustments. It is ready to listen, accommodate and support the private sector. I hope that this Council will be able to play a leading role in the difficult times ahead. God willing, together we can overcome.

The success of this Council will depend on the sense of commitment and responsibility of the Council members. I would like to thank all Council members who have consented to serve on the Council. Through your wisdom and experience, and the contributions of other sectors of our society, I am confident we can work together to formulate clear national directions and goals. I look forward to working with you in the days ahead.

It gives me great pleasure to formally launch the Malaysian Business Council.

[February 28, 1991]

Appendix 2

Malaysia: The Way Forward

Dr Mahathir Mohamad

The purpose of this paper is to present before you some thoughts on the future course of our nation and how we should go about to attain our objective of developing Malaysia into an industrialized country. Also outlined are some measures that should be in place in the shorter term so that the foundations can be laid for the long journey towards that ultimate objective.

Hopefully the Malaysian who is born today and in the years to come will be the last generation of our citizens who will be living in a country that is called "developing". The ultimate objective that we should aim for is a Malaysia that is a fully developed country by the year 2020.

What, you might rightly ask, is "a fully developed country"? Do we want to be like any particular country of the present nineteen countries that are generally regarded as "developed countries"? Do we want to be like the United Kingdom, like Canada, like Holland, like Sweden, like Finland, like Japan? To be sure, each of the nineteen, out of a world community of more than 160 states, has its strengths. But each also has its fair share of weaknesses. Without being a duplicate of any of them we can still be developed. We should be a developed country in our own mould.

Malaysia should not be developed only in the economic sense. It must be a nation that is fully developed along all the dimensions – economically, politically, socially, spiritually, psychologically and culturally. We must be fully developed in terms of national unity and social cohesion, in terms of our economy, in terms of social justice, political stability, system of government, quality of life, social and spiritual values, national pride and confidence.

Malaysia as a Fully Developed Country: One Definition

By the year 2020, Malaysia can be a united nation, with a confident Malaysian society, infused by strong moral and ethical values, living in a society that is democratic, liberal and tolerant, caring, economically just and equitable, progressive and prosperous, and in full possession of an economy that is competitive, dynamic, robust and resilient.

There can be no fully developed Malaysia until we have finally overcome the nine central strategic challenges that have confronted us from the moment of our birth as an independent nation. The first of these is the challenge of establishing a united Malaysian nation with a sense of common and shared destiny. This must be a nation at peace with itself, territorially and ethnically integrated, living in harmony and full and fair partnership, made up of one *Bangsa Malaysia* with political loyalty and dedication to the nation.

The second is the challenge of creating a psychologically liberated, secure, and developed Malaysian Society with faith and confidence in itself, justifiably proud of what it is, of what it has accomplished, robust enough to face all manner of adversity. This Malaysian Society must be distinguished by the pursuit of excellence, fully aware of all its potentials, psychologically subservient to none, and respected by the peoples of other nations.

The third challenge we have always faced is that of fostering and developing a mature democratic society, practising a form of

mature consensual, community-oriented Malaysian democracy
that can be a model for many developing countries.

The fourth is the challenge of establishing a fully moral and
ethical society, whose citizens are strong in religious and spiritual
values and imbued with the highest of ethical standards.

The fifth challenge that we have always faced is the challenge
of establishing a matured, liberal and tolerant society in which
Malaysians of all colours and creeds are free to practise and
profess their customs, cultures and religious beliefs and yet feeling
that they belong to one nation.

The sixth is the challenge of establishing a scientific and
progressive society, a society that is innovative and forward-looking, one that is not only a consumer of technology but also a contributor to the scientific and technological civilization of the
future.

The seventh challenge is the challenge of establishing a fully
caring society and a caring culture, a social system in which
society will come before self, in which the welfare of the people
will revolve not around the state or the individual but around a
strong and resilient family system.

The eighth is the challenge of ensuring an economically just
society. This is a society in which there is a fair and equitable distribution of the wealth of the nation, in which there is full partnership in economic progress. Such a society cannot be in place so
long as there is the identification of race with economic function,
and the identification of economic backwardness with race.

The ninth challenge is the challenge of establishing a
prosperous society, with an economy that is fully competitive,
dynamic, robust and resilient.

We have already come a long way towards the fulfillment of
these objectives. The nine central objectives listed need not be
our order of priorities over the next three decades. Most obviously, the priorities of any moment in time must meet the specific circumstances of that moment in time.

But it would be surprising if the first strategic challenge which
I have mentioned – the establishment of a united Malaysian nation – is not likely to be the most fundamental, the most basic.

406 MALAYSIA'S VISION 2020

Since much of what I will say this morning will concentrate on economic development, let me stress yet again that the comprehensive development towards the developed society that we want – however each of us may wish to define it – cannot mean material and economic advancement only. Far from it. Economic development must not become the be-all and the end-all of our national endeavours.

Since this Council must concentrate on the issues of economic development and economic social justice, which for this nation must go hand in hand for the foreseeable future, let me expand on the perception of the central strategic challenges with regard to these two vital objectives.

At this point it is well to define in greater detail the objective of establishing an economically just society.

Of the two prongs of the NEP [New Economic Policy] no one is against the eradication of absolute poverty – regardless of race, and irrespective of geographical location. All Malaysians, whether they live in the rural or the urban areas, whether they are in the south, north, east or west, must be moved above the line of absolute poverty.

This nation must be able to provide enough food on the table so that not a solitary Malaysian is subject to the travesty of gross under-nourishment. We must provide enough by way of essential shelter, access to health facilities, and all the basic essentials. A developed Malaysia must have a wide and vigorous middle class and must provide full opportunities for those in the bottom third to climb their way out of the pit of relative poverty.

The second prong, that of removing the identification of race with major economic function is also acceptable except that somehow it is thought not possible to achieve this without any shuffling of position. If we want to build an equitable society then we must accept some affirmative action. This will mean that in all the major and important sectors of employment, there should be a good mix of the ethnic groups that make up the Malaysian nation. By legitimate means we must ensure a fair balance with regard to the professions and all the major categories of employment. Certainly we must be as interested in quality and merit. But we must ensure the healthy development of a viable and robust Bumiputera commercial and industrial community.

A developed Malaysia should not have a society in which economic backwardness is identified with race. This does not imply individual income equality, a situation in which all Malaysians will have the same income. This is an impossibility because by sheer dint of our own individual effort, our own individual upbringing and our individual preferences, we will all have different economic worth, and will be financially rewarded differently. An equality of individual income as propounded by socialists and communists is not only not possible, it is not desirable and is a formula for disaster.

But I do believe that the narrowing of the ethnic income gap, through the legitimate provision of opportunities, through a closer parity of social services and infrastructure, through the development of the appropriate economic cultures and through full human resource development, is both necessary and desirable. We must aspire by the year 2020 to reach a stage where no one can say that a particular ethnic group is inherently economically backward and another is economically inherently advanced. Such a situation is what we must work for – efficiently, effectively, with fairness and with dedication.

"A full partnership in economic progress" cannot mean full partnership in poverty. It must mean a fair balance with regard to the participation and contribution of all our ethnic groups – including the Bumiputeras of Sabah and Sarawak – in the high-growth, modern sectors of our economy. It must mean a fair distribution with regard to the control, management and ownership of the modern economy.

In order to achieve this economically just society, we must escalate dramatically our programmes for national human resource development. There is a need to ensure the creation of an economically resilient and fully competitive Bumiputera community so as to be at par with the non-Bumiputera community. There is need for a mental revolution and a cultural transformation. Much of the work of pulling ourselves up by our bootstraps must be done ourselves. In working for the correction of the economic imbalances, there has to be the fullest emphasis on making the needed advances at speed and with the most productive results – at the lowest possible economic and societal cost.

With regard to the establishment of a prosperous society, we can set many aspirational goals. I believe that we should set the realistic (as opposed to aspirational) target of almost doubling our real gross domestic product every ten years between 1990 and 2020. If we do this, our GDP should be about eight times larger by the year 2020 than it was in 1990. Our GDP in 1990 was 115 billion ringgit. Our GDP in 2020 should therefore be about 920 billion ringgit in real (1990 ringgit) terms.

This rapid growth will require that we grow by an average of about 7 per cent (in real terms) annually over the next thirty years. Admittedly this is an optimistic projection but we should set our sights high if we are to motivate ourselves into striving hard.

We must guard against "growth fixation", the danger of pushing for growth figures oblivious to the needed commitment to ensure stability, to keep inflation low, to guarantee sustainability, to develop our quality of life and standard of living, and the achievement of our other social objectives. It will be a difficult task, with many peaks and low points. But I believe that this can be done.

In the 1960s, we grew by an annual average of 5.1 per cent; in the 1970s, the first decade of the NEP, Malaysia grew by an average of 7.8 per cent; in the 1980s, because of the recession years, we grew by an annual average of 5.9 per cent.

If we take the last thirty years, our GDP rose annually in real terms by an average of 6.3 per cent. If we take the last twenty years, we grew by an annual average of 6.9 per cent. What is needed is an additional 0.1 per cent growth. Surely if we all pull together God willing this 0.1 per cent can be achieved.

If we do succeed, and assuming roughly a 2.5 per cent annual rate of population growth, by the year 2020, Malaysians will be four times richer (in real terms) than they were in 1990. That is the measure of the prosperous society we wish and hopefully we can achieve.

The second leg of our economic objective should be to secure the establishment of a competitive economy. Such an economy must be able to sustain itself over the longer term, must be dynamic, robust and resilient. It must mean, among other things:

- [ ] A diversified and balanced economy with a mature and widely based industrial sector, a modern and mature agriculture sector and an efficient, productive and equally mature services sector;
- [ ] An economy that is quick on its feet, able to quickly adapt to changing patterns of supply, demand and competition;
- [ ] An economy that is technologically proficient, fully able to adapt, innovate and invent, that is increasingly technology-intensive, moving in the direction of higher and higher levels of technology;
- [ ] An economy that has strong and cohesive industrial linkages through-out the system;
- [ ] An economy driven by brainpower, skills and diligence in possession of a wealth of information, with the knowledge of what to do and how to do it;
- [ ] An economy with high and escalating productivity with regard to every factor of production;
- [ ] An entrepreneurial economy that is self-reliant, outward-looking and enterprising;
- [ ] An economy sustained by an exemplary work ethic, quality consciousness and the quest for excellence;
- [ ] An economy characterized by low inflation and a low cost of living; and
- [ ] An economy that is subject to the full discipline and rigour of market forces.

Most of us in this present Council will not be there on the morning of January 1, 2020. Not many, I think. The great bulk of the work that must be done to ensure a fully developed country called Malaysia a generation from now will obviously be done by the leaders who follow us, by our children and grandchildren. But we should make sure that we have done our duty in guiding them with regard to what we should work to become. And let us lay the secure foundations that they must build upon.

Some Key Public Sector Economic Policies for the Foreseeable Future

Since the early 1980s, we have stressed that this country will rely on the private sector as the primary engine of economic growth. In a way we were ahead of the rest of the world, even the developed countries in entrusting economic growth to the private sector.

In the early years, our fledgling private sector could not fully respond to the challenge that was issued. Then came the unpredictable and difficult recession and slowdown years. However, in the last three years the private sector has bloomed and responded. The policy is now bearing fruit. The outcome – in 1988, we grew in real terms by 8.9 per cent; in 1989, by 8.8 per cent; in 1990, by 9.4 per cent without expansionary budgeting by the government. Even the tiger economies of Northeast Asia have not done so well.

No nation can afford to abandon a winning formula. And this nation will not. For the foreseeable future, Malaysia will continue to drive the private sector, to rely on it as the primary engine of growth.

In the meantime the government will continue to downsize its role in the field of economic production and business. The State cannot of course retreat totally from the economic life of Malaysia. It will not abdicate its responsibility for overseeing and providing the legal and regulatory framework for rapid economic and social development.

The government will be proactive to ensure healthy fiscal and monetary management and the smooth functioning of the Malaysian economy. It will escalate the development of the necessary physical infrastructure and the most conducive business environment – consistent with its other social priorities. And where absolutely necessary the government will not be so completely bound by its commitment to withdraw from the economic role, that it will not intervene. It will play its role judiciously and actively.

The process of deregulation will continue. There can be no doubt that regulations are an essential part of the governance of society, of which the economy is a part. A state without laws and regulations is a state flirting with anarchy. Without order, there can be little business and no development. What is not required is over-regulation although it may not be easy to decide when the government is over-regulating.

Wisdom lies of course in the ability to distinguish between those laws and regulations which are productive to our societal objectives and those that are not; and it lies in making the right judgements with regard to the trade-offs. Thus governments will be neither foolish nor irresponsible, and will cater to the needs of the wider society as well as the requirements of rapid growth and a competitive, robust and resilient economy. It will be guided by the knowledge that the freeing of enterprise too – not only laws and regulations, and state intervention – can contribute to the achievement of the wider social objectives. In this light and given the fact that there are clear areas of unproductive regulation which need to be phased out, you can expect the process of productive deregulation to continue. The recent move of Bank Negara to deregulate the BLR [Base Lending Rate] regime is an example in point.

Privatization will continue to be an important cornerstone of our national development and national efficiency strategy. This policy is not founded on ideological belief. It is aimed specifically at enhancing competitiveness, efficiency and productivity in the economy, at reducing the administrative and financial burdens on the government and at expediting the attainment of national distributional goals.

In implementing our privatization policy, the government is fully aware of the need to protect public interest, to ensure that the poor are provided access to essential services, to guarantee that quality services are provided at minimum cost, to avoid unproductive monopolistic practices and to ensure the welfare of workers.

There will be problems. No endeavour comes without a price tag. But it is clear enough that this policy has thus far generated positive results and we can expect its implementation to be accelerated in the future. With the completion of the privatization Master Plan Study, I believe that many of the bottlenecks and rigidities that obstruct the progress of the needed privatization will be removed, thus accelerating its smooth implementation.

There will be in the years ahead an Accelerated Industrialization Drive, a drive that is not based on a fascination with industry but on the simple truth that if we want to develop rapidly – in a situation where the developed economies will be moving out of Industrialization into a post-industrial stage – this is the way to go. If we are to industrialize rapidly, we will need to capitalize on our national strengths and forcefully tackle our weaknesses.

In pursuit of this policy, the government will need to deal with the problem of a narrow manufacturing base. In 1988, 63 per cent of total Malaysian manufactured exports came from the electrical, electronic and textile industries. Electronics alone accounted for 50 per cent of total manufactured exports. We must diversify.

Despite the most rapid development in the free trade zones insignificant demand has been generated for local intermediate products. We will have to deal with the problem of weak industrial linkages.

There is inadequate development of indigenous technology. There is too little value-added, too much simple assembly and production. There is also a need to counter rising production costs brought about by rising costs of labour, raw materials and overheads by improving efficiency and productivity. There is a serious shortage of skilled manpower. All these and many more issues will need to be addressed.

Small- and medium-sized industries (SMIs) have an important role to play in generating employment opportunities, in strengthening industrial linkages, in penetrating markets and generating export earnings. They have a crucial role as a spawning ground for the birth of tomorrow's entrepreneurs.

The government will devise appropriate assistance schemes and will seek to raise the level of management expertise, technological know-how and skills of the employees in this very important and in many ways neglected sector of our economy.

The SMIs will be one of the primary foundations for our future industrial thrust. The government is fully committed to its healthiest development.

Just as we must diversify the products we export so must we diversify the markets we export to. Malaysian exporters must look also at the non-traditional markets. It will require new knowledge, new networks, new contacts and new approaches towards dealing with unfamiliar laws, rules and regulations. It will be uncomfortable but it would be a mistake to consider that it is not worth the discomfort to deal with these markets. Alone they may be small but cumulatively the market of the developing Asian, African and Latin American countries are big. If the developed countries find it worthwhile to export to these markets then it must be worthwhile for us also. The government will help but the private sector must play their part. Reliance on export-led growth is still the way to rapid growth.

Entry into the world market pits our companies against all comers and subjects them to the full force of international competition. This is a challenge we must accept not simply because the domestic market is too small but because in the long run it will actually enrich our domestic market and reduce our dependence on export.

We must persist with export-led growth despite the global slowdown, despite the rise of protectionism, trade blocs and managed trade. When the going is tougher, we must not turn inward. We simply have no choice but to be more lean, more resourceful, more productive and generally more competitive, more able to take on the world.

The liberalization of the Malaysian economy has had beneficial result and contributed towards a more dynamic growth.

Obviously, liberalization must be undertaken responsibly and in stages so as not to create economic uncertainty and impose excessive structural adjustment costs. We should take into the fullest consideration Malaysia's capacity to undertake liberalization. We should not dismiss the infant industry argument, but we should not bow to illegitimate pressure.

At the same time, productive liberalization ensures that our private sector will be less reliant on artificial profits and on protection, which benefits some producers at the expense of consumers and other producers. Infants must grow up. They must grow up to be sturdy and strong. And this cannot be done if they are over-protected.

For reasons that are obvious, the government will continue to foster the inflow of foreign investment. This is essential for Malaysia's Accelerated Industrialization Drive. Again, we will not abandon a winning strategy. But we will fine-tune it to ensure that measures are in place to ensure that Malaysia maximizes the net benefit from the inflow of foreign investment.

In the past, the domestic private sector has largely failed to meet the targets set in successive Malaysia Plans. Apparently domestic investors feel that the government has not devoted enough effort to the fostering of domestic investment as we have devoted to those from overseas. This is not completely true but we will redress the situation as we get better feedback.

Small and medium scale enterprises must be assisted to grow bigger. Surplus savings and domestic capital must be more productively channelled into investments. Entrepreneurs must be spawned. Where necessary, technological and training help must be extended; and infrastructural support must be given.

It is worthwhile to stress again that the development that we need cannot take place without the infrastructural underpinning. We must keep one step ahead of demand and need. In the recent Budget, we clearly stated what we will do in the shorter term. The Sixth Malaysia Plan will make clear what we will do in the medium term while the Second Outline Perspective Plan (OPP2) will indicate the direction over the long-term. The government is fully aware of the infrastructure bottlenecks and of the need for massive investments in the years to come. We will not let growth to be retarded by excessive congestion and investment indigestion, as has happened in many countries.

In our drive to move vigorously ahead nothing is more important than the development of human resources.

From the experience in the last two decades of all the economic miracles of the countries that have been poor in terms of "natural resources", it is blindingly clear that the most important resource of any nation must be the talents, skills, creativity and will of its people. What we have between our ears, at our elbows and in our hearts is much more important than what we have below our feet and around us. Our people is our ultimate resource. Without a doubt, in the 1990s and beyond, Malaysia must give the fullest emphasis possible to the development of this ultimate resource.

Malaysia has one of the best educational systems in the Third World. But for the journey that we must make over to our second generation, new standards have to be set and new results achieved.

We cannot but aspire to the highest standards with regard to the skills of our people, to their devotion to know-how and knowledge upgrading and self-improvement, to their language competence, to their work attitudes and discipline, to their managerial abilities, to their achievement motivation, their attitude towards excellence and to the fostering of the entrepreneurial spirit.

We cannot afford to neglect the importance of entrepreneurship and entrepreneurial development, which goes, of course beyond training and education. We must ensure the correct mix with regard to professionals, sub-professionals, craftsmen and artisans, and the correct balance with regard to those with competence in science and technology, the arts and social sciences.

In the development of human resources we cannot afford to neglect half the population, that is, the Bumiputeras. If they are not brought into the mainstream, if their potentials are not fully developed, if they are allowed to be a millstone around the national neck, then our progress is going to be retarded by that much. No nation can achieve full progress with only half its human resources harnessed. What may be considered a burden now can, with the correct attitude and management be the force that lightens our burden and hasten our progress. The Bumiputeras must play their part fully in the achievement of the national goal.

Inflation is the bane of all economic planners. Fortunately except during the first oil shock when inflation went up to 17 per cent, Malaysia has managed to keep inflation low. We must continue to keep it low. The government, the business sector, and the people must be committed to keeping it low. The only real way to combat inflation is to live within one's means. If we cannot afford we just don't buy. In Malaysia this is possible for we can produce practically all we need in terms of food, shelter and clothing. When recently we had a recession, life was bearable because we were able to buy our needs at roughly the same price, that is, we had practically no inflation. Now that we have more money, demand pull is slowly forcing prices up. So although we may be more prosperous now, although we may be financially wealthier now, but in terms of purchasing power we are not as well-off as we should be.

The public must understand what causes inflation and must be disciplined enough to combat it. In some countries when inflation rates go up to thousands of per cent per year, governments have been changed again and again without inflation being contained. The reason is that the people are not disciplined and prepared to restrain themselves. No government can put a stop to inflation unless the people are prepared to accept the discomfort of austerity.

In the fight against inflation nothing is more effective than education and discipline among the people.

In an interdependent trading world, the exchange rate plays a vital role. Too cheap a currency will increase import bills and debt payment but it will make exports competitive. But the full benefit of a low exchange rate on export can be negated by the cost of imported material which go into the export products. A high currency value will "enrich" our people, particularly in terms of buying imported luxuries but our exports will not be competitive and the economy will eventually be adversely affected.

Clearly the management of the exchange rate is of extreme importance to the progress of our nation. There is only a limited ability to manipulate. In the final analysis it is how we balance our trade that will determine how our currency is valued. Malaysia must learn to be competitive through higher productivity rather than through manipulating exchange rates. Again the people must understand their role, particularly with regard to productivity.

In a world of high technology Malaysia cannot afford to lag behind. We cannot be in the frontline of modern technology but we must always try to catch up at least in those fields where we may have certain advantages. We have already adopted a National Plan of Action for Industrial Technology Development. This is the easy part. We must now proceed expeditiously to the enormously difficult task of implementation.

The government will certainly provide the necessary commitment and leadership to this national endeavour. The institutional and support infrastructure will be put in place to ensure rapid, realistic, focused and market-driven development of our technological capabilities. But let us never forget that technology is not for the laboratory but the factory floor and the market. The private sector and our people must respond. Far too often the results of research are ignored in favour of the tried and tested money-spinners. It has been said that the secret of Japan's success is its skill in applying research results to marketable products. If we don't do this we are going to be left behind whatever may be the level of our technology.

While increasing our industrial manufacturing sector, Malaysia must make sure that our agriculture and services sector will not be neglected. We must advance. We must strive for efficiency, modernity and competitiveness. These should be the key guiding principles of our national policy towards agriculture, tourism and the fullest development of the entire services sector.

Nor can we afford to neglect the rural sector of our economy and society. In the years ahead, we must work for a second rural development transformation, restructuring the villages so as to be compatible with both agriculture and modern industry. Less and less farmers should produce more and more food, thus releasing manpower for an industrial society.

While doing all these we must also ensure that our valuable natural resources are not wasted. Our land must remain productive and fertile, our atmosphere clear and clean, our water unpolluted, our forest resources capable of regeneration, able to yield the needs of our national development. The beauty of our land must not be desecrated – for its own sake and for our economic advancement.

In the information age that we are living in, the Malaysian society must be information-rich. It can be no accident that there is today no wealthy, developed country that is information-poor and no information-rich country that is poor and undeveloped.

There was a time when land was the most fundamental basis of prosperity and wealth. Then came the second wave, the age of Industrialization Smokestacks rose where the fields were once cultivated. Now, increasingly, knowledge will not only be the basis of power but also prosperity. Again we must keep up. Already Malaysians are among the biggest users of computers in the region. Computer literacy is a must if we want to progress and develop. No effort must be spared in the creation of an information-rich Malaysian society.

In international relations, the emphasis should be less on politics and ideology but more on economic imperatives. Small though we may be, we must strive to influence the course of international trade. To grow we have to export. Our domestic market is far too small. It is important to us that free trade is maintained. The trend towards the formation of trading blocs will damage our progress and we must oppose it. We must therefore play our part and not passively accept the dictates of those powerful nations who may not even notice what their decision have done to us.

A country without adequate economic defence capabilities and the ability to marshal influence and create coalitions in the international economic arena is an economically defenseless nation and an economically powerless state. This, Malaysia cannot afford to be.

There are many other policies that must be in place if we are to make the 1990s the most economically productive decade in our history. Let me end by mentioning just one more – the necessity of making Malaysia Incorporated a flourishing reality.

Let me stress not all collaboration between our public and private sector is justifiable or productive. In many areas there must be a long arm's length approach. But there can be no doubt that a productive partnership will take us a long way towards our aspirations.

What The Private Sector Must Contribute

I have outlined what I think are the key economic policies that should be in place to accelerate our drive towards prosperity and a competitive economy. Let me now stress the role that the private sector must play.

This nation cannot rely on the private sector as the primary engine of growth if our private sector is inefficient and lethargic. You must be strong and dynamic, robust and self-reliant, competent and honest.

Malaysia cannot deregulate if bankers eventually behave like "banksters", if the freedom afforded to enterprise becomes merely licence to exploit without any sense of social responsibility. Our companies must have a high sense of corporate duty. Our struggle to ensure social justice – to uplift the position and competitiveness of the Bumiputeras and to achieve the other social objectives – must be your struggle too.

Privatization must not proceed if its objectives are defeated by those who think only of personal profit without social responsibility. The Accelerated Industrialization Drive that attempts to rapidly develop our small and medium scale industries must be driven by the enterprise of our entrepreneurs. They must be prepared to think longer term, to venture forth into the competitive world markets. The attraction of foreign investment should not be the responsibility of the government alone. The private sector too must engage the foreign investor in mutually beneficial partnership and joint ventures for this will help him to integrate more fully into the Malaysian economy. And the responsibility of domestic investors must be greater than that of their foreign counterparts because Malaysia is our country, not theirs. We can ask ourselves to make a sacrifice for our country but we cannot expect foreigners to do it for us.

In the development of our human resources, our private sector has the most important of roles to play. Train your own manpower. Equip them for their changing tasks. Look after their interests. Upgrade their skills. Manage them well. And reward them for their contribution.

There is obviously a lot for everyone to do. Unfortunately there is no simple one-shot formula for developing a nation. Many, many things must be done by many, many people. And they must be done as correctly as possible. We must be prepared to be self-critical and to be willing to make corrections. But God Willing we can succeed.

Conclusion

This is the agenda before us in this Council and before the nation. I hope you will discuss this agenda and criticize or improve on it. Whether we achieve perfection or consensus on this agenda is not absolutely important. No formula is perfect. But the least perfect and the least productive is the perfect agenda unimplemented.

[February 28, 1991]

Appendix 3

The Second Outline Perspective Plan, 1991-2000

Dr Mahathir Mohamad

Today is a historic day for us. Malaysians have been waiting anxiously to know the successor to the New Economic Policy (NEP) which expired at the end of 1990. Indeed, the keen interest shown by Malaysians about the shape of our new policy indicates that we all have a keen sense of responsibility form the nation and we are concerned about our future and the future of the nation. This augurs well for the nation since ultimately it is the commitment of the people to our national goals that will ensure the success of the developmental efforts for our own benefit.

It has often been said in international circles that development plans in Malaysia are meant to be followed. In other words we take our plans very seriously. Many observers have also remarked that the objectives, targets and strategies that we set in our plans are well thought out, realistic and achievable and that, by and large, we have been successful in achieving what we set out to do. This was largely so with the First Outline Perspective Plan (OPP1) and the NEP. God willing, we will continue to maintain this track record by improving further our capability to plan and to implement our plans by mobilizing all the resources of the nation to achieve our objectives.

The racial riots of 1969 shocked us into realizing the political and social imperatives of addressing and resolving the twin problems of poverty and racial socio-economic imbalances facing the nation at that time. Since the new generation of Malaysians are generally not aware of the events in 1969, it is necessary to remind them and also ourselves that in a multiracial society like ours the existence of socio-economic imbalances along racial lines is not conducive to stability or national unity. Accordingly, efforts to perpetuate socio-economic imbalances along racial lines will only lead to instability and disunity in the country.

The launching of the NEP in 1970 marked the beginning of our efforts at socio-economic engineering designed to bring about a more equitable distribution of wealth between the different races and groups in the various strata of society. The main thrust of this socio-economic engineering was embodied in a two-pronged approached aimed at:

☐ Eradicating poverty irrespective of race; and
☐ Restructuring society to reduce the identification of race with economic function.

Within a span of two decades, we targeted that the incidence of poverty in Peninsular Malaysia should be reduced from 49.3 per cent to 16.7 per cent and that the ownership of share capital in the corporate sector should be restructured such that the share of Malays and other Bumiputeras would increase from 2.4 per cent to at least 30 per cent while that of other Malaysians, form 34.3 per cent to 40 per cent. The foreigners were targeted to reduce their holdings from about 63.3 per cent to 30 per cent by 1990. Apart from these, we also agreed on the target that the employment pattern at all levels should reflect the racial composition of the population. We also resolved to undertake this socio-economic engineering so that in the process of distributing the benefits of development, no ethnic group experiences a sense of absolute deprivation.

It is pertinent to mention here that there have been many attempts in other parts of the world at socio-economic engineering. Almost without exception they have failed and they have caused untold misery and dragged down the economy of the nations involved. The objectives that we had set for ourselves in the OPP1 and the NEP were therefore fraught with all kinds of pitfalls and dangers.

Macroeconomic Progress

Let me now briefly deal with the progress we have made during the last two decades in implementing the NEP.

Since 1970, Malaysia has achieved a rapid and sustained growth. The real Gross Domestic Product (GDP) growth averaged 6.7 per cent per annum during the 1971-1990 period despite the effects of a very severe recession in the mid-1980s.

The impetus for the rapid growth achieved during the decade of the Seventies came as a result of a high level of public sector involvement in the economy. Such a high public sector profile arose from the need to continue with the social and physical infrastructure development begun since Independence. It also arose because of the overriding need to achieve the objectives of the NEP in the face of a comparatively underdeveloped private sector. As a result, public sector investment as a proportion of total investment increased steadily from 32 per cent in 1970 to a peak of 50 per cent by 1982. Despite improvements in the domestic savings rate, the increasingly high level of such investments had to be financed by external debt.

While we have been successful in achieving growth targets and in meeting many of the country's socio-economic goals, dependence on the public sector was found to be unsustainable. In addition, high public sector involvement in direct productive activities, especially by the non-financial public enterprises had not yielded the result that were expected of them. Indeed their performance in most instances was dismal, very much the way state-run enterprises in other countries disappointed their protagonists.

Our response to the serious problems of unsustainable deficits in the public sector budgets and in the balance of payments took the form of sharp painful adjustment measures undertaken from 1984 onwards. These included restraints on public sector expenditure, reduced public sector involvement in the

economy as well as a reversal of the past practices of using public
sector expenditure to boost demand and growth. In order to of-
fset the declining role of public sector expenditure, steps were
taken to stimulate private sector expenditure and investment and
to make the private sector the engine of growth for the economy.
A series of measures were undertaken to liberalize and deregulate
the economy and to embark on privatization of certain government agencies and functions so as to reduce public sector expenditure and transfer it to the private sector while making the
investment climate more attractive to them.

The new strategy to make the private sector the engine of
growth was initially affected by worldwide recession. But with the
improvement in the world economy, the strategy enabled the
Malaysian economy to recover strongly from 1987 onwards. In
the last three years between 1988-1990, robust growth of higher
than 9 per cent was recorded. Most recent estimates put the
growth rate in 1990 at 10 per cent which, we believe, is among
the highest recorded in the world for 1990. This was achieved
despite the threats and instability posed by the Gulf Crisis which
occurred in the last quarter of 1990.

Our greatest achievement is that we have restored fiscal and
financial stability in the economy, strengthened the balance of
payments and reduced the external debt burden considerably
through prepayment. The economy has returned to a high
growth path. With economic expansion, the unemployment rate
has been reduced to 7.4 per cent in 1970 to 6 per cent in 1990,
resulting in a tightening of the labour market and improvements
in wage levels for the workers. The per capita income, in nominal
terms, has increased to more than five-fold from RM1,016 in
1970 to RM6,180 in 1990.

The recent progress of the economy exceeded all our expectations. In the manufacturing sector alone, total approved
projects increased from RM9,100 million in 1988 to RM28,200
million in 1990, a three-fold increase in three years. This shows
the confidence investors, particularly foreign investors, have in
the attractiveness of our economy as well as in our pragmatic
policies. Manufactured exports and tourism earnings have shown

a remarkable performance never achieved before in the past. The inflows of export earnings and foreign capital were larger than ever experienced before, providing strength to the economy as well as enabling the country to maintain a satisfactory level of reserves, which is important for sustaining growth and keeping the inflation rate low.

Progress of the NEP

There is general consensus in the country that very substantial progress has been made in eradicating poverty and that the achievements have been better than expected. The national incidence of poverty has declined from 52.4 per cent in 1970 to 17.1 per cent in 1990. In Peninsular Malaysia, the incidence of poverty declined to 15 per cent while in Sabah and Sarawak, it declined to 34.3 per cent and 21 per cent respectively. This reduction is a significant achievement by international standards although the poverty line of RM370 for 1990 is far above those used in many developing countries to define poverty. According to international institutions such as the World Bank, we have been very generous with our definition. Obviously, if the poverty line income was lower, we will still get a much lower level of poverty, as found by the estimates made by other institutions.

A significant achievement which is most encouraging in the implementation of the NEP is in the poverty eradication programme. During the period of the last two decades, about 480,000 households in Peninsular Malaysia have been lifted out of poverty. Poverty is not a serious problem anymore in Peninsular Malaysia as it used to be in the 1970s, but in Sabah and Sarawak, although the incidence of poverty has declined sharply, it is still high compared to Peninsular Malaysia.

With the progress in eradicating poverty, the mean monthly household income for the bottom 40 per cent of households in Peninsular Malaysia has increased from RM76 in 1970 to RM421 in 1990. The mean household income for the bottom 40 per cent of households in Sabah and Sarawak also showed an increase from RM68 to RM390 and RM74 to RM436 respectively.

In fact, the mean income of the bottom 40 per cent of households has been increasing at a faster rate than that of the middle and higher income groups, resulting in an improvement in income distribution.

The most important factor influencing the improvement in rural incomes and the reduction of income inequalities is the changing pattern of employment. With economic growth and the rapid expansion of the industrial sector, there are now more employment opportunities in the non-agricultural sectors. As a result, there has been a steady trend in the country for the rural poor to leave their traditional low income agricultural activities and move into higher paying employment in the manufacturing, construction and services sector. Among most rural households today, traditional agriculture is no longer the only source of income because their children can now get other kinds of employment in the nearby cities and towns to supplement the family income. Clearly, the structure of employment and the income sources of the people, especially those in the rural areas, have changed with economic growth.

The government's rural development programmes have played a major role in enabling the poor to diversify their employment and source of income. The most important of these programmes is, of course, education as it provides the capacity for the rural poor to take advantage of the growth opportunities in the country. By investing heavily in education, health, transport and communication in the rural areas, we have increased the mobility of the rural labour force and raised the capacity of youths to participate in the urban employment market and escape from the clutches of rural poverty.

We have also made progress in restructuring the employment pattern so as to reflect more closely the racial composition in the country as envisaged in the targets set for the 1971-1990 period. In the last twenty years, the progress made by the Bumiputeras in education and employment has been encouraging although there are still also some major gaps and shortfalls. For example, the share of Bumiputera employment in manufacturing has increased substantially to 50.3 per cent by 1990 but this increase is concentrated in the lower and unskilled categories of employment. In terms of occupations, while their share in the professional and technical jobs is high, this is mostly due to their high share of employment in the nursing and teaching professions. In professional occupations such as engineers, doctors and accountants, Bumiputeras are still under-represented relative to their share of the population despite efforts made to increase the output of Bumiputera graduates from the universities and colleges.

In the case of non-Bumiputeras, while all have benefited from the growth of employment, their share in certain sectors such as agriculture, land settlement and government services has remained small in relation to their percentage of the population. As regards the Indians, their former disproportionately high share of employment in certain professional groups has been declining although in absolute terms they have increased. The Bumiputeras of Sabah and Sarawak have also not benefited as much as the Bumiputeras in Peninsular Malaysia from the growth of education, employment and income opportunities in the country. The government is aware that the minority groups are lagging behind in certain areas and therefore their needs for more excess to education and employment opportunities will be given greater attention.

It is clear that poverty can be greatly reduced and the absolute poverty can be eradicated. The notion that the poor is fated to be poor is due to ignorance, for clearly when the poor is given adequate help, they can improve themselves. And when they become rich, this too is fate or *takdir*. It is the duty of a responsible government to help the poor and eradicate poverty and Islam does not sat that such help is unIslamic.

In the effort to eradicate poverty, it is important that the poor are motivated to overcome their own poverty. Those who try to convince poor people that they should not strive against their fate are in fact undermining the spirit of the poor to work towards their own salvation. Such people are in fact trying to suppress the poor and keep them poor forever. Islam has never decreed that governments should deliberately kill the spirit of the poor to strive to better themselves. Only those who do not understand Islam or who have other motives would actively deprive the poor of the help and opportunities to better themselves.

The restructuring strategy under the NEP designed to increase Bumiputera ownership and control, especially in the commercial and industrial sectors of the economy, has also met with much success in quantitative terms. Bumiputeras' share of equity in the corporate sector has increased rapidly from 2.4 per cent in 1970 to 20.3 per cent in 1990. Although this is still below the target of at least 30 per cent envisaged under the NEP, the rate of increase has been very high as the Bumiputeras started from a much smaller base compared to other races. However, most of this progress was due to the efforts of institutions such as Permodalan Nasional Berhad (PNB), PERNAS and Tabung Haji while the equity acquired by the Bumiputeras as direct investors is relatively small. Furthermore, there has been slow progress made by the Bumiputeras to develop as a commercial and industrial community and become owners and operations of their own businesses. Although the government provided substantial support and subsidies to assist them, the incidence of business failures was rather high among them. Experience during the NEP period indicates that although equity ownership has increased, this alone has not been sufficient to create a strong Bumiputera commercial and industrial community capable of retaining their share. There must be more effective efforts to develop their management and entrepreneurial skills as well as their value system so that the quality of their participation in the economy can be significantly improved and made more permanent.

Looking at the total picture, however, there is no denying that despite the shortfalls and weaknesses, great strides have been made to achieve both growth and equity in our development and achievements, making Malaysia a unique model among developed countries. There is hardly any multiracial country in the developing world which has been able to carry out this experiment in socio-economic engineering successfully, without disrupting and reducing or even negating economic growth.

Usually, if wealth is redistributed, economic growth is retarded. If, on the other hand, economic growth is given priority, then the inequities in society will be accentuated. We can be justly proud that through the NEP, we have been able to make the employment and ownership structure in this country more multi-ethnic and to reduce poverty without sacrificing economic growth. Indeed our economic growth actually outstripped those of other countries not undergoing restructuring. And all of these are achieved in the context of a democratic system with peace and stability prevailing. When all is said and done, the NEP must be acknowledged as one of the greatest policies of independent Malaysia, enabling it to prosper without the blatant injustices of a totally materialistic society.

The New Development Policy

We have made remarkable progress but we still have more to do. The objectives of the NEP have not been fully realized. Poverty still remains, although the magnitude of the problem has been substantially reduced. There are still wide gaps among the communities and the Bumiputeras still lag behind in a number of important fields, especially in the filed of ownership and management of commercial and business enterprises and in the professions. Within the different non-Bumiputera and Bumiputera communities too, there is inequitable distribution of wealth which needs to be redressed.

We must not allow the success we have reaped to slip out of our hands because of our complacency. We must push on with policies designed to reduce further the current disparities among the races in order for national unity to be firmly established.

The OPP2 covering the period 1991-2000 has been formulated based on a new policy called the National Development Policy (NDP). This new policy will maintain the basic strategies of the NEP of eradicating poverty and restructuring society so as to correct social and economic imbalances and thereby contribute towards national unity.

National unity remains the ultimate goal of the NDP because a united society is essential to the promotion of social and political stability and sustained development. The NDP will set the pace to enable Malaysia to become a fully developed nation by the year 2020 not only economically but also in terms of social justice, moral and ethical values, political sophistication, quality of life and the administrative efficiency of the government.

In the course of implementing the NEP we were able to identify methods which were effective and those which were not. There were also many areas of weaknesses which should be remedied. Therefore, while maintaining the basic strategies of the NEP, the NDP will aim at bringing about a more balanced development encompassing the following critical aspects:

- [ ] Striking an optimum balance between the goals of economic growth and equity;
- [ ] Ensuring a balanced development of the major sectors of the economy in order that growth will be more even mutually complementary and supportive;
- [ ] Reducing, and ultimately, eliminating social and economic inequalities and imbalances to promote a fair and more equitable sharing of benefits of growth by all Malaysians;
- [ ] Promoting and strengthening national integration by reducing the wide disparities in economic development between states and between the urban and rural areas in the country;
- [ ] Developing a progressive society in which the welfare of citizens is spread to all, while being imbued with positive moral and spiritual values and an increased sense of national consciousness and pride;
- [ ] Promoting human resource development, including creating a productive and disciplined workforce and developing the necessary skills to meet the challenges of an industrial society through a culture of merit and excellence without jeopardizing restructuring objectives;
- [ ] Making science and technology integral components of socio-economic planning and development and promoting a science and technology culture compatible with the process of building a modern industrial economy;

☐ Ensuring that in the pursuit of economic development adequate attention is given to the protection of the environment and ecology so as to maintain the long-term sustainability of the country's development as well as the quality of life.

The NDP has taken into account the progress that has been made so far under the NEP and the strengths and weaknesses of our development efforts. It contains several shifts in policy to provide a new dimension to our development efforts, particularly in the efforts to eradicate poverty and restructure society. The new dimensions of the NDP will be to:

☐ Put greater emphasis in the anti-poverty strategy with a view to eradicating hardcore poverty, while at the same time reducing relative poverty;

☐ Focus more on rapid development of an active Bumiputera Commercial and Industrial Community (BCIC) as an essential strategy to increase and render permanent Bumiputera participation in the economy;

☐ Rely more on the private sector's involvement in the restructuring process; and

☐ Focus more on human resource development, including moral and ethical values in order to achieve the objectives of growth and distribution.

The new dimensions in the NDP will take into account a number of considerations. Accordingly, as there has already been substantial progress under the NEP in achieving the objectives of eradicating poverty and restructuring society, there will be less need for extensive government intervention. Instead, there will be a more selective approach which takes into account the need for quality and sustainable result. The indiscriminate distribution of wealth which is immediately frittered away does not only defeat the objectives of poverty eradication or restructuring, but they do lasting damage by creating a very dependent society which cannot manage without continuous government support.

In the process of eliminating hardcore poverty and reducing the imbalances, the stress will be given on education and training before support is given. The candidates must be ready to help themselves and face the realities of a competitive society before they receive support or opportunities.

A second major consideration in pursuing the socio-economic goals of the NDP is that it is necessary to take into account the needs of the economy to compete efficiently in the international marketplace and to face the new challenges that are already emerging. For instance, all countries including the centrally planned countries are now liberalizing their economies and competing strongly for foreign capital. In the face of this challenge, Malaysia must enhance its attractiveness for investors and businessmen to expand their activities in this country.

In the export market, there is a possibility of increased protectionism in world trade. To meet all these challenges, we must establish a liberal policy framework which encourages the private sector to be more efficient and willing to take longer term risks and to be more innovative so that we can accelerate the industrial development of the country without making monumental mistakes. Reliance on the GSP must be reduced as rapidly as possible so as to avoid the frequent threats of GSP withdrawal.

Third, Malaysia's progress towards a fully developed nation by the year 2020 must involve the participation of all communities. This means that in implementing the two-pronged strategies of the NDP, the policy should encourage the mobilization of all our resources and the utilization of the creative potentials of our multiracial society to build a strong economy and make the country more resilient against the instabilities and uncertainties of the world economy. We believe that each race has its own character and strength that can complement the others. The NDP, therefore, has been formulated to provide opportunities for all Malaysians to play their part more effectively in the development of the country.

Poverty Eradication

The growth in the economy and the creation of income and employment opportunities in the modern sectors of the economy are expected to reduce the incidence of defined poverty from 17.1 per cent in 1990 to 7.2 per cent in the year 2000. Unemployment in the country is expected to fall to 4 per cent by the year 2000 and with the consequent tightening of the labour market, productivity will have to be improved in order to justify wage increases. The standards of living will therefore generally improve.

In implementing the policies for poverty eradication, the NDP will take into account the need to make certain changes in the role of the public sector. Since unemployment and poverty in the rural areas were serious problems at the start of the NEP twenty years ago, the public sector had to intervene directly to open up new lands and to.provide large subsidies to smallholders to create new jobs and support their incomes. This was necessary because the only source of income in Malaysia then was land for agriculture. Large acreage was needed to support each Felda settler, for example. Experience has shown that it costs more to run these land schemes than similar estates run by the private sector. In addition, the children of the settlers being better educated, are disinclined to work on the rubber or oil palm holdings. They prefer, and rightly so, to work in more lucrative urban jobs. Unemployment is now resolved through the opening up of numerous factories, which employ more workers per acre of land. As agricultural produce like rubber and palm oil are still a necessary part of the economy, their production is best done by commercial estates.

Of far greater importance than subsidy to farmers is the training that should be given to the rural youths to enable them to take up skilled work which brings better pay. Subsidies and support will still be needed for padi planting and fishing, mainly to upgrade them and reduce the reliance on manual labour while increasing their productivity.

It is envisaged that within the next ten years the Felda estates will face serious labour problems. The original settlers will no longer be available and it is likely that their children will not be interested in even managing the holdings. A solution will have to be found for this. Where land is required for new estates the government will favour the experienced estate management companies to open them up.

Instead of the broad-based approach as in the past, the role of the public sector in poverty eradication programmes will concentrate on those programmes which are the responsibility of the public sector such as education and training, health, rural roads, transport and communications, housing, water and electricity. Although most areas in the country are well-served with these basic services, there is still a need to do more work to provide better access to these services in the remote *kampungs*, villages and in some estates as well as in the states of Sabah and Sarawak. In particular, these programmes will focus on meeting the specific needs of the poorest households to relieve them from poverty. Fortunately, the number of hardcore poor households who receive incomes less than half of the poverty line and whose living conditions are extremely poor is not large. It is estimated that only about 143,000 households or about 4 per cent of the total households are hardcore poor. Specific programmes targeted for this group will enable most of them to be brought above the poverty line by the end of this century.

In addition to this, consideration will be given to relative poverty which is expected to be a bigger issue in the future. When groups within a community feel that they are much worse off economically than others, even if in reality their situation has improved in absolute terms, it is quite likely that they will feel a sense of deprivation or frustration. Therefore, the government will continue to enhance income opportunities for the lower income groups of all races by improving their access to better services and amenities in both the rural and urban areas. In particular, greater efforts will be made to reduce the wide regional imbalances in the country, especially the imbalances between the states of Sabah and Sarawak and the rest of the country. As poverty and economic disparities in the less developed states of the Peninsular are still high, we will address these problems more urgently under the NDP. Migration to the urban areas also contribute towards poverty and the government will give appropriate attention to the problem of urban poverty.

Restructuring of Society

Turning next to the strategy of restructuring society, the NDP will continue with the efforts to increase the share of Bumiputeras in the economy both in terms of employment as well as in ownership and control of the economy. This is necessary since current disparities in development among the ethnic groups are still large. In particular, the Bumiputeras are still far behind the other races in business, especially in the commercial and industrial activities which, with the emphasis on industrialization, constitute the growth sectors of the economy. In continuing with these efforts, the government realizes that it is essential to pay more attention to the qualitative aspects of Bumiputera participation as these have been given less emphasis in the past. A higher quality of participation by the Bumiputeras will enable them to contribute effectively to the development process and to make them more self-reliant and less dependent on the government for support. Additionally, their capacity to retain their share will increase with qualitative improvement in Bumiputera participation.

The main emphasis in strengthening and enlarging Bumiputera participation in the modern services sector of the economy will therefore be on increasing their skills in management and entrepreneurship as these skills are the real asset of a nation. Possession of wealth without the ability to manage it will only result, sooner or later, in the loss of such wealth or the Bumiputeras just becoming an instrument to be used by others to secure higher shares in the corporate sector. While we would like to see more Bumiputera-non-Bumiputera partnerships, the "Ali Baba" type of arrangement in which Ali is not only passive but risks no capital of his own must be regarded as a form of undermining the NDP. Non-Bumiputera partners must find genuine

Bumiputera partners willing to risk their capital and involve them-selves in the day-to-day running of the business. More than that we expect the non-Bumiputera partner to actually train and ex-pose their Bumiputera partners to real-life business experience. The non-Bumiputeras must realize that the faster the NDP target is achieved and the Bumiputeras become real business people, the sooner will the need to favour Bumiputeras as a matter of policy be ended. Conversely, of course, if the "Ali Baba" partner-ship is resorted to, then the OPP2 will have to be followed by similar policies after its expiry period.

For their part, the Bumiputeras too must be serious. The NDP is not a get-rich-quick scheme for them. It is meant to vastly improve their chances of getting a fair share of the wealth that is being generated in this country and to retain and build up on that wealth. Lending their names and becoming sleeping partners will not make them good businessmen. They must risk their capital no matter how small it may be. They must be completely involved in the running of the business. They must force themselves to learn and learn fast. They must concentrate on one or two busi-nesses and not have meaningless involvement in dozens of com-panies.

It must be emphasized that we do not have all the time in the world. The Bumiputeras cannot expect economic policies to al-ways favour them. Politically split as they are, the day may not be far off when their influence in the government will diminish and the government will no longer be willing to defend and formulate policies to help them.

They must remember that there will always be competition in business. Such competition will not always be according to the rules. Like politics, business can be dirty. Complaining about being sabotaged all the time will not help. They must appreciate that such so-called sabotage are frequently with collaboration. For as long as they lean on the government to protect them, their skills will not be properly developed. There is only so much the government can do. The rest will have to be done by them.

It is time the Bumiputeras cease to expect to do business only with the government. They must go fully into the marketplace to compete. The contracts and the sales must be with the public. It is not impossible to reduce their dependence on government contracts. But they have to be efficient. They cannot expect a 5 per cent price advantage outside the government. The non-Bumiputeras, on their part, must be prepared to give contracts to the Bumiputeras even when they are not involved in government projects.

The belief that to succeed in business one has to cheat is totally erroneous. Equally erroneous is that all non-Bumiputeras cheat. Honesty pays although it will take time. Cheating will earn you some profits first time around. But there will be no second or third time. The Bumiputeras must have a longer term outlook. A small profit that will come repeatedly is much better than a one-time killing.

The government is aware of the threat often made by Bumiputera businessmen not to support the government if we do not look the other way when they misbehave. But we will not be deterred in doing what we are convinced is in the long-term interest of the Bumiputera businessmen and the Bumiputeras generally.

Nevertheless, the government will continue with its efforts to increase Bumiputera ownership and participation in the corporate sector in line with the original objective of achieving at least a 30 per cent stake. This, however, will be implemented in a flexible and liberal manner so as not to unduly affect growth. Therefore, under the OPP2, no quantitative targets and no specific time frame has been set for achieving a quantitative objective. However, at the end of the year 2000, a review will be made of the policy to support Bumiputera participation in the economy.

The development of a viable and effective Bumiputera Commercial and Industrial Community will be given higher priority under the restructuring strategy than equity ownership. Agencies such as PNB and the State Economic Development Corporations or SEDCs created to enhance Bumiputera participation in the private sector will have to adopt new and more effective strategies to enlarge the pool of Bumiputera entrepreneurs and managers to effectively participate in companies where Bumiputeras have substantial stakes. Agencies like the PNB should venture into new areas through developing venture capital companies and entrepreneurial development. It is no longer adequate for such agencies to play a passive role and to be content with mobilizing Bumiputera capital to acquire equities on behalf of the Bumiputeras at privileged prices.

The existing system of quotas and licenses which are granted to provide special assistance for Bumiputeras to enter into business activities will be implemented more selectively to ensure that only those with potential, commitment and good track record will get the assistance so that they can be viable on their own over time. This may delay the achievement of quantitative targets but as we have said we are more interested in quality. The former stress on quantity had resulted in Bumiputeras owning 100 per cent of continuously losing companies. It is the government's view that they will be better off owning 10 per cent of profitable companies.

Ultimately, the Bumiputeras must learn to participate in business in an environment of competition and efficiency so that they can integrate themselves into the mainstream of the economy and be recognized as genuine businessmen and entrepreneurs. We are glad that a few Bumiputeras have actually achieved this status under the NEP but we need more of them in order to sustain the results of the quantitative achievement of the policy.

Retail Business

A very noticeable feature of the Malaysian commercial scene is the poor representation of Bumiputeras in the retail business. This is due to various factors, among which is the difficulty of finding suitable and affordable premises and the fact that in the urban areas non-Bumiputeras make up the biggest proportion of the clientele.

While the government hopes that all Malaysians should patronize all Malaysian retail outlets without any discrimination, there is a need to train the Bumiputeras in the art of retailing. The emphasis on being a 100 per cent Bumiputera enterprise should cease. It is counter productive as the customers in the urban areas are mostly non-Bumiputeras. Instead, Bumiputera retailers in the urban areas should tailor their sales presentation so as to de-emphasize their Bumiputera character and aim for the larger market.

Another obstacle to Bumiputera involvement in the retail business in the urban areas is the unwillingness of Bumiputeras with the capital and the skill to go into retailing. Invariable those who opt for retailing are undercapitalized and unskilled in the sophistication of urban retailing. There is a notion among Bumiputeras that there is no money in retailing and one cannot get rich quick, an overwhelming obsession with many Bumiputeras.

The government will study these problems and obstacles and will try to formulate a solution. But no solution will be effective without the Bumiputeras themselves appreciating that there is no way they can achieve the Malaysianization of Malaysian towns and cities unless they are prepared to move into the retail business.

I would like to stress that while the strategy of restructuring society is primarily concerned with increasing the share of Bumiputeras in the economy, there is also a need to correct the imbalances relating to the under-representation of the non-Bumiputeras in certain sectors such as agriculture, land settlement schemes and in public sector employment. It is, therefore, proposed that more opportunities be provided to the non-Bumiputeras, especially the minority groups such as the Indians and also the Bumiputera communities in Sabah and Sarawak, to increase their representation and to make the employment pattern in these sectors more multi-ethnic. Similarly, in implementing the privatization programme, opportunities will also be given to the non-Bumiputeras to participate in the privatized projects and to won shares in these projects. Thus, where possible, the restructuring strategy will take into account the needs of all communities to have greater access to the opportunities created by the government. However, it is necessary and important for the private sector to balance government action by increasing the intake of Bumiputeras into the higher occupational levels in order to bring about a balance in the employment structure between the public and the private sectors.

Economic Growth and Structural Change

Like the NEP, the objectives under the NDP will be implemented within the context of high economic growth. For the 1990s, under the OPP2, our aim is to maintain and capitalize on our strengths and reduce our weakness so that we can achieve a rapid and sustainable growth rate of 7 per cent per annum in real terms. Such a rate of growth in the output of goods and services will result in the doubling of the output of goods and services in real terms to about RM155 billion by the year 2020. Malaysians will be able to enjoy a higher standard of living with per capita income reaching to about RM17,000 by the year 2020.

The increase in output of goods and services will be accompanied by a major structural transformation of the economy. While the share of agriculture in GDP will continue to decline, the share of the manufacturing sector and the non-government services sector will continue to increase. The agriculture sector cannot be expected to grow at rates experienced in the past because of land and labour shortages in Peninsular Malaysia and labour and infrastructural constraints in Sabah and Sarawak. Future development of the sector will require a major shift towards increased commercialization and private sector participation, higher value-added and the development of new crops. The manufacturing sector is projected to grow by 10.5 per cent per annum resulting in the share of manufacturing sector in GDP increasing from 27 per cent in 1990 to about 37 per cent in the year 2000. The structure of exports will also undergo further changes, with manufacturing exports accounting for about 80 per cent of total exports and agricultural exports declining to 6 per cent. All these structural changes indicate the emergence of an industrialized economy by the turn of the century.

An important sector that can contribute vastly to economic growth and reduce invisible deficits is the service sector. The efficient management of ports, airports, land, sea and air transportation, both domestic and international must be given serious attention. The insurance industry must be upgraded so as to be able to service international trade.

The tourist industry will have the greatest potential for growth. More than anything else the tourist industry is a service industry. The physical facilities must be complemented by service of a high standard. Prices must always be reasonable and related to cost rather than to the opportunities to exploit.

Malaysians as a people must realize that tourists can contribute to their well-being. With care we can avoid the cultural pollution that a tourist industry can bring about. It behoves upon Malaysians to make the tourists feel welcome always. And certainly those who are directly involved in the industry must fully extend themselves to ensure that visitors to Malaysia will return again and again.

It is necessary to emphasize again here that while these structural changes are essential to make us a fully developed nation, they can only happen if we adopt the right policies towards growth and the role of the private sector in the economy. Thus in the NDP, the management of economic policies will continue to provide the incentives for investors to increase their activities and for entrepreneurs to be more willing to risks and be more innovative.

It is wrong to think only of reduced taxes as incentives. The strongest incentive is a healthy and liberal environment free of official harassment and red tap for local and foreign investors to expand their businesses in the country. The management of economic policy will therefore ensure that apart from maintaining fiscal and financial stability, the investment policies will continue to be implemented in a liberal manner so as to allow investors to have majority ownership and control in their projects, particularly for export-oriented projects. However, it must be pointed out that in business, a willingness to spread opportunities will actually lessen risks. It makes good business sense to appreciate the aspirations of others.

International Economic Development

The prospects for achieving the growth targets outlined in the OPP2 are bright in the light of the recent performance of investments and exports and better management of the nation's resources. However, the external environment will continue to be a major factor in determining the pace of economic growth in view of the importance of foreign trade and investment in the economy. There are still several important international economic issues that are unresolved and which continue to create uncertainty in the prospects for growth of developing countries.

The creation of a unified market in Western Europe, the democratization of Eastern Europe, the structural changes being undertaken in the Eastern Europe, the structural changes being undertaken in the Eastern European countries along market-based principles and the end of the Gulf War provide increasing opportunities for developing countries to expand their trade. Malaysia must take advantage of the potentials of all these changes in our efforts to expand and diversify our trade.

However, these changes are not without threats against the growth of developing countries like Malaysia. Rising protectionism, lack of policy coordination among developed countries on monetary matters, the slow progress towards agreement at the new Uruguay rounds of the GATT negotiations, and above all, the emergence of new trading blocs such as in the USA-Canada and the USA-Mexico trade regimes and the unified market of EC pose dangers for free trade at a time when developing countries like Malaysia are seeking greater access to the markets of America and Europe.

As I have said more than once before, our experience shows that there is no such thing as free trade. Trade was free when we were the markets for the rich developed countries. But when we want to gain access to the market of the rich countries to sell our manufactured goods, restrictions are imposed. The very people who taught us to abide by the rules of competition are now violating these same rules for their own political and economic reasons.

While we will continue to participate actively to bring about a new international economic order, we cannot bemoan the lack of co-operation from developed countries and do nothing. We must do our best to penetrate the markets of developed countries and diversify our export markets. Our interest in South-South trade, our initiative in the G-15 movements, our active participation in regional organizations like Asean and APEC as well as our role in championing the cause of the East Asia Economic Group (EAEG) concept and the formation of trade and investment links with developing countries in Southeast and East Asia represent efforts to diversify trade links and create a fairer and mutually beneficial trading relationship between nations. These actions, we believe, will help increase world trade as well as counteract some of the negative effects of rising trade protectionism by certain developed countries.

Sectoral Strategies

The manufacturing sector will continue to spearhead the development of the economy in the next decade. With the emergence of labour shortages and the consequent tightening of the labour market, the stress will be on high technology and less labour-intensive industries. Measures must be taken to diversify and broaden our industrial base through the generation of new growth industries, especially in basic metal, fabricated metal, petroleum and transport equipment industries as well as non-metallic mineral, rubber and those wood-based industries which are less labour intensive. The small- and medium-scale industries will be further promoted and upgraded so that they will not only support the major industries but will themselves grow into industrial giants. Such growth must be well-planned and the capacity to finance and manage must be given serious consideration. The tendency to expand in every direction simply because of apparent opportunity must be avoided. It is also important that companies specialize and avoid going into certain popular businesses simply because everyone else appears to be doing so.

Within the agricultural sector, in view of land constraints in Peninsular Malaysia and shortages of labour, more emphasis will be placed on increasing productivity in the sector rather than an opening up new land. There will be greater commercial reorientation in the sector in terms of the choice of crops and management style as well as reform of the inefficient smallholder operations towards a more organized and estate-like approach. Priority will be given to the rejuvenation and conversation of forestry resources through a planned programme of reforestation and the management of logging.

In order to accelerate growth, high priority is given under the OPP2 to the development of science and technology and human resources. Further development of the industrial an agricultural sectors will require absorption of new and existing technologies and utilizing them more efficiently. This will strengthen our domestic technological capabilities and promote industrial competitiveness. The government will embark on a deliberate effort to increase private and public sector investment in Research and Development (R&D) and will aim to more than double the R&D expenditure as a percentage of GNP from the current level of 0.8 per cent. R&D must be regarded as part of the normal cost rather than as a diversion of disposable profit.

Human Resource Development

An important thrust of OPP2 is the high priority to be given to the development of human resources. Human resource development is critical for the success of every nation because more than anything else the quality of human resources determines the extent of competitiveness, productivity, innovativeness as well as efficiency of a nation's economy. We must create a productive and an efficient labour force which has strong ethical and moral values and a commitment to excellence. In the context of Malaysia, human resource development is not only critical for growth, but it is also critical for attainment of equity objectives.

Developments in the last two decades have amply demonstrated that education and training are powerful tools to increase the incomes of the poor by facilitating upward mobility and access to modern sector jobs, and in reducing social and economic disparities among the ethnic groups.

With the transformation of the nation from an agricultural economy to an industrial economy, there will be new demands not only for technical, managerial and skilled manpower but also for a labour force that is instilled with the values and culture of an industrialized society. Industrial skill will have to be developed at a rapid pace to provide support for further expansion of the manufacturing industries. While the government will continue to expand and re-oriented the education and training system, the private sector will be called upon to share a larger burden of training the human resources of the country. This is to enable the output from the training institutions to become more relevant to the actual needs of the private sector. The contents of the training programmes must be more sensitive to the technological and skill changes taking place in the economy.

I have highlighted for the consideration of Honourable Members of this House, the targets and the policies of the OPP2 and the salient features of the NDP.

The NDP takes into account the needs of all Malaysians. There should be no fear or doubts in the minds of any ethnic group that they would lose. Malaysia is rich in resources and there is enough for everyone to gain from the process of development. But it must be emphasized that if the Bumiputeras gained more than others, this is because they began with a lower base-line and more need to be done for them to bring them up to the level of development of other Malaysians. Only by doing this can we be assured of political and social stability as well as national unity, a prerequisite for progress.

We must continue with the process of reducing the glaring imbalances among the ethnic groups as long as it exists. Therefore, may I say once again, it is better that all Malaysians work together to remove these imbalances as fast as possible. The task of reducing these imbalances should not be left to the government alone. It is also the duty of the private sector to play a more sincere and effective role in providing productive opportunities for the Bumiputeras to advance themselves. The faster we move towards redressing ethnic imbalances, the lesser will be the need to have special privileges for the Bumiputeras.

The NDP has been prepared following exhaustive analyses of social and economic developments in the country after taking into account the views of various groups in society, the private sector and the National Economic Consultative Council. To all those who have contributed in one form or another to the formulation of the new policy, I wish to record the government's warm appreciation for their assistance.

Conclusion

Our task now is to make the NDP work. The next ten years will be filled with challenges both in the international economy and in the domestic economy. We must be dynamic, innovative and pragmatic in our approach and above all the private sector must play a leading and proactive role.

To overcome challenges and to survive in a competitive world we must be prepared to adjust and to change. Changes in the value system and in our attitudes, are important prerequisites for progress.

We must be prepared to work hard, be disciplined and less dependent on subsidies and welfare. The history of civilization has provided us with enough evidence about the sad fate of societies which fail to change or which change too late. Societies which fail to react quickly to changing circumstances will be left behind, stagnate and eventually fall into insignificance.

The government will ensure that its machinery at all levels will work efficiently and closely with the private sector in the spirit of Malaysia Incorporated. Further, the government will continue to hold dialogues with the private sector to maintain better co-operation and greater private sector involvement in the implementation of the NDP. In working towards the goals set by the OPP2 and the NDP, Malaysians from all walks of life must strive harder to succeed. Together, all of us, by the will of Allah and His Blessings, will continue to prosper and achieve the goal of building up a progressive, prosperous and a united nation. Let us all strive hard and dedicate ourselves to achieving the objectives and targets of the OPP2 and the NDP so that we can all contribute towards making Malaysia a fully developed nation by the year 2020.

[June 17, 1991]

Abbreviations

AID	Accelerated Industrialization Drive
AFTA	Asean Free Trade Area
APEC	Asia-Pacific Economic Co-operation
ASEAN	Association of Southeast Asian Nations
AT&T	American Telephone & Telegraph
BCG	Boston Consultancy Group
BCIC	Bumiputera Commercial and Industrial Community
BLR	Base Lending Rate
BNM	Bank Negara Malaysia
CAD	Computer-Aided Design
CADAM	Computer-Aided Design and Manufacturing
CAM	Computer-Aided Manufacturing
DAP	Democratic Action Party
EAEC	East Asia Economic Caucus
EAEG	East Asia Economic Group
EC	European Community
EEC	European Economic Community
EPF	Employees Provident Fund
EPU	Economic Planning Unit

FDIs	Foreign Direct Investments
FELDA	Federal Land Development Authority
FMM	Federation of Malaysian Manufacturers
G-7	Group of Seven Countries
G-15	Group of Fifteen Countries
GATT	General Agreement on Tariffs and Trade
GDI	Gross Domestic Investment
GDP	Gross Domestic Product
GDS	Gross Domestic Savings
GEC	General Electric Company
GNP	Gross National Product
GNS	Gross National Savings
GNS	Group of Negotiations on Services
GSP	Generalized System of Preferences
HRD	Human Resource Development
IAPG	Inter-Agency Planning Groups
IBM	International Business Machines
ICOR	Incremental Capital Output Ratio
IMP	Industrial Master Plan
IRPA	Intensification of Research in Priority Areas
ISA	Internal Security Act
ISIS	Institute of Strategic and International Studies
IT	Information Technology
IT&T	International Telephone & Telegraph
JIT	Just-In-Time
KLSE	Kuala Lumpur Stock Exchange
LDCs	Less Developed Countries
LDP	Liberal Democratic Party
MARA	Majlis Amanah Rakyat
MBC	Malaysian Business Council
MDTIs	Major Deposit-Taking Institutions
MEF	Malaysian Employers Federation
MES	Minimum Efficient Scales
MFN	Most Favoured Nation
MGS	Malaysian Government Securities
MICCI	Malaysian International Chamber of Commerce and Industry

MIDF	Malaysian Industrial Development Finance
MNC	Multinational Corporation
MPC	Marginal Propensity to Consume
NAFTA	North American Free Trade Area
NDP	National Development Policy
NDPC	National Development Planning Committee
NECC	National Economic Consultative Council
NEP	New Economic Policy
NFPA	Net Foreign Payments Abroad
NICs	Newly Industrialized Countries
OECD	Organization for Economic Co-operation and Development
OPP1	First Outline Perspective Plan
OPP2	Second Outline Perspective Plan
PAS	Parti Islam Se-Malaysia
PBS	Parti Bersatu Sabah
PDS	Private Debt Securities
PERNAS	Perbadanan Nasional Berhad
PNB	Permodalan Nasional Berhad
PSD	Public Services Department
PUNB	Perbadanan Usahawan Nasional Berhad
R&D	Research and Development
S&T	Science and Technology
SEDCs	State Economic Development Corporations
SMIs	Small- and Medium-sized Industries
SMP	Sixth Malaysia Plan
SSTS	Scripless Securities Trading System
TWG	Technical Working Group
UMNO	United Malays National Organization

Index